Contents at a Glance

SketchUp®

by Aidan Chopra and Rebecca Huehls

SketchUp® For Dummies®

Published by **John Wiley & Sons, Inc.,** 111 River Street, Hoboken, NJ 07030-5774, www.wiley.com

Copyright © 2017 by John Wiley & Sons, Inc., Hoboken, New Jersey

Media and software compilation copyright © 2017 by John Wiley & Sons, Inc. All rights reserved.

Published simultaneously in Canada

For general information on our other products and services, please contact our Customer Care Department within the U.S. at 877-762-2974, outside the U.S. at 317-572-3993, or fax 317-572-4002. For technical support, please visit https://hub.wiley.com/community/support/dummies.

Wiley publishes in a variety of print and electronic formats and by print-on-demand. Some material included with standard print versions of this book may not be included in e-books or in print-on-demand. If this book refers to media such as a CD or DVD that is not included in the version you purchased, you may download this material at http://booksupport.wiley.com. For more information about Wiley products, visit www.wiley.com.

Library of Congress Control Number: 2017931254

ISBN: 978-1-119-33615-0

ISBN (ePDF): 978-1-119-33622-8; ISBN (ePub): 978-1-119-33619-8

Manufactured in the United States of America

10 9 8 7 6 5 4 3 2 1

Table of Contents

Introduction

Years ago, Aidan was teaching a workshop on advanced SketchUp techniques to a group of extremely bright middle and high school (or so he thought) students in Hot Springs, Arkansas. As subject matter went, Aidan wasn't pulling any punches and breezing through material he wouldn't think of introducing to most groups of adults. At one point, a boy raised his hand to ask a question, and Aidan noticed that the boy looked younger than most of the others. Squinting, Aidan read the logo on the boy's T-shirt that said he was in elementary school. "You're in sixth grade?" Aidan asked, a little stunned. These kids were *motoring*, after all. The boy didn't even look up. He shook his head, double-clicked something, and mumbled, "Third." He was eight years old.

SketchUp was invented by a couple 3D industry veterans whose goal was to make it easy for people to model their ideas in three dimensions. That was it, really — they just wanted to make a piece of software that anyone could use to build 3D models. That boy from Arkansas indicates they succeeded.

About This Book

This book is for people who are new to 3D modeling and SketchUp. We don't assume you know anything about polygons, vertices, or linear arrays. The nice thing is that the people who make SketchUp don't assume you know any of those things, either. That means, I don't have to spend many words explaining theoretical concepts, which I think we both can appreciate.

If you happen to know a thing or two about modeling or SketchUp, we think you'll still find plenty of useful stuff in this book. Although we write with beginners in mind, you'll find a lot that isn't beginner-level information, so that you can grow your skills after you're comfortable with the basics.

Most of this book focuses on what *you can do* with SketchUp, and not *what SketchUp does.* With that in mind, this book errs on the side of architecture, because a lot of people want to use SketchUp to model buildings. However, you can apply the techniques that you learn in this book to modeling other things, like parts or woodworking.

One more thing: SketchUp is a *cross-platform* program (it's available for both Windows and Macintosh computers), and this book covers both. In most cases, SketchUp works the same in Microsoft Windows and on a Mac, but where it doesn't, we point out the differences. Just so you know, most figures in this book that show the SketchUp user interface show the Windows version.

Foolish Assumptions

We don't presume you know anything about 3D modeling, much less 3D modeling with SketchUp. That said, we do assume you're familiar with a few important concepts:

- » **You're familiar with the basics of working with your operating system:** For example, we assume you know how to do basic things like saving and opening files. If you're trying to model with SketchUp *and* figure out how to use a computer at the same time, Wiley has some excellent books that can help you out, such as *Windows 10 For Dummies,* by Andy Rathbone, or *Mac OS X For Dummies,* by Bob LeVitus, just to name two; visit www.dummies.com for other options.

- » **You have, and know how to work, a mouse with a scroll wheel.** SketchUp all but requires you to have a scroll-wheel mouse — especially when you're just starting out.

- » **You have at least occasional access to the Internet.** You don't have to be online to use SketchUp, but you can find great resources on the web. Also, some parts of SketchUp, like the Components panel, are much more powerful with an Internet connection.

Icons Used in This Book

This icon indicates a piece of information that will probably save you time.

TIP

When you're working in SketchUp, you need to know a lot of things. This icon highlights important concepts or features you'll want to remember.

REMEMBER

TECHNICAL STUFF

Everyone's a little bit of a nerd sometimes, and paragraphs that bear this icon indulge that nerdiness. You can skip them without fear of missing anything important, but reading them can give you something to annoy your SketchUp friends with later.

WARNING

When you see this icon, pay special attention. It occurs rarely, but when it does, something you do could harm your work.

Beyond the Book

This book has an online presence, where you'll find lots of useful stuff:

>> **Videos:** Aidan recorded a few dozen videos and put them up on YouTube. They're pretty basic, but seeing SketchUp in action is often very helpful. You can find these videos, which reflect some of the steps in this book, at `https://www.youtube.com/user/aidanchopra/playlists`.

>> **Links to other cool resources:** The web has wonderful SketchUp material — plugins, components, models, and blogs — and you find direct links to many of them.

>> **Cheat Sheet:** You can access this book's online Cheat Sheet by visiting `www.dummies.com` and searching for **SketchUp For Dummies.**

Where to Go from Here

This book is intended to be a reference. If you keep reading from this page on, right to the end of the index, you'll have a pretty good idea of how to use SketchUp to make 3D models — but you don't have to use this book that way. We recommend that you start with Chapters 1 and 2, just to get your bearings. After that, use the table of contents or the index to find what you're looking for; then proceed from there.

1
Getting Started with SketchUp

Chapter **1**

Meeting SketchUp

O nce upon a time, software for building three-dimensional (3D) models of things like buildings, cars, and other stuff was hard to use — *really* hard. People went to school for years to learn that software. And if that wasn't bad enough, 3D modeling software was expensive — so expensive that the only people who used it were professionals and software pirates (people who stole it, basically). After debuting in 2000, SketchUp changed all that.

In SketchUp, you don't think about 3D models as complex mathematical constructs (the way computers think). You build models with familiar elements: lines and shapes. To use SketchUp, you don't even need to know how to draw. In SketchUp, you just *build*, and SketchUp takes care of stuff like perspective and shading for you.

This first chapter is about putting SketchUp in context: where to get it, how it compares with other 3D software, and what you can (and can't) do with it. In the last part of the chapter, you go on a quick tour of the program, so that you know where things are.

Things You Ought to Know Right Away

Before we continue, here's some information you may need:

» **You get SketchUp by downloading it from** www.sketchup.com.

» **SketchUp works in Windows and Mac OS X.** For the most part, SketchUp looks (and works) the same way on both.

» **SketchUp has a free and a full version: SketchUp Make and SketchUp Pro.** SketchUp Make does most of the things that the full version does but is designed for noncommercial use. With SketchUp Pro, you get terrific features that folks like architects, construction pros, and other design professionals need for exchanging files with other software. SketchUp Pro also includes a whole separate application — dubbed *LayOut* — for creating presentations and construction drawings from your SketchUp models. You learn the basics of LayOut in Chapter 14.

TIP

If you know you need SketchUp Pro, go ahead and download it. You can try it for free before you have to buy a license. After the trial period ends, Pro stops working until you license it.

Comparing SketchUp to Other 3D Modeling Programs

If you're reading this book, we presume you're at least interested in two things: building 3D models and using SketchUp to do so. The following sections tell you something about how SketchUp compares with other 3D modeling programs — how long it takes to figure out how to use it and what kind of models it produces.

Jumping right in

Among the widely available 3D modeling applications, SketchUp is the easiest to use. This software has been successful for one reason: Within a few hours of launching SketchUp for the first time, you can get good enough at SketchUp to build something. You have no thick manuals to read, and no special geometric concepts to understand. Modeling in SketchUp is about grabbing your mouse and making something.

So how long should it take you to discover how SketchUp works? That depends on your background and experience. In general, you can expect to make something recognizable in fewer than four hours. That's not to say you'll be a whiz — it just means that SketchUp's learning curve is extremely favorable. You don't need to know much to get started, but you'll still pick up things years from now. In fact, we've both discovered a couple things just writing this book.

But is SketchUp *easy?* Lots of people say so, but we think it's all relative. SketchUp is, without a doubt, easi*er* than any other modeling program we've tried, but 3D modeling itself can be tricky. Some people catch on right away, and some folks take longer. But we can say this for sure: If you want to build 3D models and you have an afternoon to spare, there's no better place to start than SketchUp (and this book, of course). Chapter 2 walks you through the basics to help you start modeling in SketchUp quickly.

Understanding the difference between paper and clay

Three-dimensional modeling software comes in two basic flavors: *solids* and *surfaces.* The following points illustrate the difference:

>> **SketchUp is a surfaces modeler.** Everything in SketchUp is basically made of thin (infinitely thin, actually) surfaces — dubbed *faces.* As shown in Figure 1-1, even things that look thick (like cinderblock walls) are actually hollow shells. Making models in SketchUp is a lot like building things out of paper — really, really thin paper.

Surfaces modelers like SketchUp are great for making models quickly because all you really need to model is what things *look* like. That's not to say that surfaces modelers are less capable; they're just intended for visualization.

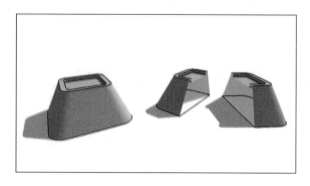

FIGURE 1-1:
SketchUp models are hollow.

>> **Using a solids modeler is more like working with clay.** When you cut a solid model in half, you create new surfaces where you cut. That's because objects are, well, solid. Programs like SolidWorks, form•Z, and Autodesk Inventor create solid models.

People who make parts — like mechanical engineers and industrial designers — tend to work with solid models because they can use them to do some pretty precise calculations. Being able to calculate the volume of an object means that you can figure how much it will weigh, for example. Also, special machines can produce real-life prototypes directly from a solid-model file.

TIP

Although SketchUp is a surfaces modeler, its Solid tools enable you to manipulate special solid objects in your models. Read all about the Solid Tools in Chapter 6.

TECHNICAL
STUFF

Yet another caveat: When we said (a few paragraphs ago) that 3D modeling programs come in two basic flavors, we sort of lied. The truth is, you can group these programs another way: by the kind of math they use to produce 3D models. You can find *polygonal* modelers (of which SketchUp is an example) and *curves-based* (NURBS) modelers. The former type uses straight lines and flat surfaces to define everything — even things that *look* curvy, aren't. The latter kind of modeler uses true curves to define lines and surfaces. Curves yield organic, flowing forms that are much more realistic than those produced by polygonal modelers, but put a lot more strain on the computers that have to run them. Curves modelers are also harder to learn how to use. Ultimately, it's a trade-off between simplicity and realism.

What You Should (and Shouldn't) Expect SketchUp to Do

Have you ever been to a hardware store and noticed the multitool gizmos on the racks next to the checkout stands? Aidan once saw one that was a combination screwdriver, pliers, saw, tape measure, and (he swears) hammer. This tool was probably great in a pinch, but we can't imagine it did any of its jobs very well.

SketchUp, however, is a specialist that does one thing really well: building 3D models. Here's a list of things (all model-building related) that you can do with SketchUp:

>> **Start a model in lots of ways:** With SketchUp, you can begin a model in whatever way makes sense for what you're building:

- *From scratch:* As Chapter 2 explains, you can start with a completely blank slate on which to model anything you want.

- *From a photograph:* Have a photo of the thing you want to build? Chapter 8 explains how to use that photo as a starting point.

- *With another computer file:* In addition to photos, you can import AutoCAD files and other specialized files, such as 3DS, DEM, IFC, and COLLADA. (If you need those specialized options, you already know what those file types do.)

- *From a geo-location snapshot:* In SketchUp, it's easy to grab a geo-location snapshot (a small chunk of the planet, basically) from Google Earth. Chapter 8 explains how to grab this snapshot and use it as a site for your model.

» **Work loose or work tight:** Your models can be super-sketchy or absolutely precise. SketchUp is just like paper in that way; the amount of detail you add is entirely up to you.

» **Build something real or make something up:** *What* you build with SketchUp really isn't the issue. You work with only lines and shapes — or in SketchUp, *edges* and *faces*. How you arrange them is your business. SketchUp isn't intended for making buildings any more than it is for creating other things. It's just a tool for drawing in 3D.

» **Share your models:** After you make something you want to show off, you can print your model, create an image file, animate a walkthrough, export the model to another 3D format, or upload your model to the 3D Warehouse (a giant, online repository of SketchUp models). Part 4 helps you start sharing in all these ways.

What *can't* SketchUp do? A few things, actually — but that's okay. SketchUp was designed from the outset to be the friendliest, fastest, and most useful modeler available — and that's it, really. Fantastic programs are available that do the things in the following list, and SketchUp can exchange files with most of them:

» **Photorealistic rendering:** Most 3D modelers have their own, built-in photo renderers, but creating model views that look like photographs is a pretty specialized undertaking. SketchUp has always focused on *nonphotorealistic rendering (NPR)* instead. NPR (as it's known) is essentially technology that makes things look hand-drawn — sort of the opposite of photorealism.

» **Animation:** A few paragraphs ago, we mention that SketchUp can export animated walkthroughs, but that's a different thing. The movies that you can make with SketchUp involve moving your "camera" around your model. True animation software lets you move things around *inside* your model. SketchUp doesn't do that, but the Pro version enables you to export to programs that do.

IS THIS MODEL A TOASTER OR A BUNGALOW?

SketchUp models are made from two basic kinds of *geometry:* edges (straight lines) and *faces* (2D surfaces bound by edges). That's it. When you use SketchUp to draw a bunch of edges and faces in the shape of a staircase, all SketchUp knows is how many edges and faces it has to keep track of, and where they all go. There's no such thing as a *stair* in SketchUp — just edges and faces.

That said, SketchUp's *dynamic components* are preprogrammed objects that know what they are. A dynamic staircase, for example, is smart enough to know that it should add or subtract steps when you make it bigger or smaller. What's that mean for you? For starters, SketchUp is easier to pick up than it's ever been. Chapter 5 goes on and on about dynamic components.

With the exception of dynamic components, things in SketchUp have no idea what they're supposed to represent. Coming to this realization has the tendency to freak out some people. If you want a model of something, you have to make it out of edges and faces. The thing to remember is that SketchUp enables you to model *anything*, not just buildings, so its tools are designed to manipulate geometry. That's good news, believe it or not, because you're not restricted in any way. You can model anything you can imagine.

Taking the Ten-Minute SketchUp Tour

In this tour, you find out where everything is in the SketchUp interface — like the way you look around a new place before you decide where you'll put your sofa, bed, and desk. When you start modeling, you'll know where to look for the tools and commands you need.

As shown in Figure 1-2, SketchUp has seven main parts:

>> **Modeling window:** See the big area in the middle of your computer screen? That's your modeling window. You build your model here, and your modeling window *always* shows a 3D view of your model, even if you're looking at it from the top or side.

>> **Menu bar:** If you've used a computer in the last 30 years, the menu bar is nothing new. Each menu contains a long list of options, commands, tools,

settings, and other goodies that pertain to just about everything you do in SketchUp. We introduce you to the commands on these menus throughout this book, and you can look up what any one of them does using this book's index.

» **Toolbars:** Click a toolbar button to activate a tool or command. SketchUp has a few toolbars, but only one is visible when you launch SketchUp the first time: the Getting Started toolbar. See the upcoming section, "Customizing the toolbar" for details about finding other toolbar options.

» **Dialog boxes and panels:** You'll find traditional dialog boxes that enable you to select an option and then disappear when you're done. The Open dialog box and Save dialog box are both good examples. On Windows, SketchUp 2016 and later has a tray of panels that help you work with components, colors, styles, and more. By default, the tray appears on the right side of the interface. You start with a default tray that contains the panels beginners use most often. To customize the tray, choose Window ⇨ Manage Trays and use the Manage Trays dialog box to reconfigure what you do (or don't) see here. On a Mac, the tools for components, colors, styles, and so on look like dialog boxes, but you can stack them like trays and keep these dialog boxes open for as long as you need them.

» **Status bar:** You can consider this your SketchUp dashboard. The status bar contains contextual information you use while you model. Most of the time, you check here to see what options may be available for whatever you're doing. *Modifier keys* (keyboard strokes that you use in combination with certain tools to perform additional functions), step-by-step instructions, and general information about what you're doing all show up in one place: right here.

» **Measurements box:** You use this box all the time as you model in SketchUp. Depending on what you're doing, this box displays information about what you're modeling or enables you to specify a precise length, angle, or other measurement. Chapters 2 and 3 help you understand all that this little unassuming box can do.

» **Context menus:** Context-clicking things in your modeling window usually causes a context menu of commands and options to open. These are always relevant to whatever you context-click (and whatever you're doing at the time), so the contents of each context menu are different. On a Windows computer, you context-click by clicking the right mouse button. On a Mac, you hold down the ⌘ button while you click.

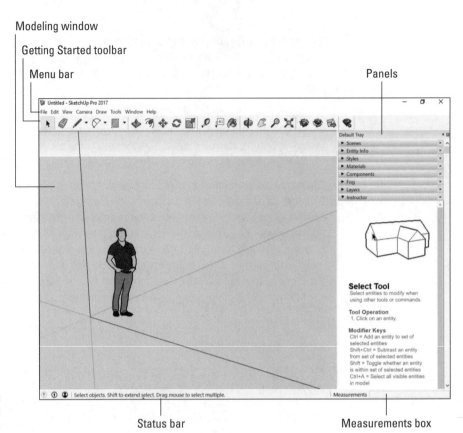

Modeling window

Getting Started toolbar

Menu bar

Panels

Status bar

Measurements box

REMEMBER

Although the following items aren't part of the SketchUp user interface (as all the stuff in the preceding list is), they're a critical part of modeling in SketchUp:

>> **A mouse with a scroll wheel:** You usually find a left button (the one you use all the time), a right button (the one that opens the context menus), and a center *scroll wheel* that you both roll back and forth and click down like a button. A mouse with a scroll wheel will improve your SketchUp experience more than any single other thing you can buy. The Mac's Magic Mouse enables you to scroll not with a wheel, but by moving your finger forward or back along the top of the mouse. However, without a scroll wheel that you can hold down to orbit, modeling the Mac with a Magic Mouse is much less efficient than adding a scroll-wheel mouse to your Mac setup.

>> **A keyboard:** This sounds silly, but some people have tried to use SketchUp without one; it's just not possible. So many things you need to do all the time (such as make copies) involve your keyboard, so you'd better have one handy if you plan to use SketchUp.

Customizing the toolbar

The Getting Started toolbar contains a small subset of the tools that you can use in SketchUp. The thinking (which we agree with, incidentally) is that seeing all the tools right away tends to overwhelm new users, so having a limited selection helps people.

TIP

To access more tools (through toolbars, anyway — you can always access everything through the menus), you do different things depending on which operating system you use:

>> **Windows:** Choose View ⇨ Toolbars. The mother lode! In the Toolbars dialog box, we recommend selecting the Large Tool Set check box to start. Then, you can add toolbars as you need them (and as you figure out what the tools do).

>> **Mac:** Choose View ⇨ Tool Palettes ⇨ Large Tool Set. To add even more tools, right-click the Getting Started toolbar (the one right above your modeling window) and choose Customize Toolbar. Now drag whatever tools you want onto your toolbar and click the Done button.

Checking out some special tools

Most graphics programs have a ton of little controller boxes, and SketchUp is no exception. Here are the ones that we think deserve special attention:

>> **Preferences:** Whereas the Model Info dialog box (see the next bullet point) contains settings for the SketchUp file you have open right now, the Preferences dialog box has controls for how SketchUp behaves — *no matter what* file you have open. Pay particular attention to the Shortcuts panel, where you can set up keyboard shortcuts for any tool or command in the program.

To set your preferences, select Window ⇨ Preferences (Windows) or SketchUp ⇨ Preferences (Mac).

TIP

Some changes to the Preferences settings don't take effect until you open another file or restart SketchUp altogether, so don't worry if you can't see a difference right away.

For a fairly comprehensive list of what every preferences option does, see this SketchUp Help Center article: `http://help.sketchup.com/en/article/3000137`.

>> **Model Info:** This dialog box is, to quote the Bard, the mother of all dialog boxes. It has controls for everything under the sun; you should definitely open

it and take your time going through it. Chances are, the next time you can't find the setting you're looking for, it's in Model Info. To open this dialog box, choose Window ⇨ Model Info.

>> **Entity Info:** This little guy is small, but it shows information about *entities* — edges, faces, groups, components, and lots of other things — in your model. On Windows, you find Entity Info in the default tray and can toggle it open or closed by clicking its arrow. On a Mac, choose Window ⇨ Entity Info.

>> **Instructor:** The Instructor does only one thing: It shows you how to use whatever tool happens to be activated. While you're learning how to use SketchUp, keep the Instructor open. You can also open it anytime by clicking its right-pointing arrow in the default tray or, on a Mac, choose Window ⇨ Instructor.

Chapter **2**

Getting a Running Start

I f you can't wait to get your hands dirty (so to speak), you've come to the right chapter. Here we help you make a simple model step by step, spin it around, paint it, and even apply styles and shadows. You don't need to read another word of this book to be able to follow along, although we do refer you to chapters where you can find out more. Above all, following along with the basic project in this chapter can help you understand how SketchUp's basic features work together and enable you to produce a knockout model in no time!

So what are you going to build? Perhaps a doghouse. The nice thing about doghouses is that they're a lot like peoplehouses in the ways that count: They have doors and roofs, and just about everybody has seen one.

REMEMBER

One last thing: Just about every other piece of this book is written so that you can jump around to the bits you need; you don't have to follow a particular order. This chapter is the exception. If you want to follow along, start on this page and work your way to the end. Otherwise, the steps just won't make sense.

Setting Up Your Workspace

We know — setup is boring. Who wants to flip through menus and options dialog boxes instead of jumping in? We completely agree, so we keep this short and sweet. This section is just about making sure you start at the right place. That's it.

Follow these steps to get ready:

1. Launch SketchUp.

The Welcome to SketchUp dialog box appears, as shown in Figure 2-1. The dialog box looks a little different in SketchUp Make versus SketchUp Pro, but the steps for setting up your workspace work the same in either version.

FIGURE 2-1:
The Welcome
to SketchUp
dialog box.

2. Open the Template area by clicking the arrow next to its name, select one of the Architectural Design templates, and click the Start Using SketchUp button.

A new SketchUp file opens.

If the Welcome to SketchUp dialog box doesn't appear, someone (maybe you) has told the dialog box not to show up automatically on startup. Choose Help ➪ Welcome to SketchUp from the menu bar, select an Architectural Design template, and click the Start Using SketchUp button. Then choose File ➪ New to open a new file with the template you selected.

3. Make sure that you can see the Getting Started toolbar.

Figure 2-2 shows the Getting Started toolbar. If it's not visible in your modeling window, choose View ➪ Toolbars ➪ Getting Started to make it show up. If you're on a Mac, choose View ➪ Show Toolbar.

FIGURE 2-2:
The Getting
Started toolbar
lives at the top
of your model-
ing window.

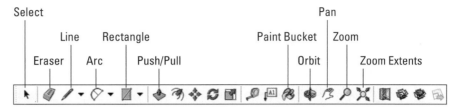

Select

Pan

Line   Rectangle   Paint Bucket   Zoom

Eraser   Arc   Push/Pull   Orbit   Zoom Extents

4. **Clear your modeling window.**

If your computer has run SketchUp already, you may see dialog boxes all over the place. If that's the case, put everything back where it belongs by resetting your workspace:

a. *Choose Window ⇨ Preferences (Microsoft Windows) or SketchUp ⇨ Preferences (Mac OS X).*

b. *In the Preferences dialog box, select Workspace panel on the left.*

c. *Click the Reset Workspace button.*

Making a Quick Model

Figure 2-3 shows what your computer screen looks like at this point. You should see a row of tools across the top of your modeling window, a little person, and three colored *modeling axes* — red, green, and blue lines.

FIGURE 2-3:
This is what
your screen
should look
like in Windows
(left) and on a
Mac (right).

Follow these steps to build a doghouse:

1. **Delete the little person on your screen.**

Using the Select tool (the arrow on the far left of your toolbar), click the little person to select him or her. (The person changes with each version of SketchUp. In SketchUp 2016, the person is Lisanne. In SketchUp 2017, you see Chris.) Then choose Edit ⇨ Delete.

2. **Choose Camera ⇨ Standard Views ⇨ Iso.**

This command switches you to an *isometric (3D)* view of your model, which allows you to build something without having to "move around."

3. **Draw a rectangle on the ground.**

Use the Rectangle tool (refer to Figure 2-2) to draw a rectangle by doing the following:

a. Click once to place one corner on the left side of your screen.

b. Click again to place the opposite corner on the right side of your screen.

Remember that you're in a 3D *perspective,* or view of the world, so your rectangle looks more like a diamond — 90-degree angles don't look like 90-degree angles in perspective. Figure 2-4 shows what you should aim for in this step.

TIP

It's important to draw the right kind of rectangle for this example (or for any model you're trying to create in Perspective view), so try it a few times until it looks like the rectangle in Figure 2-4. To go back a step, choose Edit ⇨ Undo Rectangle (or press Ctrl+Z). You can use Undo to go back as many steps as you like.

Click here to start drawing   Finish drawing here

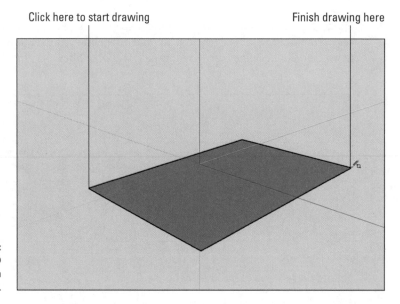

FIGURE 2-4:
Draw a 3D
rectangle on
the ground.

4. **Select the Push/Pull tool and extrude your rectangle into a box by clicking the rectangle and then clicking again somewhere above the rectangle.**

At this point, your model should look like Figure 2-5; if it doesn't, use Push/Pull again to make your box look about the right height.

TIP

If you're happily pushing/pulling away on your box and everything suddenly disappears, you pushed/pulled the top of your box all the way to the ground. Just choose Edit ⇨ Undo and keep going.

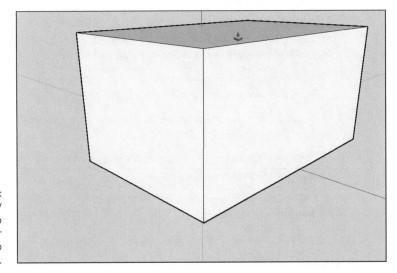

FIGURE 2-5:
Use the Push/
Pull tool to
extrude your
rectangle into
a box.

5. **Select the Line tool and draw two diagonal lines for your roof, as shown in Figure 2-6.**

Here's a step-by-step explanation of how to draw the lines:

a. *Click once at the midpoint of the top of your box's front face to start your line.*

You know you're at the midpoint when you see a small, light blue dot and the word *Midpoint* appears. In SketchUp, these tips are called *inferences.* Move slowly to make sure that you see the Midpoint inference.

b. *Click again somewhere along one of the side edges of your box's front face to end your line.*

Wait until you see a red *On Edge* inference before you click; if you don't, your new line won't end on the edge where it needs to be.

c. *Repeat the previous two steps to draw a similar but opposite line from the midpoint to the edge on the other side of the face.*

Don't worry about making your diagonal lines symmetrical; for the purposes of this exercise, it's not important that they are.

Click here to start drawing   Click here to finish your first edge

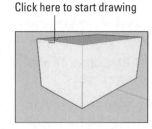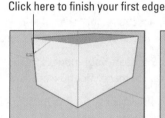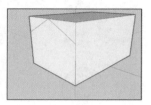

FIGURE 2-6:
Draw two
diagonal
lines that will
become your
peaked roof.

6. **Push/pull the triangles away to leave a sloped roof.**

Use the Push/Pull tool (the same one you use in Step 4) to get rid of the triangular parts of your box, leaving you with a sloped roof. Have a look at Figure 2-7 to see this in action and then follow these steps:

a. *Choose Edit ⇨ Select None to make sure you don't have anything selected in your model. If this menu option is grayed out, you're good to go.*

b. *Select the Push/Pull tool and then click the right triangular face once to start the push/pull operation.*

c. *Move your cursor to the right to push the triangle as far as it will go (so that it's even with the end of your box).*

d. *Click again (on the triangle) to end the push/pull operation and to make the triangular face disappear.*

e. *Still using the Push/Pull tool, double-click the left triangular face to repeat the previous push/pull operation, making that face disappear as well.*

7. **Draw a rectangle on your front face.**

Switch back to the Rectangle tool (which you used in Step 3) and draw a rectangle on the front face of your pointy box. Make sure that the bottom of your rectangle is flush with the bottom of your box by watching for the red On Edge inference to appear before you click. Figure 2-8 shows what your model looks like when you're done.

TIP

Using the Rectangle tool is a two-step process: You click once to place one corner and again to place the opposite corner. Avoid drawing lines and shapes by *dragging* your cursor. In SketchUp, doing so makes modeling more difficult. Practice clicking once to start an operation, such as drawing a rectangle, and clicking again to stop.

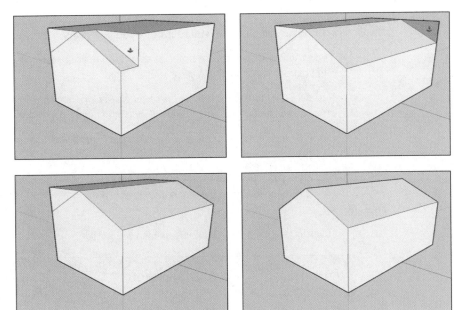

FIGURE 2-7:
Use the Push/
Pull tool
to form a
peaked roof on
your box.

Finish here

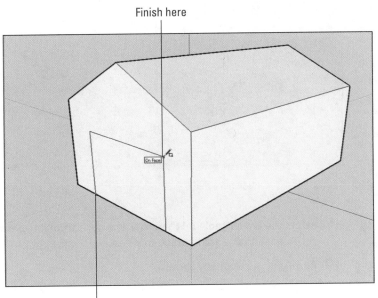

On Face

FIGURE 2-8:
A rectangle
drawn on the
front of your
pointy box.

Click here to start drawing

8. **Draw an arc on top of the rectangle you just drew.**

Use the 2 Point Arc tool to draw an arc on top of your rectangle, as illustrated in Figure 2-9. Follow these steps to draw an arc:

a. *Click the upper-left corner of the rectangle to place one endpoint of your arc. Make sure that you see the green Endpoint inference before you click.*

b. *Click the upper-right corner of the rectangle to place the other endpoint of your arc.*

c. *Move your cursor up to bow out the line you're drawing into an arc and then click when you're happy with how the arc looks.*

Click here to start   Click here second

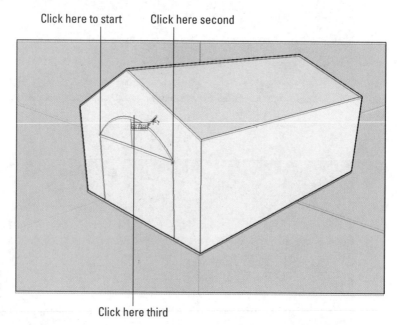

FIGURE 2-9:
Draw an arc on top of your rectangle.

Click here third

9. **Select the Eraser tool and then click the horizontal line between the rectangle and the arc to erase that line.**

10. **Push/pull the doorway inward.**

Use the Push/Pull tool (which you're an old hand with by now) to push in the "doorway" face you created in Steps 7 through 9 just a bit.

Use the Push/Pull tool by clicking a face once to start, moving your cursor to push/pull it in or out, and then clicking again to stop.

REMEMBER

11. **Erase the horizontal line at the bottom of the doorway by clicking it with the Eraser tool.**

This makes the line (and the whole face above it) disappear. Figure 2-10 shows what your finished doghouse looks like.

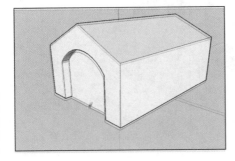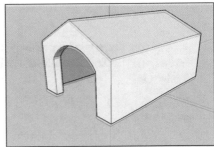

FIGURE 2-10:
Create the
door opening
by erasing its
bottom edge.

For a more detailed introduction to drawing lines and working with midpoints, angles, and more, flip to Chapter 3.

Slapping On Some Paint

We have an ulterior motive for getting you to paint your doghouse: To color it, you have to understand how to spin it around first. Moving around your model is *the most important* skill to develop when you're first figuring out SketchUp. Run through these steps to apply colors (and textures) to the faces in your model, and to find out about moving around while you're doing it:

1. **In Windows, open the Materials panel by clicking the right-pointing arrow next to its name in the Default Tray. On a Mac, choose Window ⇨ Materials.**

You see the Windows and Mac versions of the Materials panel in Figure 2-11.

2. **Click a color or texture you like.**

When you do, you automatically pick up the Paint Bucket tool and fill it with your chosen material.

3. **Paint some of the faces in your model by clicking any face with the Paint Bucket tool.**

4. **Switch materials.**

Choose another material from the Materials panel by clicking it.

Click here to see the Materials libraries

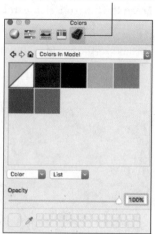

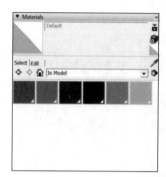

FIGURE 2-11:
The Materials
panel in
Windows (left)
and on a Mac
(right).

5. Paint the rest of the faces you can see.

Loop through Steps 2 to 4 for as long as you like. Finding the Materials panel in SketchUp is like getting a brand-new box of crayons when you were little (you know, the *big* box, with the built-in sharpener).

6. Select the Orbit tool; it's on the toolbar, just to the left of the creepy hand (also known as the Pan tool).

7. Click somewhere on the left side of your screen and *drag* your cursor over to the right, as shown in Figure 2-12. Release your mouse button when you're done.

Your model spins, or *orbits!* Orbit around some more, just to get the hang of it.

TIP

If you're orbiting, and you've dragged your cursor over as far as it will go, and you haven't orbited as much as you wanted to, don't fret. Just release the mouse button, move your cursor over to where it was when you started orbiting, and orbit some more by clicking and dragging. To see what you want to see, you usually need a bunch of separate drags (separate orbits, I guess).

FIGURE 2-12:
Choose the
Orbit tool and
drag your
cursor to spin
your model.

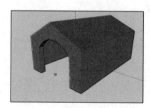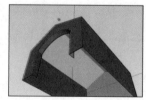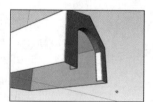

8. **Zoom in and out if you need to by selecting the Zoom tool and dragging your cursor up and down in your modeling window.**

Dragging up zooms in, and dragging down zooms out.

TIP

You can also zoom in and out by rolling the scroll wheel on your mouse. If you have a Mac with a Magic Mouse, the scrolling gestures work like a scroll wheel.

9. **If needed, move around in two dimensions with the Pan tool by selecting it and then clicking and dragging the Pan cursor inside your modeling window.**

Use Pan to slide your model around inside your modeling window without spinning it or making it look bigger or smaller. You can pan in any direction.

10. **Use the Orbit, Zoom, Pan, and Paint Bucket tools to finish painting your doghouse.**

Now that you know how to move around your model, try painting the different parts these specific colors, as shown in Figure 2-13:

- Paint the exterior walls red-brown.

- Paint the roof light blue.

- Paint the interior yellow-orange.

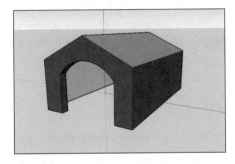
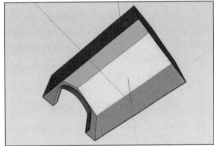

FIGURE 2-13: Orbit (spin) your model to paint all the faces.

TIP

When you're just starting out, you can easily become a little lost with the navigation tools (Orbit, Zoom, and Pan). If you find yourself in a pickle, choose Camera ➪ Zoom Extents. SketchUp plunks your model right in front of you, as shown in Figure 2-14. Just so you know, Zoom Extents is also a button on the toolbar; it's right next to the Zoom tool.

For more details about using SketchUp's drawing tools, Chapter 3 walks you through many basic drawing and modeling skills. After you're comfortable with the techniques in Chapter 3, explore the details about modeling buildings in Chapter 4 or the tips on modeling parts and shapes in Chapter 6.

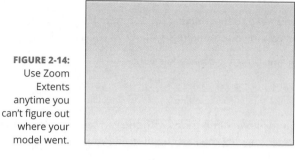
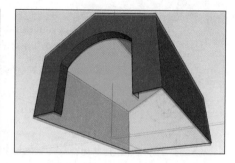

FIGURE 2-14:
Use Zoom
Extents
anytime you
can't figure out
where your
model went.

Giving Your Model Some Style

SketchUp Styles enable you to change your model's appearance — the way it's drawn, basically — with just a few mouse clicks. SketchUp also comes with a library of premade styles that you can use without knowing anything about how they work. (After you discover how styles work, you might want to try creating your own, as explained in Chapter 10.)

Follow these steps to try a couple styles on your doghouse:

1. **Open the Styles panel by clicking the right-pointing arrow next to its name in the Default Tray (Windows). Or choose Window ⇨ Styles (Mac).**

   By default, you see the Select tab, which is where you can browse and select styles. At the top of the Select tab, a drop-down list enables you to open different style libraries. The styles in each library appear in the bottom half of the Select tab.

2. **From the drop-down list, choose the Assorted Styles library, as shown in Figure 2-15.**

3. **Click a style to see how it changes your model's whole appearance.**

   You can click through the different styles to see what your options are. Figure 2-16 shows the doghouse with a few styles applied — can you figure out which ones?

 4. **Go back to your original style by clicking the In Model icon and selecting the Architectural Design style.**

   In the Styles panel, clicking the In Model icon displays a list of all the styles you've applied to your model. The Architectural Design style should be first in the list. Chapter 10 explains styles in more detail.

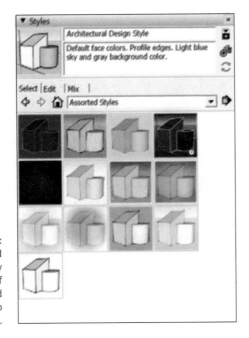

FIGURE 2-15:
The Assorted
Styles library
is a sampler of
ready-mixed
SketchUp
styles.

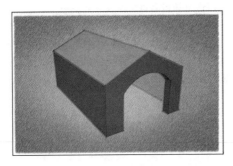

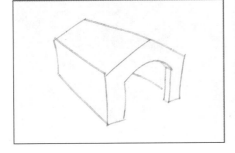

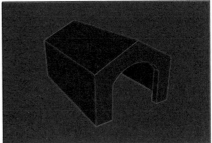

FIGURE 2-16:
The same
doghouse
with four very
different styles
applied to it.

Switching On the Sun

You're about to use what we consider to be one of SketchUp's best features: Shadows. When you turn on Shadows, you're activating SketchUp's built-in sun. The shadows you see in your modeling window are *accurate* for whatever time and location you set.

Ready to shine light on your model? Follow these steps:

1. **Use Orbit, Zoom, and Pan to get an aerial, three-quarter view of your doghouse, sort of like the view shown in Figure 2-17.**

2. **Click the right-pointing arrow next to the Shadows panel in the default tray (Windows). Or choose Window ⇨ Shadows (Mac).**

   You see the Shadow Settings panel. (Refer to Figure 2-17.)

3. **Click the Show/Hide Shadows button (in the upper-left corner) to toggle on the sun.**

   Your doghouse casts a shadow on the ground.

4. **Move the Time slider back and forth.**

   Changing the time of day means that you're moving SketchUp's sun around in the sky. When the sun moves around, so do your shadows. To see accurate shadows, you also have to *geolocate* your model, which is a fancy way of saying that you give it a latitude. Chapter 10 explains how to create accurate shadow studies.

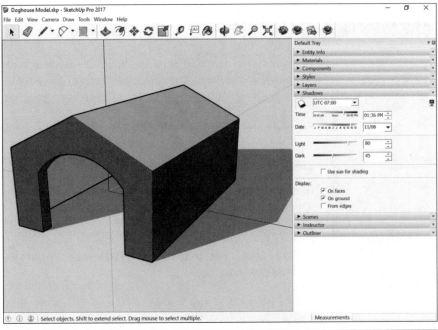

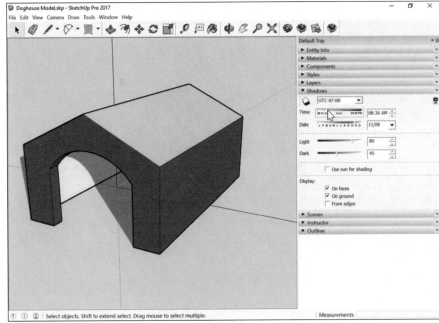

FIGURE 2-17:
Use Orbit,
Zoom, and Pan
to navigate
around until
your model
looks some-
thing like this.

Sharing Your Masterpiece

Now that you have a model that looks about the way you want it to, you probably want to show it to someone. The easiest way is to export a JPEG image that you can attach to an e-mail. Follow these steps, and you're on your way:

1. **Navigate around (using Orbit, Zoom, and Pan) until you like the view of your model that you see in your modeling window.**

2. **Choose File ⇨ Export ⇨ 2D Graphic.**

3. **In the Export dialog box that opens, choose to export the graphic as a JPEG.**

4. **Pick a location on your computer and give your exported image a name.**

5. **Click the Export button to create a JPEG image of what's visible in your modeling window.**

Exporting a JPEG file is just one way to share models. To find out about all your options, see Part 4, which explains how to share your model on the SketchUp 3D Warehouse, as a printout, as an image or animation, as part of a multipage document, or as a slick presentation that will (hopefully) impress all your friends.

Chapter **3**

Establishing the Modeling Mindset

When you were learning how to drive a car, you probably didn't just get behind the wheel, step on the gas, and figure it out as you went along. (If you did, you probably have bigger things to worry about than getting started with SketchUp.) The point is, knowing some basic concepts can make your first few hours with SketchUp *much* more productive and fun.

So here's the deal: This chapter has three main parts:

» The first part talks about edges and faces — the basic *stuff* that SketchUp models are made of.

» The second part explains how SketchUp enables you to model in 3D (three dimensions) on a 2D (flat) surface — namely, your computer screen. Understanding how SketchUp represents depth is *everything* when making models. If you've never used 3D modeling software before, pay close attention to the middle part of this chapter.

» The final part of this chapter is about the things you need to do all the time — things like navigating around your model, drawing lines, selecting things, and working with accurate measurements.

All about Edges and Faces

In SketchUp, everything is made up of one of two kinds of *elements:* edges or faces. They're the basic building blocks of every model you'll ever make.

REMEMBER

Collectively, the edges and faces in your model are *geometry.* Other modeling programs have other kinds of geometry, but SketchUp is pretty simple. That's a good thing — you have less to keep track of.

The drawing on the left in Figure 3-1 is a basic cube drawn in SketchUp; it's composed of 12 edges and 6 faces. The model on the right is a lot more complex, but the geometry's the same; it's all just edges and faces.

Edge   Face

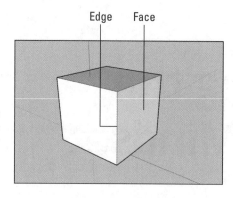

Face   Edge

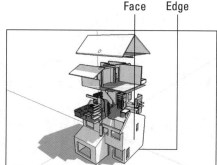

FIGURE 3-1: SketchUp models are made from edges and faces.

Living on the edge

Edges are lines. You can use lots of tools to draw them, erase them, move them, hide them, and even stretch them. Here are some things you ought to know about SketchUp edges:

>> **Edges are always straight.** Not only is everything in your SketchUp model made up of edges, but all those edges are also perfectly straight. Even arcs and circles are made of small straight-line segments, as shown in Figure 3-2.

>> **Edges don't have a thickness.** This one's a little tricky to get your head around. You never have to worry about how thick the edges in your model are because that's not how SketchUp works. Depending on how you choose to *display* your model, your edges may look like they have different thicknesses, but your edges themselves don't have a built-in thickness.

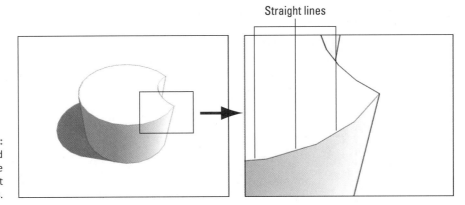

Straight lines

FIGURE 3-2:
Even curved lines are made up of straight edges.

>> **Just because you can't see the edges doesn't mean they're not there.**
Edges can be hidden so that you can't see them; doing so is a popular way to make certain forms. Take a look at Figure 3-3. On the left is a model that looks rounded. On the right, the hidden edges are visible as dashed lines — see how even surfaces that look smoothly curved are made of straight edges?

These edges are smoothed, but still there

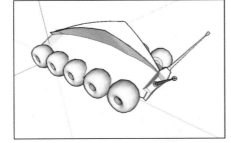
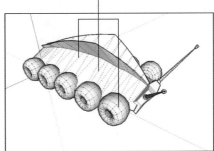

FIGURE 3-3:
Even organic shapes and curvy forms are made up of straight edges.

Facing the facts about faces

Faces are surfaces. If you think of SketchUp models as being made of toothpicks and paper (which they kind of are), faces are basically the paper. Here's what you need to know about faces:

>> **You can't have faces without edges.** To have a face, you need to have at least three *coplanar* (on the same plane) edges that are connected. In other words, a face is defined by the edges that surround it, and those edges all have to be on the same, flat *plane*. Because you need at least three straight lines to make a closed shape, faces must have at least three sides. There's no

limit to the number of sides a SketchUp face can have, though. Figure 3-4 shows how faces can disappear when you erase an edge that defines one or more faces. We started with the model on the left and deleted the edge that completed both the top face and one of the side faces. The result, shown in the right, is that both of those faces disappeared.

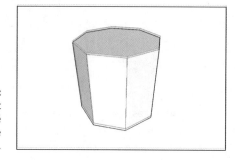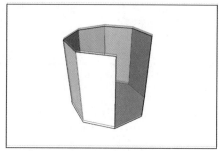

FIGURE 3-4:
You need at least three edges to make a face.

» **Faces are always flat.** In SketchUp, even surfaces that look curved are made of multiple, flat faces. In the model shown in Figure 3-5, what look like organically shaped surfaces (on the left) are really just lots of smaller faces (on the right). To make a bunch of flat faces look like one big, curvy surface, the edges between them are *smoothed*. You find out about smoothing edges in Chapter 6.

Each of these triangles is perfectly flat

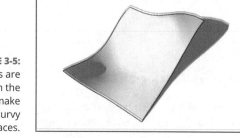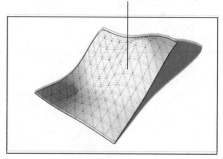

FIGURE 3-5:
All faces are flat, even the ones that make up larger, curvy surfaces.

» **Just like edges, faces don't have any thickness.** If faces are a lot like pieces of paper, they're *infinitely thin* pieces of paper — they don't have any thickness. To make a thick surface (say, a 6-inch-thick wall), you need to use two faces side by side.

Understanding the relationship between edges and faces

Now you know that models are made from edges and faces, you're most of the way to understanding how SketchUp works. Here's some information that should fill in the gaps:

>> **Every time SketchUp can make a face, it will.** There's no such thing as a "Face tool" in this software; SketchUp just automatically makes a face every time you finish drawing a closed shape out of three or more coplanar edges. Figure 3-6 shows this in action: As soon as a line connects the last edge to the first one, SketchUp creates a face.

FIGURE 3-6: SketchUp automatically makes a face whenever you create a closed loop of coplanar edges.

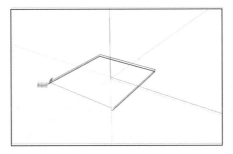 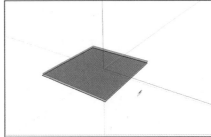

>> **You can't stop SketchUp from creating faces, but you can erase them if you want.** If SketchUp creates a face you don't want, just right-click the face and choose Erase from the context menu. That face is deleted, but the edges that defined it remain, as illustrated in Figure 3-7.

>> **Retracing an edge re-creates a missing face.** If you already have a closed loop of coplanar edges but no face (because you erased it, perhaps), you can *redraw* one of the edges to make a new face. Just use the Line tool to trace over one of the edge segments, and a face reappears, as shown in Figure 3-8.

>> **Drawing an edge all the way across a face splits the face in two.** When you draw an edge (like with the Line tool) from one side of a face to another, you cut that face in two. The same thing happens when you draw a closed loop of edges (like a rectangle) on a face — you end up with two faces, one "inside" the other. In Figure 3-9, we split a face in two with the Line tool and then extruded one face a little bit with the Push/Pull tool.

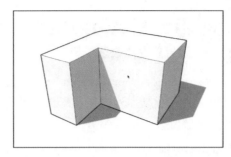

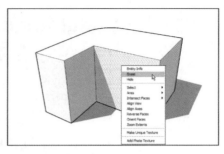

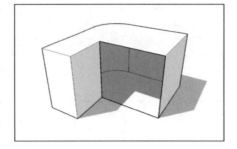

FIGURE 3-7:
You can delete a face without deleting the edges that define it.

Drawing an edge from here...   ...to here...   ...causes this face to be created

FIGURE 3-8:
Just retrace any edge on a closed loop to tell SketchUp to create a new face.

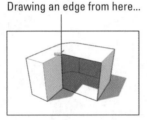
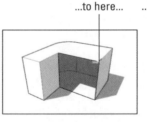
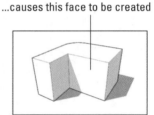

>> **Drawing an edge that crosses another edge splits both edges where they touch.** In this way, you can split simple edges you draw with the Line tool, as well as edges created when you draw shapes like rectangles and circles. Most of the time, this auto-slicing is desirable, but if it's not, you can always use groups and components to separate your geometry. Flip to the first part of Chapter 5 for more information.

FIGURE 3-9:
Splitting a face with an edge, and then extruding one of the new faces.

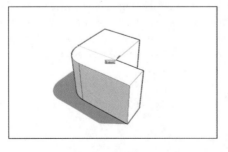
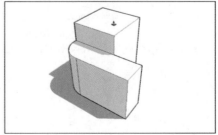

Drawing in 3D on a 2D Screen

For computer programmers, letting you draw 3D objects on your screen is a difficult problem. You wouldn't think it'd be such a big deal; after all, people have been drawing in perspective for a very long time. If some old guy could figure it out 500 years ago, why should your computer have problems?

The thing is, human perception of depth on paper is a trick of the eye. And of course, your computer doesn't have eyes that enable it to interpret depth without thinking about it. You need to give your computer explicit instructions. In SketchUp, this means using drawing axes and inferences, as we explain in the sections that follow.

DON'T WORRY ABOUT DRAWING IN PERSPECTIVE

Contrary to popular belief, modeling in SketchUp doesn't involve drawing in perspective and letting the software figure out what you mean. This turns out to be a very good thing for two reasons:

- **Computers aren't very good at figuring out what you're trying to do.** This has probably happened to you: You're working away at your computer, and the software you're using tries to "help" by guessing what you're doing. Sometimes it works, but most of the time it doesn't. Eventually, the computer's bad guesswork gets really annoying. Even if SketchUp *could* interpret your perspective drawings, you'd probably spend more time correcting its mistakes than actually building something.

- **Most people can't draw in perspective anyway.** Even if you're one of the few folks who *can,* you know darn well that most people couldn't draw an accurate 3D view of the inside of a room if their lives depended on it. Drawing just isn't one of the things people are taught, unfortunately. So even if SketchUp *did* work by turning your 2D perspective drawings into 3D models (which it most certainly doesn't), the vast majority of those who "can't draw" couldn't use it. And that would be a shame because building 3D models is a real kick.

Giving instructions with the drawing axes

See the three colored lines that cross in the SketchUp modeling window? These are the *drawing axes*, and they're the key to understanding how SketchUp works. Simply put, you use SketchUp's drawing axes to figure out where you are and where you want to go in 3D space. When you're working with the color axes, you need to keep three important things in mind:

>> **The red, green, and blue drawing axes define 3D space in your model.** If you were standing at the spot where all three axes meet — the *axis origin* — the blue axis would run vertically, passing through your head and feet. The red and green axes define the ground plane in SketchUp; you'd be standing on top of them. The axes are all at right angles to one another, and extend to infinity from the origin.

>> **When you draw, move, or copy something parallel to one of the colored axes, you're working in that color's direction.** Take a look at Figure 3-10. In the first image, we're drawing a line parallel to the *red* axis, or drawing "in the *red* direction." You know a line is parallel to the red axis because the line turns red to let you know. In the second image, we're moving a box parallel to the *blue* axis, or "moving in the *blue* direction." The dotted, blue line appears to tell you so.

>> **The colored drawing axes help you tell SketchUp what you mean.** For example, in Figure 3-11, moving the cylinder in the blue direction and the green direction both involve moving the cursor up. The drawing axes help SketchUp know whether you want to move the cylinder *up* in space (above the ground) or *back* in space.

When you work in SketchUp, you use the colored drawing axes *all the time.* They're not just handy; they're what make SketchUp work. They make modeling in SketchUp quick, accurate, and relatively intuitive. As you model, all you have to do is make sure that you're working in your intended color direction: Line up your geometry with the appropriate axis and watch the visual cues that tell you what direction you're working in.

REMEMBER

FIGURE 3-10:
Visual cues tell you when you're drawing or moving geometry parallel to a drawing axis.

Drawing in the red direction

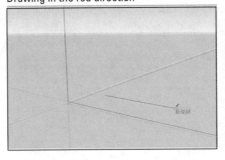

Moving in the blue direction

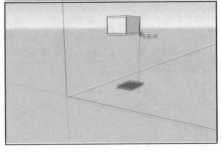

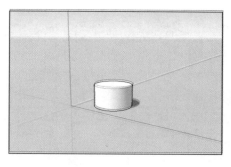

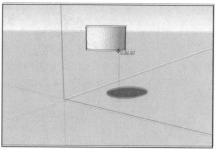

To go up, move in the blue direction

To go back, move in the green direction

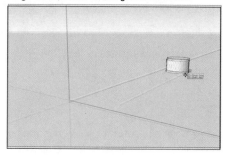

FIGURE 3-11:
The axes help
you create 3D
models on a
2D screen.

Keeping an eye out for inferences

If you've spent any time fiddling with SketchUp, you've noticed all the little colored circles, squares, dotted lines, yellow screen tips, and other doodads that show up as you move your cursor around your modeling window. All this stuff is referred to collectively as SketchUp's *inference engine,* and its sole purpose is to help you while you build models. Luckily, it does. Without inferences (the aforementioned doodads), SketchUp wouldn't be very useful.

Point inferences

Generally, SketchUp's inferences help you be more precise. *Point* inferences appear when you move your cursor over specific parts of your model. They look like little colored circles and squares, and if you pause for a second, a yellow label appears. For example, the little green Endpoint inference (which appears whenever your cursor hovers over the end of an edge) helps you accurately connect an edge that you're drawing to the end of another edge in your model.

Figure 3-12 shows the point inferences that you use most often.

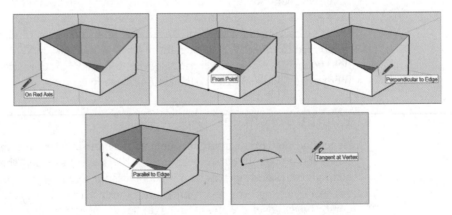

FIGURE 3-12: Point inferences appear when you hover your cursor over key points and help you draw accurately.

REMEMBER

In SketchUp, lines are called *edges,* and surfaces are called *faces.* Everything in your model is made up of edges and faces.

Linear inferences

As you've probably already noticed, color plays a big part in SketchUp's *user interface,* or the way it looks. Maybe the best example of this is in the software's *linear* inferences — the "helper lines" that show up to help you work more precisely. Figure 3-13 illustrates the important linear inferences, and here's a description of what they do:

FIGURE 3-13: SketchUp's linear inferences help you align new geometry with existing geometry.

>> **On Axis:** When an edge you're drawing is parallel to one of the colored drawing axes, the edge turns the color of that axis. In Figure 3-13, you see the On Red Axis inference.

>> **From Point:** This one's a little harder to describe. When a colored, dotted line appears as you move your cursor, your cursor is "lined up" with the point at

the other end of the dotted line. Naturally, the color of the From Point inference reflects the axis you're lined up "on." Sometimes From Point inferences show up on their own, and sometimes you have to *encourage* them; see the section "Using inferences to help you model," later in this chapter, for details.

>> **Perpendicular:** When you draw an edge that's perpendicular to another edge, the one you're drawing turns magenta (reddish purple).

>> **Parallel:** When the edge you're drawing is parallel to another edge in your model, it turns magenta to let you know. You tell SketchUp which edge you're interested in "being parallel to" by *encouraging* an inference.

>> **Tangent at Vertex:** This one applies only when you draw an arc (using the Arc tool) that starts at the endpoint of another arc. When the arc you're drawing is *tangent* to the other one, the one you're drawing turns cyan. *Tangent,* in this case, means that the transition between the two arcs is smooth.

TIP

One of the most important inferences in SketchUp is one that you probably didn't even realize was an inference: Unless you specifically start on an edge or a face in your model, you always draw on the ground plane by default. That's right — if you just start creating stuff in the middle of nowhere, SketchUp just assumes that you mean to draw on the ground.

Using inferences to help you model

A big part of using SketchUp's inference engine involves *locking* and *encouraging* inferences — sometimes even simultaneously. At first, these actions seem a little like that thing where you pat your head and rub your stomach at the same time, but with practice, they get easier.

>> **Locking inferences:** If you hold down the Shift key when you see any of the first four types of linear inferences described previously, that inference gets *locked* — and stays locked until you release Shift. When you lock an inference, you constrain whatever tool you're using to work only in the direction of the inference you locked.

>> **Encouraging inferences:** Sometimes an inference you need doesn't show up on its own. When this happens, you have to *encourage* it. To encourage an inference, hover your cursor over the part of your model you want to "infer" from and then slowly go back to whatever you were doing when you decided you could use an inference.

The following example illustrates how you might lock and encourage inferences to draw a 3D model. In Figure 3-14, say you want to draw a line on the blue axis that's parallel to the back-right corner of the house and as tall as the roof's bottom edge. Here's how you might use inferences to help you:

1. **With the Line tool selected, encourage a From Point inference by hovering the cursor over the back-right corner of the house and then slowly moving your cursor away from that corner to encourage a From Point inference.**

2. **Click to set the line's starting point and hold down the Shift key to lock the line in the blue direction as you draw the line.**

   The blue line inference becomes thicker to show the line is locked in the blue direction.

3. **When the line is close to your desired endpoint, hover your mouse cursor over that endpoint while continuing to hold down the Shift key. When the inference to the endpoint appears, click to set the endpoint of your new line.**

1. Encourage a From Point inference.

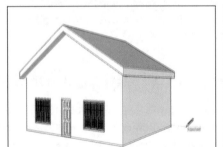

2. Lock the direction.

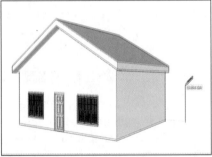

3. Encourage another point inference.

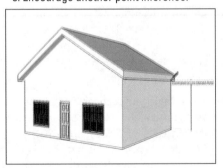

FIGURE 3-14:
Lock and encourage inferences as you draw new geometry in relationship to existing geometry.

Warming Up Your SketchUp Muscles

About eight SketchUp skills are useful every time you use SketchUp. Formal-education types would probably call them *core competencies*. Whatever you care to call these activities, we introduce them all in the following sections. Anytime you need a quick refresher, come back to this section.

Getting the best view of what you're doing

Using SketchUp without learning how to orbit, zoom, and pan is like trying to build a ship in a bottle. In the dark. With your hands tied behind your back. Using chopsticks. Get the picture?

REMEMBER

Fully half of modeling in SketchUp uses the Orbit, Zoom, and Pan tools, which let you change your view so that you can see what you're doing. Most people who try to figure out SketchUp on their own take too long to understand the importance of these navigation tools and spend hours squinting, grunting, and having an all-around miserable time trying to "get at" what they're working on. The following sections help you avoid the headache (literally).

Going into orbit

Hold a glass of water in your hand. Now twist and turn your wrist around in every direction so that the water's all over you and the rest of the room. Stop when the glass is completely empty. We think that's a pretty memorable way to find out about the Orbit tool, don't you?

Just as your wrist helps you twist and turn a glass to see it from every angle, think of using Orbit as the way to fly around your work. Figure 3-15 shows Orbit in all its glory.

TIP

Although you can find the Orbit tool on the Camera menu and an Orbit button on the toolbar, here's how you should *always* orbit: Hold down your mouse's scroll wheel and move your mouse around. See your model swiveling? Release the scroll wheel when you're done. Using your mouse to orbit means that you don't have to switch tools every time you want a better view, which saves you *truckloads* of time.

Zooming in and out

Hold your empty glass at arm's length. Close your eyes and then bring the glass rushing toward you, stopping right when it smashes you in the nose. Now throw the glass across the room, noticing how it shrinks as it gets farther away. That, in a nutshell, describes the Zoom tool.

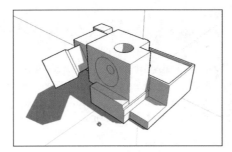
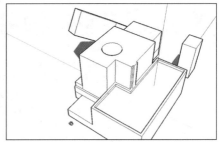
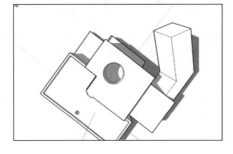
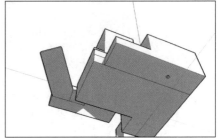

FIGURE 3-15:
The Orbit tool lets you see your model from any angle.

You use Zoom to get closer to (and farther from) your model. If you're working on something small, you zoom in until it fills your modeling window. To see everything at once, zoom out. Figure 3-16 is a demonstration.

Zoomed in   Zoomed in eve

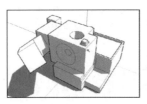

FIGURE 3-16:
Use the Zoom tool to get closer to the action.

TIP

As you're drawing in SketchUp, you zoom in and out of your model all the time, and the following tips make zooming quick and easy:

>> **To zoom in and out, roll your finger on your mouse's scroll wheel.** This method is the easiest way to zoom. You can find a Zoom tool on the Camera menu and a Zoom button on the toolbar, but zooming with your mouse's scroll wheel means that you don't have to switch tools. When you stop scrolling, you stop zooming and revert to your active tool.

>> **As you scroll, SketchUp zooms in on your cursor.** Position the cursor over whatever part of your model you want to see closer (or from farther away).

>> **Use Zoom Extents to see everything.** If you want your model to fill your modeling window (which is especially useful when you "get lost" with the navigation tools — trust us, it happens to everyone), just choose Camera ⇨ Zoom Extents. You can also click the Zoom Extents button on the toolbar.

Just panning around

Using the Pan tool is a lot like washing windows: You move the paper towel back and forth, but it stays flat and never gets any closer or farther away from you. The Pan tool is basically for sliding your model view around in your modeling window. To see something that's to the right, you use Pan to slide your model to the left. It's as simple as that.

Although you find a Pan tool on the Camera menu and a Pan button on the toolbar, here's the best way to pan: Hold down your mouse's scroll wheel button and press the Shift key. When you do both at the same time — basically, Orbit+Shift — your cursor temporarily turns into the Pan tool, and you can move your mouse to pan.

TIP

Drawing and erasing edges with ease

Here's *the* secret to modeling anything you want in SketchUp: Learn to use the Line tool without having to think too much about it. You use the Line tool to draw individual edges, and because SketchUp models are really just fancy collections of edges (carefully arranged of course), anything you can make in SketchUp, you can make with the Line tool.

SketchUp models are made up of edges and faces. Any time you have three or more edges that form a closed shape and are *on the same plane*, SketchUp creates a face. If you erase an edge that *defines,* or borders, a face, the face disappears, too. Take a look at the section "All about Edges and Faces," earlier in this chapter, for more information on the relationship between edges and faces.

REMEMBER

Drawing edges is simple. Just follow these steps:

1. **Select the Line tool.**

   You can select the Line tool from the Draw menu or the toolbar. Pressing the L key activates the Line tool, too.

2. **Click where you want your line to begin.**

3. **Move your cursor to the desired endpoint for your line and click again to end.**

   When you draw a line segment with the Line tool, notice how SketchUp automatically tries to draw another line? This is called *rubber banding* — the Line tool lets you continue to draw edge segments, automatically starting each new one at the end of the previous one you drew.

4. **When you want the Line tool to stop drawing lines, press the Esc key to snip the line at the last spot you clicked.**

TIP

SketchUp lets you draw lines in two ways: You can either use the click-drag-release method or the click-move-click one. We highly recommend training yourself to click-move-click. You'll have more control, and your hand won't get as tired. When you draw edges by clicking and *dragging* your mouse (click-drag-release), you're a lot more likely to "drop" your line accidentally. Because the Line tool draws only straight lines, think about using it less like a pencil (even though it looks like one) and more like a spool of sticky thread.

The Eraser tool is specifically designed for erasing edges. You find this tool on the Draw menu and the toolbar, or activate it by pressing the E key. To erase an edge, select the Eraser tool and click the edges you don't like to delete them. You can also *drag* over edges with the Eraser, but that's a little harder. To erase several edges at once, select them (selecting is explained in the upcoming section, "Selecting what you mean to select"); then context-click the selection and choose Erase.

Injecting accuracy into your model

Most of the time, you need to make sure that your model is accurate — that what you've modeled is precisely the size you intend it to be. In SketchUp, the key to accuracy is the Measurements box. This powerful little text box lives in the lower-right corner of your SketchUp window.

TURNING OFF RUBBER-BANDING LINES

Depending on what you're making and how you work, you may want to turn off the Line tool's rubber-banding behavior. To do so, follow these steps:

1. **Choose Window ⇨ Preferences (SketchUp ⇨ Preferences on the Mac).**

2. **Choose the Drawing panel from the list on the left in the Preferences dialog box.**

3. **Clear the Continue Line Drawing check box.**

Here are some things the Measurements box can do:

>> Make a line a certain length.

>> Draw a rectangle a certain size.

>> Push/pull a face a certain distance.

>> Change the number of sides in a polygon.

>> Move something a given distance.

>> Rotate something by a certain number of degrees.

>> Make a certain number of copies.

>> Divide a line into a certain number of segments.

>> Change your field of view (how much you can see).

TIP

Here's what you need to know about the Measurements box:

>> **You don't have to click in the Measurements box to enter a number.** This one's a big one: SketchUp beginners often assume that they need to click in the Measurements box (to select it, presumably) before they can start typing. You don't have to click it — just start typing, and whatever you type shows up in the box automatically. Whenever you're drawing, the Measurements box "listens" for you to type something that controls your geometry's precision.

>> **The Measurements box is context-sensitive.** The box accepts values based on what you're doing. If you're drawing an edge with the Line tool, the box listens for a length; if you're rotating a shape, the box listens for an angle.

>> **You can set the default units for the Measurements box and override the default when needed.**

  ● *You don't need to type a unit if you want to use the default unit.* Perhaps you want a line you're drawing to be 14 inches long. If inches are your default unit of measurement, just type **14** into the Measurements box and press Enter — SketchUp assumes that you mean 14 inches.

  ● *Do type a unit if you want to override the default unit.* For example, if your default is inches and you want to draw something 14 *feet* long, type **14'** and press Enter. You can override the default unit of measurement by typing any unit you want. If you want to move something a distance of 25 meters, type **25m** and press Enter.

  ● *You set the default units in the Model Info dialog box.* You can open this dialog box from the Window menu. Open the Units panel, and choose your new default unit from the drop-down menu.

>> **Sometimes, the Measurements box does more than one thing.** In certain circumstances, you can change the box's mode (what it "listens for") by entering a unit type after a number. For example, when you draw a circle, the default "value" in the Measurements box is the radius. If you type **6** and press Enter, a circle radius becomes 6 inches. But if you type **6s**, you're telling SketchUp that you want 6 *sides* (and not inches), so your circle becomes a hexagon. If you type **6** and press Enter, and then type **6s** and press Enter again, SketchUp draws a hexagon (a 6-sided circle) with a radius of 6 inches.

>> **The Measurements box lets you change your mind.** As long as you don't do anything after you press Enter, you can always type a new value and press Enter again; there's no limit to the number of times you can change your mind.

>> **You can use the Measurements box *during* an operation.** In most cases, you can use the Measurements box to be precise *while* you're using a tool. Here's how that works:

1. *Click once to start your operation (such as drawing a line or using the Move tool).*

2. *Move your mouse so that you're going in the correct color direction. Be sure not to click again.*

   If you're using the Line tool and you want to draw parallel to the green axis, make sure that the edge you're drawing is green (displays the green edge inference).

3. *Without clicking the Measurements box, type the dimension you want.*

   The dimension appears in the box.

4. *Press Enter to complete the operation.*

>> **You can also use the Measurements box *after* an operation.** Doing so revises what you've just done. For example, say you want to move a box, as shown in Figure 3-17, 5 meters in the red direction (parallel to the red axis). Here's what you do:

1. *With the Move tool, click the box once to pick it up.*

2. *Move the mouse until you see the red linear inference.*

3. *Type **5m** and press Enter.*

   The box is positioned exactly 5 meters from where you picked it up. However, after you see that placement, you realize the box needs to move a little farther.

4. *Type **15m** and then press Enter again. The box moves another 10 meters in the red direction.*

5. *You can keep changing the box's position until you're happy (or bored).*

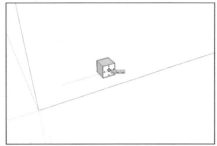
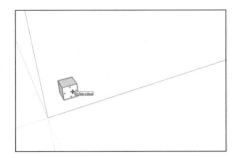

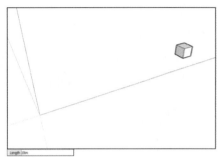
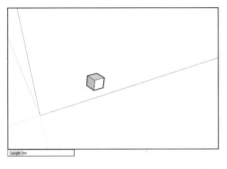

FIGURE 3-17:
You can move
the box 5
meters and
then change
your mind
and move it
15 meters
instead.

>> **The Measurements box tells you what value or values it's expecting.**
For example, select the Line tool and the Measurements box tells you it's
listening for a length. Select the Move tool, and you see the box is expecting a
distance. This feature is great because remembering everything the box can
do at any given moment is pretty difficult — even for experienced SketchUp
modelers.

RESIZING EVERYTHING WITH THE TAPE MEASURE TOOL

Consider that you've been working away in SketchUp, not paying particular attention to
how big anything in your model is, when you suddenly decide that you need what you've
made to be a specific size. SketchUp has a terrific trick for taking care of this exact situation: You can use the Tape Measure tool to resize your whole model based on a single
measurement.

Here's how this tool works: In the following figure, Aidan started to model a simple
staircase. Making sure that it's the right size will make working on it easier. Aidan knows

(continued)

(continued)

the *riser height,* the vertical distance between the steps, should be 7 inches, so this is what he does:

1. **Select the Tape Measure tool on the toolbar or the Tools menu.**

Measure from here...   ...to here

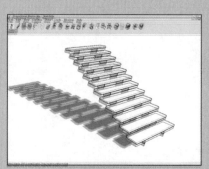 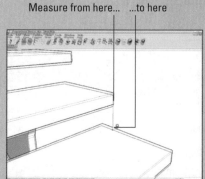

2. **To put the Tape Measure in Measure mode, press the Ctrl key (Option on the Mac) so that the plus sign (+) next to the Tape Measure cursor disappears.**

3. **Click once to start measuring the distance that will change (in this case, the riser height) and click again to stop.**

4. **Type the desired dimension (7 for 7 inches).**

5. **In the dialog box, confirm the resize by clicking Yes.**

After Aidan clicks the Yes button, his whole model is resized proportionately to the dimension he entered.

Selecting what you mean to select

If you want to move, rotate, copy, scale, or otherwise manipulate existing geometry in your model, you need to select it first. Your selection tells SketchUp what geometry you want to change.

 To select things, you use (drum roll, please) the Select tool, which looks exactly the same as the Select tool in every other graphics program on the planet — it's an arrow. That's a good thing because selecting isn't the sort of thing you should have to relearn every time you pick up a new program. Here's everything you need to know about selecting things in SketchUp:

» **Technically, every single thing you see in your modeling window is an** *entity.* **SketchUp has three different kinds of entities:**

- *Elements* are basic pieces of geometry like edges and faces.

- *Objects* are made up of elements. Components and groups, which we cover in Chapter 5, are objects. Anytime you want to make a separate *thing* with its own name and metadata, you make an object. In SketchUp, they're everywhere.

- *Annotations* are things like text, guides, dimensions, and section planes. It's kind of a catch-all category — anything that isn't an element or an object is an annotation.

» **Just click anything in your model to select it (while you're using the Select tool, of course).**

» **To select more than one thing, hold down the Shift key while you click all the things you want to select.**

The Shift key works both ways when it comes to the Select tool. You can use it to *add* to your set of selected things (which we mention earlier), but you can also use it to *subtract* something from your selection. In other words, if you have a bunch of stuff selected and you want to deselect something in particular, just hold down Shift while you click it — it isn't selected anymore.

» **Selected entities in SketchUp look different depending on what they are:**

- Selected edges turn blue.

- Selected faces change from plain gray to blue gray (if you're using the default style).

- Selected groups and components have a blue box around them.

- Selected annotations turn blue.

» **A much fancier way to select things in your model is to double- and triple-click them.** When you double-click a face, you select that face and all the edges that define it. Double-clicking an edge gives you that edge plus all the faces that are connected to it. When you *triple*-click an edge or a face, you select the whole conglomeration that it's a part of. See Figure 3-18.

» **You can select several things at once by dragging a box around them.** You have two kinds of selection boxes; the one you use depends on what you're trying to select. See Figure 3-19:

- *Window selection:* If you click and drag from *left to right* to make a selection box, you create a window selection. In this case, only things that are *entirely* inside your selection box are selected.

- *Crossing selection:* If you click and drag from *right to left* to make a selection box, you create a crossing selection. With one of these, anything your selection box touches (including what's inside) is selected.

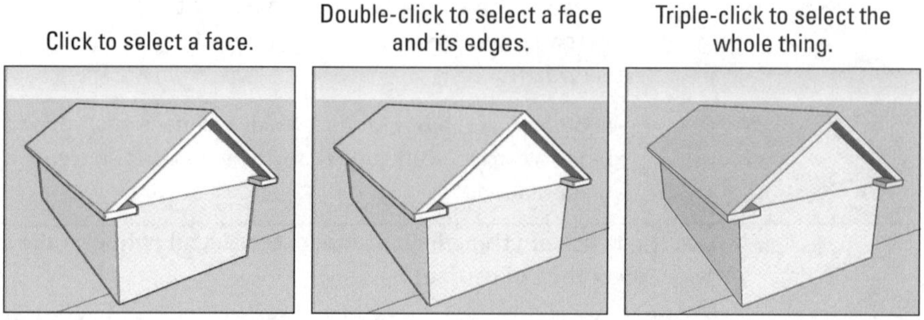

Click to select a face.

Double-click to select a face and its edges.

Triple-click to select the whole thing.

FIGURE 3-18: Try single-, double-, and triple-clicking edges and faces in your model to make different kinds of selections.

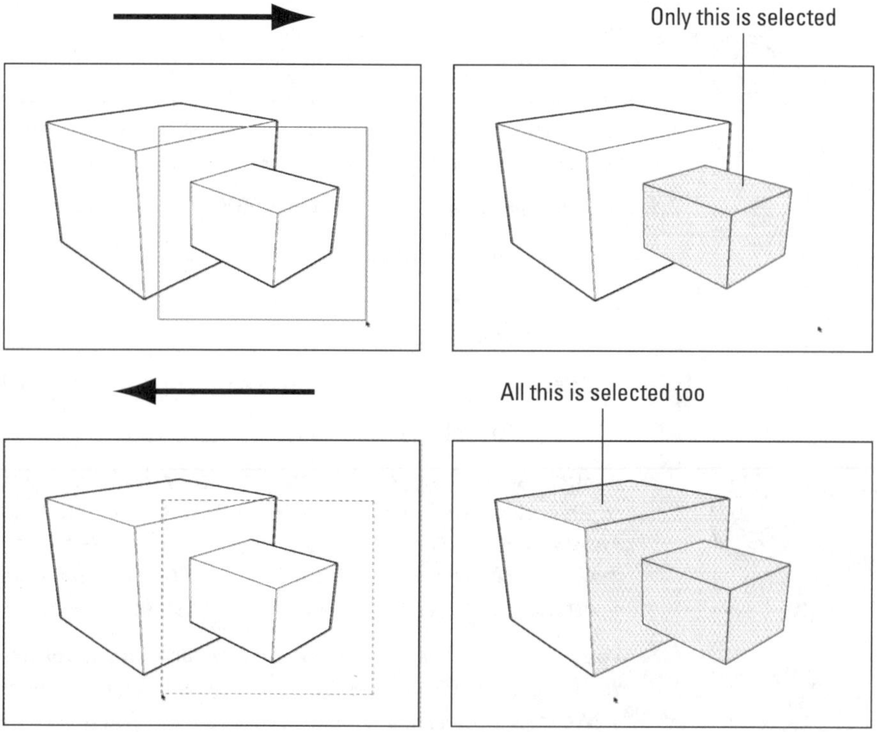

Only this is selected

All this is selected too

FIGURE 3-19: Dragging left to right selects everything inside your selection box. Dragging right to left selects everything that your selection box touches.

REMEMBER

Just because you can't see something doesn't mean it isn't selected. Whenever you make a selection, it's a very good idea to orbit around to make sure you have only what you intended to get. Accidentally selecting too much is an easy mistake to make.

CHANGING THE COLOR OF MODELING CUES

Whether you have color blindness or the default selection colors and other colored modeling cues simply don't work for you, know that you can change the selection color, the axis colors, and several other visual cues. You control these colors with SketchUp styles and preferences settings that are new in SketchUp 2017. See Chapter 10 for details.

Moving and copying like a champ

To move, stretch, or copy geometry in SketchUp, use the Move tool. That's right, the Move tool isn't just for moving, and this section explains all the Move tool secrets that will help you quickly advance to more complex 3D modeling.

Moving things

The Move tool is the one that looks like four red arrows. Using this tool involves clicking the entity you want to move, moving it to where you want it to be, and clicking again to drop it. The maneuver isn't complicated, but getting the hang of it takes a bit of time.

Here are tips for using Move successfully:

>> **Click, move, and click. Don't drag your mouse.** Many new SketchUp users are tempted to move stuff by clicking and dragging. That works, but in the long run, moving things is harder that way. Instead, practice clicking once to pick something up, moving your mouse without any buttons held down, and clicking again to put down whatever you're moving.

>> **Click a point that will let you position whatever you're trying to move.** For example, Figure 3-20 shows two boxes. To stack one on top of the other precisely, you can't just click anywhere on the first box and move it over the other one. You have to click the *bottom corner* of the soon-to-be top box and move the cursor over the *top corner* of the bottom box.

>> **Press the Esc key to cancel a move operation.** When you start to move something (on purpose or accidentally), it's tempting to use Move to put things back the way they were. Inevitably, Move messes up your model instead. Instead, press Esc, which is the quickest and easiest way to get out of a Move operation and keep your model intact.

Picking it up here...   ...doesn't let you stack properly

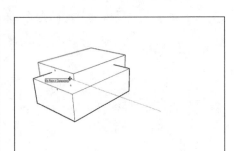

Picking it up here...   ...lets you stack precisely

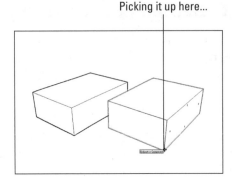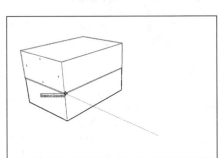

>> **Watch for helpful inferences.** To move something in one of the colored directions, wait until you see the dotted On Axis linear inference appear; then hold down Shift to lock yourself in that direction. For more information about using SketchUp's inference engine, check out the earlier section "Keeping an eye out for inferences."

>> **Move precisely with the Measurements box.** You can move things precise distances with the Measurements box; see "Injecting accuracy into your model," earlier in this chapter.

Shaping forms with the Move tool

SketchUp's Move tool isn't just for moving whole objects. You can also use this tool to change the shape of your model. To do this, move a *vertex* (where edges' endpoints come together), an edge, a face, or a combination of any of these. By moving only certain *entities* (all the things we just mention), you can change the shape of your geometry pretty drastically, as shown in Figure 3-21.

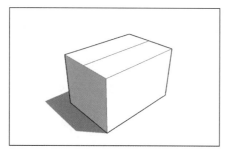

Moving a vertex

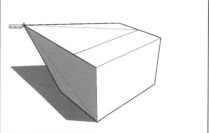

Moving an edge

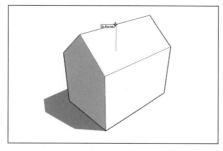

Moving a face

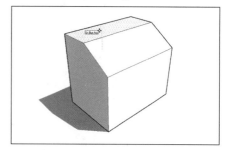

FIGURE 3-21: You can use the Move tool on vertices, edges, and faces to model different forms.

TIP

Using the Move tool to create forms (instead of just moving them around) is an incredibly powerful way to work but isn't particularly intuitive. After all, nothing in the physical world behaves like the Move tool. You can't just grab the edge of a hardwood floor and move it up to turn it into a ramp in real life. In SketchUp, you can — and should.

TELLING SKETCHUP WHO'S BOSS WITH AUTO-FOLD

This will happen to you sooner or later: As you try to move a vertex, an edge, or a face, you can't go in the direction you want. SketchUp doesn't like to let you create *folds* (when extra faces and edges are created in place of a single face) with the Move tool, so SketchUp constrains your movement to directions that won't add folds. To force the move, press and hold down the Alt key (Command on a Mac) while you move. When you

(continued)

(continued)

do this, you're telling SketchUp that it's okay to proceed — to create folds if it has to. This is called *Auto-Fold,* and the following figure shows how it works.

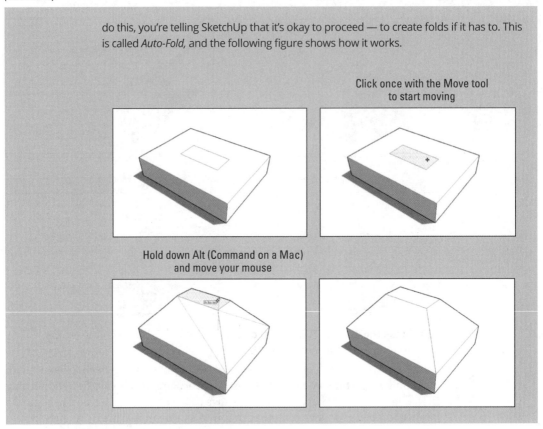

To preselect or not to preselect

The Move tool works in two different ways; you eventually need to use them both, depending on what you're trying to move:

>> **Moving a selection:** When you select one or more entities, the Move tool moves only the selection. This behavior is handy when you need to move more than one thing all at once; Figure 3-22 shows how to move selected items with the Move tool.

>> **Moving without a selection:** If you don't make a selection, you can click anything in the drawing window to move it around. Only the thing you click moves.

This isn't selected   ...so it doesn't move with the rest

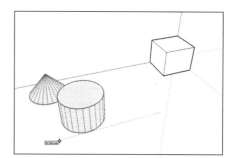

FIGURE 3-22:
Using the
Move tool
when you have
a selection
moves only the
things in that
selection.

Making copies with the Move tool

Lots of folks spend time hunting around in SketchUp, trying to figure out how to make copies. It's very simple: You just press a *modifier key* — a button on your keyboard that tells SketchUp to do something different — while you're using the Move tool. Instead of moving something, you move a copy of it. Here are a couple things to keep in mind:

>> **Press the Ctrl key (Windows) or the Option key (Mac) to create a copy.**
You can press the modifier key before or after you click the entity you want to move. When the Move tool is in Copy mode, a little + appears next to the Move cursor, and your copy moves when you move your mouse. Figure 3-23 shows this in action.

If you decide you don't want to make a copy, just press the Ctrl key (Option on a Mac) again to toggle back to Move; the + sign disappears.

>> **Copying is just like moving, except you're moving a copy.** This means that all the same rules for using the Move tool apply to making copies, too.

FIGURE 3-23:
Press Ctrl
(Option on a
Mac) to tell
SketchUp
to make a
copy while
you move
something.

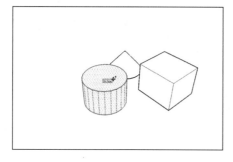 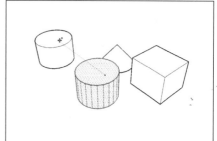

>> **To make more than one copy at a time, use the Measurements box.** For example, say you want to make five equally spaced copies of a column, as shown in Figure 3-24. First, move a copy to where you want the last column to be; then type **5/** and press Enter. This makes five copies of the column and spaces them evenly between the first and last column in the row. Neat, huh?

To set a precise distance between your copies, move a copy to set the distance between each copy. Then type **5x**, and press Enter.

TIP

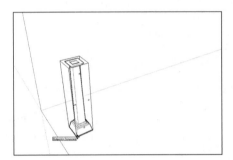
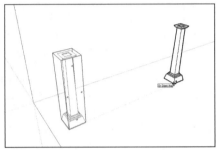

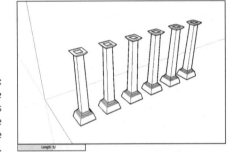

FIGURE 3-24: Use the Measurements box to make multiple copies.

Rotating the right way

The Rotate tool spins geometry based on an angle you specify. No surprises there. However, the Rotate tool also has a trick up its sleeve that most new modelers don't discover until hours after they could've used it. First things first, though:

>> **It's better to preselect.** As with the Move tool, rotating something you've already selected is usually easier.

>> **The Rotate tool can make copies, too.** Press the Ctrl key (Option on a Mac) to switch between rotating your original or rotating a copy. You can also make several copies arranged in a circle or along an arc. Check out the earlier section "Making copies with the Move tool," to read about using x and / to create multiples.

>> **You can be precise.** The Measurements box enables you to type exact angles while you're rotating. Take a look at "Injecting accuracy into your model" (earlier in this chapter) to find out more.

Using Rotate: The basic method

Follow these steps to rotate things in your model:

1. **Select everything you want to rotate.**

2. **Activate the Rotate tool.**

   The default keyboard shortcut for Rotate is Q. The Rotate tool also appears on the toolbar and the Tools menu.

3. **Click once to establish an axis of rotation.**

   Your *axis of rotation* is the theoretical line around which your selected entities will rotate; picture the axle of a wheel. Although it'd be nice if SketchUp drew the axis of rotation in your model, you just have to imagine it.

   TIP

   As you move the Rotate tool's big protractor cursor around your screen, the cursor sometimes changes orientation and color. When you hover over a face, the cursor realigns itself to create an axis of rotation that's perpendicular to that face. When the cursor is red, green, or blue, its axis of rotation is parallel to that colored axis.

   TIP

   You can (and should) use *inference locking* when you're using the Rotate tool. Just hover over any face in your model that's perpendicular to the axis of rotation you want, hold down the Shift key to lock in that orientation, and click where you want your axis to be. See "Using inferences to help you model" (earlier in this chapter) to read all about it.

4. **Click again to start rotating.**

   Clicking part of the thing you're rotating is helpful, especially if you're rotating visually instead of numerically (by typing an angle).

5. **Move your mouse; then click again to finish rotating.**

   If you like, now is a good time to type a rotation angle and press Enter. As with everything else in SketchUp, you can be as precise as you want or need to be.

Using Rotate: The not-so-basic method

The basic method of using Rotate is fine when you need to rotate something on the ground plane, but this method isn't as useful when your axis of rotation isn't vertical. Finding a face to use to orient your cursor can be tricky or impossible, and that's where a lot of SketchUp modelers get hung up.

With this not-so-basic rotation method, you can establish a precise axis of rotation (the invisible line around which you're rotating) *without having any pre-existing faces to use for orientation.* This makes rotating things about a million times easier.

In this case, using Rotate goes from being a five-step operation to a seven-step one. Check out Figure 3-25 for a visual explanation:

1. **Select everything you want to rotate.**

2. **Activate the Rotate tool (Tools ⇨ Rotate).**

3. **Click once to establish your axis of rotation, but *don't let go* — keep your finger on your mouse button.**

4. **Drag your cursor around (still holding down the mouse button) until your axis of rotation is where you want it.**

   As you drag, notice your Rotate protractor changes orientation; the line from where you clicked to your cursor is the axis of rotation.

5. **Release your mouse button to set your axis of rotation.**

6. **Click (but don't drag) the point at which you want to "pick up" whatever you're rotating.**

7. **Click again to drop the thing you're rotating where you want it.**

Making and using guides

Sometimes you need to draw temporary lines while you model. These temporary lines, or *guides,* are useful for lining up things, making things the right size, and generally adding precision and accuracy to what you're building.

In previous versions of SketchUp, guides were called *construction geometry* because that's basically what they are: a special kind of entity that you create when and where you need them. They aren't part of your model because they're not edges or faces. This means that you can choose to hide them or delete them — like other annotations, they don't affect the rest of your geometry.

Figure 3-26 shows an example of guides in action. The guides are positioned 12 inches from the wall and 36 inches apart to draw the sides of a doorway. Another guide (6 feet, 8 inches from the floor) indicates the top. With these guides in place, you can easily draw a rectangle, bounded by your guides, which you know is exactly the right size and in the correct location.

Click

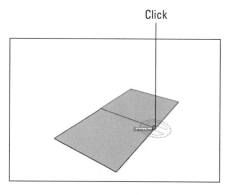

Drag to locate axis of rotation

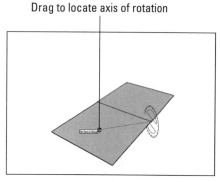

Release mouse to define axis

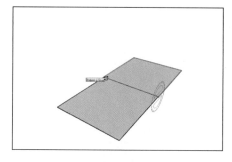

Click to rotate

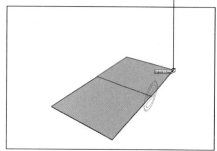

Click to finish rotating

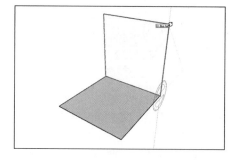

FIGURE 3-25:
Define a
custom axis
of rotation by
click-dragging
your mouse.

Creating guides with the Tape Measure tool

 You can create three kinds of guides, and you use the Tape Measure tool to make them all, as shown in Figure 3-27.

>> **Parallel guide lines:** To create a guide that's parallel to an edge, select the Tape Measure tool, and click anywhere (except the endpoints or midpoint) along an edge. Then move your mouse, and a parallel, dashed guide appears. Click again to place the guide wherever you want.

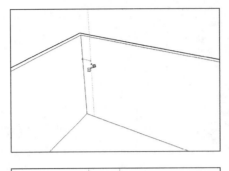
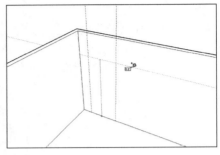
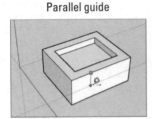
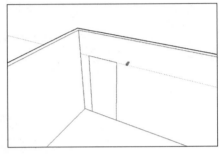

FIGURE 3-26:
Use guides to measure things before you draw.

Parallel guide   Linear guide   Guide point

FIGURE 3-27:
Use the Tape Measure tool to create guide lines and points.

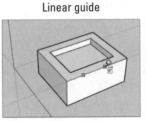
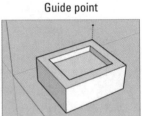

>> **Linear guide lines:** To create a guide along an edge in your model, click anywhere along the edge *except* on either endpoint. Then click again anywhere else along the edge.

>> **Guide points:** You may want to place a point somewhere in space; you can do exactly that with guide points. With the Tape Measure tool, click an edge's endpoint, and then click again somewhere else. A little *x* appears at the end of a dashed line — that's your new guide point.

REMEMBER

Here's an important point about the Tape Measure tool: It has two modes, and it creates guides in only one of them. Pressing the Ctrl key (Option on a Mac) toggles between the modes. When you see a + next to your cursor, your Tape Measure can make guides; when there's no +, it can't.

Using guides to make your life easier

As you're working along in this software, you'll find yourself using guides all the time; they're an indispensable part of how modeling in SketchUp works. Here's what you need to know about using them:

>> **Position guides precisely using the Measurements box.** Check out the section "Injecting accuracy into your model," earlier in this chapter, to find out how.

>> **Erase guides one at a time.** Just click or drag over them with the Eraser tool to delete guides individually. You can also context-click them and choose Erase from the context menu.

>> **Erase all your guides at once.** Choosing Edit ⟿ Delete Guides does just that.

>> **Hide guides individually or all at once.** Context-click a single guide and choose Hide to hide it, or deselect View ⟿ Guides to hide them all. It's a good idea to hide your guides instead of erasing them, especially while you're still modeling.

>> **Select, move, copy, and rotate guides just like any other entity in your model.** Guides aren't edges, but you can treat them that way a lot of the time.

Painting your faces with color and texture

When adding colors and textures — collectively referred to in SketchUp as *materials* — to your model, look no further than the Materials panel and the Paint Bucket tool. Chapter 2 introduces you to this winsome pair and provides a workflow for adding materials to your mode. This section offers a more in-depth introduction to your options.

The Materials panel

The Materials panel looks different in the Windows and Mac versions of SketchUp, but they do basically the same thing. By default, the Materials panel appears on the Default Tray (Windows only). If the panel is ever hidden and you need to reopen it, choose Window ⟿ Default Tray ⟿ Materials (Windows) or Window ⟿ Materials (Mac).

In SketchUp, you can choose from two kinds of materials to apply to the faces in your model:

>> **Colors:** These are simple — colors are always solid colors. You can't have *gradients* (in which one color fades into another), but you can pretty much make any color you want.

>> **Textures:** A SketchUp texture is a tiny image that is tiled to cover a face. If you paint a face with, say, a brick texture, what you're really doing is telling SketchUp to cover the surface with however many "brick photo" tiles it takes to do the job. The preview image you see in the Materials panel is actually a picture of a single texture image tile.

SketchUp comes with a whole bunch of textures, and you can always go online and choose from thousands more available for sale. And if that's *still* not enough, you can make your own (though the process is well beyond the scope of this humble tome). For details on more advanced techniques like creating a custom texture, check out the SketchUp Help Center (`http://help.sketchup.com`).

The following facts about SketchUp materials are also handy to know as you work with them:

>> **Materials can be translucent.** Sliding the Opacity slider makes the material you've selected more or less translucent, which makes seeing through windows in your model a lot easier. On Windows, you find the Opacity slider on the Edit tab.

>> **Textures can have transparent areas.** If you take a look at the materials in the Fencing library, you'll notice that a lot of them look kind of strange; they have areas of black that don't seem right. These black areas are areas of transparency: When you paint a face with one of these textures, you can see through the areas that look black.

There's actually a third thing (besides colors and textures) you can apply to the faces in your models: photos. In fact, *photo-texturing* is an incredibly important part of some SketchUp workflows. As such, we dedicate a good portion of Chapter 8 to the subject of modeling with photographs.

The Paint Bucket tool

Activating the Paint Bucket tool automatically opens the Materials panel so it's handy. Here's everything you need to know about the Paint Bucket tool:

>> **You fill it by clicking in the Materials panel.** Just click a material to load your bucket and then click the face you want to paint.

>> **Holding down the Alt key (⌘ on a Mac) switches to the Sample tool.** With the Sample tool, you can click any face in your model to load your Paint Bucket with that face's material. Release the Alt key to revert to the Paint Bucket tool.

» **Holding down the Shift key paints all similar faces.** Don't like the dark brick on your house model? Select a new material in the Materials panel, hold down the Shift key, and click any face with the brick applied. In Figure 3-28, Paint Bucket tool is ready to change the dark brick to a lighter option, which you see as the active material in the upper left of the Materials panel. When you're done, all faces in your model that match the one you click are painted with the new material. If things don't turn out the way you want, just choose Edit ⇨ Undo to go back a step.

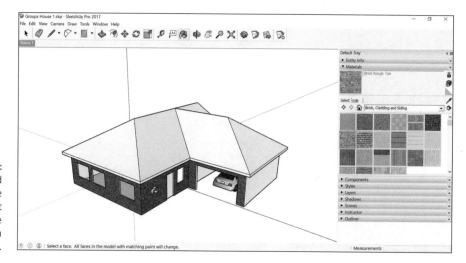

FIGURE 3-28:
Press Shift and click with the Paint Bucket to replace one material with another.

Modeling in SketchUp

Draw buildings and discover tricks for creating common elements, such as floors, walls, doors, windows, roofs, and stairs.

Simplify your modeling with components, including premade components from SketchUp as well as components you create.

Create lathed objects with Follow Me, scale shapes to create unique effects, set your model on terrain, and create new 3D shapes from other shapes with the Solid Tools.

Tidy up complex models with the Organizer and see only the elements you need with layers.

Add photos, geo-location data, or CAD data to a SketchUp model.

Find out about 3D printers and learn the basics of creating 3D-printable models.

IN THIS CHAPTER

» Drafting a simple floor plan

» Going from a 2D plan to a 3D model

» Adding floors, doors, and windows

» Modeling stairs

» Building a roof

Chapter **4**

Building Buildings

E ven though SketchUp lets you make (just about) anything you can think of, certain forms are easier to make than others. Fortunately, these kinds of shapes are exactly the ones that most people want to make with SketchUp, most of the time. That's no accident; SketchUp was designed with architecture in mind, so the whole *paradigm* — the models made of faces and edges, and the kinds of tools SketchUp offers — is perfect for making things like buildings.

But what about curvy, swoopy buildings? You can use SketchUp to make those, too, but they're a little harder, so we don't think they're a good place to start. Because *most* people live in boxy places with right-angled rooms and flat ceilings, that kind of architecture is relatively easy to understand.

In this chapter, you discover some fundamentals of SketchUp modeling in terms of making simple, rectilinear buildings. By writing about how to build certain kinds of things, instead of just describing what the individual tools do, we hope to make it easier for you to get started. Even if you're not planning to use SketchUp to model any of the things we describe, you can still apply these concepts to your creations.

TIP

One more thing: Just about every page in this chapter relies heavily on the stuff introduced in Chapter 3. Working with the colored drawing axes, making selections, navigating around your model, and drawing things accurately are pretty key to making anything in SketchUp. Be prepared to flip back and forth while you're getting used to modeling in SketchUp. Aidan likes to use paper clips as bookmarks, Rebecca tears off tiny scraps of paper, but you surely have your own method. . . .

Drawing Floors and Walls

Most floors and walls are flat surfaces, so it's easy to model them with straight edges and flat faces in SketchUp. In fact, chances are good that the first thing you ever model in SketchUp looks a lot like the floor and walls of a building.

How you approach modeling floors and walls depends entirely on the type of model you're making:

>> **Exterior:** An exterior model of a building is basically just an empty shell; you don't have interior walls, rooms, or furniture to worry about. This type of model is a slightly simpler proposition for folks who are new to SketchUp.

>> **Interior:** An interior model of a building is significantly more complicated than an exterior-only one; dealing with interior wall thicknesses, floor heights, ceilings, and furnishings involves a lot more modeling prowess.

REMEMBER

Here's the thing: Because everything in SketchUp is made of super-flat faces (they have no thickness), the only way to model a wall that's, say, 8 inches thick is to use two faces side by side and 8 inches apart. For models in which you need to show wall thicknesses — namely, interior models — you have to use this two-face approach. Exterior models are easier to make because you can use single faces to represent walls, as shown in Figure 4-1.

Single-face walls   Double-face walls

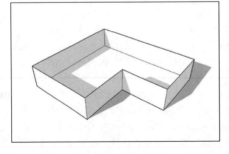 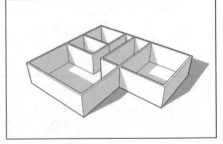

FIGURE 4-1: Use single faces for exterior models and double faces for interior ones.

TIP

Making a model that shows both the interior and the exterior of a building at the same time is, to be honest, *way* too hard. If you need both interior and exterior views, build two separate models instead: one of the interior and one of the exterior. With the two separate models, you can create the combination model in a quarter of the time you took building the first two — we guarantee it.

Starting out in 2D

You can model a building's interior in lots of ways. In this section, Aidan shares the method he developed over years of creating SketchUp models. Basically, you draw a two-dimensional floor plan that includes all your interior and exterior walls, and then pull it up to the right height (extruded). Only after your model is extruded do you worry about doors, windows, and stairs.

Switching to a 2D view

Before you draw a 2D plan, you need to orient your point of view. Drawing in 2D is easiest when you view your work from directly above, looking down at the ground plane. You also want to make sure that you're not seeing things in perspective, which distorts your view of what you have.

Follow these simple steps to set up your SketchUp modeling area for 2D drawing:

1. **Create a new SketchUp file by choosing File ⇨ New.**

   Depending on the template you have set to open when you create a new SketchUp file, you may already be in a 2D view. If all you see are the red and green axes on a white background, you can skip Step 2. Remember that you can always switch templates by choosing Help ⇨ Welcome to SketchUp and clicking the Template section of the dialog box that pops up.

2. **Choose Camera ⇨ Standard ⇨ Top.**

   This changes your viewpoint so that you're looking directly down at the ground.

3. **Choose Camera ⇨ Parallel Projection.**

   Switching from Perspective to Parallel Projection makes it easy to draw plans in 2D. At this point, your modeling window looks like the one shown in Figure 4-2.

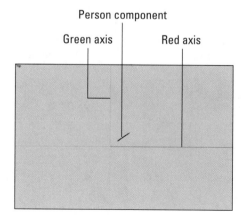

Person component

Green axis   Red axis

FIGURE 4-2:
Your modeling window should look like this before you start drawing in 2D.

TIP

Feel free to delete the person component (Chris in 2017, Lisanne in 2016, or in your version of SketchUp, whatever person component appears in every new file). In Top view, the person component is that little diagonal line. To delete the component, just context-click her and choose Erase.

Dusting off SketchUp's drafting tools

You don't need many tools to draft a 2D plan in SketchUp. Figure 4-3 shows the basic toolbar; everything you need is right there:

FIGURE 4-3:
All the tools you need to draft in 2D in SketchUp are on the basic toolbar.

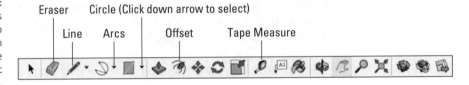

>> **Line tool:** You use the Line tool (which looks like a pencil) to draw *edges,* which are one of the two basic building blocks of SketchUp models. Fundamentally, you click to start drawing an edge and click again to finish it. (You can find lots more information about drawing lines in Chapter 3.)

>> **Eraser tool:** Use the Eraser to erase edges, as shown in Figure 4-4. Although you can't use the Eraser to delete faces, erasing an edge that defines a face automatically erases that face, too. Take a look at the section about edges and faces at the beginning of Chapter 3 for more detail on using the Eraser tool on edges. You can use the Eraser in two ways:

- *Clicking:* Click edges to erase them one at a time.

- *Dragging:* Click and drag over edges to erase them; this is faster if you want to erase lots of edges.

FIGURE 4-4:
Use the Eraser tool to erase edges. Erasing an edge that defines a face erases that face, too.

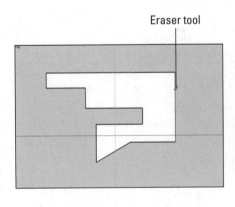
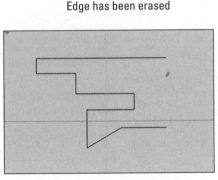

>> **Circle tool**: On the Getting Started toolbar, the Circle tool hides on the Rectangle tool's drop-down menu. Drawing circles in SketchUp is pretty easy: Click once to define the center and again to define a point on the circle (which also defines the radius). To enter a precise radius, just draw a circle, type a radius, and press Enter, as shown in Figure 4-5. For more information on typing while you draw, check out the section on model accuracy in Chapter 3.

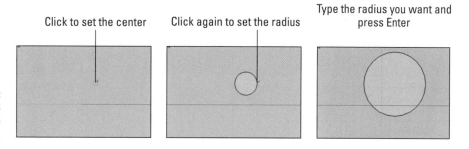

Click to set the center   Click again to set the radius   Type the radius you want and press Enter

FIGURE 4-5:
Drawing circles is easy with the Circle tool.

>> **Arc tools:** As of version 2017, SketchUp has four tools for making arcs (it used to have only one). See Figure 4-6. Here they are, in order:

- *Arc:* Click once to define the center point, click again to define the first endpoint, and click a third time to finish the arc. The result is an arc made of straight-edge segments.

- *2 Point Arc:* To use this tool, you create a line and pull out a bulge that makes the arc. Click once to define one end, again to define the other end, and a third time to define the bulge. If you want, type a radius after you draw your arc by entering the radius, the units, and the letter *r*. If you want an arc with a radius of 4 feet, draw it however big, type **4'r**, and press Enter.

- *3 Point Arc:* This tool creates an arc around a pivot point. Click to set a start point, click again to set a pivot point, and click a third time to set the arc's endpoint.

- *Pie:* The Pie tool is exactly the same as the Arc tool, but with a useful twist. It yields a pie-shaped face and all three of its perimeter edges.

>> **Offset tool:** The Offset tool helps you draw edges that are a constant distance apart from edges that already exist in your model. Pictures are usually better than words, so take a look at Figure 4-7. Using Offset on the shape creates another shape that's exactly 6 inches bigger all the way around (middle image), or 6 inches *smaller* all the way around (right image). Offsetting edges is a useful way to create things like doorways and window trim.

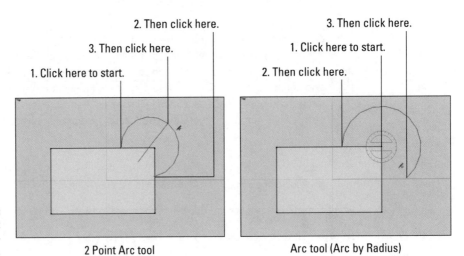

2. Then click here.

3. Then click here.

1. Click here to start.

3. Then click here.

1. Click here to start.

2. Then click here.

FIGURE 4-6:
Using an Arc
tool is a three-
step operation.

2 Point Arc tool

Arc tool (Arc by Radius)

You can use Offset in two ways; for both ways you click once to start offsetting and again to stop:

- *Click a face to offset all its edges.* If nothing is selected, clicking a face with the Offset tool lets you offset all that face's edges by a constant amount, as shown in Figure 4-7.

- *Preselect one or more coplanar (on the same plane) edges and then use Offset.* If you have selected edges, you can use Offset on just those edges; this comes in handy for drawing things like door frames and balconies, as shown in Figure 4-8.

>> **Tape Measure tool:** The Tape Measure does a bunch of things. To measure a distance, click any two points in your model. The distance readout is in the Measurements box, in the lower-right corner of your modeling window. You can also use the Tape Measure tool to size a model and to create guides, as we explain in Chapter 3.

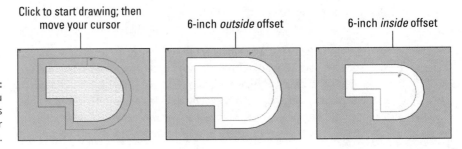

Click to start drawing; then
move your cursor

6-inch *outside* offset

6-inch *inside* offset

FIGURE 4-7:
Offset lets you
create edges
based on other
edges.

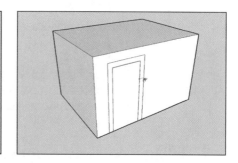

FIGURE 4-8:
Using Offset on a set of preselected edges is handy for drawing things like door frames.

Coming up with a simple plan

If all you're trying to do is model an exterior view of a building, just measure around the actual building's perimeter, draw the outline of the building in SketchUp, pull it up with the Push/Pull tool, and delete the top face if you like, as shown in Figure 4-9. Then you can add your desired roof, as explained in "Raising the Roof" later in this chapter. With this method, your walls are only a *single-face thick* (meaning paper-thin), but that's okay. You're only interested in the outside, anyway.

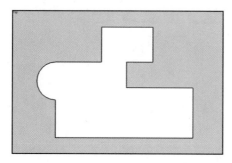
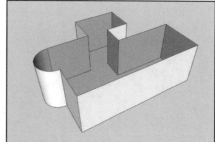

FIGURE 4-9:
To make an exterior model, just measure the outside of your building to draw an outline in SketchUp.

Measuring an existing building so that you can model an *interior* view is easier said than done. Even experienced architects and builders often get confused when trying to model the interiors of *as-builts,* which are drawings of existing buildings. Closets, ventilation spaces, interior walls, and all kinds of other obstructions inevitably get in the way of good measurements. Usually, you give the measuring your best shot and then tweak things a bit to make them right. The following sections walk you through the process.

Drawing an interior outline

When you model a building's interior, your main goal is creating accurate interior spaces. To achieve that accuracy, work from the inside out. If your tape measure is long enough, measure the major dimensions first. That is, measure the total interior width and length of the building's inside. You may not be able to, but do your best. After that, just work your way around, using basic arithmetic and logic to figure out the size of the space.

TIP

Before you start drawing an interior outline in SketchUp, make a paper drawing. The drawing helps you know what you need to draw so you can focus all your concentration for drafting on the computer. Figure 4-10 shows the paper sketch that Aidan used when modeling his house.

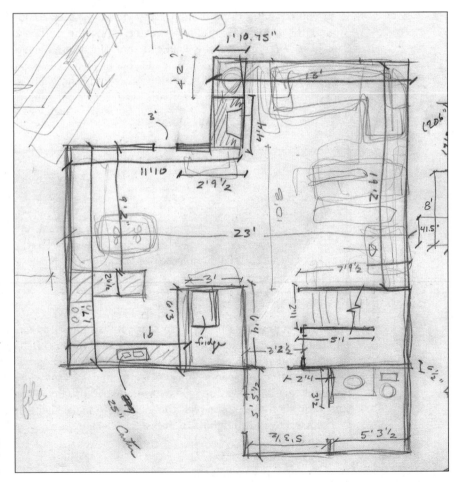

FIGURE 4-10:
Aidan's paper sketch.

From this paper drawing, here's how you draw a basic interior outline of this house:

1. **Switch to a 2D overhead view.**

   The section "Switching to a 2D view," earlier in this chapter, explains how.

2. **Using the Line tool, draw a line that represents the exact length of a wall in the house.**

   For example, Aidan starts drawing his house's eastern wall by creating an line that's exactly 17 feet long. (See the top-left image in Figure 4-11.)

   To draw a precise line, click once to start the line, click again to end the line, type **17'**, and press Enter. Remember you don't need to click anywhere before you type a precise value; the Measurements box listens for your keystrokes immediately after you draw something. After you press Enter, the line resizes itself automatically to be exactly 17 feet in length. If you want, you can use the Tape Measure to double-check the size.

3. **Connect the next edge to your first one.**

   As shown in the lower-left image in Figure 4-11, Aidan works clockwise, drawing an edge 11 feet, 10 inches long, starting at the end of the first edge and heading to the right in the red direction.

4. **Keep going all the way around the house, until you get back to where you started. See Figure 4-12.**

   If you make a mistake, use the Eraser to get rid of edges. Alternately, undo by pressing Ctrl+Z (⌘+Z on the Mac) or choosing Edit ⇨ Undo to go back a step or two.

5. **If all your measurements don't add up, adjust things so that they do — a few extra inches here and there never killed anyone, after all.**

   After you complete the outline (forming a closed loop of edges that were all on the same plane), a face automatically appears. Now you have a total of 11 edges and 1 face.

TIP

When you draft in 2D, use only Zoom and Pan to navigate your drawing (see Chapter 3). If you accidentally orbit your model into a 3D view, return to 2D by following the steps in the section "Switching to a 2D view," earlier in this chapter.

REMEMBER

If you get lost, and no amount of zooming and panning gets you back to a view of your floor plan, choose Camera ⇨ Zoom Extents or click the Zoom Extents tool. Think of Zoom Extents as an emergency lever you can pull to fill your modeling window with your geometry.

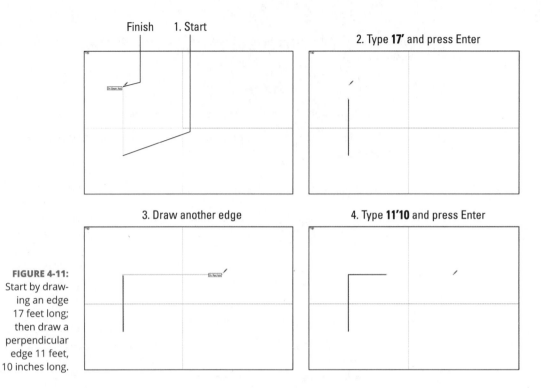

Finish   1. Start

2. Type **17′** and press Enter

3. Draw another edge

4. Type **11′10** and press Enter

FIGURE 4-11:
Start by draw-
ing an edge
17 feet long;
then draw a
perpendicular
edge 11 feet,
10 inches long.

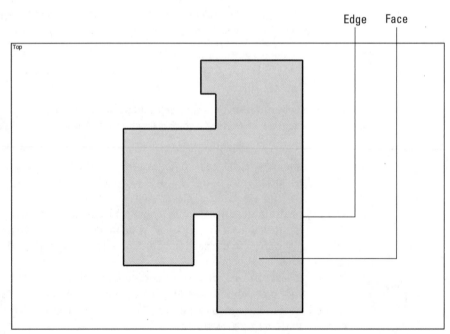

Edge   Face

FIGURE 4-12:
The completed
interior
perimeter of
Aidan's house.

Offsetting and grouping an exterior wall

With the Offset tool, you can offset an exterior wall thickness, which can make it easier to visualize your spaces. Here's how you do it:

1. **Using the Offset tool, offset your closed shape by 8 inches to the outside. See Figure 4-13, upper left.**

   An offset of 8 inches is a pretty standard thickness for an exterior wall, especially for houses in Aidan's neck of the woods. See "Dusting off SketchUp's drafting tools" earlier in this chapter for details about using the Offset tool. After you create the offset, type **8"** and press Enter.

2. **Use the Line tool to close off any alcoves, creating pockets of wall that are thicker than the rest. See Figure 4-13, upper right.**

3. **With the Eraser tool, delete the extra edges. See Figure 4-13, middle left.**

   By deleting the extra edges, you have only two faces: one that represents the floor and one that represents the wall.

4. **With the Line tool, draw edges that define the thickness of your exterior wall. See Figure 4-13, middle right.**

   For this example, Aidan separated the *bulges* (which actually represent a fireplace and a mechanical closet) from the part of the wall that goes all the way up to the roof, two stories up.

   When you're done, you end up with several faces: one for the floor, one for the exterior wall (whose thickness should be more or less uniform), and a few for the bulges.

5. **Select the face that defines the exterior wall. See Figure 4-13, lower left.**

   The easiest way to do this is to click the face with the Select tool.

6. **Make the face you just selected into a group. See Figure 4-13, lower right.**

   Chapter 5 is all about these groups (and their über-useful cousins, components), but here's all you need to know for now: Making groups lets you separate different parts of your model. Turning your exterior wall into a separate group makes it easier to edit, hide, and move. Groups also simplify the process of adding more levels to your building, if that becomes necessary.

   To turn the face you selected in Step 5 into a group, choose Edit ➪ Make Group. You see a perimeter of blue lines around your face; that's the group you just created. Congratulations — you're now officially an intermediate SketchUp user.

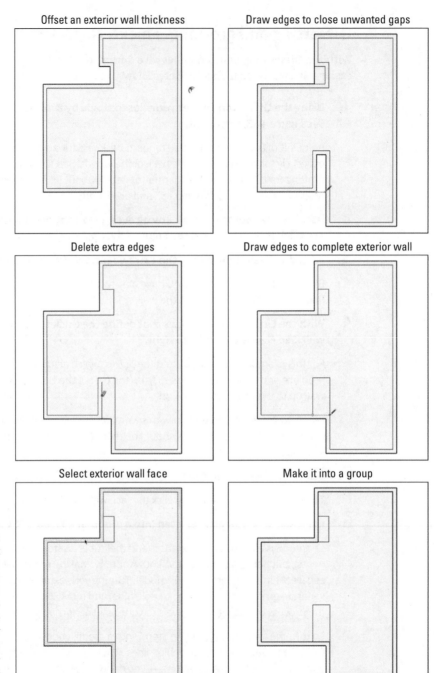

Offset an exterior wall thickness

Draw edges to close unwanted gaps

Delete extra edges

Draw edges to complete exterior wall

Select exterior wall face

Make it into a group

FIGURE 4-13:
Use Offset to create an exterior wall thickness and then clean up using the Line and Eraser tools. Finally, make the exterior wall into its own group.

Putting in the interior walls

For this part of the process, guides are your friends. Chapter 3 has a section on guides, where you find a full description of guides and how to use them.

TIP

At this point in creating an interior floor plan, Aidan ignores things like doors, windows, and stairs. Where a wall contains a doorway, he draws a solid wall. After you extrude the floor plan into a 3D figure, adding doors, windows, and stairs is much easier.

Working from your 2D drawing, here's how you create interior walls:

1. **With the Tape Measure tool, create guides to mark the precise location of the interior walls.**

   For example, the guide for the wall in the lower right of the sketch (Figure 4-10) is a parallel guide 5 feet, 3½ inches from the inside of the entryway. See Figure 4-14, left. Figure 4-14, right, shows all Aidan's guides.

   To create a parallel guide, click the edge from which you want to draw the guide, move your cursor (to tell SketchUp which way to go), type your distance (such as **5'3.5**), and press Enter.

Create a parallel guide   Create more guides

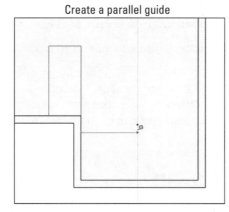
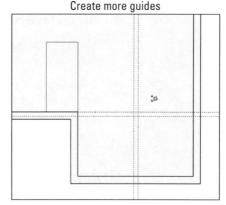

FIGURE 4-14: Draw a guide to help you locate your first interior wall, and then draw a bunch more.

2. **With the Line tool, draw edges to represent the interior walls.**

   With guides, it's easy to draw your edges correctly. Figure 4-15 shows what you have so far.

REMEMBER

   Don't forget to zoom! When you have a jumble of edges and guides and you can't see what you're doing, just zoom in. Many folks forget to change their point of view while they work, and zooming makes all the difference.

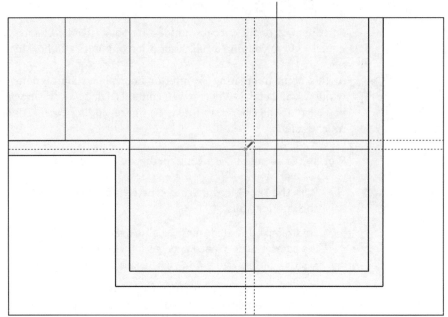

Solid lines are edges

FIGURE 4-15:
Use the
Line tool to
create edges
where guides
come together.

3. **With the Eraser tool, click your guides to delete them.**

4. **Use the Eraser to delete extra edge segments. See Figure 4-16.**

The goal is to have the smallest-possible number of 2D faces to extrude into 3D walls, a little later on.

TIP

Because the exterior-wall face — and the edges that define it — is part of a separate group, accidentally nicking it with the Eraser deletes the whole thing. If this happens, just choose Edit ⇨ Undo to go back a step, zoom in a little bit, and try again.

Going from 2D to 3D

With a 2D plan in hand, you're ready to extrude it into a 3D model. This process is enormously enjoyable and involves the tool that made SketchUp famous: Push/Pull. In the following sections, you take a simple floor plan (the one you draw earlier in this chapter) and turn it into 3D walls.

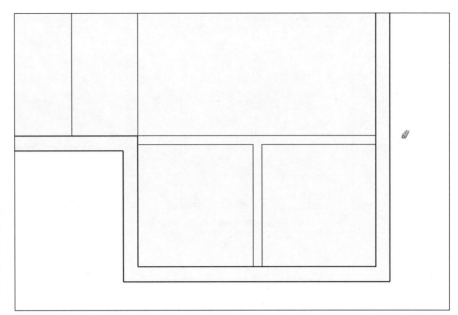

Getting a good view

Before you pop up your plan into the third dimension, change your point of view to get a better view of what you're doing. See Figure 4-17 and follow these steps:

1. **Choose Camera ⇨ Perspective.**

This turns on SketchUp's perspective engine, meaning that now you can see things more realistically — the way people really see things in 3D.

2. **Choose Camera ⇨ Standard ⇨ Iso.**

This switches you from a top view to an *isometric* (three-quarter) one. You can do this with the Orbit tool, too. SketchUp usually gives you more than one way to do something.

3. **Choose Camera ⇨ Zoom Extents.**

Zoom Extents has its own button on the Getting Started toolbar, but we're sticking with the Camera menu theme, just for consistency.

4. **Choose Camera ⇨ Field of View, type 45, and press Enter.**

You've changed the field of view from 35 to 45 degrees. By default, SketchUp's field of view is set to 35 degrees. (For more information on what this means, check out Chapter 11.)

Switch to Perspective view

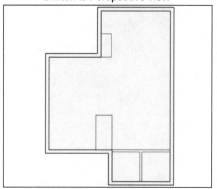

Switch to Iso view

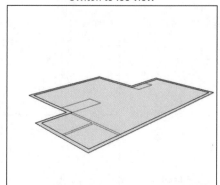

Zoom extents

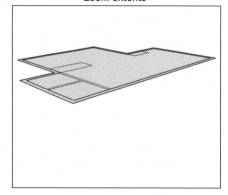

FIGURE 4-17:
Before you
start work in
3D, switch over
to a 3D view.

Pushing/pulling your way to happiness

The Push/Pull tool is a simple creature: It extrudes flat faces into 3D shapes. To use Push/Pull, click a face once to start pushing/pulling it, move your cursor until you like what you see, and then click again to stop pushing/pulling. That's it. No software tool has ever been so satisfyingly easy to use and understand. For more detail on Push/Pull, see the nearby sidebar, "More fun with Push/Pull."

Push/Pull works only on flat faces. To edit a curved face, you have to use something else — possibly the Intersect Faces feature.

TIP

The following steps outline how to use Push/Pull to extrude an interior floor plan into a 3D model, as shown in Figure 4-18:

1. **Select the Push/Pull tool from the toolbar.**

   The tool looks like a little box with a red arrow coming out the top.

1. Push/pull one interior wall

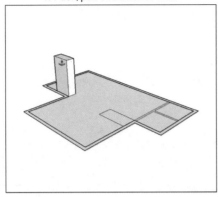

2. Push/pull remaining interior walls

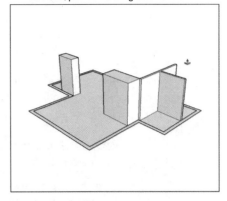

3. Double-click to select exterior wall group

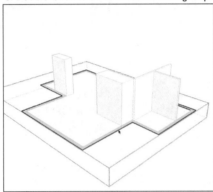

4. Push/pull exterior wall

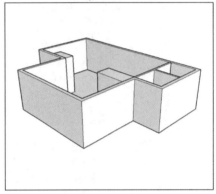

FIGURE 4-18:
Push/Pull
extrudes faces
into the walls
of Aidan's
house. Presto!

2. **Click an interior wall's face to start extruding it.**

If you click the "floor" face, you'd extrude that instead. If you accidentally choose the wrong face, press Esc to cancel the operation and try again.

3. **Move up your cursor to pull up the wall; click to stop extruding.**

How much you extrude the face doesn't matter, because you add precision in the next step.

4. **Type a ceiling height (such as 8') and press Enter.**

When you do this, the push/pull distance is revised to reflect your exact ceiling height. In this house, that's 8 feet.

5. **Repeat Steps 2 through 4 for all the interior walls.**

As explained in Chapter 3, orbiting helps you view what you're doing as you work around the model.

MORE FUN WITH PUSH/PULL

Push/Pull is the tool that most people think of when they think of SketchUp. In fact, the people who invented this software (back in the last millennium) *started* with the idea for Push/Pull — that's how closely linked SketchUp and Push/Pull are. If you'd like to know a little more about SketchUp's most distinguished tool, here are five things about Push/Pull that aren't immediately obvious when you start using it:

- **Double-click with the Push/Pull tool to extrude a face by the last distance you pushed/pulled.**

- **Press the Ctrl key (Option on a Mac) to push/pull a *copy* of your face.** As shown in the first graphic in the following figure, instead of using Push/Pull the regular way, you can use a modifier key to extrude a copy of the face you're pushing/pulling. This comes in super-handy for modeling things like multistory buildings quickly.

- **While pushing/pulling, hover over other parts of your geometry to tell SketchUp how far to extrude.** Take a look at the second graphic. Perhaps you want to use Push/Pull to extrude a cylinder that's exactly the same height as this box. Before you click the second time to stop pushing/pulling, hover over a point on the top of the box; now the cylinder is exactly that tall. To complete the operation, click while you're still hovering over the box. It's pretty simple and saves you hours of time after you're used to doing it.

- **Pushing/pulling a face into another, coplanar face automatically cuts a hole.** In fact, this is how you make openings (like doors and windows) in double-face walls. The last graphic shows this in action.

- **You can push/pull preselected faces.** Push/Pull works just like Move, Rotate, Offset, and Scale: You can preselect a face before you start using the tool. This comes in handy when you need to extrude a face that you can't see — a rare case, but handy nonetheless.

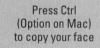
Press Ctrl
(Option on Mac)
to copy your face

Click while
you're hovering

Push/pull a face all the
way into another one
to make both disappear

6. **Push/pull the exterior wall to match the height of these interior walls.**

Because the exterior wall face is part of a group, you need to "open" the group before you can do anything to it. To open a group, double-click the exterior wall face, or context-click it and choose Edit Group. After you're able to work inside the group, you can follow Steps 2 through 4 in the preceding steps to make the exterior wall group 3D. Click anywhere outside the model to exit the group when you're done.

Adding floors to your building

Adding a second (and third, and fourth) floor to your model isn't as hard as it may seem. The key is to think of each level as a separate "tray" consisting of interior walls, a floor surface, and the ceiling of the level below. You model each floor as an individual group, making it easier to hide, edit, and move.

For the same reasons, you also make the exterior walls a separate group. They act kind of like a "box" into which your floor levels stack, as shown in Figure 4-19.

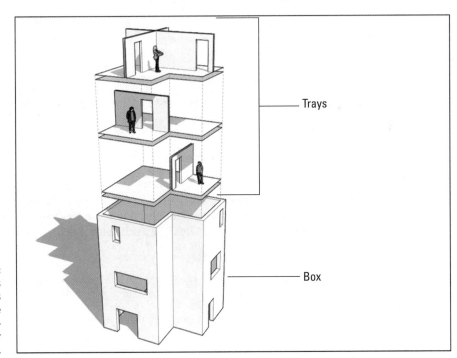

Trays

Box

FIGURE 4-19: Floor levels are like trays stacked inside a box consisting of your exterior walls.

Making groups to keep things separate

If you've been following along since the beginning of this chapter, the edges and faces that make up your exterior walls are already enclosed in a group by themselves. If they're not, seriously consider doing that now. If you take the time to group your exterior walls before you add floors to your building, you save hours of headache later. Trust us.

Otherwise-well-meaning people who have worked with other CAD or 3D modeling programs often take this opportunity to bring layers into the discussion. Yes, SketchUp has a Layers feature. And yes, floor "trays" are a lot like layers, at least conceptually. But you should *not* use Layers when modeling multiple levels of the same building. Layers in SketchUp simply don't work the way you might think they do. Chapter 7 explains how SketchUp layers work — and how using them as you would in other programs can make a mess of your 3D model.

If your exterior walls are already a group, the next step is to turn the rest of your first floor's geometry into *another* group. This is how you do just that:

1. Select the floor and interior walls of the first level.

You can accomplish this efficiently with the Select tool: Just triple-click a face on any interior wall to select everything that's attached to it. Chapter 3 has plenty of tips on selecting things.

2. Make a group by choosing Edit ⇨ Make Group from the menu bar.

Chapter 5 is all about groups and components; peruse the first few pages if you're utterly confused about what just happened.

Drawing the next floor

Modeling each new floor directly on top of the one underneath guarantees that everything in your building lines up. Some folks advocate for working "off to the side" and putting things together later, but Aidan finds that a recipe for trouble. Here's how you add a second floor to the house model. Check out Figure 4-20 to see the steps as pictures:

1. With the Line tool, trace the inside perimeter of the exterior wall to create a new face.

Keep in mind that tracing works only if everything you touch is already part of another group. If it isn't, your new edges stick to your existing ones, and your model becomes very, very messy.

2. Push/pull your new face into a thick slab.

How thick? It depends on your building, but a reasonable ceiling-to-floor distance between levels for houses is about 1 foot. You can figure yours out with a tape measure and a calculator.

TIP

The underside of the new slab is the ceiling of the first floor. Modeling buildings this way improves visibility because it enables you to hide a floor group to see the one below it.

3. **Draw the interior walls of the new floor.**

This is just like drawing the first floor. Switch to the Top view (Camera ⇨ Standard Views ⇨ Top) and then use the Tape Measure, Eraser, and Line tools to draft your floor plan. Just start at the very beginning of this chapter for a refresher.

1. Trace the inside perimeter of the exterior wall

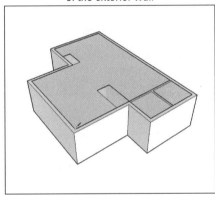

2. Push/pull into a thick slab

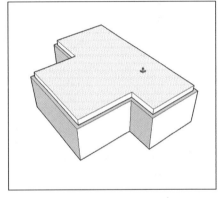

3. Draw interior walls

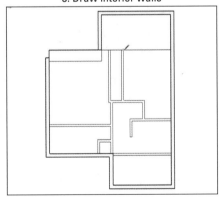

4. Push/pull interior walls

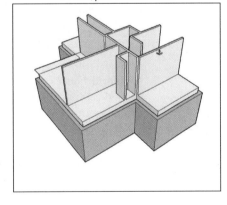

FIGURE 4-20: Draw right on top of the lower floor; then push/pull the interior walls to ceiling height.

TIP

If the floor you're drawing is bigger than the one below it, its outline overlaps the exterior walls. That's okay — just pay special attention to where your edges and faces end up as you draw. Orbit every once in a while to check that everything's copacetic.

In the event that your new floor is *smaller* than the one underneath, represent the inside boundary of the new exterior walls with a single edge. The next section explains what to do when your first and second floor plans don't match up exactly.

4. **Push/pull your interior walls to the correct height.**

   That's 8 feet, in this example.

5. **Group together your interior walls, your floor, and the ceiling of the level below.**

   If you're unsure of how to do this, take a look at the steps in "Making groups to keep things separate," a few pages back.

6. **If your upper floor isn't bigger or smaller than your lower floor, pull up your exterior walls to match your interior ones.**

   Here you're extending the box that holds your floor trays up another level. See the last step in "Push/pulling your way to happiness" earlier in this chapter for details.

TIP

Chances are your newest floor doesn't line up exactly with the one below it. Read the next section to find out what to do. If your building does happen to be one of the few with perfectly aligned floor plans, you can skip the next section entirely. Congrats! You're a lucky devil.

Creating additional exterior walls

Most buildings aren't simple extrusions; they bump in and out as they rise. Second-floor decks sit atop first-floor garages; bedrooms cantilever over gardens; intermediate roofs shelter new room additions. Buildings — especially multilevel houses — are complicated assemblies. Figuring out where walls, floors, and ceilings come together takes time, trial and error, and a good dose of spatial reasoning. It's best not to attempt the steps in this section when you're tired or distracted.

In the house Aidan models for this chapter, the second floor both overhangs and, um, underhangs (hooray for neologisms) the first floor. Wherever this happens, you need to add a new section of exterior wall, as shown in Figure 4-21.

Second floor bumps out

First floor bumps out

FIGURE 4-21: The outline of the second floor doesn't exactly match that of the first.

To begin the second floor, draw faces to define any new exterior walls. Follow these steps, which correspond to Figure 4-22:

1. **With the Line tool, trace the inside perimeter of your new exterior walls.**

2. **Hide the group that includes your second-floor interior walls by context-clicking it and choosing Hide.**

   You created this group by following the steps in the preceding section, "Drawing the next floor."

3. **Select the face that you created when you traced the inside perimeter in Step 1.**

   Don't see a face? Maybe you forgot to draw an edge somewhere.

4. **With the Offset tool, offset the edges of your selected face by the thickness of your exterior walls.**

   In this case, the thickness is 8 inches.

5. Delete the face in the center, leaving only a face that represents your new exterior wall thickness.

6. Unhide the group you hid in Step 2 by choosing Edit ⇨ Unhide ⇨ Last from the menu bar.

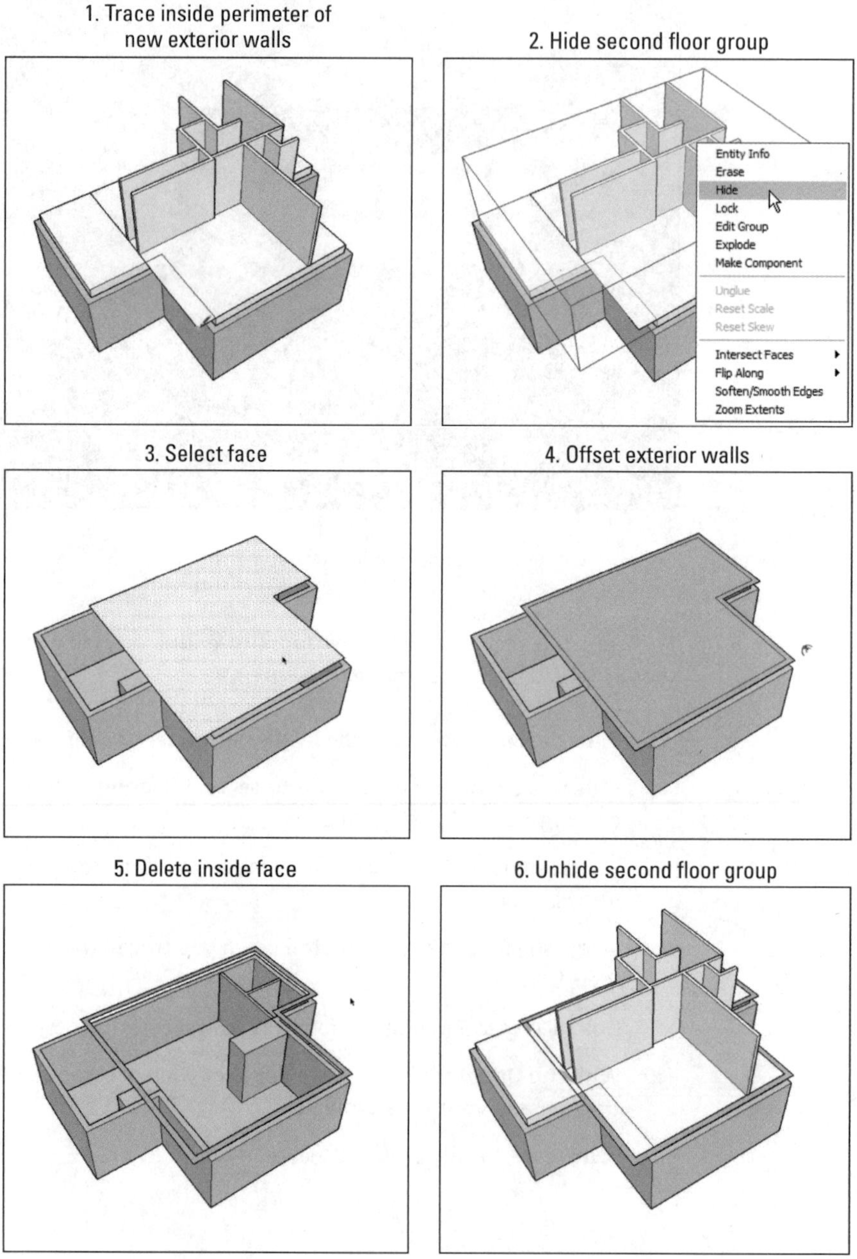

1. Trace inside perimeter of new exterior walls

2. Hide second floor group

3. Select face

4. Offset exterior walls

5. Delete inside face

6. Unhide second floor group

FIGURE 4-22:
Use Offset to draw faces that represent new exterior walls.

After you define the exterior wall face, you fine-tune how the second floor rests on top of the first floor by following these steps:

1. **Make a group out of your new exterior wall face by selecting it and then choosing Edit ⇨ Make Group.**

2. **Delete any floor geometry that doesn't belong.**

   For example, in Figure 4-23 (top), part of the second floor extends past the exterior wall on the left side of the figure. Double-click the group with the Select tool to edit it, and then use the Eraser to take away only the geometry that doesn't belong on your new floor, being careful to leave the ceiling that covers the first floor.

3. **With the Select tool, double-click the exterior wall face to open the group you created in Step 1.**

4. **Push/pull down any wall faces to meet the top of the lower floor's exterior wall. See the bottom of Figure 4-23.**

Delete unwanted floor faces

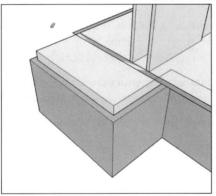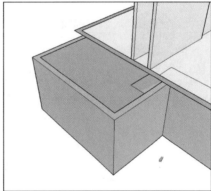

Push/pull exterior wall face down

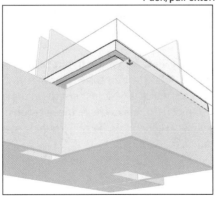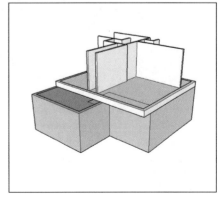

FIGURE 4-23: Delete extra floor faces; then push/pull down the walls.

Only now are you ready to ensconce your second floor in its new exterior walls. Doing so is yet another multistep process:

1. **Make *all* your exterior walls part of the same group:**

   a. *Select the group that contains your new exterior walls and then choose Edit⇨Cut.*

   b. *With the Select tool, double-click the group containing your lower exterior walls.*

   You're "inside" that group.

   c. *Choose Edit⇨Paste in Place.*

   d. *Choose Edit⇨Group⇨Explode to ungroup the edges and faces in the selected group, sticking them to those in the lower group.*

   Whew.

2. **With the Line tool, add any necessary edges. With the Eraser tool, delete any extraneous ones.**

   In Figure 4-24, you can see where the model has extra edges that need to be deleted.

   Using your SketchUp virtuosity, watch the colors as you draw, use the Shift key to lock inferences, and remember to zoom in on what you're doing. Skimming Chapter 3 provides useful pointers on these actions.

3. **With the Push/Pull tool, extrude your exterior walls up to the height of your second-floor interior walls (also shown in Figure 4-24).**

4. **Orbit around your model to make sure all is well.**

   You can see the result in the lower right of Figure 4-24.

Up, up, and away

Now that you're privy to Aidan's favorite technique for modeling multilevel build-ings, you can build up as high as you like. As you proceed, the following tidbits may be helpful:

>> **Hide things to get a clearer view for your current task.** When you context-click any entity and choose Hide, it's often easier see what you're doing. This is particularly true of groups, which is why, in the steps in the preceding sections, you to go to so much trouble to create those groups. To see stuff that's hidden, choose View⇨Hidden Geometry. To unhide something that's hidden, context-click and choose Unhide.

1. Make all exterior walls part of the same group

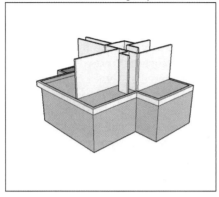

2. Delete edges between faces

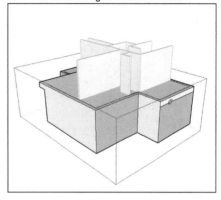

3. Push/pull exterior walls

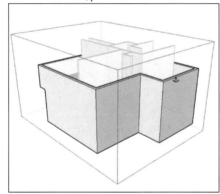

4. Orbit to make sure everything looks right

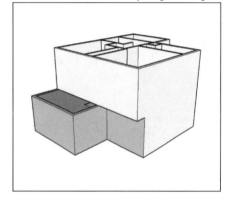

FIGURE 4-24: Do what you need to do to make your exterior walls look right.

>> **Better yet, use the Outliner.** Chapter 7 is all about making your SketchUp life easier by using certain tools to work more efficiently. If you're up for it, skip ahead and read the stuff about the Outliner. It's hyper-relevant to staying organized and seeing what's where as you create a multilevel building.

>> **There's gold in Model Info.** Choose Window⇨ Model Info and then click the Components option on the left. Next to the Fade Rest of Model slider, you can select a Hide check box. With this check box selected, everything outside the group you're currently editing becomes hidden. Smart modelers (such as yourself) make liberal use of this gem when cutting doors and windows in interior walls, which is the topic of the next section.

Inserting doors and windows

To add doors and windows, the best method depends on what kind of building you're modeling, whether you're using single-face or double-face walls, and how much detail you plan to include in your model. You can make openings in your walls in a couple ways:

>> **Cut openings with SketchUp components.** The SketchUp 3D Warehouse (read all about it in Chapter 5) contains scores of doors and windows that you can download and use in your models. Some of them cut their own openings when you insert them in a face. Here's the catch, though: SketchUp's cut-opening components work only on single-face walls, which means that they're only really useful for exterior building models. If you're building an interior model, you have to cut your own openings.

>> **Cut openings yourself.** For double-face walls, this is your only option; luckily, it's easy to do. Basically, draw the opening's outline and then use Push/Pull to create the opening. The process is the same for doors and windows.

Using SketchUp's handy-dandy components

As long as you're making an exterior model, you can use the door and window components from SketchUp's 3D Warehouse. Without going into a ton of detail, here's what you need to know about them:

>> **Components are accessible from the Components panel.** The Components panel appears on the Default Tray, but if you don't see it, check whether Components is selected on the submenu that appears when you choose Window⇨Default Tray. On the Components panel, click the drop-down menu next to the In Model icon and select Architecture, which contains the Doors, Windows, and DC Doors and Windows collections. Components that can cut their own openings generally contain *gluing* or *cutting* in their descriptions. Keep in mind that you need to be online to access the 3D Warehouse.

>> **You can find hundreds more online.** If you're connected to the Internet, you can type any search query (such as *revolving door*) into the little search box at the top of the Components panel. This scours the 3D Warehouse for your search term and shows the results below. Some advice: The 3D Warehouse holds so much stuff that making your query specific helps you sort through the results.

>> **Components are editable.** You find details in Chapter 5, but here's the gist: If you don't like something about a component you find online, you can change it.

>> **Some components are dynamic.** Dynamic Components have special capabilities that make them easier to resize and otherwise reconfigure. You can read all about Dynamic Components in Chapter 5.

>> **When components cut their own openings, the openings aren't permanent.** When you move or delete a hole-cutting door or window component you've placed in a model, the opening goes with the component.

Follow these steps to add a door or window component to your model:

1. With the Tape Measure tool, create guides to help you line up your doors or windows.

Guides are the best way to ensure that everything's in the right spot. In Figure 4-25, two horizontal guides (which are 2.5 feet from the bottom of the exterior wall) mark where to place the bottom of the windows. One vertical guide marks where to place the right edge of the door. After Rebecca placed the door, she created a guide 4 feet from each side of the door, to help place the windows symmetrically. Chapter 3 explains how to create guides.

2. In the Components panel, select the component that you want to place in your model.

For help navigating the Components panel, see Chapter 5.

3. In the drawing area, click to place the component where you want it to be.

In Figure 4-25, you see one door and four instances of the window component.

4. If you don't like where your component is, use the Move tool (read all about it in Chapter 3) to reposition your component.

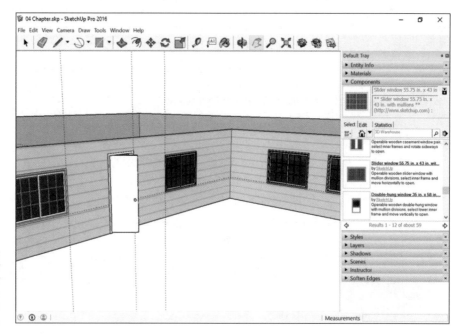

FIGURE 4-25: Placing window and door components in your model is a breeze.

Making your own openings

Most of the time, you can't get away with using SketchUp's built-in door and window components. Because these components can't cut through two-faced walls, they're limited to external use only. That's okay though; cutting your own holes in walls is quick and easy, and you end up with exactly what you want.

To cut a precise opening in a double-face wall, here's what you need to do; Figure 4-26 shows the basic steps:

REMEMBER

1. **Mark where you want your opening to be with guides.**

For a refresher on using guides, have a look at Chapter 3.

If you're drawing on a wall that's part of a group, you need to edit that group in order to punch holes in the wall. To edit a group, double-click it with the Select tool. To stop editing, click somewhere off to the side of your model. Chapter 5 has more info about working with groups.

2. **Draw the outline of the opening you want to create, making sure to create a new face in the process.**

Use the Line tool, and keep an eye out for the colored inferences, which let you know where you are.

3. **With the Push/Pull tool, extrude your new face back into the thickness of the wall until it touches the face behind it.**

If everything goes well, your face disappears, taking with it the corresponding area of the face behind it. Now you have an opening in your wall. If your face doesn't disappear, and no opening is created, it's probably for one of the following reasons:

- *Your faces aren't parallel to each other.* This technique works only if both faces are parallel. Keep in mind that just because two faces *look* parallel doesn't mean that they are.

- *You hit an edge.* If you push/pull your face into a face with an edge crossing it, SketchUp gets confused and doesn't cut an opening. Use Undo, get rid of the pesky edge (if you can), and try again.

Create guides   Draw edges   Push/pull all the way through

FIGURE 4-26:
With guides and the Push/Pull tool, create an opening through parallel faces.

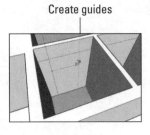
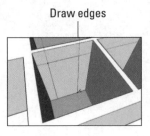
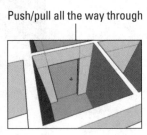

TIP

Don't forget to orbit! If you can't quite push/pull what you mean to push/pull, orbit around until you can see what you're doing.

Staring Down Stairs

You can make stairs probably a million different ways in SketchUp, and in the following sections, you find two methods that work equally well.

Chapter 5 contains a third, slightly trickier (but way more powerful) way of making stairs using components. SketchUp's Dynamic Components have some pretty neat implications for models that need stairs. A so-called *dynamic stair component* automatically adds or subtracts individual steps as you make it bigger or smaller with the Scale tool. Depending on what you want to accomplish, a premade dynamic stair component may save you a bunch of time. Find out more about them in Chapter 5.

Before you dive in, here's some simple stairway vocabulary, just in case you need it. Figure 4-27 provides a visual reference:

>> **Rise and run:** The *rise* is the total distance your staircase needs to climb. If the vertical distance from your first floor to your second (your *floor-to-floor* distance) is 10 feet, that's your rise. The *run* is the total *horizontal* distance of your staircase. A set of stairs with a big rise and a small run would be really steep.

>> **Tread:** A *tread* is an individual step — the part of the staircase you step on. When someone refers to the size of a tread, he's talking about the *depth* — the distance from the front to the back of the tread. Typically, this is anywhere from 9 to 24 inches, but treads of 10 to 12 inches are most comfortable to walk on.

>> **Riser:** The *riser* is the part of the step that connects each tread in the vertical direction. Risers are usually about 5 to 7 inches high, but that depends on your building. Not all staircases have actual risers (think of steps with gaps between treads), but they all have a riser *height*.

>> **Landing:** A *landing* is a platform somewhere around the middle of a set of stairs. Landings are necessary in real life, but modeling them can be a pain; figuring out staircases with landings is definitely more complicated. Sometimes, modeling a landing is easier if you think of it as a really big step.

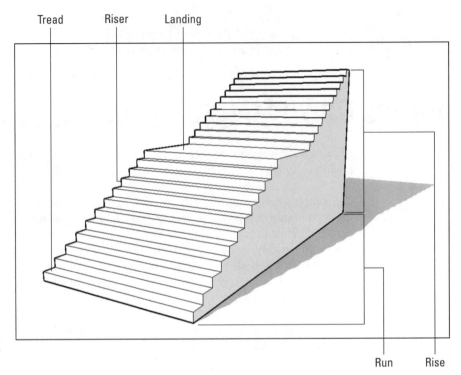

Tread   Riser   Landing

Run   Rise

FIGURE 4-27:
The anatomy
of a staircase.

TIP

Model steps as a group, separate from the rest of your building, and move them into position when they're done. You can read all about groups in Chapter 5.

The Subdivided Rectangles method

The Subdivided Rectangles method is how most people think to draw their first set of stairs. This method is intuitive and simple, but a bit more time-consuming than the other methods in this book.

TIP

The key to the Subdivided Rectangles method is a special trick you can do with edges: Called *Divide*, it lets you pick any edge and divide it into as many segments as you want. If you know how many steps you need to draw but not how deep each individual tread needs to be, the Divide command comes in really handy.

Here's how the Subdivided Rectangles method works. See Figure 4-28:

1. **Draw a rectangle the size of the staircase you want to build.**

2. **With the Select tool, context-click a long edge of your rectangle and choose Divide.**

    If your staircase is wider than it is long, context-click a short edge instead.

Divide edge into smaller edges, marking off treads

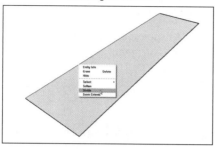

Connect new endpoints

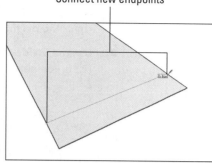

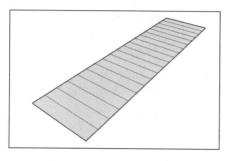

Divide vertical edge marking off vertical risers

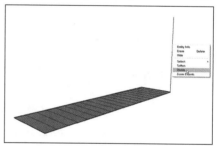

Infer to the endpoints on this divided edge

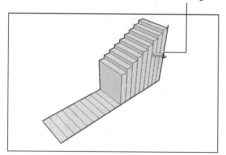

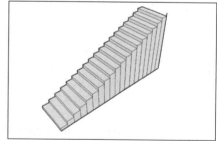

FIGURE 4-28: The Subdivided Rectangles method of building stairs.

3. **Before you do anything else, type the number of treads you want to create and press Enter.**

   This command automatically divides your edge into many more edges, eliminating the need to calculate how deep each of your treads needs to be. Essentially, each new edge becomes a side of one of your treads.

4. **Draw a line from the endpoint of each new edge, dividing your original rectangle into many smaller rectangles.**

   You can use the Line or the Rectangle tool to do this.

5. **From one of the corners of your original rectangle, draw a vertical edge that's the height of your staircase's total rise.**

6. **Use the Divide command to split your new edge into however many risers you need in your staircase (generally your number of treads, plus one).**

   Repeat Steps 2 and 3 to do this. The endpoints of your new, little edges tell you how high to make each step.

7. **Push/pull the rectangle that represents your last step to the correct height.**

   Here's where you need to use the hover-click technique that we describe in the sidebar "More fun with Push/Pull," earlier in this chapter. Just click once to push/pull, hover over the endpoint that corresponds to the height of that tread, and click again. Your step is automatically extruded to the right height.

   Extrude your highest step first, but remember that it doesn't go all the way to the top. You always have a riser between your last step and your upper floor.

REMEMBER

8. **Repeat Step 7 for each remaining step.**

9. **Use the Eraser to eliminate extra edges you don't need.**

   Don't accidentally erase geometry on the part of your staircase you can't see. Turning on Back Edges (View ⇨ Edge Style ⇨ Back Edges) is a nice way to see "through" your model without resorting to X-Ray mode.

TIP

The Copied Profile method

This method for modeling a staircase relies, like the last one, on using Push/Pull to create a 3D form from a 2D face, but this method is more elegant. In a nutshell, draw the *profile* — the side view, sort of — of a single step and then copy as many steps as you need, create a single face, and extrude the whole thing into shape. The first time you do this is breathtakingly satisfying — one of those "guaranteed to make you smile" SketchUp operations you'll want to repeat for friends (assuming you have nerdy friends like us).

Follow these steps to make a staircase using the Copied Profile method, as shown in Figure 4-29:

1. **Start with a large, vertical face; make sure that it's big enough for the flight of stairs you want to build.**

   You're going to end up pushing/pulling the whole shebang out of the side of this face, just so you know.

Start with a vertical face

Draw the profile of a single step

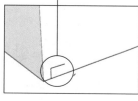

Copy it up

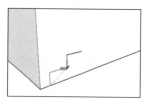

Type the number of copies, then **x**, and press Enter

Push/pull the stair into 3D

FIGURE 4-29: The Copied Profile method.

2. **In the bottom corner of the face, draw the profile of a single step.**

   The Line tool is a great choice, although you may want to use an arc or two, depending on the level of detail you need. For a refresher on drawing lines accurately, check out Chapter 3.

3. **Select all the edges that make up your step profile.**

   TIP

   You can hold down the Shift key while clicking with the Select tool to select multiple entities. Chapter 3 has lots of selection tips.

4. **Make a copy of your step profile and place it above your first one.**

   If you're unfamiliar with how to make copies using the Move tool, see Chapter 3.

5. **Type the number of steps you want to make, type** x, **and then press Enter.**

   For example, if you want ten steps, type **10x**. This technique repeats the copy operation you just did by however many times you tell it to; the *x* after the number tells SketchUp to make copies.

6. **If you need to, draw an edge to make sure that all your step profiles are part of a single face.**

7. **Push/pull the staircase face to reflect the desired width of your staircase.**

   This part seems like magic to most folks; we don't think it ever gets old.

TIP

This method of stairway building also works great in combination with the Follow Me tool, covered in Chapter 6. Figure 4-30 whets your appetite. Follow Me is cool beans, all the way around.

Profile   Extrusion path for Follow Me

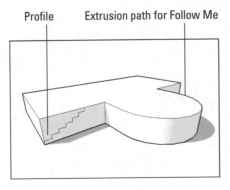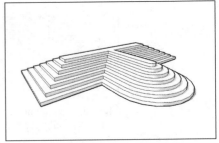

FIGURE 4-30:
Using Follow Me with the Copied Profile method produces some impressive geometry, indeed.

Raising the Roof

If you're lucky, the roof you want to build is fairly simple. Unfortunately, home builders sometimes go a little crazy, creating roofs with dozens of different *pitches* (slopes), dormers, and other doodads that make modeling them a nightmare. For this reason, this section keeps things pretty simple: The following sections show you how to identify and model basic roof forms. After that, you discover a great tool — *Intersect Face* — that you can use to assemble complicated roofs from less-complicated pieces.

TIP

The tricky thing about roofs is that they're hard to see. If you want to make a model of something that already exists, it helps to get a good look at it — but that's not always possible with roofs. Google Maps offers a neat way to view an existing roof you're trying to build.

WARNING

Always, *always* make a group out of your whole building before you work on your roof. If you don't, your geometry starts sticking together, you end up erasing walls by accident, and eventually, you lose your mind. On top of that, the ability to separate your roof from the rest of your building whenever you want is handy. You can also group your roof, if that makes sense for what you're doing. Check out Chapter 5 for a full rundown on making and using groups.

Before you dive in, here's a brief guide to general roof types and terminology that may come in handy for the explanations later in this chapter. Figure 4-31 illustrates each of the following terms:

>> **Flat roof:** *Flat roofs* are just that, except they aren't — if a roof were really flat, it would collect water and leak. That's why even roofs that look flat are sloped very slightly.

>> **Pitched roof:** Any roof that isn't flat is technically a *pitched roof.*

>> **Shed roof:** A *shed roof* is one that slopes from one side to the other.

>> **Gabled roof:** *Gabled roofs* have two planes that slope away from a central *ridge.*

>> **Hip roof:** A *hip roof* is one where the sides and ends all slope in different directions.

>> **Pitch:** The angle of a roof surface.

>> **Gable:** A *gable* is the pointy section of wall that sits under the peak of a pitched roof.

>> **Eave:** *Eaves* are the parts of a roof that overhang the building.

>> **Fascia:** *Fascia* is the trim around the edge of a roof's eaves where gutters are sometimes attached.

>> **Soffit:** A *soffit* is the underside of an overhanging eave.

>> **Rake:** The *rake* is the part of a gabled roof that overhangs the gable.

>> **Valley:** A *valley* is formed when two roof slopes come together; this is where water flows when it rains.

>> **Dormer:** *Dormers* are the little things that pop up above roof surfaces. They often have windows and make attic spaces more usable.

>> **Parapet:** Flat roofs that don't have eaves have *parapets* — extensions of the building's walls that go up a few feet past the roof itself.

Building flat roofs with parapets

Good news! SketchUp was practically made for modeling these kinds of roofs. By using a combination of the Offset tool and Push/Pull, you can make a parapet in less than a minute. Follow these steps, as shown in Figure 4-32:

1. **With the Offset tool, click the top face of your building.**

2. **Click again somewhere inside the same face to create another face.**

3. **Type the thickness of your parapet and then press Enter.**

This redraws your offset edges to be a precise distance from the edges of your original face. How thick should your parapet be? It all depends on your building, but most parapets are between 6 and 12 inches thick.

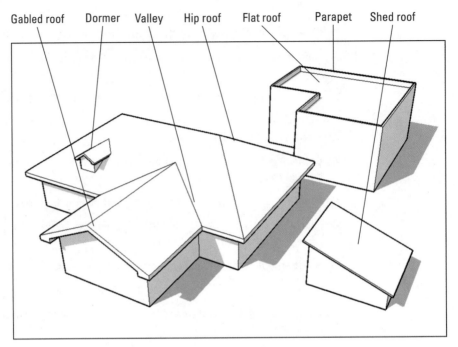

Gabled roof Dormer Valley Hip roof Flat roof Parapet Shed roof

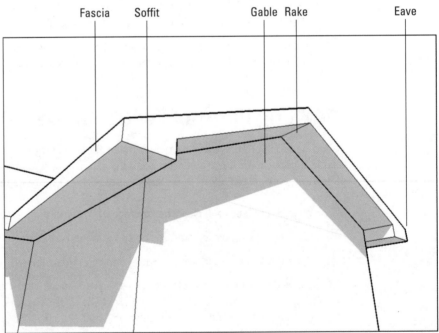

Fascia Soffit Gable Rake Eave

FIGURE 4-31: Some different kinds of roofs, and their various and sundry parts.

PITCHED ROOFS CAN MAKE YOU CRAZY

That fact notwithstanding, a few tips might make building your next pitched roof a little easier:

- **Start by making the rest of your building a group.** As we warn you elsewhere in this section, you should always make a group out of your whole building before you start working on your roof.

- **Draw a top view of your roof on paper first.** Working out the roof's basic shape in your mind can help you figure out how to manage the roof's details. Adding measurements and angles is even better because these details help you know what to do in SketchUp.

- **Figure out how to use the Protractor tool.** This tool (which is on the Tools menu) is for measuring angles and, more importantly, creating angled guides. Because sloped roofs are all about angles, you probably need to use the Protractor sooner or later. To find out how this tool works, open the Instructor panel and then activate the Protractor tool. Chapter 3's section on rotating can also help you, because, in many ways, the Protractor tool behaves like the Rotate tool.

4.   **Push/pull your outside face (the one around the perimeter of your roof) into a parapet.**

5.   **Type the height of your parapet and then press Enter.**

Offset to the inside   Push/pull your parapet up

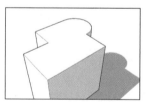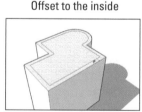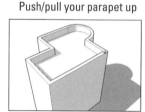

FIGURE 4-32: Modeling parapets on flat-roofed buildings is easy.

Creating eaves for buildings with pitched roofs

Aidan's favorite way to create *eaves*, or roof overhangs, is to use the Offset tool. Follow these steps to get the general idea and see Figure 4-33:

1.   **Make a group out of your whole building before you start modeling the roof.**

Keeping your roof separate makes your model easier to work with.

2. **With the Line tool, create an outline of the parts of your roof that will have eaves of the same height.**

   The goal is a single face that you can offset. A lot of buildings have complex roofs with eaves of all different heights; for the sake of this step, just create a face that, when offset, will create roof overhangs in the right places.

3. **With the Offset tool, create an overhanging face.**

   For instructions on how to use Offset, see the section "Dusting off SketchUp's drafting tools," earlier in this chapter.

4. **Erase the edges of your original face.**

   Here's a quick way to do this with the Select tool:

   a. Double-click inside your first face.

   This selects both the face and the edges that define it.

   b. Press Delete to erase everything that's selected.

5. **Push/pull your overhanging roof face to create a thick fascia.**

   Different roofs have fasciae of different thicknesses; if you don't know yours, just take your best guess.

Offset an overhang   Delete the inside face   Push/Pull a fascia thickness

FIGURE 4-33:
Eaves are
the parts of
the roof that
overhang a
building's
walls.

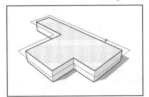  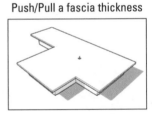

Constructing gabled roofs

You can construct a gabled roof in a bunch of ways (every SketchUp expert has her favorite), but one method works particularly well.

Follow these steps to build a gabled roof, which is shown in Figure 4-34:

1. **Create a roof overhang, following the steps in the preceding section.**

   Most gabled roofs have eaves, so you probably need to create them for your building.

Create an angled guide with the Protractor

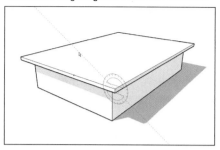

Draw a vertical edge

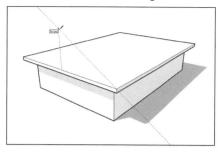

Complete the roof profile

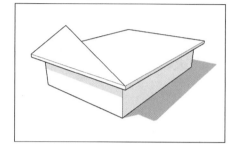

Push/pull it back

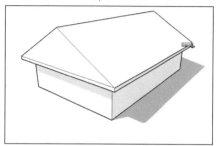

FIGURE 4-34: Gabled roofs are relatively easy to make in SketchUp.

2. **With the Protractor tool, create an angled guide at the corner of your roof.**

   The nearby sidebar, "Pitched roofs can make you crazy," points you to help with the Protractor.

   TECHNICAL STUFF

   Architects and builders often express angles as *rise over run ratios.* For example, a 4:12 (pronounced *4 in 12*) roof slope rises 4 feet for every 12 feet it runs. A 1:12 slope is very shallow, and a 12:12 slope is very steep. When you are using the Protractor tool, SketchUp's Measurements box understands angles expressed as ratios as well as those expressed in degrees. Typing **6:12** yields a slope of 6 in 12.

3. **With the Line tool, draw a vertical edge from the midpoint of your roof to the angled guide you created in Step 2.**

   The point at which your edge and your guide meet is the height of your roof ridge.

4. **Draw two edges from the top of your vertical line to the corners of your roof.**

   This creates two triangular faces.

5. **Erase the vertical edge you drew in Step 3 and the guide you drew in Step 2.**

6. Push/pull back your triangular gable.

If your gabled roof extends all the way to the other end of your building, push/pull it back that far. If your roof runs into another section of roof, as shown in Figure 4-35, extrude it back until it's completely "buried." The section "Sticking your roof together with Intersect Faces," later in this chapter, has more information on how to make a complex roof.

Push/pull it all the way into the other roof pitch

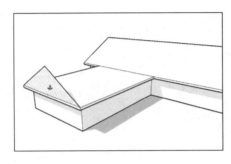
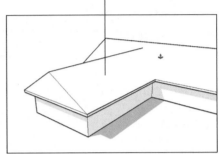

FIGURE 4-35:
If your gabled roof is part of a larger roof structure, it may just run into another roof pitch. Let it.

7. Finish your eaves, fascia, soffit, and rake(s) however you want.

Gabled roofs have more details than we can cover, but Figure 4-36 shows a few common ones.

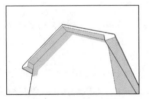
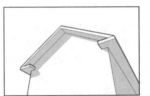
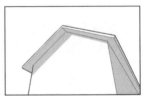

FIGURE 4-36:
Some common gabled roof details.

Making hip roofs

Believe it or not, building a hip roof is easier than building a gabled one. *Hip roofs* don't have rakes, which makes them a lot less complicated to model. Follow these steps to find out for yourself:

1. Follow Steps 1 through 5 in the preceding section "Constructing gabled roofs."

2. Measure the distance from the midpoint of the gable to the corner of the roof.

Because hip roofs have pitches that are the same on all sides, you can use a simple trick to figure out where to locate the hip in your roof. It's a lot easier than using the Protractor.

3. **With the Tape Measure, create a guide the distance you just measured from the end of the gable, as shown in Figure 4-37.**

4. **Draw edges from the point on the ridge you just located to the corners of your roof, as shown in Figure 4-37.**

This does two things: It splits the sides of your roof into two faces each and creates a new face (which you can't see yet) under the gabled end of your roof.

5. **Erase the three edges that form the gabled end of your roof, revealing the "hipped" pitch underneath.**

Neat, huh? Now all three faces of your roof are the same pitch — just the way they should be.

6. **If appropriate, repeat the process on the other end of your roof.**

Measure half-width of your gable

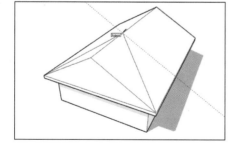

Create a guide that distance from end of gable

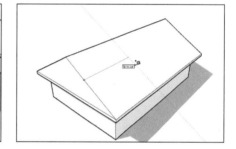

Draw edges connecting ridge and corners and erase 3 edges that form gable

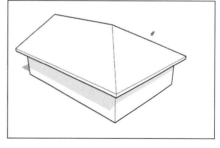

Now you have a hip

FIGURE 4-37: To make a hip roof, start with a gabled one.

Sticking your roof together with Intersect Faces

In general, the newer and more expensive a house is, the more roof slopes it has. Who knows why this is the case? Maybe folks think complex-roofed houses look more like French chateaus. Whether crazy roofs are a good thing isn't relevant to this book, but they're a pain in the, um, gutters to model.

Luckily, SketchUp has a relatively little-known feature that often helps when it comes to making roofs with lots of pitches: *Intersect Faces.* Here's what you need to know about this terrific little tool:

>> **Intersect Faces makes new geometry from existing geometry.** It takes faces you've selected and creates edges wherever they intersect. Figure 4-38 shows what we mean: Perhaps you want to make a model that's a cube with a cylinder-shaped chunk taken out of it. You'd model the cube and model the cylinder. After positioning them carefully, you can then use Intersect Faces to create edges where the two shapes' faces come together. After that, the Eraser can remove the edges you don't want — the rest of the cylinder, in this case.

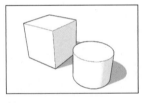 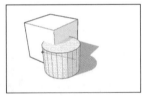 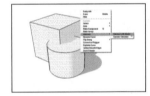

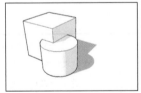 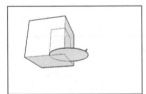 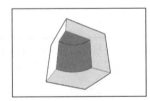

FIGURE 4-38: Using Intersect Faces to cut a partial cylinder out of a cube.

» **Intersect Faces and the Eraser tool go hand in hand.** Anytime you use Intersect Faces, you need to follow up by deleting unwanted geometry. To find it all, orbit, zoom, and pan around your model, zapping stray lines and faces with the Eraser as you go.

» **Most of the time, choose Intersect Faces with Model.** This tool has three modes, but the majority of the time, you use the basic one. Here's what all three modes do:

- *Intersect Faces with Model:* Creates edges everywhere your selected faces intersect with other faces in your model — whether the other faces are selected or not.

- *Intersect Faces with Selection:* Only creates edges where *selected* faces intersect with other *selected* faces. This is handy if you're trying to be a little bit more precise.

- *Intersect Faces with Context:* Choosing this option creates edges where faces *within the same group or component* intersect; that's why it's available only when you edit a group or component.

» **Intersect Faces doesn't have a button.** To use it, you have to either

- *Context-click and choose Intersect Faces.*

- *Choose Edit ⇨ Intersect Faces.*

When creating roofs, you can use Intersect Faces to combine a whole bunch of gables, hips, dormers, sheds, and so on into a single roof. Doing so is no cakewalk, and it requires a fair amount of planning, but it works great when nothing else will.

Figure 4-39 shows a complicated roof with several elements. Gabled roofs have been pushed/pulled into the main hip roof at all different heights, but edges don't exist where all the different faces meet. In the steps that follow, use Intersect Faces to create the edges you want and then use the Eraser to clean up the mess:

1. **Select the whole roof.**

TIP

If you grouped your building and roof the way we recommend earlier in this chapter, here's a timesaving trick: Hide the group that contains the rest of your building and then draw a big selection box around the whole roof with the Select tool.

2. **Choose Edit ⇨ Intersect Faces ⇨ With Selected.**

This tells SketchUp to create edges everywhere faces *intersect* — that is, everywhere faces pass through each other without an edge.

3. **With the Eraser, *carefully* delete the extra geometry on the inside of your roof, as shown in Figure 4-39.**

Although this erasing can be a lot of work, it's a whole lot easier than using the Line tool and SketchUp's inference engine to figure out where complex roof details should go.

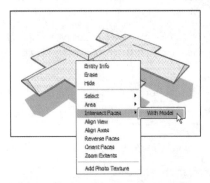
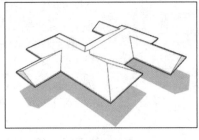

Erase from underside stuff that doesn't belong

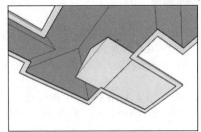

FIGURE 4-39:
Here's a typically complex roof that Intersect Faces can unify.

WHEN ALL ELSE FAILS, USE THE LINE TOOL

Fancy tools like Follow Me and Intersect Faces are useful most of the time, but for some roofs, you just have to resort to drawing good old edges. If that's the case, you'd better get familiar with most of the stuff at the beginning of Chapter 3 because you're going to be inferencing like there's no tomorrow. SketchUp users who really know what they're doing can draw *anything* with the Line and Eraser tools, which is beautiful to watch but beyond the scope of this book.

All the same, the following figure shows how the Line tool and SketchUp's venerable inference engine help you draw a gabled dormer on a sloped roof surface. With practice, you can do it.

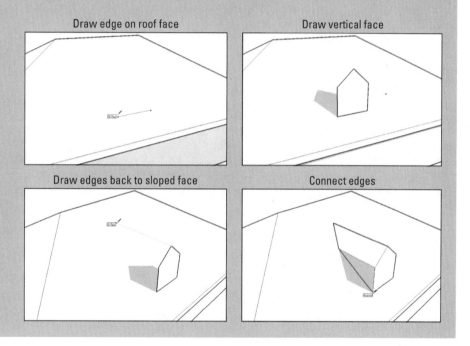

Draw edge on roof face

Draw vertical face

Draw edges back to sloped face

Connect edges

IN THIS CHAPTER

» **Organizing geometry into groups**

» **Discovering the wonder and majesty of components**

» **Getting familiar with Dynamic Components**

» **Using components to make symmetrical models**

» **Building stairs with component instances**

Chapter **5**

Falling in Love with Components

I f we had our way, this chapter would begin with the word *COMPONENTS* printed 4 inches high and colored neon green. Components are *that* important.

Making a component or a group is like gluing together geometry in your model. Edges and faces that are grouped together act like mini-models inside your main model. You use components and groups to more easily select, move, hide, and otherwise work with parts of your model that need to be kept separate. For example, if the roof of a house model is a component or group, you can easily hide or move the roof so that you can peer inside the house from above.

Now that you know how components and groups are alike, here's how they're different:

» *Groups* are simple conglomerations of edges and faces.

» *Components* are basically groups with an all-important, added benefit: Changes you make to one *instance* (copy) of a component automatically apply to all the other component instances in your model. So change one window component, and you change all instances where that window component appears in your model.

Learning to use groups and components is the single biggest thing you can do to get better at SketchUp.

This chapter is about creating and using SketchUp groups and components to make your life a whole lot simpler. We begin by talking about groups (which have a lot in common with components). After that, we jump into components — finding them, managing them, and making your own.

In the last section of this chapter, you learn a couple of modeling techniques that take advantage of component behavior. They're guaranteed to save you time and effort, and using them will make you feel like a rock star — one who makes 3D models, at least.

Grouping Things Together

SketchUp geometry (the edges and faces that make up your model) is *sticky.* In other words, stuff in your model wants to stick to other stuff. The people who invented SketchUp built it this way on purpose, but also knew you'd sometimes need to separate geometry, too. Suffice it to say, making and using groups are the keys to keeping the stuff in your model from sticking together. Here are a few reasons for you to make groups:

>> **Grouped geometry doesn't stick to anything.** Perhaps you've modeled a building, and you want to add a roof. You want to move the roof out of the way with the Move tool, but every time you try, you pull the top part of the house along with it (like the middle image in Figure 5-1). Making the roof a separate group enables the roof to sit on top of your house without sticking to the walls, as shown in the right image in Figure 5-1.

The house is being stretched

FIGURE 5-1: Making the roof into a group means that it won't stick to the rest of your building.

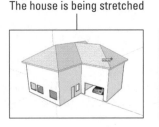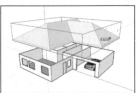

>> **Using groups makes working with your model easier.** You can select all the geometry in a group by clicking it once with the Select tool. You can move groups and make copies with the Move tool.

>> **You can name groups.** If you turn a selection of geometry into a group, you can give it a name. In the Outliner (covered in Chapter 7), you can see a list of the groups (and components) in your model, and if you've given them names, you can see what you have.

>> **Groups can be solids.** Basically, a *solid* is any group (or component) whose geometry can be thought of as *watertight* — continuous, with no holes. Solids are important for two reasons:

  - *If an object is a solid, SketchUp can calculate its volume.* You can see a solid's volume in the Entity Info panel.

  - *The Solid Tools let you perform nifty modeling tricks using two or more solids.* You can read all about the Solid Tools toward the end of Chapter 6.

Follow these steps to create a group:

1. **Select the geometry (edges and faces) you want to turn into a group.**

For help with making selections, check out Chapter 3.

2. **Choose Edit ⇨ Make Group.**

You can also context-click and choose Make Group from the context menu that pops up.

To ungroup the geometry in a group, you need to explode it. Context-click the group and choose Explode from the context menu. The edges and faces that were grouped together aren't grouped together anymore.

TIP

To edit the geometry inside a group, double-click it with the Select tool. In edit mode, the rest of your model appears to fade back, and the box around the group (also known as the group's *context*) changes from solid lines to dashed lines. To close the group's context when you're done editing, click outside it, somewhere else in your modeling window.

Working with Components

Components make 3D modeling fast, fun, and easy, and this section explains all their special capabilities. After you discover components' special magic, you might actually get excited about diving into the nitty-gritty of how components work:

using the features in the Components panel, keeping your components organized, making your own components, and finding dynamic components that move when you click them.

What makes components so great?

If components were a sports team, we'd hold season tickets in the front row and attend every game wearing fan jerseys and carrying homemade posters to cheer on our favorites. (Go Architecture Collection!) Here's why we're big fans of using components whenever you can:

» **Everything that's true about groups is true about components.** That's right: Components do everything that groups do. Components don't stick to the rest of your model, you can give them meaningful names, and you can select them, move them, copy them, and edit them easily — just like you can with groups.

» **Components update automatically.** Unlike with groups, when you use multiple copies (called *instances*) of the same component in your model, they're all spookily linked. Changing one makes them all change, which saves loads of time. For example, in Figure 5-2, when Aidan adds something (in this case, shutters) to one instance of his window component, *all* the instances are updated. After Aidan changes one component, all three windows have shutters.

These windows are instances
of the same component

FIGURE 5-2:
Changing one
instance of a
component
changes all
the other
instances, too.

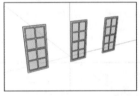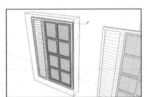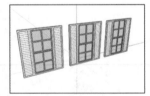

» **The Components panel has special component-management features.** You can use the Components panel to count, select, substitute, and otherwise manage all the component instances in your model. (Groups don't appear in the Components panel at all.) Figure 5-3 shows a basic building with a window component. In the lower left corner of the Component panel's Statistics tab, you can see there are 18 instances of the window. On the Component panel's Select tab, you can context-click to select all instances of the window and replace it with another component with only a few clicks. We chose a white sedan.

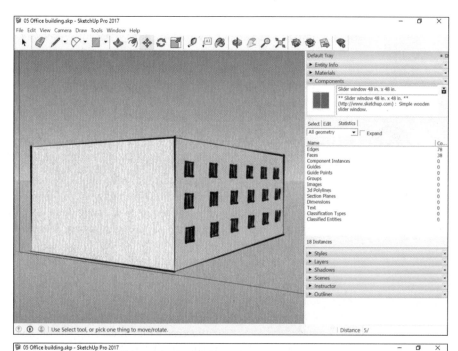

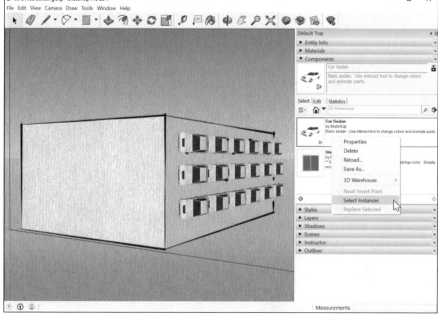

FIGURE 5-3:
Quickly count
all the window
instances in
your model
(top), or even
swap them out
for another
component.

>> **Components can cut an opening automatically.** Perhaps you've made a window, and you want that window to poke a hole through whatever surface you stick it to. On the Edit tab, explained a little later in this section, you can set up SketchUp components to cut their own openings in faces. Even better, these openings depend on the existence of the component; if you delete the component, the hole disappears.

Components that cut openings can do so only through a single face. If your wall is two faces thick, your components cut through only one of them.

REMEMBER

>> **You can use your components in other models.** It's simple to make any component you build available for use whenever you work in SketchUp, no matter what model you're working on. If you have a group of parts or other things you always use, making your own component collection can save you a lot of time and effort. For more information about creating your own component collections, see the upcoming section, "The Select tab."

>> **Components are great for making symmetrical models.** Because you can flip a component instance and keep working on it, and because component instances automatically update when you change one of them, using components is a great way to model anything that's symmetrical. If you look around, you'll notice that most things people use are symmetrical. The "Modeling symmetrically: Good news for lazy people" section near the end of this chapter dives headlong into modeling symmetrical things like couches and hatchbacks; Figure 5-4 shows examples.

FIGURE 5-4:
What do all these things have in common? They're symmetrical.

124   PART 2 **Modeling in SketchUp**

» **Components keep file sizes down.** When you use several instances of a single component, SketchUp has to remember the information for only one of them. This means that your files are smaller, which in turn means you have an easier time e-mailing, uploading, and opening them on your computer.

» **Components show in the Outliner.** If you're at all interested in *not* wasting time hunting for things you've misplaced, create lots of components. Doing so means that you can see, hide, unhide, and rearrange them in the Outliner, which is covered in Chapter 7.

» **Components can save your sanity.** Hooray! You've finished a model of the new airport — and it took only three weeks! Too bad the daylighting consultant wants you to add a sunshade detail to every one of the 1,300 windows in the project. If you made that window a component, you're golden. If, on the other hand, that window *isn't* a component, you're going to spend a very long night holding hands with your computer mouse.

» **Components can be dynamic.** Dynamic Components are components with special abilities. They can be set up with multiple configurations, taught to scale intelligently, programmed to perform simple animations, and more. Anyone can use existing DCs, but only people with SketchUp Pro can create new ones. Check out "Discovering Dynamic Components" later in this chapter for the whole story.

THE SketchUp 3D WAREHOUSE

Imagine a place online where everyone in the world can share SketchUp models for free. That's the 3D Warehouse in a nutshell. It's hosted by Trimble (SketchUp's parent company), it's available in several languages, and it's searchable — which is a very good thing because it's jam-packed with models. Millions of 'em.

You can get to the 3D Warehouse in a couple ways:

• **On the web:** Just type http://3dwarehouse.sketchup.com into your web browser.

• **Through SketchUp:** The Components panel is hooked up directly to the 3D Warehouse as long as you're online. You can also open the 3D Warehouse in a separate window by choosing File ⇨ 3D Warehouse ⇨ Get Models.

Anything in the 3D Warehouse is available for you to download and use in your own models. You can also upload anything you make so that other people can use it. Find out more about sharing your work on the 3D Warehouse in Chapter 12.

Exploring the Components panel

The Components panel gives you a place to keep any components you make. You can also search for components that other people have made, which is a great way to spiff up your model without building everything yourself.

TIP

You can bring any SketchUp model on your computer into your current file as a component. That's because components are really just SketchUp files embedded in other SketchUp files. When you create a component in your model, you're effectively creating a new, nested SketchUp file. Neat, huh?

The Components panel is made up of four major areas, each covered in the following sections.

Info and buttons

We don't really know what to call this part of the Components panel, so we call it like it is: It's for information and buttons. Figure 5-5 points out its elements, and here's what everything does:

>> **Name:** The name of the component you select appears here. If your component is in your model, it's editable. If the component is in one of the default collections, it's not. A component is considered to be in your model if it appears in your In Model collection, which you can read about in the next section, "The Select tab."

>> **Description:** Some, but not all, components have descriptions associated with them. You can write one when you create a new component, or you can add one to an existing component in your model. Just like the name, you can edit descriptions for models only in your In Model collection.

 >> **Display Secondary Selection Pane button:** Clicking this button opens a second view of your collections at the bottom of the Components panel. Use this view to manage the components on your computer.

The Select tab

This tab is where your components live (if they can be said to live anywhere). Use the Select tab to view, organize, and choose components. Refer to Figure 5-5 to see the Select tab in all its glory.

 >> **In Model button:** SketchUp automatically keeps track of the components you've used in your model and puts a copy of each of them in your In Model collection. Each SketchUp file you create has its own In Model collection, which contains the components that exist in that model. Clicking the In Model button displays the components in your In Model collection, if you have any.

Name

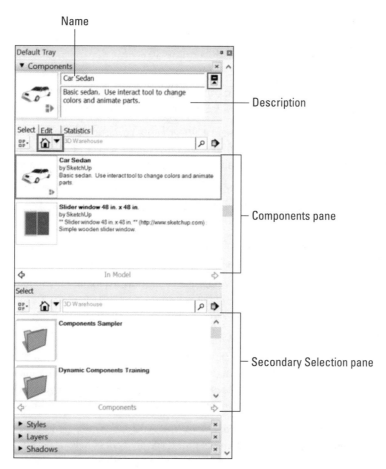

Description

Components pane

Secondary Selection pane

FIGURE 5-5:
The
Components
panel is
chock-full o'
goodness.

>> **Collections drop-down menu:** You open this menu by clicking the down arrow next to the In Model button. The components listed in the Favorites area of this menu are a mix of two collection types:

- *Local* collections are folders of components that live on your hard drive. You can access them anytime because they refer to files on your computer.

- *Online* collections are groupings of components that live in the 3D Warehouse (see the nearby sidebar). Unlike local collections, you can access online collections only when you're — you guessed it — online.

Unfortunately, the Collections drop-down menu doesn't indicate which collections are local and which are online. If you click the name of a collection and see a progress bar before you see any models, that collection is online.

>> **3D Warehouse search box:** It works just like any regular search box: Type what you're looking for and press Enter. Models in the 3D Warehouse that

match your search terms appear in the Components pane. Naturally, you need to be online for this feature to work.

>> **Components pane:** This pane displays the components in the currently selected component collection, or the results of a 3D Warehouse search you've just performed. Click a component to use it in your model.

TIP

Components that have a little green arrow icon next to them are special; they're Dynamic Components. They have special abilities. You can read about DCs later in this chapter, in the "Discovering Dynamic Components" section.

>> **View Options button:** Pretty simple, really. This is where you decide how to view the components (or subcollections) in the Components pane. You can choose different thumbnail image sizes or a list view.

>> **Collection Details menu:** Here's where you manage your component collections. Here's a brief introduction to your options:

- *Open a Local Collection:* Lets you choose a folder on your computer system to use as a component collection. Any SketchUp models in that folder show up in the Components pane, ready to be used as components in your models.

TIP

- *Create a New Collection:* Allows you to create a folder somewhere on your computer system that you can use as a component collection. A collection is handy if you have a number of components that you use all the time; putting them all in one place makes them easier to find.

- *Save as a Local Collection:* When you choose this option, SketchUp lets you save the components that currently appear in your Components pane as a brand-new local collection. If the components you're viewing are online, copies of them are downloaded to your computer. If you're viewing your In Model collection, the contents are copied and included in a new folder. If you're already viewing a local collection, this option isn't available.

- *View in 3D Warehouse:* If you're viewing an online collection, this option opens that collection in a separate window that displays the 3D Warehouse in much more detail.

- *3D Warehouse Terms of Service:* Choose this option if you're having trouble sleeping. If you're wondering who owns the stuff on the 3D Warehouse, this is where it's at.

- *Add to Favorites:* Choosing this option adds whatever you're viewing in the Components pane to the Favorites section of the Collections list. That goes for local collections (folders on your computer); online collections (from the 3D Warehouse); and 3D Warehouse searches. That's right — you can save a search as a favorite collection. The models in a Favorite Search collection are always different, depending on what's in the 3D Warehouse.

The next two options appear only when you're viewing your In Model collection:

- *Expand:* Because components can be made up of other, nested components, a component you use in your model may really be *lots* of components. Choosing Expand displays all the components in your model whether or not they're nested inside other components. Most of the time, you probably want to leave Expand deselected.

TIP

- *Purge Unused:* Choose this option to get rid of any components in your In Model collection that aren't in your model anymore. Be sure to use this before you send your SketchUp file to someone else; it significantly reduces your file size and makes the file a whole lot neater.

SELECT AND REPLACE ALL YOUR TROUBLES AWAY

On top of all the buttons, menus, and windows you can immediately see in the Select tab of the Components panel, you can also find hidden options tucked away on a context menu. The menu pops up when you context-click an In Model collection component:

- **Select Instances:** Perhaps you have 15 *instances* (copies) of the same component in your model, and you want to select them all. Just make sure that you're viewing your In Model collection and then context-click the component (in the Components pane) whose instances you want to select all. Choose Select Instances, and your work's done. This trick can save you tons of time, particularly if you have component instances all over the place. The feature even selects hidden instances and ones on layers that are turned off.

- **Replace Selected:** You may want to swap in a different component for one that's in your model. Simply select the component instances (in your modeling window) that you want to replace and then context-click the component (in the Components pane) that you want to use instead. Choose Replace Selected from the context menu to perform the swap.

Ready for an even better tip? Use Select Instances and Replace Selected together to help you work more efficiently. Instead of placing 20 big, heavy tree components in your model (which can slow down your work), use a smaller, simpler component instead (such as a stick). When you're finished modeling, use Select Instances to select all the stand-in components at once and then use Replace Selected to swap in the real component. Figure 5-3 (earlier in this chapter) shows the mechanics of this operation, albeit using windows and cars.

The Edit tab

Because the options in this part of the Components panel are similar to the ones you get when you make a new component, check out the section "Creating your own components," later in this chapter, for the whole scoop.

TIP

You can use the options in the Edit tab only on components in your In Model collection — everything is grayed out for components that live in any other place.

The Statistics tab

Can you remember who won the 1975 Super Bowl? How many home runs did Hank Aaron hit in his career? Do you always check the nutrition information panel on food packaging? You may be a sucker for statistics, and if so, welcome home. . . .

Even if you're not, the Statistics tab is a useful place for keeping track of all the details related to whatever component you have selected in the Components panel. (See Figure 5-6.) This tab is especially useful for doing the following things:

>> **Checking the size of your components:** The information in the Edges and Faces areas of this tab lets you know how much geometry is in a component. If you're worried about file size or your computer's performance, try to use small components — ones with low numbers of faces and edges.

>> **Seeing what components are inside your components:** The Component Instances line lists how many component instances are in your selected component. If you switch from All Geometry to Components in the drop-down list at the top of the tab, you can see a list of all the constituent components: subcomponents within your main component.

SAVE TIME — GO SHOPPING

Why spend hours modeling an oak tree when you can buy a fantastic one for a reasonable price? If you can't find what you need among the zillions of components that you can download for free from the 3D Warehouse, try Aidan's favorite paid option. Form Fonts (www.formfonts.com) is a website that sells components "all you can eat, buffet-style." You pay a (surprisingly low) monthly fee, and you have access to *thousands* of high-quality models of just about anything. Form Fonts's international team of modelers even takes requests — if you need something that they don't have, they can probably make it if you ask nicely. Even if you're not interested in signing up, it's worth checking out the website just to see the beautiful models Form Fonts makes.

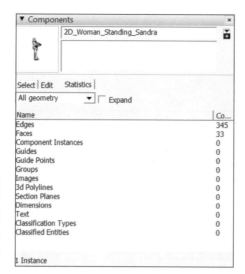

FIGURE 5-6:
The Statistics
tab of the
Components
panel: Geek
out on
numbers.

The Statistics tab *doesn't* show details for components you have selected in your actual model; it shows only information about the component that's selected in the Select tab of the Components pane. To see information about whatever component (or other kind of object) you have selected in your modeling window, use the Entity Info panel (in the Default Tray).

Creating your own components

Creating simple components is a pretty easy process, but making more complicated ones — components that automatically cut openings, stick to surfaces, and always face the viewer — can be a little trickier. Follow these steps no matter what kind of component you're trying to make:

1. Select one or more entities you want to turn into a component.

You can select edges, faces, images, guides, section planes — even other groups and components. For more information on making selections, see Chapter 3.

2. Choose Edit ⇨ Make Component.

The Create Component dialog box opens. (See Figure 5-7.)

3. Give your new component a name and description.

Of these two, the name is by far the most important. Choose a name that will enable you to understand what the component is in the Outliner or when you open your model a year from now.

4. Set the alignment options for your new component.

Wondering what the heck all this stuff means? Check out Table 5-1.

TABLE 5-1 **Component Alignment Options**

Option	What It Does	Tips and Tricks
Glue To	Makes a component automatically stick to a specific plane. For example, a chair will almost always sit on a floor. It will almost *never* be stuck to a wall, turned sideways. When a component is glued to a surface, using the Move tool moves it only on that surface — never perpendicular to it (up and down, if the surface is a floor).	Use this feature for objects that you want to remain on the surface you put them on, especially objects you want to rearrange: Furniture, windows, and doors are prime examples. If you want to unstick a glued component from a particular surface, context-click it and choose Unglue from the context menu.
Set Component Axes	Sets a component's *axis origin* and *orientation.* This option is important primarily if you have SketchUp Pro and plan to make this component into a Dynamic Component. If that isn't your plan, you can safely leave this option alone.	Click the Set Component Axes button to choose where you want your component's axis origin to be (where the red, green, and blue axes meet). Click once to center your axes, again to establish the red direction, and again to establish the green and blue directions. If you're creating a Dynamic Component, this is something you absolutely must know how to do.
Cut Opening	For components "in" a surface, such as a window, select this check box to automatically cut an opening in surfaces to which you stick the component.	As with premade components, this opening is dependent on the component's existence: If you delete the component instance, the opening disappears. If you move the component instance, the opening moves, too.

Option	What It Does	Tips and Tricks
Always Face Camera	Makes a component *always* face you no matter how you orbit around. To make your 2D Face-Me components (that's what they're called) work correctly, rotate your component-to-be so that it's perpendicular to your model's green axis before you choose Make Component.	Using flat 2D components instead of complex 3D ones is a great way to have lots of people and trees in your model without bogging down your computer.
Shadows Face Sun	Available only when the Always Face Camera check box is selected. It is selected by default.	Leave this check box selected unless your Face-Me component meets the ground in two or more separate places, as shown in Figure 5-8.

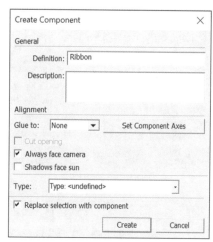

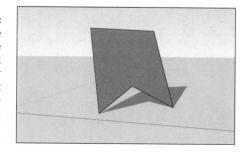

FIGURE 5-8: Deselect the Shadows Face Sun check box if your component touches the ground in more than one place.

5. **Select the Replace Selection with Component check box if it isn't already selected.**

   This step drops your new component into your model right where your selected geometry was, saving you from inserting it from the Components panel.

6. **Click the Create button to create your new component.**

REMEMBER

Components can cut through only one face at a time. If your model's walls are two faces thick, you have to cut your window and door openings manually.

Editing, exploding, and locking component instances

Context-clicking a component instance in your modeling window opens a context menu that offers lots of useful choices. Here's what some of them let you do:

>> **Edit Component:** To edit all instances of a component at once, context-click any instance and choose Edit Component from the context menu. The rest of your model fades back, and you see a dashed bounding box around your component. When you're done, click somewhere outside the bounding box to finish editing; your changes have been made in every instance of that component in your model.

>> **Make Unique:** Sometimes you want to make changes to only one or a few of the instances of a component in your model. In this case, select the instance(s) you want to edit, context-click one of them, and choose Make Unique from the context menu. This option turns the instances you selected into a separate component. Now edit any of them; only those instances you made unique reflect your changes.

>> **Explode:** When you explode a component instance, you're effectively turning it back into regular ol' geometry. Explode is a lot like Ungroup in other software programs (in SketchUp, you use Explode to disassemble both components and groups).

>> **Lock:** Locking a group or a component instance means that nobody — including you — can mess with it until it's unlocked. Lock parts of your model that you don't want to change accidentally. To unlock something, context-click it and choose Unlock.

MAKING YOUR OWN DOORS AND WINDOWS

If you're kind of nerdy like Aidan is, nothing beats making your own window and door components. Here's what you need to know (check out the illustration in this sidebar for visual instructions):

1. **Draw a rectangle on a vertical surface, such as a wall.**

2. **Delete the face you just created to make a hole in your vertical surface.**

3. **Select all four edges of the hole you just created; then context-click one of the edges and choose Make Component from the context menu.**

4. **Make sure that Glue to Any, Cut Opening, and Replace Selection with Component are all selected; then click the Create button to create your new component.**

5. **With the Select tool, double-click your new component (in the modeling window) to edit it.**

   The rest of your model appears to fade back a bit.

6. **Use the modeling tools just like you always would; keep building your door or window how you want.**

7. **When you're done, click outside your component to stop editing it.**

If the opening you create ever closes, one of two things probably happened:

• **A new surface was created.** Try deleting the offending surface to see whether that fixes things; it usually does.

• **The cutting boundary was messed up.** The cutting boundary consists of the edges that define the hole your component is cutting. If you take away those edges,

(continued)

(continued)

SketchUp doesn't know where to cut the hole anymore. Drawing them back in usually sets things straight.

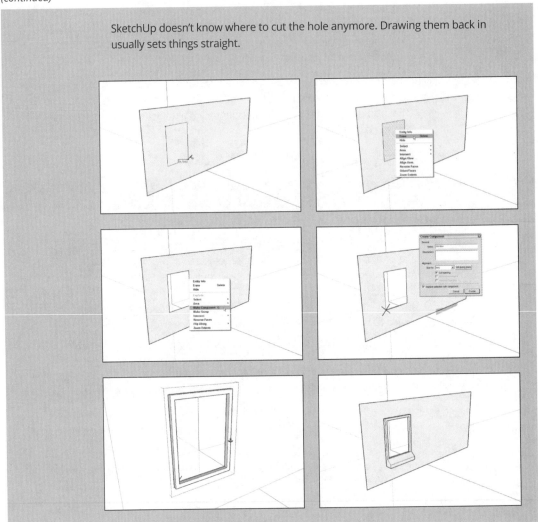

Discovering Dynamic Components

Once upon a time, the smartest thing a component could do was cut its own hole in a surface. "Wow!" all SketchUp aficionados thought, "Components are *geniuses!*" And so they were — until Dynamic Components came along in version 7.

Until version 7, SketchUp components were basically dumb. If you wanted to make a staircase longer, you had to make copies of the steps and place them in the right spot. If you needed to change the color of a car, you had to dig out the Paint Bucket and dive in to the geometry. The problem was that components didn't know what they were supposed to represent; they were just groupings of faces and edges in the shape of an object.

Dynamic Components (DCs) are models that have an idea of what they are; they know what to do when you interact with them. This section outlines what DCs represent for SketchUp modelers and how to use them.

Before you start working with Dynamic Components, here's what you need to know:

>> **DCs can do all sorts of things.** Describing what DCs *do* is tricky because they're all different. The simple (but totally unsatisfying) answer is that they do what they've been programmed to do. Figure 5-9 shows some examples, which are explained in the following list:

- A dynamic door component may be set up to swing open when you click it with the Interact tool, which you find on the Dynamic Components toolbar.

- The same dynamic door may also be configured into different sizes, styles, and finishes by using simple drop-down lists in the Component Options dialog box.

- A dynamic chair may be scaled into a sofa but without stretching the arms. The dynamic programming would also add cushions as you make the component longer.

- A dynamic stair component may automatically add or remove steps as you use the Scale tool to make the staircase taller or shorter.

- The little person who appears by default when you start a new SketchUp file is also dynamic: Click the person's shirt with the Interact tool to cycle through various colors. You can replace the default person with another character, too, and his or her shirt also changes color.

>> **Anyone can use DCs.** Both the free and Pro versions of SketchUp can read and use Dynamic Components. The SketchUp team invented them (at least partially) to make SketchUp easier for new modelers to learn.

>> **You need Pro to make your own DCs.** If you need to build your own Dynamic Components (or modify ones that other folks have made), you need a copy of SketchUp Pro.

>> **DCs are free.** People are adding new DCs to the 3D Warehouse every day. As you can imagine, companies that make things like furniture and building products (windows, kitchen cabinets, and flooring) are really excited about the possibilities that DCs offer. Many of them are in the process of producing DCs of everything in their catalogues and posting them to the 3D Warehouse. That's good news for you; soon you can download and use a configurable model of almost anything you need.

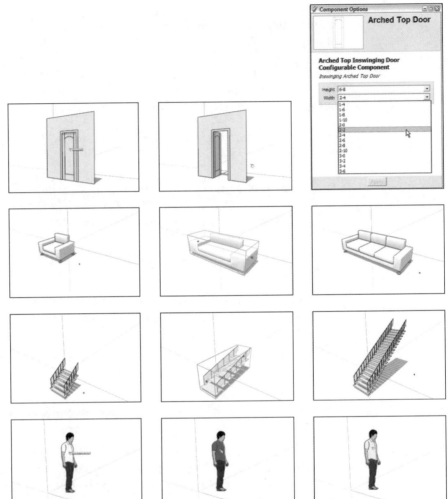

FIGURE 5-9:
Dynamic
Components
can do all kinds
of things.

>> **They have a special icon.** When you download SketchUp, you find a few sample DCs in the Components panel. They're the ones with the little green dynamic icon next to them (that looks kind of like an arrow).

Using Dynamic Components

In SketchUp, you can interact with Dynamic Components in three basic ways. Depending on what a particular DC has been set up to do, it may respond to one, two, or all three of the following interactions.

SMART SCALING

DCs designed to react intelligently to the Scale tool are the closest things to true magic that SketchUp offers. Instead of stretching and getting all distorted when you scale them, the parts that are supposed to change dimensions, do; the other parts don't.

Take a look at Figure 5-10. The center image shows what happens when you scale a nondynamic window component to make it wider. See how the frame stretches? Yuck. The image on the far right shows the dynamic version of the same window. It gets wider when you scale it, but the frame stays the same thickness. The component is smart enough to know that only some parts of it should get wider when you scale it.

FIGURE 5-10:
Scaling a nondynamic window (center) stretches the whole thing. The DC version scales properly.

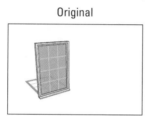
Original

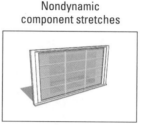
Nondynamic component stretches

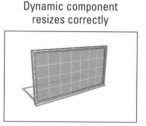
Dynamic component resizes correctly

There's another way that DCs can scale smartly: by adding or subtracting pieces as they get bigger or smaller. Dynamic stairs are a perfect example of this, as shown in Figure 5-11. When you use the Scale tool to make the staircase taller, the staircase adds steps instead of stretching.

TIP

You can turn on the Dynamic Components toolbar, which is a quicker way to work with DCs than constantly using the menu bar. Just choose View ⇨ Toolbars ⇨ Dynamic Components, and you're all set.

COMPONENT OPTIONS

In the Component Options dialog box, you can configure DCs that have been hooked up to this dialog box by choosing options from drop-down lists, typing dimensions, and performing other simple tasks. To open the dialog box, choose Window ⇨ Component Options. When you change a setting in Component Options, the DC you've selected updates to reflect the change, kind of like modeling by remote control.

REMEMBER

The Component Options dialog box looks different for every DC.

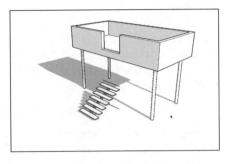

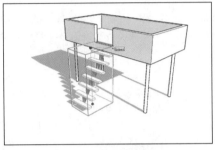

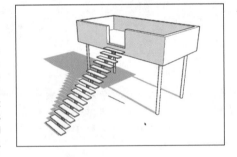

FIGURE 5-11:
When you make the staircase taller, this dynamic staircase adds steps instead of stretching.

Figure 5-12 shows a simple drop-down list for selecting a color. However, a straight staircase might enable you to choose a riser height and a tread depth from preprogrammed lists.

THE INTERACT TOOL

Activate the Interact tool by choosing it from the Tools menu or displaying the Dynamic Components toolbar (View ➪ Toolbars). Using this tool couldn't be simpler: When a DC is set up to react to the Interact tool, it does stuff when you click it. Its actions depend on what you've programmed it to do.

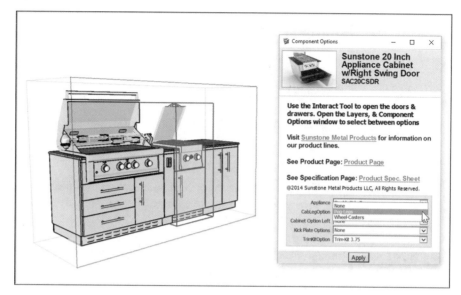

FIGURE 5-12:
The Component Options dialog box looks different for every Dynamic Component.

Check out the truck in Figure 5-13; it's been designed to react to the Interact tool in a few ways:

>> Clicking the back of the truck cycles through the following options: box, flatbed, or flatbed with rails.

>> Clicking the front wheels turns them from side to side.

>> Clicking the doors makes them open and close.

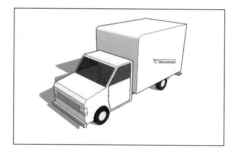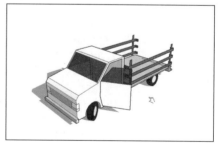

FIGURE 5-13:
Clicking stuff with the Interact tool makes things happen.

TIP

When you're hovering over a DC that's been connected to the Interact tool, your cursor (it was originally called the Magic Finger) glows a little yellow at the end.

Poking around to see what happens

You can't know which interactions you can use with any particular DC just by looking at it. If you know you're dealing with a DC, the best way to figure out what it does is to experiment:

>> Select it and open Component Options to see whether anything's there.

>> Hover over it with the Interact tool to see whether a glow appears at the end of your cursor.

>> Click it with the Select tool to show its scale *grips* (little green boxes). If any show up, grab one and scale to see what happens. If none show up, your DC can't be scaled with the Scale tool.

TECHNICAL
STUFF

Although developing your own dynamic components is beyond the scope of this book, SketchUp provides great online resources to help you get started. Check out the introduction to developing dynamic components in the SketchUp Help Center (http://help.sketchup.com/en/article/3000123) and the SketchUp team's DC Function Examples collection in the 3D Warehouse (https://3dwarehouse. sketchup.com).

Taking Advantage of Components to Build Better Models

A huge amount of the stuff in the galaxy is made of some kind of *repeated element.* In the case of bilaterally symmetrical objects (like most furniture), that element is a mirrored half. For things like staircases, it's a step or tread. The *whole* is composed of two or more instances of a single *part.* This makes modeling a heck of a lot easier because you don't often have to model things in their entirety — especially if you use components.

In the following sections, you discover two methods for modeling with components. The first method involves symmetrical objects, and it covers about 50 percent of the things you might ever want to model. The second technique applies to things like stairs and fences, which are both perfect examples of why components were invented in the first place.

Modeling symmetrically: Good news for lazy people

And smart people, too! First off, take a hard look at the shape of the things you may want to model. Then think about all the objects in the universe. We'll wait a couple of minutes while you do that. Done so soon? Good. Everything in the world can be categorized as either of the following formal types:

» **Symmetrical:** Objects that exhibit *bilateral symmetry* are made of mirrored halves. You're (more or less) bilaterally symmetrical, and so is your car. Another kind of symmetry is *radial symmetry*. Radially symmetrical objects can be (conceptually, anyway) cut into identical wedges that all radiate from a central axis. Starfish are good examples of this, as are umbrellas and apple pies. If you were going to build a model of something that exhibits some form of symmetry, building one part and making copies would be a smarter way to do it.

» **Asymmetrical:** Some things — puddles, oak trees, and many houses — aren't symmetrical. There's no real trick to making these things; you just have to get some coffee, settle in, and get to work.

You can take advantage of both bilateral and radial symmetry with SketchUp components. To do so, assemble those components as follows, depending on what type of symmetry your object has (also take a look at Figure 5-14):

» **Bilateral symmetry:** To make a model of something that's bilaterally symmetrical, build half, make it into a component, and flip over a copy.

» **Radial symmetry:** You can use components to model radially symmetric things, such as car wheels and turrets, by building a single wedge and rotating a bunch of copies around a central point.

Working smarter by building only half

Bilaterally symmetrical forms are everywhere. Most animals you can name, the majority of the furniture in your house, and your personal helicopter — they can all be modeled by building half, creating a component, and flipping over a copy.

Follow these steps to get the general idea of how to build a bilaterally symmetrical model in SketchUp (see Figure 5-15):

1. **Make a simple box.**

   You can do this however you want, but the easiest way is to draw a rectangle and push/pull it into 3D.

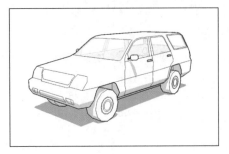

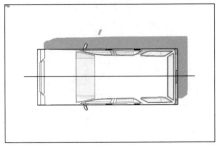

Axis of symmetry

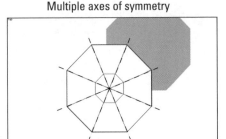

Multiple axes of symmetry

FIGURE 5-14:
Bilateral symmetry (top) and radial symmetry (bottom) make your SketchUp life a lot easier.

2. **Draw a diagonal edge on the corner of your box.**

   The point of this step is to mark one side of your box so that when you flip it over, you don't get confused about which side is which.

3. **Turn your box into a component.**

   See "Creating your own components," earlier in this chapter, if you wonder how to do this.

4. **Make a copy of your new component instance.**

   Chapter 3 has information about moving and copying objects in SketchUp.

   Make sure that you move in either the red or the green direction; it makes things easier in the next step.

5. **Flip over the copy.**

   To do this, context-click the copy and choose Flip Along from the context menu. If you moved your copy in the red direction in the preceding step, choose Flip Along ⇨ Component's Red. Choose Component's Green if you moved in the green direction.

6. **Stick the two halves back together.**

   Using the Move tool (this time without Copy toggled on), pick up your copy *from the corner* and move it over, dropping it *on the corresponding corner* of the original. Take a look at the last image in Figure 5-15. Doing this precisely is important if you want your model to look right.

Make a box   Turn it into a component   Move a copy over

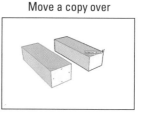

Flip the copy   Stick the two halves together

FIGURE 5-15:
Getting set
up to build
a bilaterally
symmetrical
model.

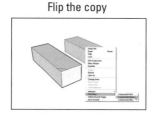

Now you're set up to start building symmetrically. If you want, you can do a test to make sure things went smoothly. (See Figure 5-16.) Follow these steps:

1. **With the Select tool, double-click one of the halves of your model to edit it.**

2. **Draw a circle on the top surface and push/pull it into a cylinder.**

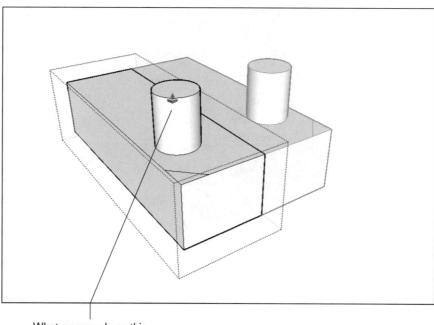

FIGURE 5-16:
Test your setup
to make sure
that everything
works.

Whatever you do on this
side should happen on the
other side, too

If the same thing happens on the other side, you're good to go. If the same thing *doesn't* happen on the other side, it's possible that:

>> **You're not really editing one of your component instances.** If you aren't, you're drawing *on top of* your component instead of *in* it. You know you're in edit mode if the rest of your model looks grayed out.

TIP

MAKING TWO HALVES LOOK LIKE ONE WHOLE

Looking carefully at the little boat in the figure that follows, notice how the edges in the middle clearly show that it's made out of two halves? If you were to erase those edges, the whole model would disappear because those edges are defining faces, and without edges, faces can't exist.

Instead of erasing those unwanted edges, you can hide them by using the Eraser while pressing the Shift key. See the second and third images of the boat? When you hold down Shift while dragging over the edges that you want to hide with the Eraser, they disappear.

Keep in mind these two important details about hidden edges:

- **Hidden edges aren't gone forever.** Actually, this applies to any hidden geometry in your model. To see what's hidden, choose View ⇨ Hidden Geometry. To hide it again, just choose the same thing.

- **To edit hidden edges, you have to make them visible.** If you need to make changes to your model that involve edges you've already hidden, you can either view your hidden geometry (see the preceding point) or unhide them altogether. Just show your hidden geometry, select the edges you want to unhide, and choose Edit ⇨ Unhide ⇨ Selected.

Distracting edges   Use Eraser to hide

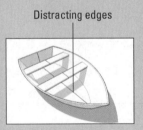 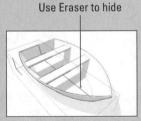 

>> **You never made a component in the first place.** If your halves don't have blue boxes around them when you select them, they're not component instances. Start a new file and try again, paying particular attention to Step 3 in the previous steps.

The coolest things since radially sliced bread

You can model objects that exhibit radial symmetry just as easily as those with bilateral symmetry. You just start slightly differently. Before you start, the only thing you have to decide is how many wedges — that is, how many identical parts — you need to make the whole object.

To model something with radial symmetry, start with one wedge, make it into a component, and then rotate copies around the center. Follow these steps to get the hang of it:

1. **With the Polygon tool, draw a polygon with as many sides as the number of segments you need for the object you're modeling.**

   Here's the easiest way to draw a polygon in SketchUp, as shown in Figure 5-17:

   a. *Choose Tools ⇨ Polygon to select the Polygon tool. You can also select it from the Shapes menu on the toolbar.*

   b. *Click once to establish the center (Aidan likes to place the center on the axis origin), move your cursor, and then click again to establish the radius.*

      Don't worry about being accurate right now.

   c. *Before you do anything else, type the number of sides you want your polygon to have and press Enter.*

FIGURE 5-17:
Draw a
polygon to
start, draw two
edges to create
a wedge, and
erase the
rest of your
polygon.

Make a polygon   Define a wedge   Erase the rest

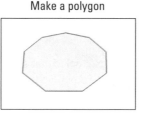 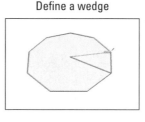 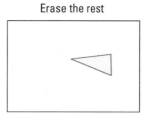

2. **Draw edges from the center of your polygon to two adjacent vertices (endpoints) on the perimeter, creating a wedge.**

   To find the center of a polygon (or a circle), hover your cursor over the outline for a couple seconds and move the cursor toward the middle; a center inference point appears.

3. **Erase the rest of your polygon, leaving only the wedge.**

The first three steps in this list are all about making sure that your wedge is the correct angle; if it isn't, this technique won't work.

4. **Turn your wedge into a component.**

Check out "Creating your own components," earlier in this chapter, if you're unsure of how to do this.

 5. **Make copies of your wedge component instance with the Rotate tool. (See Figure 5-18.)**

Click to define center of rotation

Click to start rotating

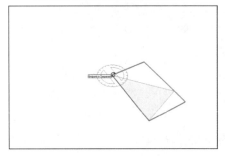 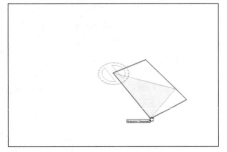

Press Ctrl (Option on Mac) to rotate copy

Make more copies

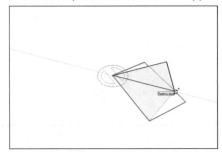 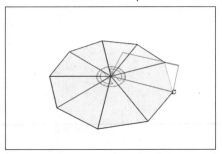

FIGURE 5-18: Use the Rotate tool to make copies of your wedge component instance.

As with the Move tool, you can use the Rotate tool to make copies. You can even make an *array* (more than one copy at a time). Here's how:

a. *Select your wedge's edges (heh, heh) and select the face, too.*

b. *Choose Tools ⇨ Rotate to select the Rotate tool.*

c. *Press the Ctrl key (Option on a Mac) to tell SketchUp you want to make a copy.*

A plus sign (+) appears next to your cursor.

d. *Click the pointy end of your wedge to set your center of rotation.*

e. *Click one of the opposite corners of your wedge to set your rotation start point.*

f. Click the other corner to make a rotated copy of your wedge.

g. Type the number of additional wedges you want, followed by the letter **x**, and then press Enter.

6. **(Optional) Test your setup.**

Follow the steps associated with Figure 5-16 to test whether updates to a single component in your new object updates all instances of the component.

REMEMBER Hiding the edges in your component instances makes your finished model look a whole lot better. Take a look at the sidebar "Making two halves look like one whole," earlier in this chapter, to discover how.

Modeling with repeated elements

A staircase is a perfect example of an object that's composed of several identical elements. If, when you hear the phrase "several identical elements," a big, flashing neon sign that screams "COMPONENTS!" doesn't appear in your head, you're not using SketchUp enough. On the other hand, maybe we need to get out more often....

The following example demonstrates two handy SketchUp modeling tricks:

>> Using components to model more efficiently

>> Building a set of stairs the smartest way (for readers of Chapter 4)

The Treads Are Components method involves (you guessed it) making each *tread* (step) in your staircase into an instance of the same component. Basically, you build one simple tread that's the right depth, make it into a component, and copy a bunch of instances into a full flight of stairs. Because every step is linked, anything you do to one automatically happens to them all. If you don't know the first thing about components, now would be a terrific time to start from the beginning of this chapter.

Go through these steps to build a staircase using the Treads Are Components method:

1. **Model a single step, including the tread and the riser.**

You can make the step very simple at this stage if you want to; all that matters is that the tread depth and the riser height are correct. You can fiddle with everything else later. See Figure 5-19.

FIGURE 5-19:
Model a single
step, making
sure that the
depth and
height are
accurate.

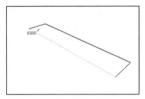
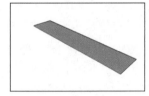
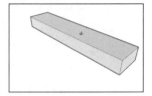

2. **Make a component out of the step you just built.**

   Take a look at "Creating your own components," earlier in this chapter, if you need help.

3. **Move a copy of your step into position, above the first one, as shown in Figure 5-20.**

4. **Type the total number of steps you want, type an x, and then press Enter.**

   You're creating a *linear array,* meaning that you're making several copies at regular intervals, in the same direction you moved the first one. Typing **12x** generates 12 steps the same distance apart as the first step and its copy. See the last image in Figure 5-20.

5. **With the Select tool, double-click any one of your steps to edit all instances of your component.**

   Everything besides the component instance you're editing fades out a little.

6. **Go nuts.**

   This really is the fun part. Having your staircase made up of multiple component instances means that you have all the flexibility to make drastic changes to the whole thing without ever having to repeat yourself. Add a *nosing* (a bump at the leading edge of each tread), a *stringer* (a diagonal piece of structure that supports all your steps), or even a handrail by getting creative with how you modify a single component instance. Figure 5-21 shows some of what you can do.

Create a component

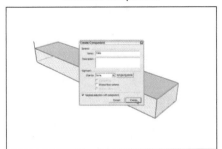

Move up a copy

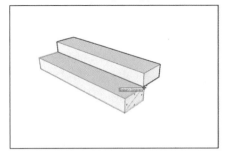

Type the number you want,
then **x**, and press Enter

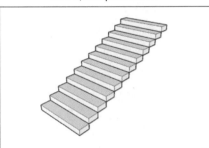

Edit one instance

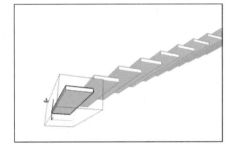

All components change

FIGURE 5-20:
Make your
step into a
component
instance,
move a copy
into position
above the
original, and
then create
an array.

Series of component instances

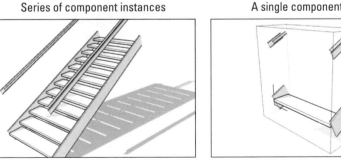

A single component instance

FIGURE 5-21:
A flight of
stairs with side
stringers and
a handrail.
On the right,
a single
component
instance.

IN THIS CHAPTER

» **Extruding around circles and along paths with Follow Me**

» **Mastering the Scale tool**

» **Creating 3D terrain with the Sandbox tools**

» **Using the Solid Tools for additive and subtractive modeling**

Chapter **6**

Going Beyond Buildings

Here's something you already know: There's more to life than modeling buildings. Even though SketchUp is *really good* at letting you make models of built structures, you can use SketchUp to build just about anything you can imagine. All you need is time, ingenuity, and the ability to step back and break down things into their basic parts. SketchUp provides fantastic tools for creating forms that aren't the least bit boxy, but those tools aren't as obvious as Push/Pull and Rectangle, so most people never find them. This chapter is devoted to helping you discover SketchUp's "rounder" side.

Another reason for pushing past basic boxes? Many people see 3D printing (sound of futuristic music and warp drives engaging) as the next vanguard of human innovation, and 3D modeling — like you do with SketchUp — is half of that equation. If you're going to be printing your own bike helmets and vacuum cleaners in the next decade, you'd better get good at modeling organic shapes. (Chapter 9 offers an introduction to 3D printing with SketchUp.)

In this chapter, you discover tools, techniques, and other tips for creating forms that are distinctly unbuilding-like. Our hope is that you'll use them to push the limits of what you think SketchUp can do.

Extruding with Purpose: Follow Me

Follow Me is probably the best example of a powerful SketchUp tool with kind of an underwhelming name. When the software designers were trying to figure out what to call their new baby, the problem that they faced was this: This tool does what other 3D modeling programs dedicate two or three other tools to doing. The designers chose an unconventional name because Follow Me is a wholly unconventional tool.

As shown in Figure 6-1, you can use Follow Me to create all sorts of shapes:

>> **Bottles, spindles, and spheres:** These are all examples of *lathed* forms. You can create these by spinning a 2D *profile* (shape) around a central axis to create a 3D model.

>> **Pipes, gutters, and moldings:** If you look closely, all three of these things are basically created by extruding a 2D face along a 3D path; the result is a complex 3D form.

FIGURE 6-1:
Follow Me lets you create all kinds of different shapes.

>> **Chamfers, fillets, and dados:** Without explaining what all these things are (that's what Internet search engines are for), know this: You can use Follow Me to *cut away* profiles, too.

Using Follow Me

At its core, Follow Me lets you create forms that are extrusions. It's a little bit like Push/Pull, except that it doesn't just work in one direction. You tell Follow Me to follow a path, and it extrudes a face all along that path. So, you need three things to use Follow Me:

>> **A path:** In SketchUp, you can use any edge, or series of edges, as a path. All you have to do is make sure that they're drawn before you use Follow Me.

>> **A face:** Just like with Push/Pull, Follow Me needs a face to extrude. You can use any face in your model, but the face needs to be created before you start using Follow Me.

>> **Undo:** Imagining what a 2D face will look like as a 3D shape isn't easy. Getting a Follow Me operation right usually takes a couple tries. That's what Undo is for, after all.

Follow these steps to use Follow Me; Figure 6-2 shows a basic example of how it works:

1. **Draw a face to use as an extrusion profile.**

   In this example, you create a pipe, so the extrusion profile is a circular face.

2. **Draw an edge (or edges) to use as an extrusion path.**

   Although the edge (or edges) is touching the face in this case, it doesn't have to for Follow Me to work.

3. **Select the complete extrusion path you want to use.**

   Check out the section on making selections in Chapter 3 for pointers on using the Select tool to best advantage.

4. **Activate the Follow Me tool by choosing Tools⇨Follow Me.**

   To see Follow Me on your toolbar, select the Large Tool Set. On Windows, choose View⇨Toolbars, select the Large Tool Set check box in the dialog box that appears, and click Close. On a Mac, choose View⇨Tool Palettes⇨Large Tool Set.

5. **Click the face you want to extrude.**

   Magic! Your face (extrusion profile) is extruded along the path you chose in Step 3, creating a 3D form (in this case, a section of pipe).

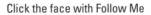
Select the whole path   Click the face with Follow Me

FIGURE 6-2: Using Follow Me to create a simple extruded shape.

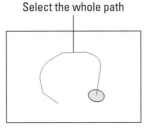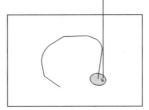

TIP

If you want to use Follow Me all the way around the perimeter of a face, you don't need to spend time selecting all the individual edges. Just select the face and then use Follow Me; the tool automatically runs all the way around any selected face.

TECHNICAL STUFF

You can use Follow Me another way, too: Instead of preselecting a path (as in Step 3 of the preceding list), you can click any face with Follow Me and attempt to drag it along the edges in your model. Although this dragging method works on simple things, preselecting a path works a lot better — it's really the only option for using Follow Me in a predictable way.

Making lathed forms like spheres and bottles

And nuclear power plant chimneys. A surprising number of things can be modeled by using Follow Me to perform a lathe operation. A *lathe* is a tool that carpenters (and machinists) use to spin a block of raw material while they carve into it — that's how baseball bats are made (the good ones, anyway).

A simple example of a lathed object is a sphere. Here's how you might make one with Follow Me:

1. Draw a circle on the ground.

2. Rotate a copy of your circle by 90 degrees, as shown in Figure 6-3.

If you're wondering how to do this, follow these steps:

a. Select the face of your circle with the Select tool and then choose Tools ⇨ Rotate to activate the Rotate tool.

b. Press the Ctrl key (Option on a Mac) to tell SketchUp you want to make a copy.

c. Click a green endpoint inference along the edge of your circle and hold down your mouse button to drag. Don't let go just yet.

d. Still dragging, move your cursor to the endpoint on the exact opposite side of your circle; then release your mouse button.

Your *axis of rotation* is a line right through the center of your circle.

e. Click anywhere on the edge of your circle and then move your mouse over a little bit.

*f. Type **90** and press Enter.*

You can read all about the Rotate tool in Chapter 3.

TIP

Click and hold down mouse button

Drag here

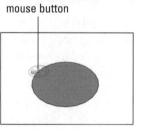
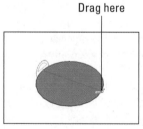
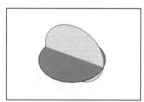

FIGURE 6-3:
Using the Rotate tool to make a rotated copy of a circle.

3. **Make sure that one of your circles is selected.**

4. **With the Follow Me tool (choose Tools ⇨ Follow Me), click the circle that's not selected, as shown in Figure 6-4.**

   Now you have a sphere. The Follow Me tool lathed your circular face around the path you selected — the other circle.

Select one circle
Click the other with Follow Me

FIGURE 6-4:
Clicking one circle with Follow Me while the other one is selected produces a sphere.

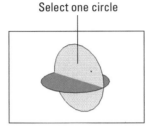

TIP

If you really need a sphere, the easiest way to get one is in the Components panel. Type **sphere** into the 3D Warehouse search box, and then press Enter on your keyboard. Something useful should appear.

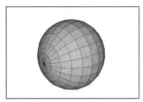

If you want to make your curved surfaces look *smooth* (hiding the edges between them), check out the sidebar "Smoothing those unsightly edges," later in this chapter.

FIGURE 6-5:
A few examples of lathed objects created with Follow Me.

Under typical circumstances, you only have to model half a profile to use Follow Me to make it three-dimensional. Figure 6-5 shows a few examples of 3D objects created by using Follow Me.

Creating extruded shapes like gutters and handrails

A lot of the time, you want to use Follow Me to create geometry (edges and faces) that's attached to another part of your model. An example of this may be modeling a gutter that runs all the way around the roof of your house. In this case, you already have the path along which you want to extrude a profile (the edge of the roof).

When you use Follow Me to extrude a face along a path that consists of edges that already exist as part of your model, *always* do two things:

» **Before using Follow Me, make the rest of your model a separate group.**
Take our word for it — Follow Me can sometimes mess up your model, so keep the geometry Follow Me creates separate, just in case.

» **Make a copy of your extrusion path outside your group.** There's a consequence to working with Follow Me on top of a group: The edge (or edges) you want to use as an extrusion path aren't available because you can't use Follow Me with a path that's in a separate group or component.

What to do? You need to make a copy of the path *outside* the group and then use the *copy* to do the Follow Me operation. Here's the best way to make a copy of the path:

a. With the Select tool, double-click your group to edit it.

b. Select the path you want to use for Follow Me and then choose Edit ⇨ Copy.

c. Exit (stop editing) your group by clicking somewhere else in your modeling window.

d. Choose Edit ⇨ Paste in Place.

    You have a copy of the path you want to use, and it's outside your group.

The Weld Ruby script is a SketchUp extension that's super-useful for creating extrusion paths for Follow Me. Chapter 16 introduces the Extension Warehouse, where you find SketchUp extensions.

When you use an existing edge (or series of edges) as an extrusion path, the hard part is getting your profile in the right place. You can proceed in two ways; which one you choose depends on what you need to model:

» **Draw the profile in place.** Do this only if the extrusion path is parallel to one of the colored drawing axes.

» **Draw the profile on the ground and then move it into position.** If your extrusion path doesn't start out parallel to a colored drawing axis, you should probably draw your profile somewhere else and move it into place later.

Drawing your profile in place

Consider that you have a model of a house. You want to use Follow Me to add a gutter that goes all the way around the perimeter of the roof. You decide to draw the profile in place (right on the roof itself) because the edges of the roof are drawn parallel to the colored drawing axes. This means that you'll have an easier time using the Line tool to draw in midair.

WHY YOUR COMPUTER IS SO SLOW

When you use Follow Me with an extrusion profile that's a circle or an arc, you create a piece of 3D geometry that's very big. In this case, *big,* means that the geometry has lots of faces, and faces are what slow down your computer. Without going into detail about how SketchUp works (we don't really know that anyway), keep this in mind: The more faces you have in your model, the worse your computer's performance will be. At a certain point, you'll stop being able to orbit, your scenes (introduced in Chapter 11) will stutter, and you'll be tempted to do something terrible out of frustration.

The first pipe in the figure that follows has been extruded using Follow Me; it was made with a 24-sided circle as an extrusion profile, and it has 338 faces. Hidden Geometry is turned on (in the View menu) so that you can see how many faces you have.

The second pipe uses a 10-sided circle as an extrusion profile. As a result, it has only 116 faces. What an improvement!

The third pipe also uses a 10-sided circle as an extrusion profile, but the arc in its extrusion path is made up of only 4 segments, instead of the usual 12. This pipe has a total of 52 faces. Even better.

The second image in the figure shows all three pipes with Hidden Geometry turned off. Is the difference in detail worth the exponential increase in the number of faces? Most of the time, the answer is no.

To change the number of sides in a circle or an arc, just before or just after you create it, follow these steps:

1. **Type the number of sides you want to have.**

2. **Type an s to tell SketchUp that you mean "sides."**

3. **Press Enter.**

338 faces   116 faces   52 faces

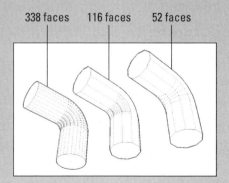
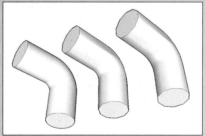

The trick to drawing an extrusion profile that isn't on the ground is to start by drawing a rectangular face. You then draw the profile on the face and erase the rest of the rectangle. Figure 6-6 shows how you'd draw the profile of a gutter directly on the corner of a roof; the steps that follow explain the same things in words:

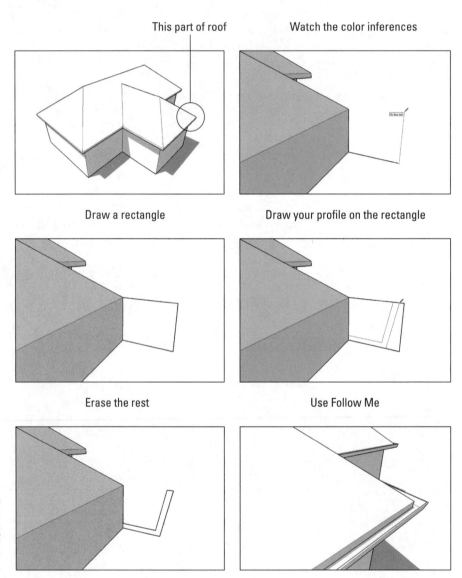

This part of roof

Watch the color inferences

Draw a rectangle

Draw your profile on the rectangle

Erase the rest

Use Follow Me

FIGURE 6-6:
Drawing an extrusion profile in place by starting with a rectangle.

1. **Zoom in on what you're doing.**

   Many people try to work without filling their modeling windows with the subject at hand. Not doing so is like trying to do a crossword puzzle while looking the wrong way through a pair of binoculars. Get close — SketchUp models don't bite!

2. **Using the Line tool, draw a rectangle whose face is perpendicular to the edge you want to use for Follow Me.**

   Pay careful attention to SketchUp's inference engine, introduced in Chapter 3. Watch the colors to make sure that you're drawing in the right direction.

3. **Use the Line tool (and SketchUp's other drawing tools) to draw your profile directly on the rectangle you just drew.**

   The important thing here is to make sure that your extrusion profile is a single face; if it's not, Follow Me won't work the way you want it to.

TIP

4. **Erase the rest of your rectangle, leaving only the profile.**

Drawing your profile somewhere else

The awful thing about handrails is that they're almost always at funny angles, not parallel to a colored axis. When drawing your extrusion profile in place isn't convenient, draw it on the ground and move it into position after.

Here's the trick: Draw a *tail* — a short edge — perpendicular to your extrusion profile. This tail helps you line up your profile with the edge that you want to use as an extrusion path for Follow Me. The following steps and Figure 6-7 describe how you'd draw and position a profile for a handrail:

1. **Draw your extrusion profile flat on the ground.**

2. **Draw a short edge perpendicular to the face you just drew.**

   This tail should come from the point where you want your profile to attach to the extrusion path.

3. **Make your profile and its tail into a group.**

   This makes it easier to move and rotate around all at once. See Chapter 5 for information on creating and using groups.

4. **Using the Move tool, place your profile at the end of the extrusion path.**

   To make sure that you position your profile accurately, pick it up by clicking the point where the tail meets the face and then drop it by clicking the end of the extrusion path.

5. **With the Rotate tool, rotate your profile into position.**

   Here's where you need to use a bit of skill. (See Chapter 3 for guidance.) The Rotate tool is easy to use — after you get the hang of it.

6. **Context-click the group you made in Step 3 and choose Explode; delete your tail.**

Extrusion path

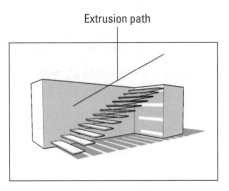

Draw a tail

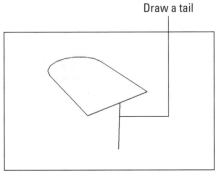

Box indicates   Extrusion   Move handrail profile
a group   path   to bottom of extrusion path

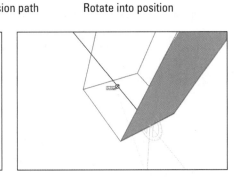

Rotate into position

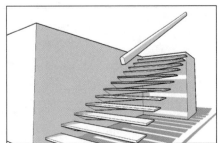

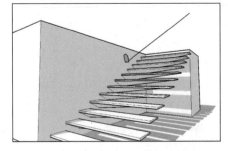

Subtracting from a model with Follow Me

What if you want to model a bar of soap? Or a sofa cushion? Or anything that doesn't have a sharp edge? The best way to round off edges in SketchUp is to use Follow Me. In addition to using Follow Me to *add* to your model, you can also *subtract* from your model.

Here's how it works: If you draw an extrusion profile on the end face of a longish form, you can use Follow Me to remove a strip of material along whatever path you specify. Figure 6-8 demonstrates the concept on the top of a box.

TIP

If the extrusion path you want to use for a Follow Me operation consists of the entire perimeter of a face (as is the case in Figure 6-8), you can save time by just selecting the face instead of all the edges that define it.

But what if you want to create a corner that's rounded in *both* directions, as so many corners are? That one's a little trickier to do. The basic technique involves using Follow Me on a corner you've already rounded with the Push/Pull tool. After you round a corner with an arc of the correct radius, you can use copies (or component instances, if you're clever) of that corner several times, wherever you need them. Although we wouldn't call this solution elegant, it works.

Draw an arc

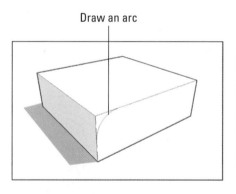

Select a path

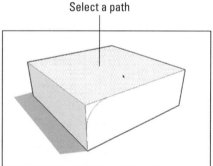

Click the face with Follow Me

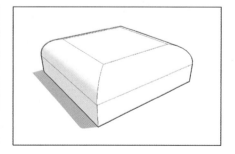

FIGURE 6-8:
Creating a rounded edge with Follow Me.

Figure 6-9 gives a step-by-step, visual account of the process, while the following steps explain it in words, as follows:

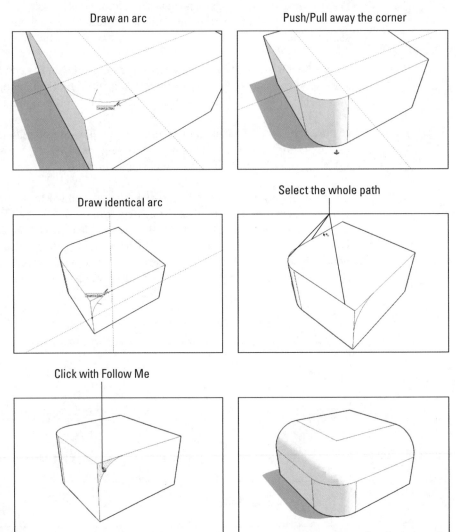

Draw an arc

Push/Pull away the corner

Draw identical arc

Select the whole path

Click with Follow Me

FIGURE 6-9:
Making a corner that's rounded in both directions.

1. **Draw a box.**

   The box should be big enough for the round you want to apply.

 2. **With the 2 Point Arc tool, draw an arc on the corner of the box.**

   When you're drawing an arc on a corner, keep an eye out for the inferences that help you draw properly:

   - After clicking to place one endpoint of your arc, as you cut across the corner, the point at which your line turns magenta is where your endpoints are *equidistant* (the same distance) from the corner across which you're cutting.

   - After clicking to place your second endpoint, you see a point at which the arc you're drawing turns magenta — this means your arc is *tangent to* (continuous with) both edges it's connected to. You want this to be the case, so you should click when you see magenta.

   Reduce the number of sides on your arc before you start rounding away. See the sidebar "Why your computer is so slow," earlier in this chapter, to find out why.

REMEMBER

3. **Push/pull down the new face to round off the corner.**

4. **Draw another *identical* arc on one of the corners directly adjacent to the corner you just rounded.**

   This is where you refer to Figure 6-9. Pictures are better than words when explaining things like adjacent corners.

5. **Select the edges shown in Figure 6-9.**

6. **Choose Tools ➪ Follow Me.**

7. **Click the arc corner face to extrude it along the path you selected in Step 5.**

8. **Hide or smooth any edges that need it.**

   For information about hiding edges, see Chapter 5. Check out this chapter's "Smoothing those unsightly edges" sidebar for the whole scoop on how to smooth edges.

After you have a fully rounded corner, you can use a bunch of them to make anything you want; it just takes a little planning. Figure 6-10 shows a simple bar of soap created out of eight rounded corners, copied, and flipped accordingly. The text (in case you're wondering) was created with SketchUp's 3D Text tool, which you can find on the Tools menu.

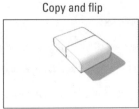
Copy and flip

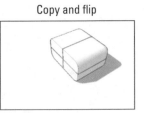
Copy and flip

Copy and flip

Hide and smooth edges; then add text

FIGURE 6-10:
Assembling
a bunch of
rounded
corners to
make objects is
relatively easy.

SMOOTHING THOSE UNSIGHTLY EDGES

If you're wondering how to get rid of all the ugly lines that appear when you use Follow
Me, the answer is pretty simple: You can *smooth* edges, just like you can hide them. (See
Chapter 5 for more information about hiding edges.) The difference between hiding and
smoothing is illustrated by the images of the cylinders in the figure that follows:

- **When you *hide* an edge between two faces,** SketchUp treats those faces as though
  your edge is still there — it just doesn't show the edge. Materials you've applied to
  each face stay separate, and each face is lit separately by SketchUp's sun. The latter
  fact is the reason why simply hiding the edges between faces that are supposed to
  represent a smooth curve doesn't make things look smooth — you still end up with a
  faceted look, as you can see in the second cylinder.

- **When you *smooth* an edge between two faces,** you're telling SketchUp to treat
  them as a single face — with a single material and smooth-looking shading. The difference is pretty huge, as you can see in the third cylinder in the figure.

You can smooth edges in two ways:

- **Use the Eraser.** To smooth edges with the Eraser tool, hold down the Ctrl key
  (Option on the Mac) while you click or drag over the edges you want to smooth.

- **Use the Soften Edges panel.** Located on the Window menu, this panel lets you smooth a bunch of selected edges all at once, according to the angle of their adjacent faces. To get started: Select the edges you want to smooth and then move the slider to the right until you like the way your model looks.

To unsmooth edges, follow these steps:

1. **Choose View ⇨ Hidden Geometry so that the Hidden Geometry menu option is selected.**

   This makes hidden edges visible.

2. **Select the edges you want to unsmooth.**

3. **In the Soften Edges panel, move the slider all the way to the left.**

Visible edges   Hidden edges   Smoothed edges

Modeling with the Scale Tool

Real heroes are rarely obvious. The Scale tool is the single most misunderstood member of SketchUp's mercifully limited toolkit. New modelers assume that Scale is for resizing things in your model. That's technically true, but most folks only use it to resize *whole* objects; the real power of Scale happens when you use it on *parts* of objects to change their shape. Figure 6-11 illustrates how Scale can distort basic shapes into more complex ones.

Getting the hang of Scale

The basic principle of this technique is pretty simple: You select the geometry (edges and faces) in your model that you want to resize, activate the Scale tool, and go to town.

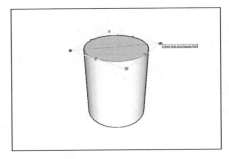
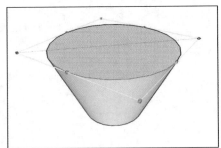
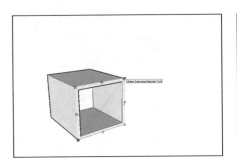
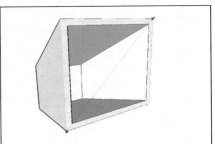
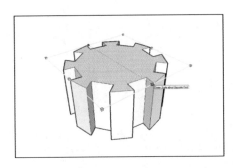
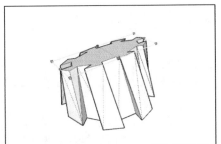
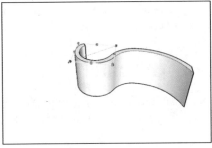
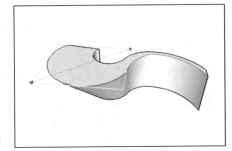

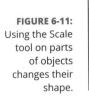

FIGURE 6-11:
Using the Scale
tool on parts
of objects
changes their
shape.

Here's a list of steps, just so it's crystal clear. Figure 6-12 tells the story in pictures:

1. **Select the part of your model that you want to scale.**

   Use the Select tool to do this; check out Chapter 3 for details about making selections.

2. **Activate the Scale tool by choosing Tools ⇨ Scale.**

   You can also make Scale active by clicking its button on the toolbar or by pressing the S key on your keyboard. After you activate Scale, the geometry you selected in Step 1 should be enclosed in a box of little green cubes, or *grips.*

3. **Click a grip and then move your mouse to start scaling your selected geometry.**

   Keep reading for the lowdown on the different grips.

4. **When you're finished scaling, click again to stop.**

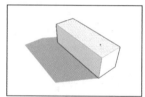
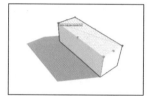
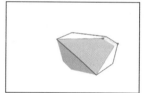

FIGURE 6-12:
The Scale tool is a cinch to use.

While we're on the subject of Scale, here are a few more things you should know:

>> **Use different grips to scale different ways.** Which grip (the little green boxes that appear when you activate the Scale tool) you use determines how your geometry scales:

  - *Corner* grips scale proportionally — nothing gets distorted when you use them.

  - *Edge* and *side* grips distort your geometry as you scale — use them to squeeze what you're scaling.

>> **Hold down the Shift key to scale proportionally.** This happens automatically if you're using one of the corner grips, but not if you're using any others. If you don't want to distort what you're scaling, hold down Shift.

>> **Hold down the Ctrl key (Option on a Mac) to scale about the center of your selection.** You might find yourself doing this more often than not.

>> **Type a scaling factor to scale accurately.** To scale by 50 percent, type **0.5**. Typing **3.57** scales your geometry by 357 percent, and typing **1.0** doesn't scale it at all. Take a look at Chapter 3 to read more about using the Measurements box while you work.

>> **Type a specific measurement.** If you know the final dimension you're trying to achieve with the Scale tool, you can type it in, followed by the units. To scale a 4-foot box until it's 10 feet wide, type **10'**.

>> **Which grips appear depend on what you're scaling.** Have a look at the differences in Figure 6-13.

- Most of the time, you see a scaling box enclosed by 26 green grips.

- If you're scaling flat, *coplanar* geometry (faces and edges that all lie on the same plane) and that plane is perfectly aligned with one of the major planes in your model, you see a rectangle consisting of 8 grips instead of a box with 26.

- If what you're scaling is a Dynamic Component, you may see anywhere from 0 to all 26 grips, depending on how the builder set up the component. Chapter 5 introduces Dynamic Components.

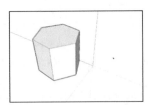
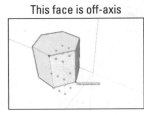
This face is off-axis

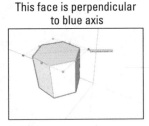
This face is perpendicular to blue axis

FIGURE 6-13: Grips depend on what you're trying to scale.

TIP

>> **You can't make a copy while you scale.** Both the Move and Rotate tools let you make copies by holding down a button on your keyboard while you're using them, but Scale doesn't work this way. If you need to make a scaled copy, try this instead:

a. *Select the geometry that you want to scale and copy, and then make it into a group.*

See Chapter 5 for more information on making groups.

b. *Choose Edit ⇨ Copy from the menu bar and then choose Edit ⇨ Paste in Place from the menu bar.*

c. *Scale the copied group as you would anything else.*

Scaling profiles to make organic forms

Here's where it gets really interesting. We need to thank über-SketchUpper Justin Chin (who goes by the handle monsterzero online) for demonstrating the power of scaling profiles to make organic forms. The method is great because it's easy to understand *and* powerful enough to be applied all over the place.

So what is this method? You use the Scale tool in combination with a series of 2D profiles to create curvy, lumpy, distinctly un-boxy 3D shapes. An awful lot of the stuff in the universe fits squarely in this category: us, you, slugs, intergalactic alien fighter vessels, bananas — just about everything that wasn't made by a machine can be modeled using the scaled profiles method of 3D modeling.

On the Extension Warehouse, you find the FredoScale SketchUp extension, which is hyper-relevant to the material in this section. After you're comfortable with the techniques we describe in this section, check out the extension. We introduce the Extension Warehouse in Chapter 16.

Combining Scale and Push/Pull

The simplest way to use this method is in association with Push/Pull. Here's a very simple example of how it works. Check out Figure 6-14 for an illustrated view:

1. Create a 2D shape.

TIP

This shape may be something simple (such as a circle) or something more complex; it all depends on what you're trying to model. The shape may also be a half-shape if what you're trying to make exhibits bilateral symmetry. Take a look at the last section in Chapter 5 for more information on using components to build symmetrical models.

2. Push/pull your 2D shape into a 3D form.

3. Scale the new face you created so it's slightly bigger (or slightly smaller) than the original 2D shape from Step 1.

See the previous section in this chapter for more specifics about using the Scale tool. Pay special attention to the points about using *modifier keys,* or keyboard buttons, to scale proportionally or about the center of what you're working on.

4. Push/pull the face you scaled in the preceding step.

TIP

Try to make this extrusion about the same as the one you made in Step 2.

You can usually double-click a face with the Push/Pull tool to repeat the last Push/Pull operation you did.

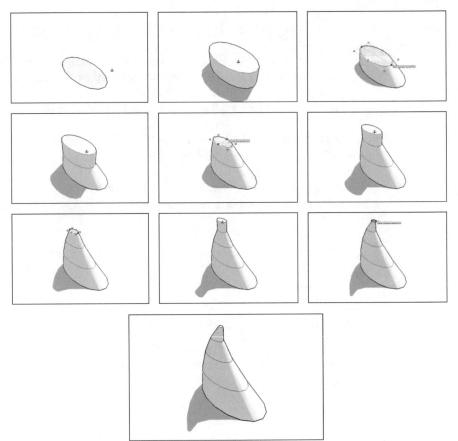

FIGURE 6-14:
Using Scale
and Push/Pull
together is a
simple way to
make organic
forms.

5. **Repeat Steps 3 and 4 until you're done.**

    You can add skillful use of the Rotate tool into the mix if you like; doing so allows you to curve and bend your form as you shape it.

Keep the following tidbits in mind as you explore this technique:

>> **Watch your polygon count.** *Polygons* are faces, basically — the more you have, the "heavier" your model becomes, and the worse it performs on your computer. Try to minimize the number of faces you're working with by reducing the number of edges in your original 2D shape. Have a look at the sidebar "Why your computer is so slow," earlier in this chapter, for the whole scoop.

>> **Don't be afraid to go back and tweak.** The beauty of this method is its flexibility. While you're working, you can select any of the 2D *profiles* (shapes) in your model and use the Scale tool to tweak them. Just select the loop of edges along the perimeter of the profile you want to scale and take it from there. Figure 6-15 illustrates an example of how you can tweak a shape by scaling.

FIGURE 6-15:
You can go
back and scale
any profile at
any time while
you work.

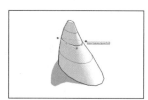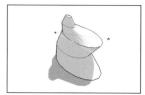

Combining Scale and Follow Me

Another way to create extruded forms is to use Follow Me. (See the first part of this chapter if you need a refresher.) This technique is ideally suited to making long, curvy, tapered things like tentacles and antlers; it's a little time-consuming but works like a charm.

Modeling a simplified bull's horn is a good, straightforward illustration of how the Follow Me variation of this method works. Here's how to go about it; take a look at Figure 6-16 to see the story in pictures:

1. **Draw a circle.**

This is the extrusion *profile* for Follow Me. Strongly consider reducing the number of sides in your circle from the standard 24 to something more like 10 or 12. See the sidebar "Why your computer is so slow" (earlier in this chapter) to find out how and why you should do this.

2. **Draw a 10-sided arc that starts perpendicular to the center of the circle you drew in Step 1.**

Type **10s** and press Enter right after you click to finish drawing your arc.

This tells SketchUp to make sure your arc has 10 sides (instead of the default 12). Why 10 sides? It makes the math easier a few steps from now.

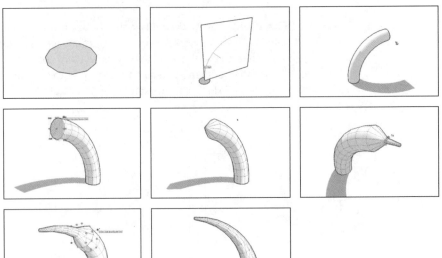

FIGURE 6-16:
Use Scale with
Follow Me to
create long,
tapered forms
like this bull's
horn.

TIP

The easiest way to create a halfway-accurate arc in 3D space is to start by drawing a rectangle. When you're sure this rectangle is properly situated, use one of the arc tools to draw on top of the rectangle and then delete everything but the arc.

3. **Select the arc you just drew.**

This is the extrusion *path* for Follow Me.

4. **Activate the Follow Me tool by choosing Tools ⇨ Follow Me from the menu bar.**

5. **Click the circle you drew in Step 1 to extrude it along the path you drew in Step 2.**

6. **Choose View ⇨ Hidden Geometry from the menu bar.**

Showing the hidden geometry in your model lets you select the edges that were automatically *smoothed* (made hidden) when you used Follow Me in Step 4.

7. **Scale the face at the end of your new extrusion by a factor of 0.1.**

See "Getting the hang of Scale," earlier in this chapter, for instructions on how to do this. Use any of the four corner grips on the scaling box, and don't forget to hold down the Ctrl key (Option on a Mac) while you're scaling — this forces SketchUp to scale about the center of the face you're resizing.

8. **Select the edges that define the next-to-last profile in your extruded form.**

TIP

Depending on the angle of your arc, making this selection can get tricky. Here are some tips that may help:

- See Chapter 3 for tips on making selections.

- Choose View ⇨ Face Style ⇨ X-Ray or View ⇨ Edge Style ⇨ Back Edges from the menu bar to make it easier to see what you've selected.

- Hold down the Ctrl key (Option on a Mac) while you orbit to turn off SketchUp's "blue is up/down gravity bias." While orbiting this way, try drawing lots of tight, little circles with your mouse to get your view to tilt in the direction your want. This is by no means simple stuff, but getting the hang of temporarily disabling the Orbit tool's tendency to keep the blue axis straight up and down is a very nifty way to work. Doing so makes it infinitely easier to get just the right angle for making a window selection. This in turn makes selecting the edges that define profiles a whole lot easier, and that's what becoming a Zen master of the Orbit tool is all about.

9. **Scale the edges you selected in the preceding step by a factor of 0.2.**

Starting to see what's happening?

10. **Repeat Steps 8 and 9 for each of the remaining profiles in your form, increasing the scaling factor by 0.1 each time.**

Of course, you can absolutely choose to sculpt your form however you like, but this method (counting up by tenths) yields a smooth taper.

The Santa-Claus-and-reindeer project illustrates the kind of fancy, not-a-box models you can build after you master the Scale tool. It's not beginner-level material, but it's worth the time when you're ready.

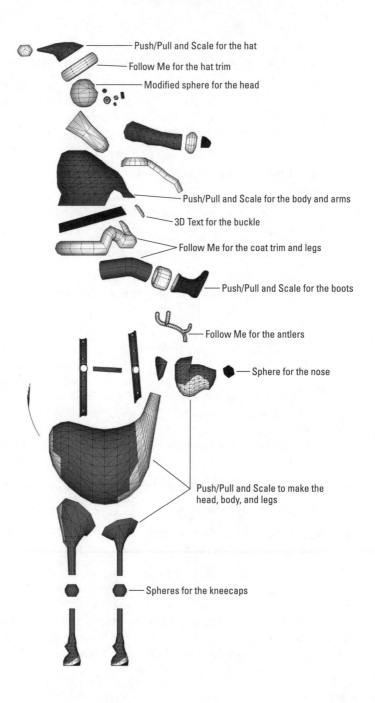

Push/Pull and Scale for the hat

Follow Me for the hat trim

Modified sphere for the head

Push/Pull and Scale for the body and arms

3D Text for the buckle

Follow Me for the coat trim and legs

Push/Pull and Scale for the boots

Follow Me for the antlers

Sphere for the nose

Push/Pull and Scale to make the head, body, and legs

Spheres for the kneecaps

Making and Modifying Terrain

Continuing in the grand tradition of building extremely powerful tools and then hiding them so you'll never find them, the people at SketchUp introduced the *Sandbox* way back in version 5 of the software. We introduce the Sandbox here because it helps people to model *terrain* — the stuff your buildings sit on (or in, if what you're making is underground).

The Sandbox isn't new, but owing to its less-than-obvious location, most SketchUp users have never used it. Here are the facts:

» **The Sandbox is a collection of tools.** Each tool serves a fairly specific purpose and is meant to be used at a particular stage of the terrain-modeling process. That said, like all SketchUp's tools, they're incredibly flexible. You can use them to model anything you want.

» **The Sandbox is in both Make and Pro.** Despite what many people think, the Sandbox tools aren't just for Pro users; people who use the free version of SketchUp can use them, too. They're just hidden, which brings you to our next point.

» **The Sandbox is hidden.** The reasons for this are complicated, but the tools in the Sandbox are a little bit special; they're *extensions* — you have to find them and turn them on before you can use them. If you're using SketchUp Pro, you can skip the first two steps in the following list — they're already turned on.

Follow these steps to switch on the Sandbox tools:

   a. *Choose Window➪Preferences from the menu bar to open the Preferences dialog box.*

   Choose SketchUp➪Preferences if you're on a Mac.

   b. *In the Extensions panel, make sure the Sandbox Tools check box is selected and then close the Preferences dialog box.*

   c. *Choose View➪Toolbars➪Sandbox from the menu bar to show the Sandbox toolbar.*

Creating a new terrain model

Whether you're modeling a patch of ground for a building or redesigning Central Park, you need one of two terrain-modeling methods:

» **Starting from existing data:** This existing data usually arrives in the form of *contour* or *topo* lines; see the next section to read more about them.

>> **Starting from scratch:** If you don't have any data to start or if you're beginning with a perfectly flat site, you can use SketchUp's From Scratch tool to draw a grid that's easy to form into rolling hills, berms, and valleys. Skip ahead to "Modeling terrain from scratch" for more information.

There's a neat trick Aidan learned for modeling small (yard-sized) amounts of terrain — the piece of land immediately surrounding a building, for example. You *could* use the From Scratch tool to start with a flat site, but there's a better way: See "Roughing out a site" a little later in this chapter.

Modeling terrain from contour lines

You know the squiggly lines on topographical maps that show you where the hills and valleys are? They're *contour lines* (or *contours*) because they represent the contours of the terrain; every point on a single line is the same height above sea level as every other point on that line. Where the lines are close together, the ground between them is steep. Where the lines are far apart, the slope is less steep. Cartographers, surveyors, engineers, and architects use contour lines to represent 3D terrain in flat formats like maps and site drawings.

Sometimes, you have contour lines for a building site that you want to model in 3D. You can use the From Contours tool in the Sandbox to automatically generate a three-dimensional surface from a set of contour lines, as shown in Figure 6-17.

Select your lines

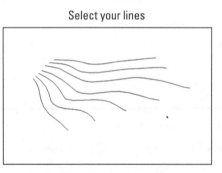

Choose From Contours

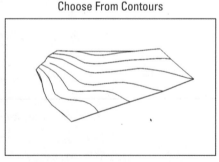

Show Hidden Geometry

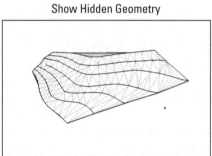

Separate your lines from your surface

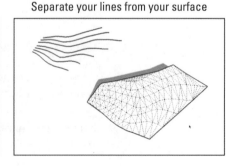

FIGURE 6-17:
Use the From Contours tool to turn a set of contour lines into a 3D surface.

Here are some things to keep in mind about the From Contours tool:

>> **It's a two-step tool.** Using From Contours is simple after you get the hang of it:

   a. *Select all the contour lines you want to use to create a surface.*

   b. *Choose Draw ⇨ Sandbox ⇨ From Contours from the menu bar (or click the From Contours tool button, if the Sandbox toolbar is visible).*

   Note: If you can't see the Sandbox tools in your menus, you haven't turned them on yet. See the beginning of this section, "Making and Modifying Terrain," to rectify the situation.

>> **Your contour lines need to be lifted up.** The From Contours tool creates a surface from contour lines that are already positioned at their proper heights in 3D space. Most of the time you work with contours that are part of a 2D drawing, and that means you probably have to lift them up yourself using the Move tool — one at a time. It's tedious but necessary. Just oil up the Select tool, put on some music, and get to work. For a refresher on selecting things, take a look at the last part of Chapter 3.

>> **Download and install Weld.** The Weld SketchUp extension turns selections of individual line segments into *polylines* — this makes them much, much easier to work with. If you work with contour lines imported from a computer-aided drawing (CAD) file, using Weld makes your life a little easier. To add Weld to SketchUp, visit the Extension Warehouse, introduced in Chapter 16.

>> **You end up with a group.** When you use From Contours, SketchUp automatically makes your new surface (the one you generated from your contour lines) into a group. It leaves the original lines themselves completely alone; you can move them away, hide them, or delete them if you want. We recommend making another group out of them, putting them on a separate layer (see Chapter 7 for more on this), and hiding that layer until you need it again.

   To edit the faces and edges inside a group, double-click it with the Select tool. Chapter 5 has all the details on groups and components.

>> **To edit your new surface, turn on Hidden Geometry.** The flowing, organic surface you just created is actually just a bunch of little triangles. The From Contours tool smooths the edges that define them, but they're there. To see them, choose View ⇨ Hidden Geometry from the menu bar.

>> **Try to keep your geometry reasonable.** The From Contours tool is super useful, but it has its limits. The trouble is that it's too easy to use it to create enormous amounts of geometry (faces and edges) that can really bog down your system. If it takes forever for your contours to turn into a surface, or if that surface is so big that your computer turns blue and curls up into a fetal

position (so to speak), you need to go back a few steps and do one (or perhaps all) of the following:

- *Work on a smaller area.* As nice as it'd be to have the whole neighborhood in your SketchUp model, you may have to narrow your scope. Creating only what you need is good modeling policy.

- *Use only every other contour line.* Doing this effectively halves the amount of geometry in your resulting surface.

- *Dumb down the contour lines.* This is a little bit hard to explain, but here goes: The From Contours tool works by connecting adjacent contour lines together with edges that form triangles. How many triangles it creates depends on how many individual edge segments are in each contour line; Figure 6-18 provides an illustration. Unless you created the contour lines to begin with — there's a good chance you imported them as part of a CAD file — you have no control over how detailed they are. Redrawing each contour line is a major bummer, but luckily, you can download a great Simplify Contours extension that makes the process much simpler.

» **You don't have to start with existing contour lines.** In fact, drawing your own edges and using From Contours to generate a surface from them is one of the most powerful ways to create organic, nonboxy forms in SketchUp. The next section, "Modeling terrain from scratch," has more details.

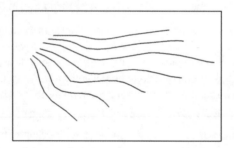
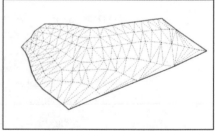

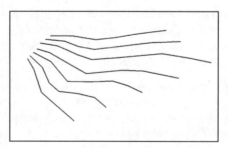
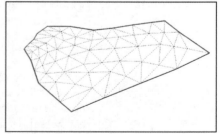

FIGURE 6-18: How many triangles are created depends on the number of edge segments in the contour lines you start with.

Low-detail lines yield fewer triangular faces

DON'T FLIP OUT — FLIP EDGE

The Sandbox's Flip Edge tool is a simple beast, but it's indispensable if you're working with the From Contours tool. Basically, you use Flip Edge to clean up the surfaces that From Contours creates. When you turn contour lines into a surface, lots and lots of triangular faces appear. Sometimes, the From Contours tool decides to draw an edge between the wrong two line segments, creating two triangular faces that form a "flat spot" in your surface. See the following image.

You get rid of these flat spots manually by flipping the edges that create them. Doing so changes the resulting triangular faces, usually making them end up side by side (instead of one above the other).

To use the Flip Edge tool (choose Tools ⇨ Sandbox ⇨ Flip Edge), just click the edge you want to flip. If you're not sure about an edge, go ahead and flip it; then see if things look better. If they don't, you can always undo or flip it back.

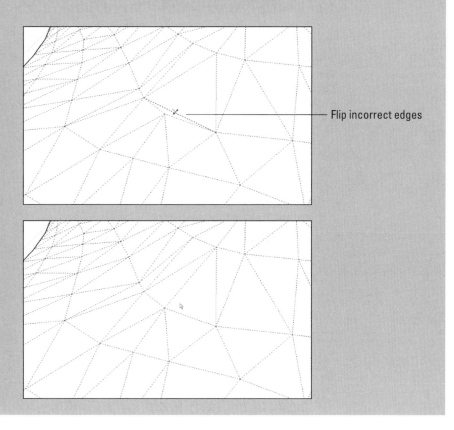

Flip incorrect edges

>> **Get ready to do some cleanup.** The surfaces that From Contours creates usually need to be cleaned up to some extent. Use the Eraser to delete extra geometry (you'll find lots along the top and bottom edges of your surface). Use the Flip Edge tool to correct the orientation of your triangular faces. See the nearby sidebar "Don't flip out — Flip Edge" for the lowdown.

Modeling terrain from scratch

Without contour lines that define the shape of the terrain you want to model, you have to start with a level surface. Use the From Scratch tool to create a big, flat rectangle that represents a chunk of ground. Because the rectangle is already divided into triangular faces, it's easy to use the Smoove tool (discussed next in this chapter) to shape the rectangle into hills, valleys, sand traps, and whatever else you have in mind.

Here's the thing, though: It's a very rare occasion that you have *carte blanche* with a piece of land. Unless you design something like a golf course in the middle of a dry lake bed or terraform a new planet for colonization, you probably have preexisting terrain conditions to contend with. And if that's the case, you're prob-ably better starting off with a set of contour lines that describe those conditions, as discussed earlier in this chapter.

So although the From Scratch Tool works great, you probably won't need to use it much. All the same, here's how to do so, just in case.

Follow these steps to create a new terrain surface with the From Scratch tool and take a look at Figure 6-19 while you're at it:

1. **Choose Draw ⇨ Sandbox ⇨ From Scratch from the menu bar to activate the From Scratch tool.**

2. **Type a grid spacing amount and press Enter.**

   The default grid spacing amount is 10 feet, which means the tool draws a rectangle made up of squares that are 10 feet across. The grid spacing you choose depends on how big an area you're planning to model and how detailed you plan to make the terrain for that model.

TIP

   If Aidan were modeling a single-family house on a reasonably sized lot, he would probably use a grid spacing of 2 feet — that'd provide enough detail for elements like walkways and small berms without creating too much geometry for a computer to handle. If he were laying out an 18-hole golf course, on the other hand, he'd choose a grid spacing closer to 50 feet and then add detail to certain areas later.

3. **Click to position one corner of your new terrain surface where you want it.**

4. **Click to determine the width of the surface you're drawing.**

5. **Click to establish the length of your new terrain surface.**

   When you're done, the great big rectangle you've created will automatically be a group. Double-click with the Select tool to edit it and get started. You'll probably decide to use the Smoove tool next; jump ahead to "Making freeform hills and valleys with Smoove" (later in this chapter) to find out how.

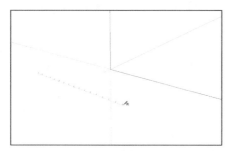
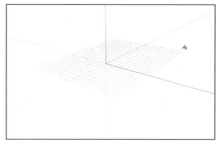

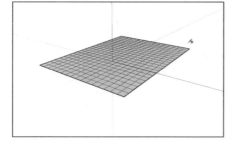

FIGURE 6-19: Use the From Scratch tool to create big swatches of flat terrain. Ah, the possibilities!

Roughing out a site

Perhaps you want to model a smallish chunk of nonflat terrain that surrounds a building. Maybe you're trying to reproduce existing site conditions, or maybe you're in the process of designing the landscape for a project. There's a neat technique for cases like this one: You can use From Contours to quickly generate a surface from just a few simple outlines.

Follow these steps to model a simple terrain surface with the From Contours tool, as shown in Figure 6-20:

1. **Extend the bottom of your building down so the exterior walls drop below ground level.**

2. **Make your building into a group.**

   See Chapter 5 if you need help.

3. Use the Tape Measure and Line tools to draw the outline of the chunk of terrain you want to model around the building.

Keep in mind that the resulting horizontal face is flat; just pretend you're drawing in 2D space. It doesn't matter if the outline you draw is below, above, or in line with the building, as you see in the next step.

4. Use the Push/Pull tool to extrude the face you drew in Step 3 into a box that extends above and below your building, and then delete the top and bottom faces of the box you just drew.

5. Paint the walls of your box with a translucent material.

You can find some in the Translucent library, in the Materials panel. See Chapters 2 and 3 for help.

6. Draw edges on the sides of the box that represent where the ground should intersect them.

7. Draw edges on the sides of the building that represent where the ground meets the building.

8. Delete the box you created in Step 4, leaving the edges you drew in Step 6.

9. Select all the edges you drew in Steps 6 and 7.

10. Choose Draw ⇨ Sandbox ⇨ From Contours from the menu bar to generate a surface based on the edges you selected in the preceding step.

Take a look at the section "Modeling terrain from scratch" for tips on using From Contours; at this point, you need to use the Flip Edge tool and the Eraser to clean up your terrain model — particularly where your building is supposed to go.

Editing an existing terrain model

No matter how you make a terrain model, there's a 99-percent chance that it consists of lots and lots of triangles. Switch on Hidden Geometry (choose View ⇨ Hidden Geometry) to see them. As long as you have triangles, you can use the Sandbox's terrain editing tools. This section shows you how to do the following:

» Shape (or reshape) your terrain with the Smoove tool.

» Create a flat spot for a building with the Stamp tool.

» Draw paths and roads with the Drape tool.

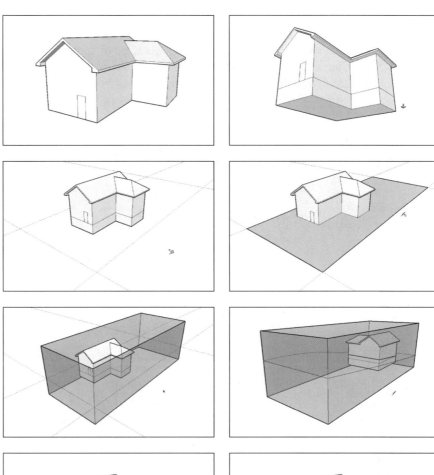

FIGURE 6-20:
You can create irregular terrain surfaces very quickly with the From Contours tool.

REMEMBER

Keep in mind that both From Contours and From Scratch create terrain objects that are groups. To edit a group, double-click it with the Select tool. When you're done, click somewhere else in your modeling window.

Making freeform hills and valleys with Smoove

Smoove is a tool *for moving smoothly* — get it? Smooth + Move = Smoove. We'll wait while you compose yourself.

Smoove is actually one of the coolest tools in SketchUp; it lets you shape terrain (or any horizontal surface that's made up of smaller, triangular faces) by pushing and pulling (sort of) bumps and depressions of any size. Smoove is fun to use and yields results that you'd be hard-pressed to produce with any other tool in SketchUp. Figure 6-21 shows what Smoove can do.

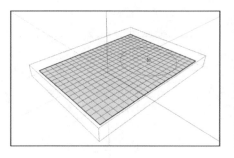 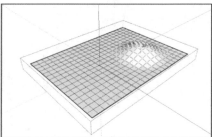

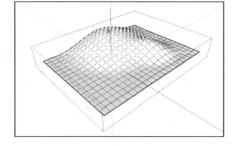 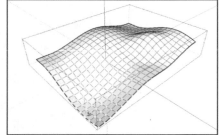

FIGURE 6-21: Smoove creates shapes that are unlike anything else you can make with SketchUp.

Follow these steps to shape a surface with Smoove:

1. **Double-click the group containing your terrain to edit it.**

   If your terrain isn't part of a group, forget this step.

2. **Choose Tools⇨Sandbox⇨Smoove from the menu bar to activate the Smoove tool.**

3. **Type a radius and press Enter.**

   Smoove creates lumps, bumps, and dimples that are circular. The radius you enter here determines how big those lumps, bumps, and dimples should be.

4. **Click somewhere on your terrain surface to start smooving.**

5. **Move your mouse up or down (to create a bump or a depression, respectively), and then click again to stop smooving.**

Fun, huh? Here are some more things to keep in mind when you use Smoove:

» **Use the From Scratch tool beforehand.** You don't have to, but creating a surface with the From Scratch tool (described earlier in this chapter) is by far the easiest way to end up with terrain that you can smoove easily.

» **Try smooving to edit other terrain surfaces.** You can also use Smoove after you create a terrain surface with the From Contours tool.

» **Double-click to repeat your previous smoove.** As with Push/Pull, double-clicking tells SketchUp to carry out the same operation as you did the last time you used the tool.

» **Preselect to smoove shapes other than circles.** Any faces and edges you select before you use the Smoove tool will move up (or down) by a constant amount. This means you can use Smoove to create things like ridges and ditches by selecting the right geometry beforehand. Figure 6-22 provides a much-needed picture.

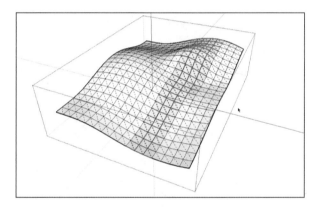

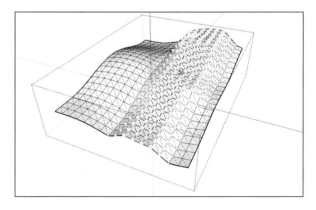

FIGURE 6-22: Preselect faces and edges to smoove shapes other than circles.

NEED MORE TRIANGLES? ADD DETAIL

Like the Flip Edge tool, Add Detail is kind of a one-trick pony. Use it to add triangles to areas of your terrain surface that need more detail. That way, you can save geometry (and file size, and waiting) by having lots of faces only in the areas of your terrain that require it. As Aidan mentions elsewhere in this chapter, if he were designing a golf course, he'd use very big triangles for the vast majority of it. He'd use the Add Detail tool to add triangles to areas where he planned to have smallish things like sand traps.

You can use the Add Detail tool in two ways:

- **Add detail to faces one at a time.** To be honest, you may never have a reason to use the tool this way, but here goes: You can activate the tool (see the next bullet) *without* having any geometry selected. Then click faces or edges on your terrain to divide them into more faces. This method might be handy when you model something very precisely.

- **Add detail to an area all at once.** Simply select the faces on your terrain you want to subdivide and choose Tools ⇨ Sandbox ⇨ Add Detail from the menu bar. Take a look at the figure to see what happens when you do.

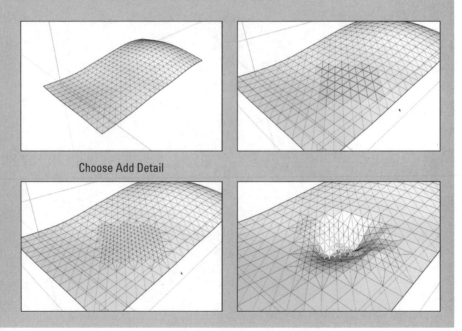

Choose Add Detail

Placing a building on your terrain with Stamp

Eventually, you may need to plunk down a building (or some other structure) on the terrain you've lovingly crafted. The Stamp tool provides an easy way to — you guessed it — stamp a building footprint into a terrain surface, creating a flat "pad" for something to sit on. This tool also provides a way to create a gently sloping offset around the perimeter of your stamped form. This creates a smoother transition between the new, flat pad and the existing terrain.

Follow these steps to use the Stamp tool; check out Figure 6-23 to see the corresponding pictures:

1. **Move the building you want to stamp into position above your terrain surface.**

   The building shouldn't touch the terrain but float in space directly above it. Also, turn the building into a group before you start moving anything; take a look at Chapter 5 to find out all about groups and components.

   If you're having trouble moving your building into position accurately, move it to the correct height first and then switch to a top, no-perspective view to finish the job. Look in the Camera menu for both these commands.

   TIP

2. **Choose Tools⇨Sandbox⇨Stamp from the menu bar to activate the Stamp tool.**

3. **Click the floating object to tell SketchUp what you want to use as the stamp.**

4. **Type an offset distance and press Enter.**

   The *offset distance* is the amount of space around the perimeter of whatever you're stamping that SketchUp uses to smooth the transition between the flat spot it's creating and the existing terrain. The offset amount you choose depends entirely on what you're stamping. Go nuts, and thank your lucky stars for Undo.

5. **Move your cursor over your terrain surface and click again.**

6. **Move (but don't drag) your mouse up and down to position the flat pad in space. Click again to finish the operation.**

Here are a couple things that are handy to know when you use Stamp:

>> SketchUp uses the bottommost face in your stamp object as the template for the flat pad it creates in your terrain.

>> Read the "Don't flip out — Flip Edge" sidebar, earlier in this chapter; Stamp creates triangular faces that sometimes need cleaning.

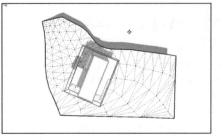
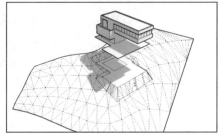

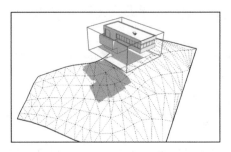
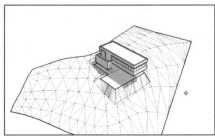

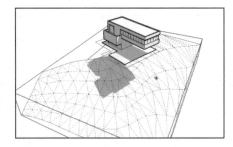
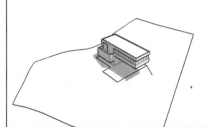

FIGURE 6-23:
Use the Stamp
tool to create
a nice, flat
spot for your
building.

Creating paths and roads with Drape

The Drape tool works a little like a cookie cutter; use it to transfer edges from an object down onto another surface, which is directly beneath it.

Perhaps you have a gently sloping terrain and you want to draw a meandering path on it. The path has to follow the contours of the terrain, but because you want to paint it with a different material, it needs to be a separate face. In this case, you'd draw the path on a separate face and use the Drape tool to transfer it to your terrain surface.

Taking the preceding example, follow these steps to use the Drape tool to draw a path on a nonflat terrain surface. Figure 6-24 illustrates the steps:

1. **Use the Line tool (see Chapter 2) to draw a flat face somewhere directly above your terrain surface.**

   If you can, make your flat face exactly the same size as your terrain. Just make sure it's big enough for whatever you plan to draw next (in this example, a path).

2. **Paint the face you just created with a translucent material.**

   I find that a light gray works well; there's a good one in the Translucent library, inside the Materials panel.

3. **Use the Line tool to carry up any important points on your terrain surface.**

   In this case, make sure the path begins precisely at the door of the building, so draw vertical lines from the sides of the door to the flat face directly above. That way, you have something to inference to in Step 6.

4. **Choose Camera ⇨ Standard Views ⇨ Top from the menu bar to switch to a top view.**

5. **Choose Camera ⇨ Parallel Projection from the menu bar to turn off perspective.**

6. **On the upper face, draw the edges you want to drape.**

   Make sure that your edges form closed loops to create faces. If they don't, you'll have a miserable time trying to paint the path (in this case) after it's draped onto your terrain surface.

REMEMBER

7. **Orbit your model so you can see both the upper and lower surfaces.**

8. **Soften/smooth the edges of the triangles in your terrain surface (if they aren't already).**

   To do this, follow these steps:

   a. *Select all the edges and faces in your terrain, and then choose Window ⇨ Soften Edges from the menu bar.*

   b. *In the Soften/Smooth Edges panel, move the slider to the far right and make sure that both the Smooth Normals and Soften Coplanar check boxes are selected.*

9. **Select the edges you want to drape.**

   If your edges define closed faces, you can select those faces instead; sometimes that's easier than selecting a bunch of individual edges. Take a look at Chapter 3 for tips on selecting things.

10. Choose Draw ⇨ Sandbox ⇨ Drape from the menu bar to activate the Drape tool.

11. Click once on your terrain surface to drape the edges you selected in Step 9.

It doesn't matter if your terrain is inside a group — the Drape tool works anyway.

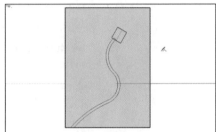

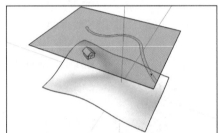

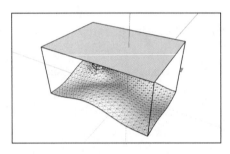

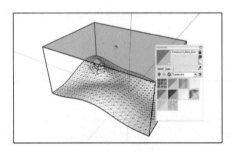

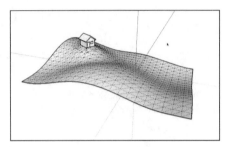

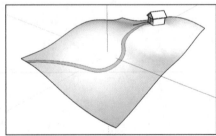

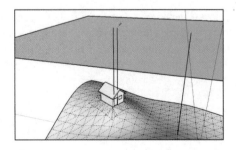

FIGURE 6-24:
Use Drape to transfer edges onto your terrain surface.

TECHNICAL STUFF

Daniel Tal (a landscape architect and SketchUpper extraordinaire who regularly builds models that defy explanation) has written *SketchUp for Site Design: A Guide to Modeling Site Plans, Terrain and Architecture* (published by Wiley), which is available online and at your local bookstore. If you're a site designer, we *highly* recommend checking it out.

Building a Solid Tools Foundation

So-called *solid modeling operations* (fancy people refer to them as *Boolean operations*) give you the ability to create the shapes you need by adding or subtracting other shapes to or from each other. In the next few pages, you discover how to use all six of SketchUp Pro's Solid Tools, giving detailed examples for the three that are the most useful.

REMEMBER

Five of the six Solid Tools are only in the Pro version of SketchUp. Take a look at Table 6-1 (later in this chapter) to see what's available to you.

Understanding solids

Before you can use the Solid Tools, you need *solids*. Here are six things you need to know about solids; you can think of them as the Solid Rules:

>> **A solid is nothing more than an object that's completely enclosed.** It has no holes or other gaps; if you filled it with water, none would leak out. For this reason, solids are sometimes referred to as being *watertight*. Here's another way to think about it: Every edge in a solid must be bordered by two faces.

>> **No extra edges or faces allowed.** You wouldn't think that one or two edges or faces would make much of a difference, but it does — solids can't contain *any* extra geometry, period. Figure 6-25 shows some examples of things that can disqualify otherwise completely enclosed shapes from being solids.

A few SketchUp extensions make it easier to figure out why a particular group or component isn't solid. For starters, check out Solid Inspector[2] by ThomThom. For an introduction to the Extension Warehouse, see Chapter 16.

>> **Only groups and components can be solids.** This one's a biggie. For SketchUp to *realize* something is a solid, you have to make it into either a group or a component first. Another thing: Solid groups and components can't have other groups and/or components nested inside them.

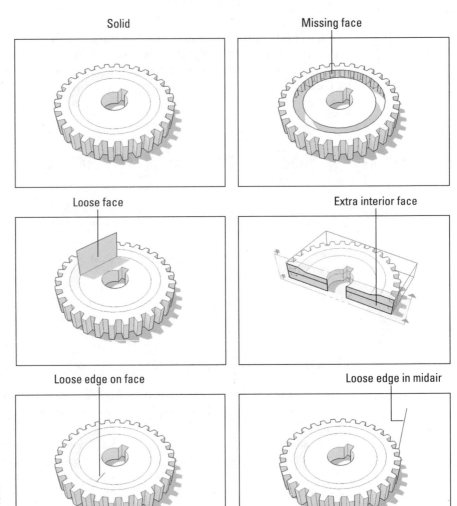

Solid

Missing face

Loose face

Extra interior face

Loose edge on face

Loose edge in midair

FIGURE 6-25:
Solids can't
contain any
extra edges or
faces.

>> **Making a solid doesn't require any special tools.** You don't have to pick
from a special list of objects to create solids; you make them with the same
SketchUp tools you use all the time. Case in point: Every time you've pushed/
pulled a rectangle into a box, you've created a solid.

>> **Check Entity Info to see if your object is a solid.** The easiest way to
tell whether a group or component is a solid is to select it and choose
Window ⇨ Entity Info. If it's solid, this panel will say either "Solid Group"
or "Solid Component." Figure 6-26 shows you where to look.

>> **Solids have volumes.** Manually calculating the volume of a simple shape like a rectangular box is straightforward, but try it for anything more complicated and you'll see why the Volume readout in Entity Info is so great. Figure 6-26 shows where to look.

Check whether your selection is a solid.

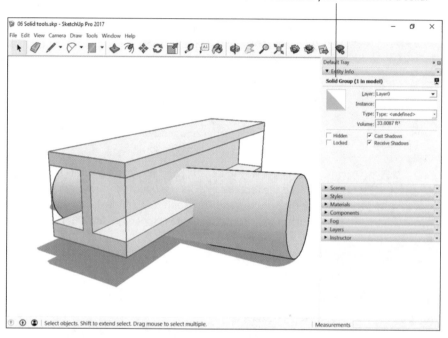

FIGURE 6-26: Check the Entity Info panel to see whether your selection is a solid.

TECHNICAL STUFF

>> **Solids can be made up of multiple shapes.** This one is confusing at first. As long as each individual cluster of geometry within a group or component is completely enclosed, SketchUp considers that group or component to be a solid. It doesn't matter that they're not connected or touching in any way; what's important is that an area of space is fully surrounded by faces.

Checking out the Solid Tools

When you have a solid object or objects, you can use SketchUp's Solid Tools in powerful ways to create shapes that'd otherwise be very complicated and time-consuming to make. For example:

>> Add two solids together to create a new one.

>> Use one solid to cut away part of another one.

TIP

With the SketchUp Intersect Faces tool, you can achieve many of the same things that the Solid Tools do. Intersect Faces takes longer because it requires an awful lot of cleanup; however, it's still useful for two very important reasons: It's available in both the free and Pro versions of SketchUp, and it works on any face in your model — not just on solids. You can read about Intersect Faces in Chapter 4.

Two things you need to know before you start using the Solid Tools:

>> **Open the dedicated toolbar.** Choose View ➪ Toolbars ➪ Solid Tools to open the toolbar that contains all six tools. You can also find them on the Tools menu. Keep in mind that five of them — all but the Outer Shell tool — are available only if you have SketchUp Pro.

>> **To use the Solid Tools, preselect — or don't.** Pick the tool you want to use either *before* or *after* you've told SketchUp which solid objects you want to affect. Like most "order of operations" issues (are you listening, Follow Me tool?), this can be confusing for some folks.

TIP

The easiest way to use the Solid Tools is to preselect the solids and *then* choose the tool to carry out the operation. The glaring exceptions to this rule are the Subtract and Trim tools; both of these depend heavily on the *order* in which you pick your solids. Take a peek at Table 6-1 for more specifics.

Without further ado, here's Table 6-1 with a rundown of the Solid Tools. (Check out Figure 6-27 for a visual.)

TABLE 6-1 ## The Solid Tools

Tool	What It Does and How to Use It	Start With	End With
Union	*What:* Combines two or more solids into a single solid. Deletes overlapping geometry. Preserves internal pockets.*	Two+ solids	One solid
	How: Select the solids you want to use and then activate the tool.		
Outer Shell	*What:* Combines two or more solids into a single solid. Deletes overlapping geometry, including internal pockets.*	Two+ solids	One solid
	How: as Union tool.		
Intersect	*What:* Makes a single solid in which two or more solids overlap. Deletes everything else.	Two+ solids	One solid
	How: Same as Union tool.		
Subtract	*What:* Uses one solid to cut away part of another solid. Deletes the first solid when it's done.	Two solids	One solid
	How: Activate the tool, click "cutting" solid, and then click solid to be cut.		

Tool	What It Does and How to Use It	Start With	End With
Trim	*What:* Uses one solid to cut away part of another solid. Keeps what's left of both solids. *How:* Same as Subtract tool.	Two solids	Two solids
Split	*What:* Cuts two solids where they overlap and creates a new solid from the overlap. Doesn't delete anything. *How:* Same as Union tool.	Two solids	Three solids

An internal pocket is like a solid within a solid — it's a completely enclosed volume that happens to be located inside the main volume of a solid. Picture a SketchUp model of a tennis ball. Because tennis balls have a thickness, you'd need two surfaces to model one: one for the inside, and one for the outside. If you selected both and made a group, you'd have a solid with an internal pocket inside.

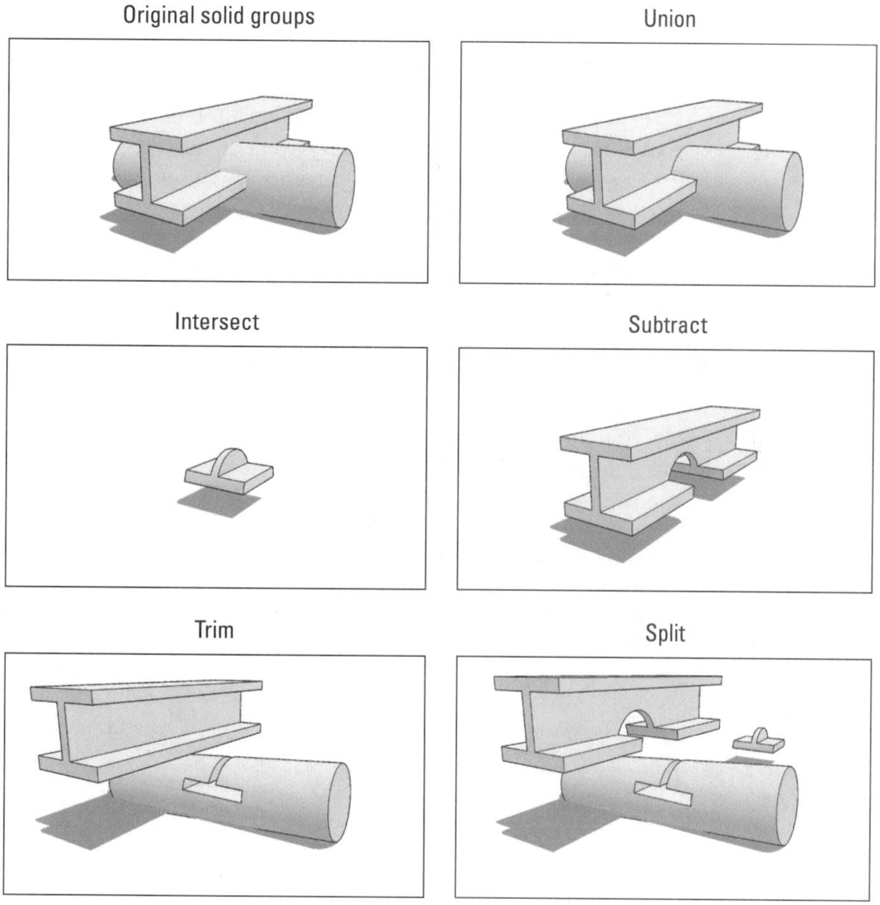

FIGURE 6-27: The Solid Tools let you do additive and subtractive modeling operations.

Note that the Split tool actually does three operations every time you use it: It yields two subtractions and an intersection. That is to say, using Split is like using both Subtract *and* Intersect on your solids. For this reason, you might want to use Split full-time. It's easier to keep track of what's going to happen, and the only downside is that you have to delete a couple extra objects when you're done.

Putting the Solid Tools to work

In this section, you find a few examples of everyday modeling challenges that the Solid Tools can help make less challenging. You're almost certain to encounter these tricky situations while you climb the ladder toward ultimate SketchUp ninjahood.

Assembling complex objects with Union or Outer Shell

Chapter 4 has a section about using the Intersect Faces tool to combine multiple roof pitches into a single, solitary roof. If all those gables, hips, dormers, and other roof elements are solids, you can absolutely use SketchUp's Union or Outer Shell tools to make quick work of the problem.

The same goes for anything that's composed of several disparate elements that you've assembled by moving them together until they overlap. In the spacecraft in Figure 6-28, the *hull* (or body) combines different pieces. Notice the lack of edges where the components intersect? We think edges add detail and definition, especially when a model is displayed using a lines-only style (as it is here). There's also the issue of all the geometry hidden inside the hull. Combining everything together into a single solid helps it shed weight and look better, all at the same time.

FIGURE 6-28:
Using Union or Outer Shell to combine several solids gets rid of internal geometry and adds edges where faces intersect.

Start with several solids

Use Union to put them together

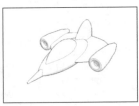

Using Intersect in combination with front, top, and side views

Anyone who's ever tried to model a car with SketchUp knows it's a tricky undertaking. The problem is that cars (and most other vehicles) are kind of curvy; worse yet, they're curvy in several directions.

One trick lots of modelers use to block out a basic shape for things like cars is to start with *orthographic* — straight-on top, front, and side — views of the thing they're trying to model. Here's how the method works:

1. **Position each 2D view where it belongs in 3D space.**

2. **Push/pull them all so their extrusions overlap.**

3. **Use the Intersect tool (Tools ⇨ Solid Tools ⇨ Intersect) to find the object that the extrusions all have in common.**

This method doesn't always produce perfect results, but it's a lot better than guessing. Plus, it's fun. Figure 6-29 shows the technique in action.

Modeling close-fitting parts with Trim

Woodworkers and industrial designers, take heed: SketchUp Pro's Trim tool saves you literally hours of work. Anytime you need to build a model with parts that interlock or otherwise fit together closely, Trim is where you should look first.

Trim basically tells one part to "take a bite" out of another, which is perfect for joinery (dovetails, finger joints, dadoes, and so on), machine parts, ball-and-socket joints, and any other positive/negative conditions where two parts meet.

Figure 6-30 shows how to build a small wooden box with dovetailed sides and a dadoed bottom.

REMEMBER

The only tricky thing about using the Trim tool is remembering which solid to pick first. Remember that the first thing you pick (or click) is the one you want to use to cut with. In the case of the box in Figure 6-30, that would be the side with the dovetails. When you select the dovetails and then select the blank side, the Trim tool cuts the dovetails into the second piece. You get the hang of it after a few tries.

Create solids from front,
top, and side views

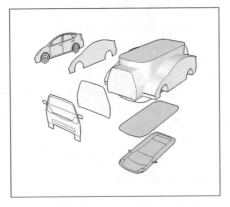

Position them precisely

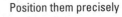

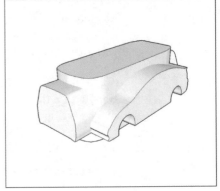

Use Intersect to find shape
they have in common

Smooth edges and use Intersect
Faces with Model to transfer details

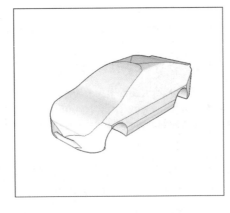

FIGURE 6-29:
If you have
orthographic
views of the
thing you're
trying to
model, you can
use Intersect to
give yourself a
head start.

The Trim tool has a neat trick up its sleeve: You can keep using your cutting solid on multiple other solids. To cut the *dado* (or groove) into the sides of the box in Figure 6-30, follow these steps:

1. Choose Tools ⇨ Solid Tools ⇨ Trim to activate the Trim tool.

Your cursor has the number 1 on it.

2. Select the box bottom.

Your cursor changes to show the number 2.

3. Select one side on the box.

You just cut a dado using the box bottom you picked in Step 2. Your cursor still says 2.

Start with sides as solid components

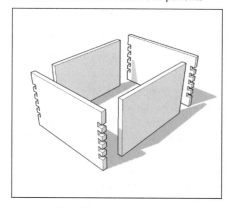

Fit everything together

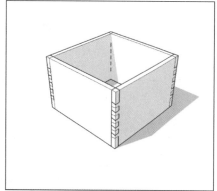

Use Trim to cut dovetails
into other two sides

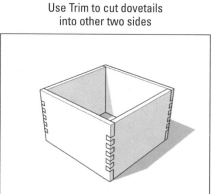

Create bottom to fit

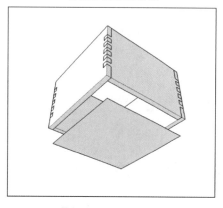

Position bottom and use Trim
to cut dadoes in sides

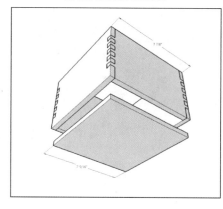

Take everything apart
to make sure it looks right

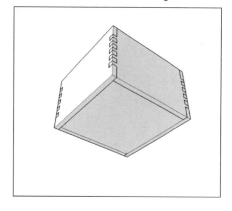

FIGURE 6-30:
The Trim tool
is perfect for
modeling
joinery
and other
close-fitting
parts.

4. Select another of the box's sides to create another dado.

5. Select the remaining two sides to cut dadoes in them, too.

Fun!

TIP

A question that comes up pretty frequently concerning what happens when you use one of the Solid Tools on a component instance. Why doesn't the effect of what you just did affect all the other instances of that component? It should, shouldn't it? Anyone who's read Chapter 5 of this book should know that . . . .

Here's the thing: As soon as you use a Solid Tool on a component instance, SketchUp makes that instance unique; it's still a component — it just isn't connected to the other instances anymore.

Chapter **7**

Keeping Your Model Organized

L iving life can be a messy ordeal, and modeling in SketchUp is no exception. As you crank away at whatever it is you're modeling, you'll reach a time when you stop, orbit around, and wonder how your model got to be such a pigsty. It's inevitable.

Big, unwieldy, disorganized models are a pain. They can slow your computer, or even cause SketchUp to crash. Luckily, SketchUp includes a bunch of different ways to keep your geometry — edges and faces — from getting out of control. This chapter presents SketchUp's two main tools for organizing your model: the Outliner and layers. After we introduce each tool, we explain how to use it and how *not* to use it (are you listening, layers?). This chapter ends with a detailed example of how you can use both tools together to make modeling easier.

Taking Stock of Your Tools

When sorting out the thousands of edges and faces in your model, it's all about lumping things together into useful sets. After you organize geometry into sets, you can name them, hide them, and even lock them so that you (or somebody else) can't mess them up.

TIP

If you haven't read about groups and components yet, now would be a good time to take a look at Chapter 5 — the stuff in this chapter is best understood if you have a firm grasp on the stuff in that one.

You have two organizational methods at your disposal in SketchUp:

>> **Outliner:** The Outliner is basically a fancy list of all the groups and components in your SketchUp model. In the Outliner, you can see which groups and components are nested inside other ones, assign names for them, and easily hide parts of your model that you don't want to see. If you use a lot of components (and you should), the Outliner may well become your new best friend.

>> **Layers:** For people who are used to organizing content in other software programs, layers are usually where it's at — you put different kinds of things on different layers, name the layers, and then turn them on and off when you need to. It's a pretty simple concept. In SketchUp, layers are similar — but the ways in which SketchUp layers work differently are important for modelers to know.

WARNING

In SketchUp, using layers the wrong way can seriously mess up your model. We're not kidding. If you plan to use layers, read the section "Discovering the Ins and Outs of Layers," later in this chapter. Not doing so can result in serious injury or even death — depending on how upset you get when your 50-hour model gets ruined.

IS YOUR MODEL CLASSY?

The folks at SketchUp added an enormously powerful, enormously complicated feature to SketchUp 2014 Pro: Classifications. Basically, it lets you tag groups and components in your model with special identifiers that make them more useful — in very specific circumstances.

If you're using SketchUp Pro as part of a BIM (Building Information Modeling) workflow, *and* you want to imbue your model with juicy metadata while it's still in SketchUp, you can. All you have to do is load an existing classification *schema* and apply Type metadata to the component definitions you want to classify. Not lost yet? If you like, you can even make your own *schemata* (the plural form of "schema") using properly formatted XML to create your own .xsd files. Oof.

Needless to say, Classifications is a feature way beyond the scope of this book. You don't need to use it for basic, everyday modeling; you might not even need to use it if you're designing a new habitation module for the moon. But for folks who *do* need it (and there are more and more of them every year), this feature is a giant step forward for keeping SketchUp Pro integrated with modern, connected BIM software.

Seeing the Big Picture: The Outliner

We both love to make lists. Not only that, but we love to *look at* lists — information arranged neatly into collapsible rows is the kind of thing that comforts our hearts and brings a tear to our eyes.

Now, before you decide that we're so boring that we add zest to our lives by color-coding spreadsheets, consider this: Most halfway-complicated SketchUp models consist of dozens, if not hundreds, of groups and components. These groups and components are nested inside each other like Russian dolls, and many are heavy, computer-killing behemoths like three-dimensional trees and shrubs.

Moreover, the Outliner's list helps you keep track of all your groups and components, hide what you don't want to see, and (more importantly) *unhide* what you *do.* Ready to dive in? We thought so!

Taking a good look at the Outliner

You can open the Outliner panel by choosing Window ⇨ Default Tray ⇨ Outliner (Windows) or Window ⇨ Outliner (Mac). Figure 7-1 shows what the Outliner looks like when a model consists of a simple room with some furniture in it. Each piece of furniture is a separate component from the SketchUp 3D Warehouse.

The Outliner panel has the following features:

>> **Search filter box:** If you type a word or phrase into this box, the Outliner shows only the items in your model that include that word or phrase in their names. For example, type **coffee**, and only the coffee table component is visible.

>> **Outliner Options flyout menu:** This handy little menu contains three options:

- *Expand All:* Choose this option to have the Outliner show *all* the nested groups and components in your model — every last one of them (provided they're on visible layers).

  The Outliner shows only groups and components that exist on visible layers in your model. In other words, anything on a hidden layer doesn't appear in the Outliner, so be extra careful if you're using both the Outliner and layers to organize your model. You can read all about layers in the "Discovering the Ins and Outs of Layers" section, later in this chapter.

REMEMBER

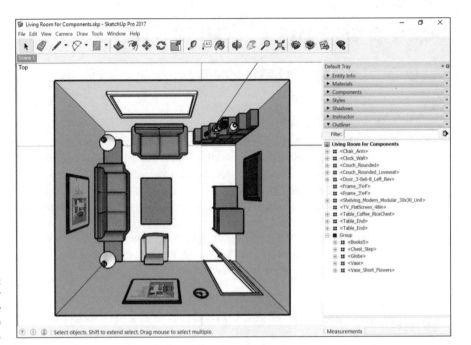

FIGURE 7-1:
The Outliner lists the components in a model.

- *Collapse All:* This option collapses your Outliner view so that you see only *top-level* groups and components — ones that aren't nested inside other groups and components.

- *Sort by Name:* Select this option to make the Outliner list the groups and components in your model alphabetically.

>> **Outliner List window:** All the groups and components in your model are listed here. An icon with four little boxes indicates a component, whereas an icon that's a bigger solid box indicates a group. An Expand/Collapse toggle arrow appears next to a group or component that holds nested groups or components. (You see an example of a group with nested components in Figure 7-1.) You can keep the nested list closed or expand it so that the constituent groups and components appear in the list.

Making good use of the Outliner

REMEMBER

If you use lots of groups and components (and you should), having the Outliner open on-screen is one of the best things you can do to model efficiently.

Here's why:

>> **Use the Outliner to control visibility.** Instead of context-clicking groups and components in your model to hide them, use the Outliner instead. Just context-click the name of any element in the Outliner and choose Hide. When you do, the element is hidden in your modeling window and its name is grayed out and italicized in the Outliner. To unhide it, just context-click its name in the Outliner and choose Unhide.

>> **Drag and drop elements in the Outliner to change their nesting order.** Don't like having the component you just created nested inside another component? Simply drag its name in the Outliner to the top of the list. This moves the component to the top level, meaning that it's not embedded in anything. You can also use the Outliner to drag groups and components into other ones, too.

>> **Find and select things using the Outliner.** Selecting something in the Outliner highlights that something's name and selects it in your modeling window. With this technique, selecting nested groups and components is easy, especially if you're working with a complex model.

Discovering the Ins and Outs of Layers

Layers are a very useful part of SketchUp, and they can make your life a lot easier. Layers can also be a major source of heartache because they can *really* mess up your model if you're not careful. This section can set you on the right track.

What layers are — and what they're not

In a 2D program like Photoshop or Illustrator, the concept of layers makes a lot of sense: You can have content on any number of layers, sort of like a stack of transparencies. You find a distinct order to your layers, so anything on the top layer is visually in front of everything on all the other layers, as shown in Figure 7-2.

But SketchUp isn't a 2D program; it's a 3D program. So how can it have layers? How can objects in three-dimensional space be layered on top of each other so that things on higher layers appear in front of things on lower ones? In short, they can't — it's impossible. Layers in SketchUp are different from layers in most other graphics programs, and that's confusing for lots of people.

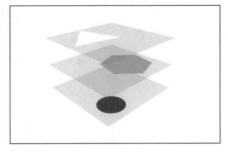

FIGURE 7-2:
In 2D
software,
layers are
pretty
straightforward.

**TECHNICAL
STUFF**

SketchUp has a layers system because some of the very first SketchUp users were architects, and many, *many* architects use AutoCAD drawing software. Because AutoCAD uses layers extensively, layers were incorporated into SketchUp to maximize compatibility between the two products. When you import a layered Auto-CAD file into SketchUp, its layers show up as SketchUp layers, which is pretty convenient. For more information about importing CAD files into SketchUp Pro, take a gander at the last part of Chapter 8.

REMEMBER

So what are SketchUp layers for? Layers control visibility. Use them to gather particular kinds of geometry so that you can easily turn it on (make it visible) and turn it off (make it invisible) when you need to. That said, layers *don't* work the same way as groups and components; your edges and faces aren't isolated from other parts of your model, which can cause major confusion if you're not careful. To find out more, take a look at the section "Staying out of trouble," later in this chapter.

Navigating the Layers panel

The Layers panel, shown in Figure 7-3, is a pretty simple piece of machinery. You open it by choosing Window ➪ Default Tray ➪ Layers (Windows) or Window ➪ Layers (Mac). Here's a quick introduction to the panel features:

- » **Add Layer:** Clicking this button (the plus sign) adds a new layer to your SketchUp file.

- » **Delete Layer:** Click this button (the minus sign) to delete the currently selected layer. If the layer you're trying to delete contains anything, SketchUp asks what you want to do with it; choose an option and click Delete.

- » **Layer Options flyout menu:** This menu offers the following useful options:

  - *Purge:* When you choose Purge, SketchUp deletes all the layers that don't contain geometry. This is a handy way to keep your file neat and tidy.

  - *Color by Layer:* Notice how each layer in the list has a little material swatch next to it? Choosing Color by Layer temporarily changes all the colors in your SketchUp model to match the colors (or textures) assigned to each layer. To see what's on each layer, go straight to this option.

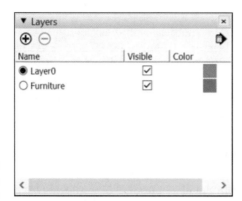

FIGURE 7-3:
The Layers
panel.

>> **Layers list:** This lists all the layers in your SketchUp file. You need to know about these three columns:

- *Name:* Double-click a layer's name to edit it. Giving your layers meaningful names is a good way to quickly find what you want.

- *Visible:* This check box is the heart and soul of the Layers panel. When it's selected, the geometry on that layer is visible; when the check box isn't selected, the layer's geometry isn't visible.

- *Color:* You can choose to view your model using Color by Layer, described earlier in the list. You can choose which material (color or texture) to assign to each layer by clicking the Color swatch.

Moving entities to a different layer

Moving things from one layer to another involves using the Entity Info panel. Follow these steps to move an *entity* (an edge, face, group, or component) to a different layer:

1. **Select the entity or entities you want to move to another layer.**

Move only groups and components to other layers; have a look at the next section in this chapter to find out why.

REMEMBER

2. **Open the Entity Info panel in the Default Tray (Windows) or choose Window ⇨ Entity Info (Mac).**

You can also open it by context-clicking your selected entities and choosing Entity Info.

3. **In the Entity Info panel, choose a layer from the Layer drop-down list.**

Your selected entities are now on the layer you chose from the list.

The Entity Info panel offers another, slightly trickier, way to add a new layer and move entities to a new layer. In the Entity Info panel, type a new layer name into the Layer field and press Enter. SketchUp both creates a new layer with that name and moves whatever geometry is currently selected onto it. We suggest you save this particular time-saver until you have experience working with layers. Nothing about Layers is as straightforward as it seems.

Staying out of trouble

Layers can be really helpful, but you need to know how to use them; if you don't, bad things can happen. Check out the following do's and don'ts before you start working with layers:

>> **Do all your modeling on Layer0.** Always make sure that Layer0 is your current layer when you're working. Keeping all your loose geometry (that's not part of a group or component) together in one place is the *only* way to make sure that you don't end up with edges and faces all over the place. SketchUp, unfortunately, lets you put geometry on whatever layer you want, which means that you can end up with a face on one layer, and one or more of the edges that define it on another. When that happens, working out where everything belongs is next to impossible; you'll spend hours trying to straighten out your model. This property of SketchUp's layers system is a major stumbling point for new SketchUp users; knowing to keep everything on Layer0 can save you a lot of anguish.

>> **Don't move anything but groups and components to other layers.** If you're going to use layers, follow this rule: *Never* put anything on a layer other than Layer0 unless it's a group or a component. Doing so ensures that stray edges and faces don't end up on separate layers.

>> **Use layers to organize big groups of similar things.** More complicated SketchUp models often include things like trees, furniture, cars, and people. These kinds of things are almost always already components, so they're perfect for organizing on separate layers. For example, you can make a Trees layer and put all your tree components on it. Because trees are usually big, complicated components with lots of faces, hiding all your trees at once with the layers feature is a handy way to improve your computer's performance.

>> **Don't use layers to organize interconnected geometry; use the Outliner instead.** By *interconnected geometry,* we mean things like building floor levels and staircases. These model parts aren't meant to be physically separate from other parts in the way that vehicles and people are. When you put Level 1 on one layer and Level 2 on another, more often than not, you become confused about what belongs where: Is the staircase part of Level 1 or Level 2? Instead, make a group for Level 1, a group for Level 2, and a group for the staircase — you'll need less headache medicine at the end of the day.

TIP

>> **Feel free to use layers to iterate.** *Iteration* is the process of doing multiple versions of the same thing. Lots of designers work this way to figure out problems and present different options to their clients. Using layers is a great way to iterate: You can move each version of the thing you're working on to a different layer, and then turn the layers on and off to show each in turn. Just remember to follow the rule about using groups and components only on separate layers (mentioned previously), and you'll be fine.

TIP

Check out the sidebar "Using Scenes to control layers" (later in this chapter) for a nifty way to quickly flip through layers that represent design iterations in your model.

Putting It All Together

In this chapter (and in Chapter 5), we talk about each of SketchUp's organizational methods in isolation: discussing how they work, why they're special, and when to use them. When you're actually working in SketchUp, you probably use a combination of them all, so we thought you'd find an example of all the organizational tools in action especially helpful.

Figure 7-4 shows a model of a house that Aidan created. Here's how all the organizational tools are working together to keep the model organized:

>> **Each floor level is a group.** Organizing each floor into a group enables you to hide whichever one you're not working on, so you can see what you're doing and SketchUp runs a little faster. Aidan included the house's only staircase in the first floor group, because that turned out to be the easiest thing to do, but you might also make the staircase a separate group, too.

TIP

Aidan included the interior walls on each level in that level's group. For most buildings, you can probably do the same, unless you plan to study different floor plans with different interior wall arrangements.

>> **The roof and exterior walls are groups inside of another group.** To remove the roof and the exterior walls separately, each needs to be a group. However, to hide and unhide them both at the same time, Aidan made a Shell group that includes them both. With this setup, he can selectively show or hide just the geometry he wants to see. See Figure 7-5.

REMEMBER

The floor levels, roof, and exterior walls are groups instead of components because they're *unique*. A house has only one first floor, so that floor doesn't need to be a component.

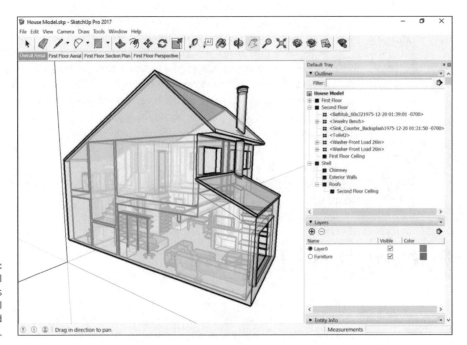

FIGURE 7-4:
Aidan used all of SketchUp's organizational tools to build this model.

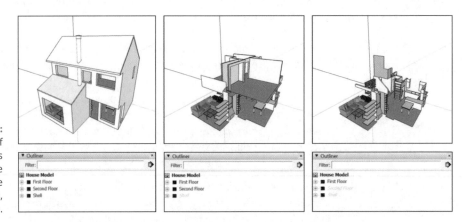

FIGURE 7-5:
Each floor of the house, as well as the roof and the exterior walls, is a group.

>> **All the furniture and plumbing fixtures are components.** To furnish the house, Aidan created furniture components himself or used components from the Components panel and 3D Warehouse.

TIP

When you have only one couch, why make it a component instead of a group? By making every piece of furniture in a model a component, you can see the furniture listed in the In Model collection of the Components panel. You can also save your furniture as a separate component collection on your computer. The next time you move, you have all your furniture in a single place, ready to drop into a model of your new house.

USING SCENES TO CONTROL LAYERS

In SketchUp, *scenes* are basically saved views of your model. Instead of fiddling with navigation tools and panels every time you want to return to an important view, you can click a scene tab.

Although you learn the details about scenes in Chapter 11, scenes are relevant in this chapter because scenes don't just save different camera positions; you can also use them to control layer visibility. Being able to click a scene tab to instantly change which layers are showing is a crazy-powerful way to do *iterative design:* creating and presenting different options within the same design.

A very simple example: You've modeled a living room and want to try three different furniture configurations:

1. **Make three layers — Option 1, Option 2, and Option 3.**
2. **Do three separate furniture arrangements, one per layer.**

   Of course, this means that you have three copies of each object you move.

3. **Use the Layers panel to show Option 1, and hide Option 2 and Option 3.**
4. **Create a new scene and name it Option 1 using the Scenes panel.**
5. **Repeat Steps 3 and 4 for the other two configurations.**

Now all you have to do is click a scene tab to switch among the three options; this is much more elegant than having to fiddle with the Layers panel during a presentation.

To make this technique really sing, you need a working knowledge of the Properties to Save check boxes in the Scenes panel. Although this technique combining layers and scenes isn't beginner-level stuff, you can probably easily get the hang of it after you have some practice with both layers and scenes. After you get the hang of this technique, it's an elegant way to work. Pick your way through Chapter 11, when you're ready.

One more useful tidbit: The Layer Tools plugin lets you (among other things) create a new layer that isn't visible in any of the scenes you've made previously. This plugin comes in handy when you need to add a new iteration *after* you've already made a bunch of scenes. You find plug-ins in the Extension Warehouse, introduced in Chapter 16.

» **All the furniture is on a separate layer.** Furniture components can be a little *heavy* — that is, they tax your computer system. With the furniture on a layer, you can easily hide it all. This setup also enables you to see your space without furniture. Remember that you can control the visibility of a layer with a single mouse click.

TIP

But why not just create a group from all the furniture components and use the Outliner to hide and unhide them all, instead of bothering with layers? Good question. Changing a component's layer is easier than adding a component to an existing group. To add something to a group, you need to use the Outliner to drag and drop that something in the proper place; with complex models, this can be a hassle. Changing a component's layer is just a matter of using the Entity Info panel to choose from a list.

IN THIS CHAPTER

» Applying photos to a model's faces

» Building a model from scratch with SketchUp's photo-matching tools

» Using photo-matching to match your model to a photograph

» Giving your model a geographic location

» Starting out with a 2D CAD file in SketchUp Pro

Chapter **8**

Modeling with Photos and Other Resources

uilding a model from scratch is all fine and well, but to help you along, SketchUp can import a whole lot of information — in the form of digital photos, 3D terrain data, and even existing 2D CAD.

If you have a model you want to paint with photographs, you can do that. You can apply photos to faces and then use the information in the pictures to help with modeling. Building windows is a lot easier when they're painted right on the wall. That's what we talk about in the first part of this chapter.

If you want to use a photo as a basis for modeling something that exists in the real world, you can do that in SketchUp, too. With the Match Photo feature, you can import a picture and trace what you see with SketchUp's modeling tools.

If you're modeling a building or other structure that you plan to build on land, you can find your desired location on an online map and import the terrain right into your model — well, a digital representation of the terrain. (You can also import certain types of terrain files if you have those instead.)

If you're working with SketchUp Pro, you can import a CAD file to use as a starting point for a 3D model. The import process isn't hard, but it's helpful to understand a few hints before you try it for the first time.

Painting Faces with Photos

Technically, painting surfaces with pictures using 3D software is called *mapping,* as in "I *mapped* a photo of your face to the underside of the pile-driver model I'm building." Different software programs have different methods for mapping pictures to faces. Luckily, in SketchUp, the process is pretty straightforward.

The following sections deal with mapping photos to two kinds of faces: flat and curved. The tools are similar, but the methods aren't. We explain both, because you never know what you're going to run into.

TIP

SketchUp uses lots of terms to refer to the stuff you can paint faces with; generically, they're all *materials.* Materials can be colors or textures; *textures* are image-based, and *colors* are a single, solid hue. When you import an image to map it to a face, the images becomes a texture — just like any of the other textures in your Materials panel. Read more about using materials in Chapter 3.

Adding photos to flat faces

When mapping photos onto flat faces, you can choose the hard way or the easy way. Unfortunately, the hard way is the method you end up using the vast majority of the time, so we describe it first. Importing images by using the File menu lets you take any image and map it to any flat face in your model.

The easy way is designed for one particular case: It gives you access to Google's huge collection of Street View imagery, letting you paint your models with building facades photographed by Google's roving fleet. The feature is cool, but also very specific.

Importing images: Use your own photos

Before you follow these steps, make sure you have at least one face in your model; you map your texture to a face. When you're ready, here's how to place the image onto that face:

1. **Choose File ⇨ Import.**

    The Import dialog box opens.

2. **Select the image file you want to use as a texture.**

You can use JPEGs, TIFFs, and PNGs as textures in SketchUp; all these are common image file formats.

3. **In the Use Image As area, select the Texture option, as shown in Figure 8-1.**

FIGURE 8-1:
Tell SketchUp you want to use the image as a texture.

4. **Click the Import button.**

The Import dialog box closes, Paint Bucket becomes your active tool, and its cursor is loaded with the image you chose to import.

5. **Click once in the lower-left corner of the face you want to paint. (See Figure 8-2.)**

Your click tells SketchUp where to position the lower-left corner of the image you're using as a texture. Although you can click anywhere on the face you're trying to paint, clicking the lower-left corner keeps things simple.

6. **Click somewhere else on the face you're painting. (See Figure 8-2.)**

Unless the proportions of your image perfectly match the face onto which it was mapped, your image repeats. Don't worry — that's normal. SketchUp automatically tiles your image to fill the whole face. If you want to edit your new texture so that it doesn't look tiled (and you probably do), skip to the later section, "Editing your textures." You can scale, rotate, skew, or even stretch your texture to make it look however you want. See the nearby sidebar, "When is an image a texture?" for more background details.

WHEN IS AN IMAGE A TEXTURE?

Time for a little bit of theory: Image textures in SketchUp are made up of *tiles*. To make a large area of texture, such as a brick wall, SketchUp uses a bunch of tiles right next to each other. In the case of a brick wall, the face of a model may look like thousands of bricks, but the effect is really just the same tile of about 50 bricks repeated over and over again.

Because SketchUp treats imported image textures just like any other texture, what you're really doing when you click to locate the upper-right corner of your image is this: You're telling SketchUp how big to make the tile for your new photo texture. Don't worry too much about getting the size right the first time. You can always tweak things later.

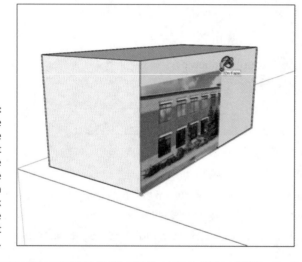

FIGURE 8-2:
Click once to locate the lower-left corner of the image you're using as a texture. Click again to locate the upper-right corner.

Get photo texture: Use online imagery

Google Street View offers an immersive and spookily cool way to experience the outside world from the lazy comfort of your computer screen.

Google Street View and SketchUp got wired together back in SketchUp 8, when Google owned SketchUp. Since then, you've been able to grab imagery from the former and use it in the latter. If your goal is to build photo-textured models of real-world buildings, you're in luck.

TIP

To use this feature, you must meet two important prerequisites:

» **Your model must be *geo-located.*** You must have already told SketchUp precisely where your model is by adding a geo-location snapshot to your file. If the preceding sentence makes no sense to you, consult the section "Geo-locating your model," later in this chapter.

» **Street View data must exist for the thing you're trying to texture.** Google has photographed an awful lot of places, but it's always possible that wherever you're working isn't one of them.

Follow these steps to paint a flat face in your model with Google Street View imagery:

1. **Select the face you want to paint with Street View imagery.**

   Selecting a rectangle-shaped face helps. You see why in a couple steps.

2. **Choose Edit⇨Face⇨Add Photo Texture.**

   The Photo Textures window pops up. If Street View data isn't available for the location where you're modeling, this is when you find out.

3. **Frame the imagery you want to use in the window:**

   - Click and drag to swivel the "camera."
   - Click the arrows superimposed on the photo to move up and down the street.
   - Zoom in and out using the + and − buttons.
   - If you need to, resize the whole window to get a better view.

4. **Click the Select Region button in the upper-right corner of the window.**

   A rectangle with blue pins at the corners appears, and the fun part begins.

5. **Drag the blue pins to define an area to paint on the face you selected in Step 1. (See Figure 8-3.)**

6. **Click the Grab button to paint the face you selected in Step 1 with the imagery you defined in Step 5.**

7. **Close the Photo Textures window.**

The photo textures you apply using Add Photo Texture are like any other photo textures in your model. You can edit the texture in exactly the same way, as we explain in the next section.

FIGURE 8-3:
You can use the Google Street View imagery to photo-texture your model.

Editing your textures

After you successfully map an image to a face, you probably want to change the image somehow: Make it bigger, flip it over, rotate it — you get the idea. This is where the Position Texture tool comes in.

The Position Texture tool is actually more of a mode; we call it Texture Edit mode. Within this mode, you can be in either of two *submodes*. Their names are less important than what they do, so that's how we describe them:

>> **Move/Scale/Rotate/Shear/Distort Texture mode:** Use this mode to move, scale, rotate, shear, or distort your texture (surprised?). Technically, this mode is called *Fixed Pin mode*. You see why in a moment.

>> **Stretch Texture mode:** Stretch Texture mode lets you edit your texture by *stretching* it to fit the face it's painted on. If you want to map a photograph of a building facade to your model, this is the mode you want to use. In the SketchUp Help documentation, Stretch Texture mode is called *Free Pin mode*, in case you're interested.

REMEMBER

You can edit textures only on flat surfaces; the Position Texture tool doesn't work on curved surfaces. For details about working with textures and curved surfaces, see "Adding photo textures to curved surfaces" later in this chapter.

Moving, scaling, rotating, shearing, and distorting your texture

The title of this section pretty much says it all — doing the aforementioned things to your texture involves Texture Edit mode, which is a little bit hidden, unfortunately. Follow these steps to move, scale, rotate, or skew your texture:

1. **With the Select tool, click the face with the texture you want to edit.**

2. **Choose Edit ⇨ Face ⇨ Texture ⇨ Position.**

   This command enables (deep breath) the Move/Scale/Rotate/Shear/Distort Texture mode. You see a transparent version of your image, along with four pins, each a different color, as shown in Figure 8-4. If all your pins are yellow, you're in Stretch Texture mode. Context-click your textured face and select Fixed Pins to switch to the correct mode.

FIGURE 8-4: Dragging each colored pin does something different.

TIP

   A quicker way to get to Texture Edit mode is to context-click the textured face and then choose Texture ⇨ Position from the context menu.

3. **Edit your texture.**

   At this point, you can edit your texture in two ways: by using the options on a context menu or by dragging the colored pins.

Context-clicking your texture opens a context menu with the following options:

- *Done:* Tells SketchUp you're finished editing your texture.

- *Reset:* Undoes all the changes you've made to your texture.

- *Flip:* Flips your texture left to right or up and down, depending on which suboption you choose.

- *Rotate:* Rotates your texture 90, 180, or 270 degrees, depending on the suboption you choose.

- *Fixed Pins:* When this option is selected, you're in Move/Scale/Rotate/Shear/ Distort Texture mode (Fixed Pin mode). Deselecting it switches you over to Stretch Texture mode, discussed in the upcoming section "Stretching a photo over a face."

- *Undo/Redo:* Goes back or forward a step in your working process.

Dragging each of the colored pins has a different effect (refer to Figure 8-4):

- *Scale/Shear (Blue) pin:* Scales and shears your texture while you drag it. *Shearing* keeps the top and bottom edges parallel while making the image "lean" to the left or right.

- *Distort (Yellow) pin:* Distorts your texture while you drag it; in this case, the distortion looks kind of like a perspective effect.

- *Scale/Rotate (Green) pin:* Scales and rotates your texture while you drag it.

- *Move (Red) pin:* Moves your texture around while you drag it. Of all four colored pins, this one is the most useful. It's great for precisely positioning brick, shingle, and other building material textures in a model.

4. **In your modeling window, click anywhere outside your texture to exit Texture Edit mode.**

   You can also press Enter or context-click and choose Done from the context menu.

Stretching a photo over a face

Imagine a photograph printed on a piece of fabric that you can stretch until the photo looks the way you want and that you hold in place with pins. That's basi-cally how Stretch Texture mode (also known as Free Pin mode) works.

Follow these steps to stretch your texture using the Position Texture tool's Stretch Texture mode:

1. **With the Select tool, click the face with the texture you want to edit.**

2. **Choose Edit ⇨ Face ⇨ Texture ⇨ Position.**

   A quicker way to get to Texture Edit mode is to context-click the textured face and choose Texture ⇨ Position from the context menu.

3. **Context-click your texture and clear the check mark next to the Fixed Pins option. (Make sure that no check mark is next to it.)**

   You switch to Stretch Texture mode. Instead of four differently colored pins with little symbols next to them, you see four white pins. (The pins used to be yellow.)

4. **Click and drag each pin to reposition it until your photo stretches over the face in a way you like.**

   TIP

   If you're repositioning a photo of a building, click a pin to pick it up, and then click to place the pin at a corner of the building, as shown in Figure 8-5. Then, drag each pin to a corner of the face to stretch the photo.

FIGURE 8-5:
Place the pin at the corresponding corner (upper left to upper left, for instance) of the building in your photo.

If you need to, feel free to orbit, zoom, and pan around your model to get the best view of what you're doing; just use the scroll wheel on your mouse to navigate without switching tools.

5. **Press Enter to exit Texture Edit mode.**

If you don't like what you see, go back and edit the texture again; you can muck around as many times as you like.

Scaling your model until the photo looks right

When you're happy with the way your texture is stretched to fit the face, one of two things will be true:

>> **The proportions are correct.** By this, we mean that the photo doesn't look stretched or squashed. This is the case only if the face to which you applied the photo texture was already exactly the right size.

>> **The proportions aren't correct.** If the photo texture you just "tweaked" looks stretched or squashed, the face it's on is the wrong size. No worries — you just need to adjust the whole face until the texture looks right. Better yet, if you know how big the face is *supposed* to be (in real life), you can stretch it until it's correct.

Follow these steps to stretch a face until the texture looks right:

1. **Use the Tape Measure tool to create guides that you can use to accurately stretch your face.**

   If you don't know how many feet wide your building is, take your best guess and see how the result looks. Chapter 3 explains how to use the Tape Measure tool and guides.

2. **Select the face you want to stretch — or your whole model if you're just roughing out your model.**

   If your model is at a fairly early stage, it's easiest to select the whole kit and caboodle. Triple-click the face with the Select tool to select it and everything attached to it.

 3. **Choose Tools ⇨ Scale to activate the Scale tool. Or select the Scale tool on the toolbar.**

   When the Scale tool is active, the SketchUp scaling box surrounds your model. Its 27 little green cubes (or *grips*) and thick, yellow lines are hard to miss.

4. **Scale your selection to the right size. (See Figure 8-6.)**

   Use the Scale tool by clicking the grips and moving your cursor to stretch whatever's selected (including your texture). Click again to stop scaling.

 To scale something precisely using a guide, click a scale grip to grab it and then hover your pointer over the relevant guide to tell SketchUp that's where you want to scale *to*. Click again to finish the scale operation.

TIP

FIGURE 8-6:
Use the Scale tool's grips to stretch your selection (texture and all).

It's perfectly normal to want to keep modeling with your photo-textured faces; tracing a window and pushing it in a bit with the Push/Pull tool is one of the most satisfying things you can do in SketchUp. Flip ahead a few pages and take a look at the "Modeling on Top of Photo Textures" section to discover everything you need to know.

Editing the pixels in a texture image

Perhaps there's something *in* a photograph you're using, and you don't want it to be there. You can use Edit Texture Image to open the texture you've selected in an image-editing program, where you can edit the texture directly.

Follow these steps to use Edit Texture Image:

1. **Context-click the texture in your model you want to edit and choose Texture ⇨ Edit Texture Image.**

2. **In the program that opens, make whatever changes you need to make.**

   Be sure not to change the *proportions* of the image — that can really mess things up.

3. **Save (don't Save As and change the filename) the image you're editing and close it if you like.**

4. **Back in SketchUp, check to make sure your edits have been applied.**

Which image-editing program actually opens depends on what you have installed on your computer; you specify which one to use in the Applications panel of the Preferences dialog box. For what it's worth, most designers use Adobe Photoshop, but you can use whatever you have.

TIP

Need to radically reduce the size of your SketchUp model file? Context-click any textured face in your model and choose Make Unique Texture to create a copy of the texture you've selected and *crop* (trim away everything that isn't visible) that copy according to the face it's on. Why is this important? Just because you can't see part of an image doesn't mean it's not there; SketchUp saves the whole photo with the model, even if you use only a little bit of it. In a complex model with dozens of photo textures, all that invisible, extra photo data adds up. Making your textures unique can make your models much, much smaller.

Adding photo textures to curved surfaces

Notice how the title of this section ends with *surfaces* and not with *faces?* That's because (as you know by now) individual faces in SketchUp are always flat — no exceptions. When you see a non-flat surface, it's actually made up of multiple faces. You can't see the edges between them because they've been *smoothed.* Choosing View ⇨ Hidden Geometry exposes all curved surfaces for what they really are. Refer to Chapter 3 for a refresher.

How you go about mapping an image to a curved surface in SketchUp depends on what type of curved surface you have. With that in mind, curved surfaces fall into two general categories (see Figure 8-7):

>> **Single-direction curves:** A cylinder is a classic example of a surface that curves only in one direction. In SketchUp, a cylinder is basically a series of rectangles set side by side. Most curved walls you see on buildings are the same way; they don't taper in or out as they rise.

TIP

Another way to think about single-direction curves is to consider how they might have been made. If the curved surface you're staring at could be the result of a single push/pull operation (such as turning a circle into a cylinder), there's an excellent chance it's single-direction.

For mapping an image to a single-curve surface, you can use the Adjacent Faces method; it works well and doesn't stretch your image.

>> **Multi-direction curves:** Terrain objects, saddles, and curtains are all prime examples of surfaces that curve in more than one direction at a time. They're always composed of triangles — never basic rectangles.

To map an image to this type of curved surface, you must use the Projected Texture method. Skip ahead a couple pages to read all about it.

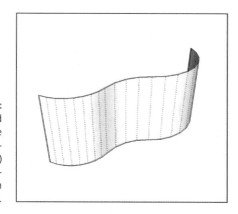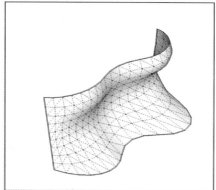

FIGURE 8-7:
All curved surfaces are either single-direction (left) or multi-direction (right).

TIP

Please keep in mind that we totally made up names for the Adjacent Faces and Projected Texture methods of mapping images to non-flat surfaces. We had to call them *something*, and these sounded descriptive without seeming too technical.

The Adjacent Faces method

If you need to paint an image onto a surface that curves only in a single direction (such as a cylinder), you can use this technique. Follow these steps to find out how and take a look at Figure 8-8 to see the process in action:

1. **Choose View ⇨ Hidden Geometry to turn on Hidden Geometry so you can see the individual faces in your model.**

2. **"Load" your cursor with an imported image.**

   Follow Steps 1–4 in "Importing images: Use your own photos" (earlier in this chapter) to import an image as a texture.

3. **Paint the leftmost sub-face entirely with the image.**

   Your curved surface is composed of sub-faces. Here's how to paint the correct one:

   a. *Hover your loaded cursor over the lower-left corner of the sub-face farthest to the left. Don't click yet.*

   b. *When the image is oriented in the right direction, click once.*

   c. *Click again on the upper-right corner of the same sub-face.*

   This places the image; it should be cropped on the right.

4. **Select the Paint Bucket tool, hold down the Alt key (Command on a Mac), and click the first sub-face to sample the texture (image) you just placed.**

   This "loads" your Paint Bucket tool with the texture.

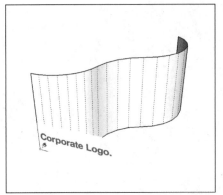

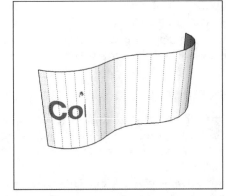

FIGURE 8-8:
The Adjacent Faces method lets you map images to simple curved surfaces.

5. **With the Paint Bucket tool, click once on the face immediately to the right of the face you painted in Step 3.**

   If everything's working correctly, the image you placed appears on the face you just clicked.

6. **Keep painting sub-faces until you're done.**

   Remember to work your way from left to right; skipping a sub-face messes up things. To fix a problem, just use Undo and keep going.

The Projected Texture method

For painting an image onto a complex curved surface, there's no substitute for this method. Chunks of terrain are good examples of complex curved surfaces — bumpy, twisted, rippled, and multi-directional. If the curve you're dealing with is more complicated than a simple extrusion, you need to use this image-mapping technique.

The key is to line up a flat surface with the curved surface to which you want to apply the photo texture. You then "paint" the flat surface with the texture, make it projected, sample it, and finally, paint the curved surface with the projected, sampled texture. Whew.

Follow these steps to get the basic idea (see Figure 8-9):

1. **Create a flat surface that lines up with your curved surface.**

You can use the Line tool and SketchUp's inferencing system to draw a flat face that lines up with (and is the same size as) your curved surface.

2. **Apply a photo texture to your flat surface and make sure that it's positioned correctly.**

For help, see "Adding photos to flat faces" earlier in this chapter.

Hidden Geometry off

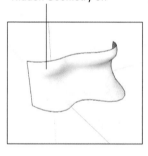
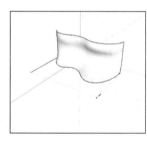
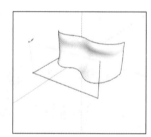
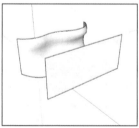
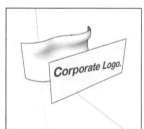

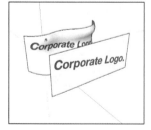
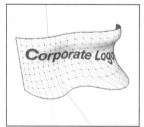

FIGURE 8-9: Mapping projected textures to curved surfaces is possible, but it ain't easy.

3. **Context-click the textured face and choose Texture ⇨ Projected.**

   This ensures that the texture is projected, which is the key to this whole operation.

4. **Select the Paint Bucket tool, hold down the Alt key (Command on a Mac), and click the projected texture to sample it.**

   This "loads" your Paint Bucket tool with the projected texture.

5. ***Without* pressing anything on your keyboard, click the curved surface to paint it with the projected texture.**

   The pixels in the image likely look stretched in some places.

6. **Delete the flat surface that you originally mapped the image to; you don't need it anymore.**

TIP

If you're trying to do this task on your own curved surface and things don't seem to be working, your curved surface is probably part of a group or component. Either explode or double-click to edit the group or component before you do Step 5 and see whether that helps. Chapter 5 explains how to edit groups and components.

Modeling Directly from a Photo: Introducing Photo-Matching

The first time we saw SketchUp's photo-matching feature in action, we giggled and clapped our hands like toddlers at a petting zoo. We're not ashamed of it, either. Sometimes technology that's so useful, so *unexpectedly satisfying*, comes along, and you just can't help yourself.

So what does photo-matching do? If you have a good photograph (or multiple photographs) of the thing you want to model, SketchUp's photo-matching feature can help you create your model. This application is how 99 percent of modelers use this feature, and the technique we focus on in this section. (You can also match an existing model to a photo.)

REMEMBER

You can edit any texture in your model — including ones produced by photo-matching — by opening them in image-editing software (such as Photoshop) directly from SketchUp. This trick is handy for taking out stuff you might not want in your photos, such as trees, cars, and ex-husbands. Take a look at the section "Editing the pixels in a texture image," earlier in this chapter, for all the juicy details.

Choosing a Match Photo-friendly image

Photo-matching works only on photographs of objects with at least one pair of surfaces that are at right angles to each other. Luckily, this includes millions of things you may want to build. But still, if the thing you want to photo-match is entirely round, or wavy, or even triangular, this method won't work.

Here are tips for choosing a photo for this process:

>> **Watch out for lens distortion.** When you take a picture with a wide-angle lens, some straight lines in the image bow a little bit, depending on where they are in the frame. Try to use photos taken with a normal or telephoto lens: 50mm to 100mm is a good bet.

>> **Make sure that the edges of two perpendicular surfaces are visible in the shot.** You need to see planes that are at right angles to each other in order to use photo-matching properly.

>> **Shoot at a 45-degree angle if you can.** Because of the way perspective works, your results are more accurate if you use a photograph in which you can see both perpendicular surfaces clearly; if one of them is sharply distorted, you have a harder time.

The following types of photos, illustrated in Figure 8-10, work especially well with SketchUp's Match Photo feature:

>> An interior view of a room in which a corner meets at a right angle

>> An aerial shot

>> An exterior view taken from a human vantage point and in which a corner (or corners) meet at a right angle

Inside   Above   Outside

FIGURE 8-10:
Choose the style that best describes your photograph's camera position.

Modeling by photo-matching

The Match Photo feature helps you build a model based on a photograph. Here are two basic concepts:

>> **The process is iterative, not linear.** Building a model using a matched photo entails going between drawing edges, orbiting around, drawing more edges, going back to your matched photo scene, and drawing yet more edges. Every photo is different, so the ones you work with will present unique challenges that you'll (hopefully) have fun figuring out.

>> **Don't forget the photo textures.** By far one of the coolest features of photo-matching is the ability to automatically photo-texture your model's faces by using your photograph as "paint." It's a one-button operation, and it's guaranteed to make you smile.

Follow these steps to start building a model from a photo:

1. **Choose Camera ⇨ Match New Photo.**

   A dialog box opens.

2. **Select the image on your computer that you want to use and click the Open button.**

   The dialog box closes, and you see the image you chose in your modeling window. You also see a jumble of colorful techno-spaghetti, as shown in Figure 8-11. Don't worry — it's all part of the photo-matching interface.

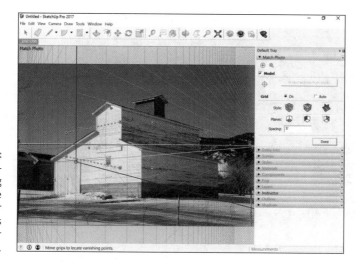

FIGURE 8-11:
The photo-matching interface includes your picture, plus lots of other things.

3. **In the Match Photo panel, choose the style that matches your photograph: Inside, Above (for an aerial view), or Outside (for an outdoor view taken at ground level).**

   For the barn shown in this example, we selected Outside.

4. **Click and drag the end points of the green perspective bars so that each bar lines up with edges in the photo that should be parallel to the model's green axis.**

   The tops and bottoms of windows are good candidates, as are rooflines, tabletops, and ceiling tiles. In our example, we align the green perspective bars with the barn's roofline.

   The following tips can help you position the bars correctly:

   TIP

   - Zoom in and out (using the scroll wheel on your mouse) to better view your photograph while you place your perspective bars. The more accurately you place the bars, the better things will turn out.

   - Match your perspective bars to nice, long edges in your photograph; you get better results that way.

5. **Click and drag the endpoints of the red perspective bars so that they line up with edges in the photo that should be parallel to the model's red axis.**

   REMEMBER

   The edges must be perpendicular to the first set of edges, or photo-matching doesn't work. In our example, we align the red perspective bars to edges on the barn's siding that are also perpendicular to the green perspective bars. You can see the result in Figure 8-12.

FIGURE 8-12:
The perspective bars are aligned with the roofline and siding.

6. **Drag the *axis origin* (the little square where the axes come together) to a place where your building touches the ground and right at the intersection of two perpendicular edges, as shown in Figure 8-13.**

Setting the axis origin is how you tell SketchUp where the ground plane is. After you set the axis origin in the right place, notice that the horizon line, which is the horizontal yellow bar, lines up with the horizon in your photo.

As long as you place the perspective bars correctly, the horizon line bar typically takes care of itself. However, now you know what the yellow horizon line bar does in case you need it.

FIGURE 8-13:
The axis origin is on a corner that touches the ground.

7. **(Optional) In the Match Photo panel, set the grid spacing so that you can roughly scale your model to your photo.**

In our example, we leave the Spacing option set to the default of 5 feet. We know the barn is about 20 feet tall. 4 gridlines are all we need to scale the model to the photo (because $4 \times 5 = 20$).

If you're photo-matching an arena or a skyscraper, you probably need to adjust the grid spacing so that the grid can scale to such a large width or height.

8. **Click the Done button in the Match Photo panel.**

When you click the Done button, you stop editing your matched photo. All the colorful lines and grips disappear, and you're left with the photo you brought in, your model axes, and your thoughts. It may have seemed like a lot of magic, but what you did was pretty simple: You used photo-matching to create a scene (explained in Chapter 11) with a camera position and lens settings that match the ones used to take the picture that's on your screen. In effect, you're now "standing" exactly where the photographer was standing when the photograph was taken.

9. **Select the Line tool and, starting at the axis origin, trace one of the edges in your photograph.**

Make sure that you're drawing in one of the three main directions: red, green, or blue. If you accidentally orbit so that your photo disappears, click the scene tab to see the photo again. (We talk a little more about orbiting as you draw in the tips that follow Step 11.)

10. **Keep tracing with the Line tool until you have a rectangular face, watching the color of your edges as you draw.**

You always want your lines to turn red, green, or blue when you're starting.

REMEMBER

11. **Use SketchUp's drawing tools to continue to trace the photograph in three dimensions.**

In Figure 8-14, you see two rectangular faces, one drawn on the green axis and the other drawn along the red axis.

TIP

Here are pointers for successfully tracing your photo with SketchUp's drawing tools:

- *Always start an edge at the end of an edge you've already drawn.* Doing so helps to assure that your results are what you expect.

- *Never draw an edge in midair.* Okay — this is the same as the last one, but it bears repeating: When you draw edges based on other edges, you get the best results.

FIGURE 8-14:
As you begin tracing your model, align your edges with the drawing axes to create basic shapes.

- *To start, be careful not to orbit while you draw.* You can zoom and pan all you want, though. If you orbit away from the vantage point you set up, your photograph will disappear, and you see only the geometry you've drawn, as shown in Figure 8-15. You can easily get back by clicking the scene tab for your matched photo. The tab is labeled with the name of your photo at the top of your modeling window.

If you orbit away from the photo, click the scene tab to see it again.

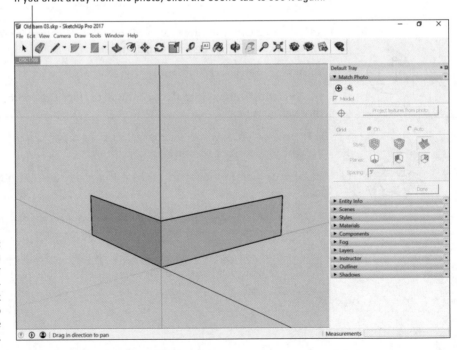

FIGURE 8-15:
When you orbit, your photo disappears. Click the scene tab to see the image again.

- *After your model begins to take shape, orbit frequently to see what's going on.* You'll be surprised what you have sometimes — tracing a 2D image in 3D is tricky business. Get in the habit of orbiting around to check on the results and draw certain edges. Click the matched photo scene tab to return to the proper view.

- *Use other tools (such as Push/Pull and Offset) when appropriate.* Nothing prevents you from using the full complement of SketchUp's modeling tools. However, tracing the basic skeleton of a model with the Line and Eraser tools keeps the process simple.

- *Pay attention to the colors.* With a color photograph as an overlay, seeing what you're doing can be tricky. Watch to make sure that you're drawing the edge you intend to draw.

- *Draw angles by connecting the dots.* If you need to trace an edge in your photo that doesn't line up with any of the colored axes (an angled roofline, for example), figure out where the endpoints are by drawing perpendicular edges and connecting them with an angled line, as shown in Figure 8-16. You can delete the line or lines that you don't need later.

- *Show or hide your photograph.* Doing so sometimes helps you see your work. The next section explains where to find the controls on the Styles panel.

To draw this diagonal edge, create a temporary line and connect the endpoints.

FIGURE 8-16: Draw a temporary line to create an edge for a roofline or other edge that doesn't align with a colored axis.

After you finish drawing your model, you can scale it precisely by using the Tape Measure tool. (Chapter 3 explains how.)

Making your matched photo reappear (or disappear)

After you match a photo to your model, the following tips are handy to know:

» **Click the matched photo scene tab:** When you create a new matched photo, you create a new scene. (You can read all about scenes in Chapter 11.) Clicking a matched photo scene tab returns your view to the one you set up when you created (or edited) that matched photo. It also makes the associated photograph reappear — handy if you've orbited into another view.

» **Manage photo visibility settings in the Styles panel:** Deep, deep down in the bowels of the Styles panel, on the Edit tab, in the Modeling Settings section, you can control the visibility of your matched photo. Chapter 10 is where you find out about Styles.

MAKING MULTIPLE MATCHES

If you have more than one photo of your modeling subject, you can have multiple matched photos in the same SketchUp file. Just get as far as you can with the first photo and then start again with the next by using the geometry you created as an "existing building." See the section "Matching a photo to an existing model," earlier in this chapter, and follow the steps to line up an existing model with a new photograph.

The following shows a model Aidan started to build of Habitat 67, in Montreal. He used two pictures to create two matches in the same SketchUp file. Making more than one photo match is a great way to build more of a model than you could see in a single picture.

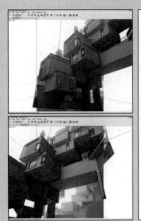
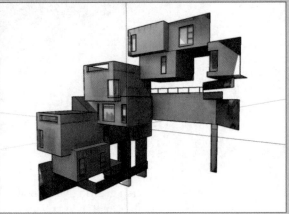

Modeling on Top of Photo Textures

After you place a photo texture on the right face and in the right place on that face (yeah, we've been reading a lot of Dr. Seuss), you can use the information in your photograph to help with adding geometry to your model. It's a great way to be roughly accurate without having to measure much, and the combination of photo textures and a few simple push/pull operations can be very convincing.

Making a texture projected

Modeling with photo-textured faces isn't hard, but you *have* to take one critical step before you can do it: You have to make sure that your texture is *projected.*

Figure 8-17 shows what happens when you try to push/pull an opening in a photo-textured face: On the left, when the texture *isn't* projected, the inside faces are painted with random parts of the texture, making your model look like a sticker-laden eye puzzle. On the right, when it *is* projected, note how the "inside" faces that the push/pull operation creates are a plain, easy-to-discern gray. The result is typically more appropriate for what you're doing.

Textures not projected

Wallpaper effect

Textures are projected

Stretched Pixels effect

No Textures

FIGURE 8-17:
Pushing/
pulling an
opening in a
textured face
when the
texture *isn't*
projected (left)
and when it *is*
projected.

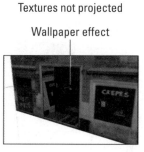
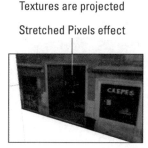
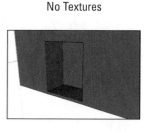

REMEMBER

Make sure that your face's texture is projected *before* you start drawing on top of it. Happily, telling SketchUp to make a photo texture projected is just a matter of flipping a switch. Context-click the face with the photo texture and choose Texture ⇨ Projected from the context menu. If you see a check mark next to Projected, your texture is already projected; don't choose anything.

Modeling with projected textures: A basic workflow

Follow these steps to get the hang of working with projected textures (and see the steps in action in Figure 8-18):

1. **Make a basic rectangular box and then apply a photo texture to one of the side faces.**

    Check out the section, "Adding photos to flat faces," earlier in this chapter.

2. **Context-click the textured face and choose Texture ⇨ Projected from the context menu.**

    Make sure that Projected has a check mark next to it.

3. **Draw a rectangle on the textured face and push/pull it inward.**

    Notice the stretched pixels effect?

4. **(Optional) Add other angles or features to your model.**

    Notice the angled face we created in Figure 8-19.

Stretched pixels

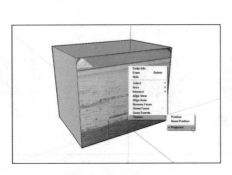

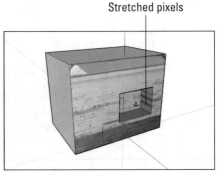

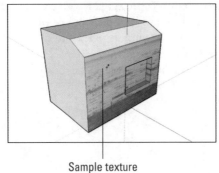

Sample texture

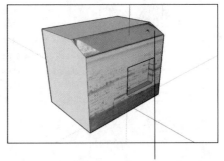

Paint texture on sloped surface

FIGURE 8-18: Working with projected textures.

5. **Switch to the Paint Bucket tool, hold down the Alt key (Command on a Mac), and click somewhere on the textured face to sample the texture. (Your cursor looks like an eyedropper when you do this.)**

   This step loads your Paint Bucket with the projected texture.

6. **Release the Alt (Command) key to switch back to the Paint Bucket cursor and then click the angled face once to paint it with the projected texture.**

   You see the stretched pixels effect here, too.

Adding Geographic Data

When you add geographic data to your model (also called *geo-locating* your model), you give it a specific latitude, longitude, and cardinal orientation based on an address, cross streets, or other information. That doesn't sound like much at first, but here are three things geo-location enables you to do:

» **Perform accurate shadow studies.** For most designer-types, this is probably the biggest benefit of geo-locating a model. With a latitude, a longitude, and a cardinal orientation, SketchUp's shadow engine can display crazy-accurate shadows for any time of day, any day of the year. You can find all the juicy details in the second half of Chapter 10.

» **Build photo-textured context models.** If you're designing a building, it's probably surrounded by other buildings, and those other buildings are probably major influences on the design of *your* building, no? Wouldn't it be nice to have them in your model? You can combine high-res, color, aerial (taken by airplanes or satellites) imagery with street-level photography to build the quickest, most useful context models you've ever had. Heck — you might not even need to visit the site in person. Try a web search for *"Site Modeling in SketchUp video"* (or just point your browser to this web address: https://youtu.be/nVhM3IYMF8o) to find an in-depth YouTube tutorial that Aidan put together on just this subject.

» **View your model in Google Earth.** After your model understands where on the planet it belongs, you can easily export the model file and send it to your copy of Google Earth. Flying from the Eiffel Tower to the Taj Mahal and then to your proposed new tool shed gives your design a level of seriousness that proclaiming, "Look what I've spent the last 37 hours working on!" to your spouse simply can't match. It's also impressive to clients.

The sections that follow outline the nitty-gritty steps for telling SketchUp where on Earth your model is (literally), looking at it in Google Earth, and saving it as a Google Earth file that you can share with other humans.

Geo-locating your model

Follow these steps to add a geo-location snapshot to your SketchUp file:

1. **Make sure you're online.**

All geo-data is stored on far-flung servers; if you don't have an Internet connection, you can't use the geo-data.

2. **Open the SketchUp file you want to geo-locate.**

You can add a geo-location snapshot to your model anytime as you work on it. If you haven't started modeling yet, it's perfectly okay to add a geo-location to an empty file.

3. **Choose File ⇨ Geo-Location ⇨ Add Location from the menu bar.**

A new window that you may recognize opens: It's a simplified version of Google Maps.

4. **Find the area where you want your model to be located.**

You can type an address into the search bar in the upper-left corner if you like. You can also just use your mouse or the controls on the left side of the window to navigate around. Scroll your mouse wheel to zoom; click and drag to pan.

When you're zoomed in close enough, you see a white, 1 km x 1 km square: This is the largest snapshot you can import all at once. That's still a very big area, so you probably want to keep zooming.

5. **Click the Select Region button to display a cropping rectangle.**

6. **Drag the pins to specify the precise corners of your geo-location snapshot, as shown in Figure 8-19.**

Try to frame an area that's just big enough to provide a base for your model. Importing too much terrain data can bog down your computer. You can always bring in more terrain data later.

7. **Click the Grab button to add a geo-location to your SketchUp file.**

The separate window closes, and a big, colorful rectangle appears in the middle of your model. That's your new geo-location snapshot.

8. **If you're geo-locating a model you've built already, move it into position on the snapshot.**

Use the Move tool (and maybe the Rotate tool) to pick up your model and place it where it belongs. You're not done yet, though — you still need to make sure your model is *vertically* situated on the terrain. Follow these steps to do just that:

a. *Choose File ⇨ Geo-location ⇨ Show Terrain to switch to the 3D version of your geo-location snapshot.*

b. *Select everything you want to move and use the Move tool to start moving; tap the up- or down-arrow key to constrain your move to the blue axis.*

c. *Sink your model into the terrain until it sits properly — avoid the dreaded floating model syndrome at all costs.*

REMEMBER

If you want to import another snapshot into SketchUp, you can. SketchUp automatically tiles all the snapshots you take to form a patchwork in your model. This feature is super-handy if you find that you didn't get everything you needed the first time.

FIGURE 8-19:
The area you frame with the pins is imported into your model as a geo-location snapshot.

ALL ABOUT GEO-LOCATION SNAPSHOTS

When you import a geo-location snapshot, you access Google's huge repository of geographic data. The snapshots are a lot more than pretty pictures. In addition to geo-locating the model's position, a snapshot has the following features:

- **Everything is already the right size.** Perhaps you take a snapshot of a football field; when you measure that football field in SketchUp, it is exactly 100 yards long. That's because SketchUp scales your snapshot to the correct size as part of the import process.

- **Snapshots look flat but contain terrain data, too.** The snapshot that SketchUp imports is more than just a color aerial photo. The snapshot also includes a chunk of topography — terrain. The *terrain* is flat when you first import it because it's easier to build on that way, but you can toggle between flat and 3D (not flat) views by choosing File ⇨ Geo-Location ⇨ Show Terrain. Don't fret if you don't see any difference when you flip between the views — you probably just chose a flat site.

Viewing your model in Google Earth

After you make (or simply position) a model on top of a geo-location snapshot, exporting the model so you can view it in your copy of Google Earth is a simple operation. You can also e-mail the KMZ file to all your friends. If you model for clients instead of friends, you can send the file to them, too.

When someone opens the KMZ file, Google Earth opens on his computer (if he has Google Earth), and he's "flown in" to look at the model you made. Try sending directions to your next party this way; your friends will think you're a genius.

Follow these steps to export a SketchUp model to a KMZ file:

1. **In SketchUp, select File ⇨ Export ⇨ 3D Model.**

2. **In the Export Model dialog box that appears, choose where on your hard drive you want to save the KMZ file.**

3. **Give the file a name and select the KMZ file type.**

4. **Click the Export button to save your model as a KMZ file.**

Working with Imported CAD files

On the SketchUp Spectrum of Fun, importing and preparing CAD files is located right between latrine digging and cat milking — it's not something many folks look forward to doing. This section is a collection of tips and tricks Aidan has learned in his many years of dealing with other people's CAD files.

Importing a CAD file into SketchUp Pro

This would probably be a great time to let you know (just in case you missed the heading right above this paragraph) that only SketchUp Pro can import 2D CAD files in DWG and DXF format; SketchUp Make doesn't include this functionality.

Your CAD file may be one you made yourself, but more likely you've received one from someone else. In that case, the absolute best thing to do is to open it in the same software that created it. If you have an AutoCAD file, open it in AutoCAD and take a look at its layer structure. Make a copy of the file, delete everything you don't need to bring into SketchUp Pro, and proceed from there.

Simple, right? But what if (like Aidan) you don't have AutoCAD? That's okay — most folks don't. You'll have a fair amount of cleanup work to do in SketchUp after you've imported the CAD data, but it's manageable. The section after this one describes a series of things you can do to wrangle the drawing into shape before you can start modeling.

Actually importing CAD data into SketchUp Pro isn't very complicated. Follow these steps, and you'll do just fine:

1. **Open a fresh, new SketchUp file.**

   You can't just open a DWG or DXF file in SketchUp Pro; you have to import the data into an existing model. We strongly recommend starting with a new SketchUp file because most CAD files are super complex. Bringing all that complexity — thousands of edges and tons of layers — into an already-complex SketchUp model is just asking for trouble. Keep things separate and stay sane.

2. **Choose File ⇨ Import.**

   The File Import dialog box opens.

3. **Select AutoCAD files (*.dwg, *.dxf) from the Formats drop-down list.**

   For some reason, you have to tell SketchUp what kinds of files you want to import before it will let you select them on your file system.

4. **Locate the CAD file (DWG or DXF) that you want to import and select it.**

   Don't click Import just yet.

5. **Click Options.**

   The DWG Import Options dialog box opens.

6. **Set the Units to match the default measurement units of the CAD file you're about to import.**

   If the CAD file is from someone in the U.S., there's a good chance the units are Inches or Feet. Other countries (wisely) use the metric system. If you have no idea what units to choose here, so start with Inches and see whether that works.

7. **Decide what to do about the other three options in the dialog box:**

   - *Merge Coplanar Faces* tells SketchUp to automatically combine adjacent faces that are coplanar into a single face. This can save you cleanup time if the CAD file you're importing actually has faces in it, but CAD files rarely do. If you select this check box and your import fails (it happens), try deselecting it the next time.

   - *Orient Faces Consistently* instructs SketchUp to do its best to make sure that the faces in your imported data (if there are any) are all facing the same way. Again, this might save you some cleanup time, but it also might throw a wrench into your import process.

   - *Preserve Drawing Origin* is useful if you'll be importing more than one CAD file into the same SketchUp model. You might do this if you're importing multiple floor plans of the same building and you want them to line up.

8. **Click OK to close the DWG Import Options dialog box.**

9. **Click Import . . . .**

   . . . and cross your fingers. With a few tries, you're usually able to import the CAD data. If you get a failure message, try again with a different Units setting in the Import Options dialog box (Step 6). If that doesn't work, the file might have been saved in a CAD format that's newer than the ones that your copy of SketchUp Pro can import. Contact the person who sent you the file and ask her to save another copy for you in an older CAD format.

10. **Take a look at the Import Results dialog box to see where you stand.**

If, after the import progress bar goes all the way to the right and the import itself is successful, SketchUp Pro will present you with a dialog box with statistics about what it imported and what it ignored. The simple version is that CAD layers, blocks (which translate to components in SketchUp), and edges of all sorts are importable. Text objects, dimensions, and hatches (of the sort that denote different materials) aren't. When you're satisfied, click OK and breathe a sigh of relief.

TIP

After you've gone through the CAD import process and SketchUp has plunked the resulting geometry into your model, make sure everything went according to plan: Measure a couple of things with the Tape Measure tool to see whether they're the sizes you expect them to be. Doorways are a good place to start; if you measure one and it's many times smaller or bigger than it should be, your Units (in Step 6 of the preceding steps) were set wrong. Close the file, open a new one, and try again.

Cleaning up imported CAD data

Most of the time, your imported CAD file looks something like the mess shown in the top image of Figure 8-20. Walls, annotations, grid lines, and other stuff are all jumbled up, and it seems like you're going to have to spend the rest of the week deleting edges. Probably not, actually — the following sections explain improvements you can make.

Switch to a style that's easier to read

If you're using a display style that includes lots of edge embellishments (such as Profiles, Extensions, and Endpoints), dense geometry of the sort in most CAD drawings looks like your model received an unwelcome visit from the Mascara Fairy. Yuck. Use the Styles panel to apply a style that's plain and simple. We recommend either Shaded or Shaded with Textures, both of which you can find in the Default Styles collection. You can read all about styles in Chapter 10. Figure 8-20 shows what a difference a style can make.

Turn off layers you don't need

Most of the drawing symbols and other annotations you brought into SketchUp aren't things you need, at least right away. The simplest and safest way to get rid of them is to turn off their layers. Remember that SketchUp Pro also imports all of the layer information associated with the CAD data you brought in; now's the time to use all of that complexity to your advantage.

Architectural Design Style

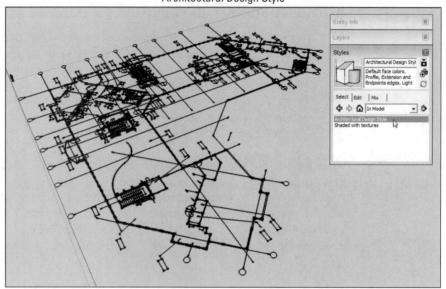

Shaded with Textures

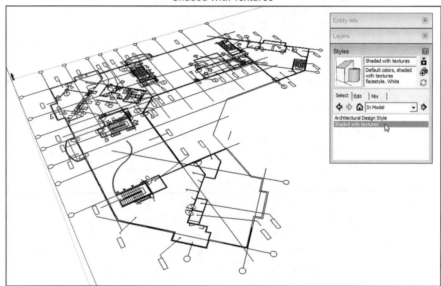

FIGURE 8-20:
Applying a
simple display
style to a
model with
imported CAD
data makes it
a lot easier to
work with.

Follow these steps to identify and hide the stuff you don't need:

1. **Open the Layers panel.**

   CAD files usually come with dozens of layers. Make the Layers panel nice and big so you can see more of them.

2. **Open the Entity Info panel.**

   The Entity Info panel tells you which layer a selected entity is on.

3. **Context-click any part of the imported CAD drawing and choose Edit Component.**

   As long as your model contains at least one entity when you do a CAD data import, SketchUp Pro automatically puts all the imported geometry into a single component. Whatever you do, try not to explode this component — you find out why later on in this chapter.

4. **Select an entity that you don't want to see right now.**

   In Figure 8-21, a grid line that we don't think we'll need for awhile (or at all) is selected.

5. **Look at Entity Info to see what layer contains your selected entity.**

   In this case, the selected grid line is on layer A-GRID. Okay, maybe we didn't need Entity Info to tell us that.

6. **Find the offending layer in the Layers panel and turn it off.**

   In the second part of Figure 8-21, switching off the A-GRID layer temporarily hides all the entities on that layer. Better already! If you're positive you won't need the contents of a particular layer, you can delete it altogether. Rebecca loves throwing out unneeded stuff, digital or otherwise, but Aidan's the kind of person who holds onto things (and has the basement to prove it).

7. **Repeat Steps 4–6 for all of the entity types you want to hide.**

   This part of the cleanup process is pure SketchUp catharsis. It takes time, but the results are immediately visible. The last part of Figure 8-21 shows the result of hiding a bunch of layers.

TIP

Of course, you can also dive right into the Layers panel and start turning off individual layers, especially if you know what entities they contain. The preceding steps are useful for situations where layers aren't named descriptively or for when you're overwhelmed and don't know where to begin.

In Entity Info, see which layer
the selected entity is on

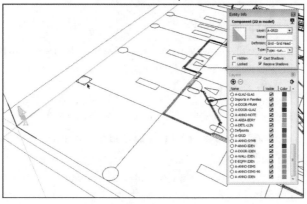

Use Layers to hide that layer

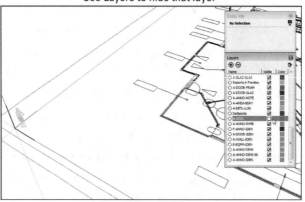

Repeat for all unnecessary entities

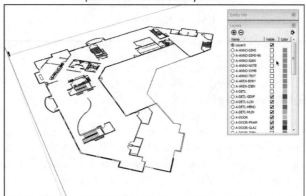

FIGURE 8-21:
Select things
you don't
need and hide
the layers
they're on.

Modeling on top of imported CAD data

So you've successfully imported a CAD drawing and stripped down its style and visible layers to make it more manageable. Kudos — it's time to start having some fun. Building a 3D model based on underlying (literally) CAD linework can be a surprisingly Zen experience *if* you follow one simple rule:

Keep the imported CAD data isolated inside of its own component and build your model on top of it. *Don't* be tempted to use the imported edges to create faces directly.

Here are three reasons why:

>> **CAD data is almost always full of gaps.** Lines that should extend all the way to their neighbors are sometimes short by tiny, invisible amounts, meaning you'll spend hours drawing edges and trying to figure out why faces won't appear where you want them to.

>> **CAD lines that should be parallel to one of the colored axes often aren't.** Think that edge is parallel to the red axis just because it looks like it might be? Not necessarily. Blithely turning imported edges into faces and then pushing/pulling them into 3D geometry is like building a house on quicksand; things get wonky quick.

>> **Imported CAD drawings aren't always flat.** Sometimes different parts of your imported linework are located at slightly, maddeningly different heights. We're talking thousandths of an inch — not enough to notice initially but certainly enough to mess up your work.

Instead of trying to use the imported edges as part of your 3D model, use them as references for new geometry that you draw on top of them. Tracing the imported geometry doesn't take as much time as you'd think, and the result is a model whose geometry is far more accurate and predictable. The following two sections talk about strategies for "tracing" imported CAD content.

Modeling straight, vertical walls based on imported CAD edges

There's a technique for modeling simple walls and other straight elements on top of imported CAD linework that's so simple and *enjoyable*, that audiences regularly applaud when Aidan demonstrates it. The credit for this method goes to our friend (and colleague) Mike Tadros.

Before you get started, make sure you're not editing the component that contains your imported CAD linework. Remember that you're using the CAD drawing as a reference underlay for your own 3D modeling activities. You'll be working "on top" (outside) of the component.

The Push/Pull tool is the hero of this method. Follow these steps (and see Figure 8-22) to model a straight wall based on edges in an imported CAD drawing:

1. Reposition axes if necessary

2. Draw rectangle

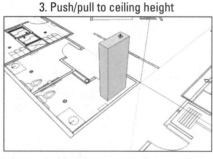
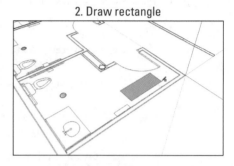

3. Push/pull to ceiling height

4. Push/pull flush with one side of wall

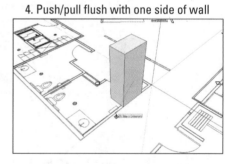

5. Push/pull flush with other side of wall

6. Push/pull flush with each end of wall

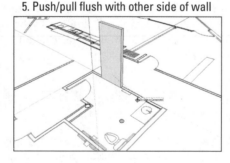
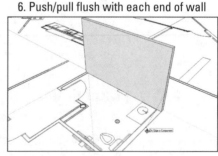

FIGURE 8-22: Modeling a simple wall based on a couple of edges in an imported CAD drawing.

1. **Use the Axes tool to line up the colored modeling axes with the wall you're about to model.**

   If the axes are already parallel to the wall, you can skip this step. If not, just choose Tools ⇨ Axes and line up the modeling axes with an edge in the CAD drawing that represents the wall you're working on. If you're not familiar with the Axes tool, "Matching a photo to an existing model" earlier in this chapter walks you through an example of aligning the axes with a model.

2. **Draw a rectangle next to the wall.**

   It doesn't matter how big it is; you'll see why in a moment.

3. **Use the Push/Pull tool to extrude the rectangle up to the height of the wall you're modeling.**

   If you don't know it just yet, just guess. It's easy to change this later.

4. **Use the Push/Pull tool to extrude the box you just made so that it's flush with one side of the wall.**

   If you drew the rectangle in Step 3 to the *outside* of the wall, push/pull the face so it's flush with the *inside* of the wall. (See Figure 8-22.)

   The key to this step is pure SketchUp Inferencing 101: Click to start pushing/pulling, hover your pointer over the edge (or its endpoint) that you're aiming for, and then click again to stop pushing/pulling. You're using the imported CAD edge as an inferencing reference for your tool. It's cake after you've done it once or twice.

5. **Use the Push/Pull tool to make the opposite face of the box flush with the other side of the wall.**

   See what's happening? You're using the Push/Pull tool and carefully chosen inferences to turn the box *into* the wall.

6. **Push/pull the ends of the 3D wall so they match the underlying drawing.**

   We told you this was fun.

What happens when walls meet up at corners? Well, that can happen at right angles (which is common) or at other angles (which isn't uncommon).

MODELING RIGHT-ANGLED WALLS

For 90-degree corners, all you have to do is draw a rectangle on the inside face of your wall and use the Push/Pull tool to extrude it out. After that, use the same tool to make it flush with the edges in the CAD drawing. Figure 8-23 provides a visual.

1. Draw rectangle on wall	2. Push/pull rectangle into 3D
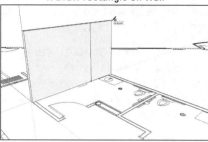	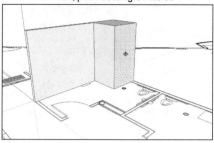

3. Push/pull flush with inside of wall	4. Push/pull flush with end of wall
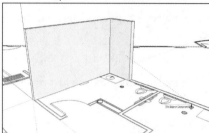	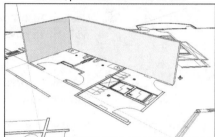

FIGURE 8-23: Use the Rectangle and Push/Pull tools to model walls that meet at right angles.

MODELING WALLS THAT MEET AT NON-RIGHT ANGLES

If you're dealing with a corner that isn't 90 degrees, you can proceed in a few different ways; using the Intersect Faces tool is a great place to start. The following steps (and Figure 8-24) elaborate on the technique:

1. **Model each straight wall segment independently but don't overlap their ends just yet.**

Follow the steps in the section "Modeling straight, vertical walls based on imported CAD edges," a few pages earlier, to build each wall so it's parallel with the CAD edges to which it corresponds. Don't worry about the two wall ends that will eventually meet; keep them apart for now.

2. **Use the Push/Pull tool to extend each wall well past the point at which it should meet the other.**

You're modeling something that looks like an *X* from above.

3. **Select the inside and outside faces of each wall.**

You should have a total of four faces selected.

4. **Choose Edit ⇨ Intersect Faces ⇨ With Selection.**

This action tells SketchUp to draw an edge wherever two faces intersect. If you had four faces selected, you should now have two new edges.

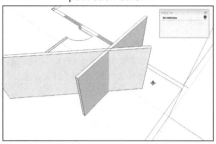

Extend wall ends
past each other

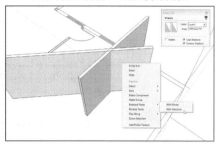

Select faces and choose
Intersect Faces→With Selection

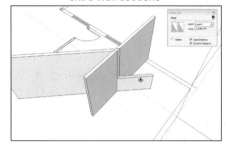

Push/pull away
extra wall sections

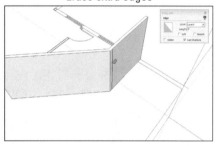

Erase extra edges

FIGURE 8-24:
Use Intersect
Faces to model
walls that form
non-90-degree
corners.

5. **Use Push/Pull to push away the wall segments you don't need.**

   Pushing their top faces all the way down to their bottom faces makes them disappear.

6. **Use the Eraser tool to get rid of any extra edges.**

Modeling curved and irregular forms from CAD data

For rectilinear walls, stairs, and other shapes, SketchUp's Rectangle and Push/Pull tools are rock stars. Rounded forms (such as concrete patios and castle turrets) and irregular lines (such as riverbeds and Frank Gehry buildings) call for other, more drastic measures.

The following steps give a general example dealing with features in your CAD file that aren't worth painstakingly tracing with the Line tool but which need to appear in your SketchUp model. In these situations, you can rely on the handy Paste in Place command:

1. **Dive into the component that contains the imported CAD linework.**

   By "dive into," we mean edit it, which you can do by double-clicking it with the Select tool.

2. **Select the edges you want to reuse.**

3. **Make a group out of the edges.**

   Choose Edit ⇨ Make Group to do this. Grouping your selection accomplishes two things: Grouping makes reselecting it easier (in case things go awry), and it keeps things nice and separate for the next couple of steps.

4. **Choose Edit ⇨ Copy.**

5. **Stop editing the CAD linework component.**

   You can exit a component (or a group) by double-clicking with the Select tool somewhere outside its bounding box.

6. **Choose Edit ⇨ Paste in Place.**

   Voilà! The edges in question are now a part of your model, and (thanks to Step 3) are quarantined from the rest of your geometry by means of a group.

For shapes that are made up of simple arcs (segments of circles), your best bet is to try to re-create them by using SketchUp's own Arc tools. Why not just use the Paste in Place method (described in the preceding steps) to copy them? For arcs, it's nice to have control over their number of sides, and drawing them from scratch is the only way to do that.

Follow these steps to accurately trace an arc from underlying CAD linework (see Figure 8-25):

1. **Draw an edge that's perpendicular to one of the arc's line segments, heading in the direction of the arc's center point.**

   You can use SketchUp's Perpendicular linear inference to help you draw a perpendicular edge. This is the first step in figuring out the precise location of the arc's center point.

2. **Repeat Step 1 for another of the arc's line segments, crossing your new edge over the one you just drew.**

   The point at which these two edges intersect is the center point.

3. **Erase two of the edges that you just drew, leaving a small V that points to the arc's center point.**

   Look at the third image in Figure 8-25 to see which two edges I'm referring to.

4. **Choose Draw ⇨ Arcs ⇨ Arc to activate the Arc tool.**

   What is now called *2 Point Arc* used to be SketchUp's *only* Arc tool; it works by first setting endpoints and then setting a bulge. The new(ish) Arc tool, which is called simply *Arc,* lets you start by defining a center point; this is much more useful for situations like the one you're in now. If you have SketchUp 2014 or later, you have this new Arc tool.

1. Draw edge perpendicular
to arc segment

2. Repeat for another arc segment

3. Erase edges to leave a V
pointing at the center

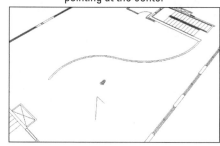

4. Use Arc tool to trace arc

FIGURE 8-25:
The Arc tool
lets you easily
draw arcs with
a given radius.

5. **Click once to set the center point of your new arc.**

This is, of course, at the tip of the V you drew in Step 3.

6. **Complete the arc by clicking to set each of its endpoints.**

7. **(Optional) Change the number of edge segments in your new arc.**

Before you move onto anything else, type the number of segments you want, followed by the letter **s**, and then press Enter. Most likely, you want more than the default 12 segments on arcs that represent major features in your design.

Chapter **9**

3D Printing with SketchUp Models

Seeing your masterpiece in SketchUp is cool. You can twist and turn and view it from every angle. But wouldn't the world be so much cooler if you could hold your creation in your hands?

This chapter talks about using SketchUp with a 3D printer.

To follow along with this chapter, you need a working understanding of SketchUp and its tools. We assume you've heard about 3D printers and are curious to learn more. The focus is on desktop 3D printers, the most common class of 3D printers on earth. You get a look at 3D printing technology in general and touch briefly on a few types of professional machines.

Most of this chapter discusses guidelines, methods, and tools to help you modify your SketchUp models to be 3D printed. We also point out a few limitations of 3D printers, and how you can work within them.

Building Up a View of 3D Printing

It may sound like magic, but 3D printing is a process that uses the 3D information from your SketchUp model to build a physical version of that model in the real world. It's science fiction come true.

3D printing got its start as the hot new technology of the mid-1970s — and spent 35 years stuck as the high-priced plaything of prototyping engineers and the lucky people who build fighter jets. And that's where it stayed until the first DIY desktop 3D printers appeared in 2009. Overnight, the cost of a 3D printer fell from $500,000 to $500. What was once the coveted technology of the chosen few is now found on the desk of any well-equipped designer, engineer, or model maker.

Building a Model in Layers

There are many different 3D printing technologies and manufacturers, but they all use a process called *additive manufacturing:* An object is built from thin horizontal slices of material, with each new layer extruded slightly above the previous layer and then fused to it. Layer by layer, the printer builds up the object until it's finished.

Supporting layers from below

SketchUp's world is an amazing place where you can rapidly build a 3D model while ignoring little things like the laws of physics. An object being 3D printed, however, is subject to all the forces of the physical world, including that pesky omnipresent one, gravity. New layers can't be printed floating in open space; they need to have something below them.

REMEMBER

The need to support each layer is the most important guideline to keep in mind while you're designing objects for 3D printing. You can use either of two strategies to support new layers as you're printing objects:

>> **Use the 3D printer's support-material function,** which creates a secondary structural lattice around the part. The lattice holds up any layers that would otherwise be free-floating in space. Support material may be dissolvable after printing or have to be manually removed with fingers and tweezers, depending on your type of 3D printer. Either way, removal of support material can become the most labor-intensive part of 3D printing; it also increases the amount of materials used and the time it takes to print the object.

>> **Design and print your parts in a way that limits the conditions that allow unsupported layers to exist.** Smooth transitions and sweeping curves not only look awesome; they can also be easily printed without resorting to the use of support material.

Designing to avoid support material

With a little forethought, you can avoid the use of support material entirely by adhering to a few basic guidelines:

>> **Think about your parts orientation.** Orient the part so that it prints with the smallest number of overhangs. This may mean printing your object upside down or on its side. The capital T in Figure 9-1 could be printed standing upright, but laying it on its back allows it to print much faster — without support material.

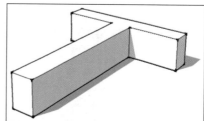

FIGURE 9-1: Re-orienting a part can make it print faster and leave less support material to clean up.

>> **Try rethinking your angle.** Most printers can print a slope between 45 and 60 degrees from vertical without using support material. Keep this limit in mind as you design. Chamfers and fillets are great for supporting features and smoothing out rough transitions. In Figure 9-2, a chamfer turns a part with an unsupported overhang into an easily printable part. As an added bonus, fillets and chamfers make your part stronger by eliminating stress points.

>> **Consider breaking your object into multiple prints.** The sphere in Figure 9-3 could be printed using support material, but it will print faster and with less cleanup if you split it in half and attach it back together afterwards. Later in the chapter, you learn about systems to make the parts lock together quickly.

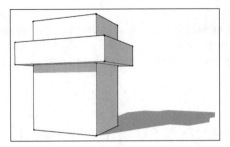
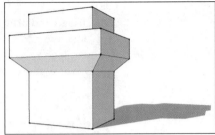

FIGURE 9-2:
A chamfer can turn an unprintable 90-degree angle in to a printable 45-degree one.

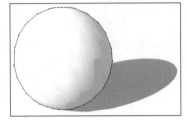

FIGURE 9-3:
Often a subdivided part is faster and cleaner to print than a part printed all at once.

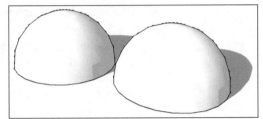

Bridging

Bridging is a feature on 3D printers that lets you print a structure across a gap without using support material. To bridge a gap, the structure being printed must be parallel to the build platform and have a secure point of attachment on either side, as with the top of the door frame shown in Figure 9-4. The printer will attach plastic to one side of the gap and stretch a line across to the other side. The process is repeated until the gap is filled. Future layers are printed on top as usual.

FIGURE 9-4:
When is a door frame a bridge? When it's 3D printed.

Preparing a SketchUp Model for 3D Printing

The longer you work on a SketchUp model, the more it tends to fill with illogical intersections, free-floating cantilevers, and other quick shortcuts. When you're making an image or walkthrough, these are minor trade-offs that help get a big job quickly. Drawing something that looks right on the outside in SketchUp doesn't necessarily mean it can be 3D printed with one click of a button. A 3D printer can't interpret that mishmash of geometry to guess what you were really thinking.

In this section, you discover how to clean up that SketchUp madness and make it into a 3D printable object. The cleanup process uses tools discussed in earlier chapters, but the way you use these tools differs. Cleaning up a messy SketchUp model can look like a daunting task when you start. Remind yourself that it's just like eating an elephant: Divide the job into manageable chunks and work on them one at a time . . . even if the trunk can be a bit chewy.

Before you start cleaning up geometry to make your model 3D-printable, make sure you've saved a separate copy of your SketchUp file, just to be safe.

Peeking inside a model

Although you can use the Section Plane tool to create sectional views through your model, this awesome tool has another use: It can show you what's going on inside your model's geometry. 3D printers see a SketchUp model as a series of 2D horizontal slices. Figure 9-5 moves the Section Plane through the model horizontally to show what the 3D printer is going to see.

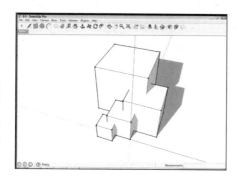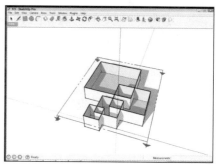

FIGURE 9-5: Using a section plane to look at all overlapping parts that make up your model.

To get a watertight solid object, all groups need to be combined into one, and all that extraneous geometry has to be eliminated from the model. Chapter 11 discusses the Section Plane tool in detail.

Knowing what makes a solid model

To 3D print your parts successfully, they need to be solid objects, or as close to solid as possible. No missing or extra faces, overlapping sections, or extraneous bits allowed. Your SketchUp model needs to describe all aspects of the outer surface of the shape. For example, to print an egg, a SketchUp model would need to describe 100 percent of the outside of the egg's shell. That's not as simple as it sounds.

A solid model that's 3D-printable meets the following criteria:

>> **The model walls have a thickness.** Zero thickness = Zero printing. A wall that is a single face has a thickness of zero and will not print. You need to make sure all the walls have some thickness.

>> **The model has only an outer surface.** In SketchUp, you can create a model quickly (in the abstract, anyway) by pushing parts through each other and building revisions on top of old geometry. To your 3D printer, however, such models are an illogical mess that would make M.C. Escher cry. Your 3D printer doesn't stand a chance. You'll need to clean everything up so that only the outer surface remains. Fortunately, SketchUp tools and extensions discussed later in this chapter can help.

>> **Groups and components are merged.** Chapter 5 explains groups and components, and how to use them to keep your SketchUp model organized as you work. Groups and components are great for keeping parts from sticking together as you work, but to make your SketchUp model a solid shell that can be 3D printed, you need to merge everything together.

TIP

Before you start exploding things and sticking them together, spend a moment thinking about how you want your actual 3D printed model to work. For most projects, you need to merge all your groups and components into one printable object before exporting your model from SketchUp. For larger projects, think about assembling the blocks into sections that you can 3D print and attach together later.

The upshot is that 3D printers aren't very smart. If you make them guess what your part should look like, they will usually guess wrong. Figure 9-6 is a testament to the carnage.

FIGURE 9-6:
This poor print never stood a chance.

Using Solid Tools to combine groups

Chapter 6 explains how to use SketchUp's Pro's Solid Tools to perform Boolean operations. Solid Tools are great for unifying groups made up of simple solid parts. They can save significant time. Unfortunately, complex shapes cause the Solid Tools to act unexpectedly — and, after multiple iterations, to break down.

In Figure 9-7, Solid Tools had no problem intersecting several simple cubes together, but adding a complex shape to the object caused the tools to break down. The accompanying sidebar takes a closer look at why this happens.

FIGURE 9-7:
Booleans are great for simple things. But don't rely on them for complex cleanup.

WHAT'S WRONG WITH SOLID TOOLS?

You may have been looking at the Outer Shell button in the Solid Tools menu and thinking, "Wow, making this into one outer shell is going to be easy." So you decided to save your work, select your whole model, and click Outer Shell. Oops. (Come back when you're done screaming.)

In the discussion of Solid Tools in Chapter 6, you find out that they are also called Boolean operations. Boolean operations started out as computer programming tools that help sort and manipulate data. In the early days of computer graphics,

(continued)

(continued)

programmers used Boolean operations to work directly with the data that makes up 3D models. Boolean operations still exist in every piece of 3D modeling software today. If you take a class in 3D Modeling, they'll be the first thing you'll learn, and then you'll be told to never use them ever again.

The problem is Boolean operations are the blunt instruments of 3D. They work within a narrowly defined set of parameters, and are notorious for the way they indifferently modify geometry. After a few uses, the damage caused by the tool itself starts to compound, and the model becomes too garbled for the Boolean to interpret again. Basically, after being confounded by the sum total of its own mistakes, it gives up in failure. Outer Shell is trying to run a whole series of Boolean operations at once, and if your model is made up of anything except simple shapes, those operations won't succeed.

Unfortunately, cleaning up your model just isn't going to be single-click simple.

CleanUp³ and Solid Inspector²

Two tools from the SketchUp Extension Warehouse are essential for 3D printing: CleanUp³ and Solid Inspector², both created by Thomas Thomassen.

CleanUp³ checks and simplifies the geometry of your SketchUp model. It combines multiple faces, eliminates extraneous data, and erases any lines that don't make a face. Two of the most useful CleanUp³ options are Erase Duplicate Faces and Repair Split Edges, which can be enabled in the CleanUp³ menu. Duplicate faces and split edges are errors that inevitably appear in your model as you work in SketchUp, and they drive 3D printers nuts. Both errors are hard to recognize and repair manually.

CleanUp³ is also great at simplifying STL files (3D-printable files) you import into SketchUp. In Figure 9-8, which shows the triangulated data you get from an imported STL file, the faces have been broken into hundreds of triangles. By removing that triangulation, CleanUp³ makes files downloaded from 3D printing communities (such as Thingiverse at `www.thingiverse.com`) easier to edit in SketchUp.

TIP

Solid Inspector² finds and highlights problems that are preventing your model from being a solid shell, and we can't overemphasize its usefulness. It highlights problem areas and helps you automatically move from one error to next, making repairs much faster (see Figure 9-9). It's a tool that everyone using SketchUp for 3D printing should have.

FIGURE 9-8:
An imported
STL file,
before and
after running
CleanUp³.

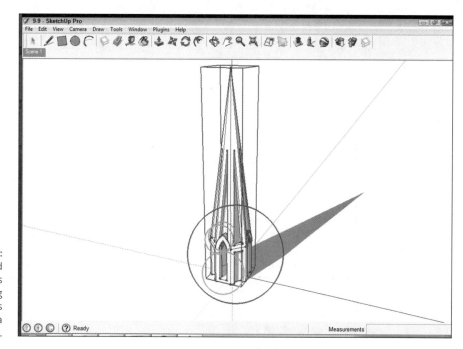

FIGURE 9-9:
Solid
Inspector² is
great at finding
problems
that need a
quick fix.

REMEMBER

As you work on your model, get in the habit of running CleanUp³ periodically. Run Solid Inspector² before you export from SketchUp to 3D print. It will catch any errors that would cause the print to fail.

Combining groups with Intersect Faces

An alternative way to assemble your groups into one object is to use the Intersect Faces command, introduced in Chapter 4. For 3D printing, Intersect Faces can eliminate overlapping geometry and leave behind a solid object. You can use Intersect Faces on very complex objects and groups that aren't already solid.

In a complex model, isolate and work on one small part of the SketchUp model at a time, making each section into one solid part. Repeat the process on those sections until you have one solid model. The following steps outline this process in more detail:

1. **Select the groups you want to combine and group them together.**

Your original groups are now subgroups that exist together inside a new group.

2. **Choose Edit ⇨ Intersect Faces with Context.**

Doing so opens your new group and selects all the subgroups, drawing lines at all the places that groups intersect. These new lines of intersection exist outside the subgroups and aren't stuck to anything yet, as shown in Figure 9-10.

Intersect Faces creates new lines where lines intersect

Lines of intersection pasted onto the object

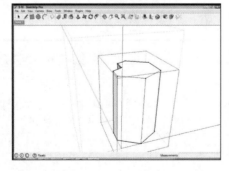
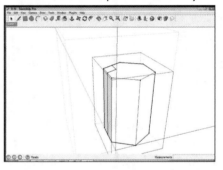

Erase overlapping geometry

Final outer shell

FIGURE 9-10:
Erase overlapping geometry to create an outer shell.

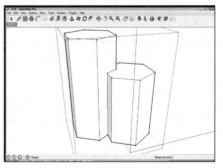

3. **Select the lines of intersection and copy them by choosing Edit ⇨ Copy.**

4. **Open each of the subgroups and paste the lines of intersection into them, using Edit ⇨ Paste in Place.**

Figure 9-10 shows the procedure.

5. **Open each subgroup and erase all the areas of overlap beyond the lines of intersection.**

   Work deliberately, moving back and forth between the subgroups to make sure you're erasing the right areas.

6. **Back in the main group, select all the subgroups, context-click the selection, and choose Explode on the menu that appears.**

   You end up with one outer shell of an object in its own group. Figure 9-10 shows this result.

7. **Run CleanUp³ on the new part and use Solid Inspector² to check for any accidental holes.**

   Individual faces and short line segments can get lost during this process. You may need to make minor touch-ups with the Line tool.

TIP

Checking a model's normals

From a highly technical computer-science perspective, every face in your model has two sides: an inside and an outside. The two sides are set apart by a bit of data called the face's *normal*.

SketchUp is smart enough that it doesn't matter how the normals (also known as the front and back) are oriented; both sides are treated the same. 3D printers aren't that clever; they need to have all the normals oriented so the outsides are pointing out and the insides are pointing in.

To check your model's normals, you'll need to look at it styled with SketchUp's default texture. Choose View ⇨ Face Style ⇨ Monochrome to hide any colors or textures you've added to the model and see the default material. (Chapter 10 covers styles in detail.)

Any faces that are shaded the default blue have reversed normals. These faces will need to be corrected, or the 3D printer will see them as missing.

>> **To correct a single face,** context-click the face and select Reverse Faces from the menu that appears.

>> **To correct several misaligned faces,** context-click one of the faces that is white and select Orient Faces. Doing so flips all the faces in the model to match the view shown in Figure 9-11.

FIGURE 9-11:
A correct
normal is a
happy normal.

TIP

If the Orient Faces tool causes everything to flip randomly, it's a sign that you have extraneous faces inside your model. Use the Section Plane tool to look inside, find the face, and erase it.

Checking your model's size

Every 3D printer has a minimum and maximum size of object it can build, as shown in Figure 9-12. These sizes are usually set by the size of the tool printing the material and by the overall size of the printer. To build something bigger, you have to get creative. To build something smaller, you'll need a more expensive 3D printer.

FIGURE 9-12:
Too big and
too small.
There is
something
there on the
right; it's just
very small.

Too small to print

In the SketchUp world, you can design a skyscraper small enough to fit on the head of a pin, but the 3D printer can't print it. Every 3D printer has a minimum size for what it can build; anything smaller than that won't be printed. You find these values listed as Minimum Feature Size and Minimum Wall Thickness. Feature Size and Wall Thickness can turn into stumbling blocks when you're trying to 3D print a SketchUp model that was constructed at full size and then scaled down.

>> Minimum Wall Thickness tells you how thin a freestanding piece of geometry can be and still be printed. That thickness is typically between 1.0mm and 0.5mm.

>> Minimum Feature Size is the smallest size that a feature can be on the surface of the object that will be printed. It's typically between 0.7mm and 0.2mm.

If you're modeling a small object for 3D printing, create the model in small units, such as millimeters, from the beginning. To set or change the default units in your SketchUp model template, choose Window ⇨ Preferences (SketchUp ⇨ Preferences on a Mac) and select a template that uses millimeters. You can also adjust the default units in the Model Info window by choosing Window ⇨ Model Info and selecting the Units option on the left.

Too big to print

The biggest object you can 3D print at one time is set by the printer's *build volume.* If your model won't fit in the build volume, you have to either scale your object down, or print it in parts. The next section talks about how to split up a model so you can print it in parts.

REMEMBER

Although the maximum size of any single part is limited by the size of your 3D printer, the size of what you can 3D print is limited only by your creativity and patience. A man in New Zealand is 3D-printing himself an Aston Martin, one 6-inch cube at a time.

Here are some handy hints for making best use of build volume:

>> The build volume, or *envelope,* is given by manufacturers as measurements of X, Y, Z. X and Y are the width and depth of the build surface; Z is the maximum height.

>> It's helpful to create a representation of your 3D printer's maximum build volume in your SketchUp model. Make a translucent block representing the maximum build volume and check to see whether your SketchUp model or its components will fit inside that volume.

>> A 3D printer's build platform is much longer diagonally than it is on any one side. To take advantage of the extra length, rotate long parts so they stay inside the build volume.

>> Printing large objects comes with its own issues and complexities. Large objects are more prone to failure and breakdowns. Make sure you're comfortable with your 3D printer before you start printing your own sports car.

Breaking Your Model into Parts

As you do more 3D printing with SketchUp, you'll run into the need to split your model into parts. Some ideas are just too big to fit into your 3D printer's build volume. Other ideas want to be 3D printed in a rainbow of colored plastic. And sometimes a model just needs to be split to make it easy to print.

Where to cut

When subdividing a SketchUp model into printable parts, start by thinking about what you're going to do with the seams. If you're going to sand, paint, and finish the model, then have at it and cut wherever you want. But sanding and finishing is a huge amount of work, especially if you've never done it before. It's much easier to make your cuts and seams look like they're intentional parts of the model.

REMEMBER

For a seam to look intentional, it has to work with the logic of the object. Every object has its own logic, an underlying order that informs how it's shaped and structured. For example, in Figure 9-13, the object is symmetrical left and right. A seam on the axis of symmetry is less objectionable than one that runs randomly in another direction. By following a line that's already conceptually present in the object, the seam reinforces what the eye already perceives.

FIGURE 9-13:
The line is far less objectionable when it's well thought out.

Another good place to hide a cut is at a change in elevation, curvature, or color, as shown in Figure 9-14. Placing a seam where the surface of a part is already interrupted or in transition will make it far less noticeable. This is the strategy most commonly employed for injection-molding parts. Pick up something around you that's made of plastic and find the seams where the parts come together. If you can imitate that type of seam, people will readily accept that your object is a "real" thing. It will feel correct among manufactured things in our injection-molded world, and you'll fool people into thinking your 3D printed part came from a factory somewhere.

FIGURE 9-14:
Do the seams look out of place?

For very large constructions, the only option may be to establish a grid and cut into build-volume-size blocks. Sanding, finishing, and painting can work well on large parts, but expect to spend substantial time doing it right. If you've spent the energy to build something that big, it's worth the extra time to make it amazing.

How to cut

Cutting a model into parts is very similar to using the Intersect Faces tool to combine groups (discussed earlier in the chapter). You use a piece of geometry as a cutter that will be intersected with the larger object and become the new edges of the cut.

If your model is fairly simple and you have SketchUp Pro, you can use the Solid Tools to short-circuit this process. Create a solid block as a cutting object and use the Solid Tools ⇨ Trim command. Remember to run CleanUp[3] and Solid Inspector[2] on the new parts when you're done. For more complex models, or users with SketchUp Make, use the Intersect Faces method:

1. **Select the group you want to cut and make a new group around it.**

   The original group becomes a subgroup.

2. **Working inside the new group, create geometry in the shape of the cut you want to make.**

   Work on top of the subgroup, so you place the cut correctly, as shown in Figure 9-15.

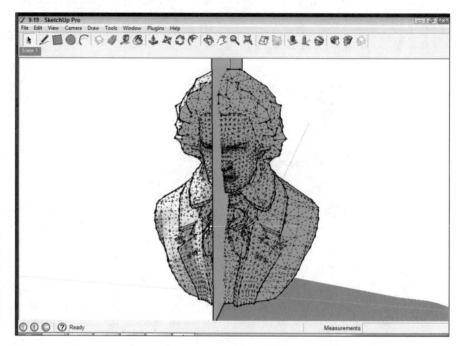

FIGURE 9-15:
The cutter
object can be
a single plane;
it's going to
become part
of the solid
object.

3. **When you're done placing cuts, make the new geometry into its own group.**

4. **Select the Cutter object and choose Edit ⇨ Intersect Faces with Context (or choose Edit from the context-click menu).**

   Doing so draws a line at every place where groups touch. These new lines of intersection exist outside the subgroups and aren't stuck to anything yet, as shown in Figure 9-16.

5. **Inside each group, use Explode to stick the intersection lines, cutting object, and base object together.**

   The surface of the cutting object becomes the sides of the new part.

6. **Move back out to the master group and make as many copies of that group as the number of parts you're dividing it into (see Figure 9-17).**

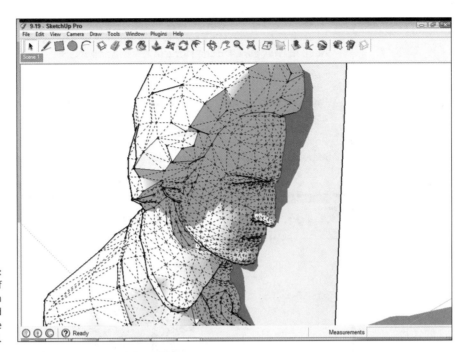

FIGURE 9-16:
Lines of intersection created between the two groups.

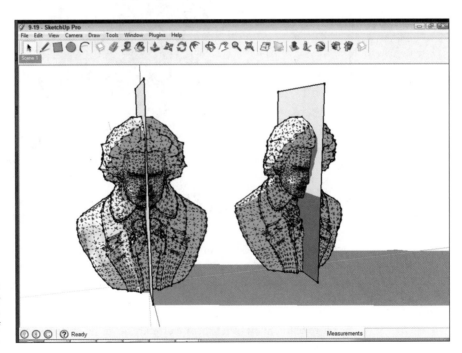

FIGURE 9-17:
Make one copy of the group for each part of your model.

7. **In each copy, open the group for editing and erase everything you don't need in that part. Do the same in the other parts.**

   Just make sure you don't erase what the object needs to do its job.

8. **Run CleanUp³on the new parts and use Solid Inspector² to check for any accidental holes.**

9. **Position the parts back together to make sure everything lines up as expected, as shown in Figure 9-18.**

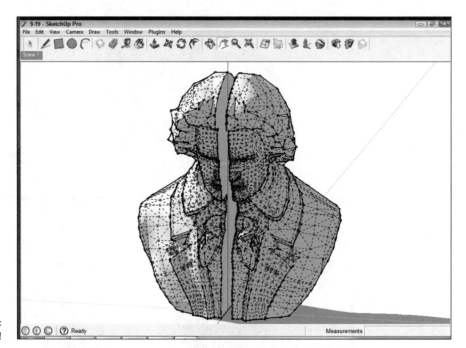

FIGURE 9-18:
It still fits!

Exporting Your SketchUp File

After you've cleaned up your SketchUp model and you're ready to print it, you have to get your 3D model out of SketchUp and into your 3D printer's control software. Before your 3D printer can open your model, you have to export the model in either the STL or OBJ file format.

If you're using SketchUp Pro, you already have the option of exporting an OBJ file. To export an STL file from either version of SketchUp, you'll need to install a free extension from the SketchUp Extension Warehouse called SketchUp STL. It's a great tool created by the SketchUp team to make 3D printing easier.

Knowing Your 3D Printers

3D printers are available that print objects in materials ranging from plastic to titanium. The medical research world has even created machines that can build structures from human tissue. All that separates these technologies is cost. Affordable desktop 3D printers are limited to printing in plastics. So that 3D printer you bought for $500 can't print you a new kidney. (Not yet, anyway, but don't hold your breath.)

The two main ways 3D printers are compared to each other are in terms of *cost per cm³* (that is, cost per cubic centimeter of printed object) and *minimum layer height*. Cost per cm³ is the cost of one cubic centimeter of printed volume; it's typically the number used when comparing the cost of one 3D printing technology to that of another. Minimum layer height is the thickness of one layer in the object. The smaller the height between layers, the smoother the surface of the finished object will look and feel.

Desktop 3D printers

Desktop 3D printers are still an emerging technology. When starting out with your first desktop 3D printer, don't expect it to work perfectly the first time out of the box. The machines haven't reached that level of polish yet. It helps to see a 3D printer as a tool you're learning to use, rather than as an appliance you just plug in. Before you dive into printing your own creations, spend some time going through the printer's training materials. Print a few test objects and get a feel for using the machine.

Desktop 3D printers tend to be based on tried-and-true technologies that have been used in industrial machines for decades. The two technologies that are available now are fused deposition modeling and stereolithography. The following sections give you an overview.

Fused deposition modeling (FDM)

FDM printers represent the mostly widely available type of desktop 3D printer. They build objects using solid plastic fed through a fancy robotic glue gun-style nozzle. FDM printers are inexpensive to buy, with desktop models ranging from $500 to $2,500. FDM-printed parts are done the moment the printer is finished; no secondary process is needed to finish or strengthen the object. The parts that FDM printers make can be as strong as parts from injection molding, and cost around $0.04 per cm³. On the downside, FDM 3D printers have limited maximum resolution and tend to have a lot of moving parts, which can impact their reliability.

FDM printers consume plastic filament as they build objects. Filament is drawn into the printer, heated, and then fused to form the object. Filament comes coiled on spools that look a bit like brightly colored weed-whacker wire. Spools are available inexpensively through vendors online and are starting to become available in large office supply stores.

Examples of FDM 3D printers are MakerBot Replicator (`www.makerbot.com`), Ultimaker (`www.ultimaker.com`), 3D Systems Cube (`http://cubify.com`), Affinia H-Series (`www.afinia.com`), and Solidoodle (`www.solidoodle.com`).

Stereolithography

SLA 3D printers represent one of the oldest 3D printing technologies. They use a laser to build solid parts in a vat of liquid resin, selectively hardening the resin layer by layer. Desktop SLA machines cost between $2,500 and $8,000, but you'll hear ongoing speculation about a printer emerging at a price below $1,000. Stereolithography offers superior printing resolution, which gives finished parts a glassy smooth surface. The machines are typically small and nearly silent, with a few moving parts. Prints from an SLA machine typically cost around $0.15 per cm³ and require some cleanup after printing. Also, due to the resin's toxicity, printed objects must be washed in isopropyl alcohol before handling.

Stereolighography's consumable resin is an amazing bit of chemical engineering. It's a liquid at room temperature until it's exposed to intense ultraviolet light, which hardens the resin into a solid plastic. Resin comes as a bottle of liquid; usually you have to buy it from the maker of your 3D printer to ensure compatibility. Resin has a set shelf life and needs to be stored with some care; it can begin to harden if left in sunlight.

Two examples of SLA machines are Formlabs Form 1 (`http://formlabs.com`) and B9 Creator (`http://b9creator.com`).

TECHNICAL STUFF

As this book goes to press, DLP (digital light processing) printers are emerging on the desktop 3D printer market, with price points from $3,000 to $5,000 but likely to fall in the near future. The technology is similar to SLA, but uses less material.

Do-it-yourself and kit printers

Both FDM and SLA printers are available as kits and open-source DIY plans. In general, these 3D printers are good options for people who are interested in exploring printer technology and modifying their printers. Kits are cheaper than buying a printer, but often less reliable. The saying is, "If you build it yourself, you fix it yourself."

Two examples of DIY and kit machines are RepRap (http://reprap.org) and Printrbot (http://printrbot.com).

Professional 3D printers

Professional 3D printers are typically housed in a dedicated department and operated by full-time employees. They are expensive, with prices in the hundreds of thousands of dollars, but offer capabilities beyond what is available in desktop models. As desktop 3D printing grows, and patents continue to expire, expect to see these technologies becoming cheaper and move into the desktop realm. Here's the current lineup:

>> **Selective laser sintering (SLS):** *Selective laser sintering* uses a laser to melt and fuse a finely powdered plastic. SLS machines can reproduce fine detail without adding any supporting structure to the model. (By and large, lasers that can manage these feats are still relatively expensive.)

>> **Inkjet, powder-based:** Similar to SLS machines, these 3D printers use a powder that is selectively hardened by liquid glue sprayed from an inkjet printhead. The ink can be colored and mixed; this is one of the few technologies that can offer full-color 3D printing.

>> **Inkjet, resin-based:** These machines are an expansion of stereolithography technology. They use an inkjet printhead to spray fine layers of a UV-sensitive resin, which is then hardened by a powerful UV light. Advertising materials for these printers talk about layer heights measured in atoms.

>> **Paper-based:** These printers build objects out of copy paper by gluing the sheets together then cutting away the excess. The parts are immensely strong, and can be treated like wood after printing.

3D printing services

3D printing services offer access to professional-level machines on a pay-per-print basis. Cost is based on volume of material printed, and you receive your printed object by mail in a few working days. Each company offers detailed instructions on minimum part sizes, wall thicknesses, and feature size. Pay attention to these rules. The services know what their machines can do, and you don't want to be stuck waiting a week for a part that didn't come out right.

Two examples of 3D printing services are Shapeways (www.shapeways.com) and Ponoko (www.ponoko.com).

Using Your 3D Printer

Your new 3D printer's manufacturer will have documentation to help you learn how to use the printer and the software, so we don't go into detail on specific machines. The following sections touch on a few general concepts of 3D printing that are often not explained well. For a closer look at 3D printers, check out *3D Printing For Dummies* by Kalani Kirk Hausman and Richard Horne.

Print early, print often

Desktop 3D printing is cheap. Really, unbelievably, remarkably cheap. Cost for running a typical desktop 3D printer is about 60 cents an hour. Once you've started the printer, it doesn't need any more input from you, which frees you to continue working on the design. With such an amazing tool that's so cheap to use, don't be afraid to print constantly. Print your SketchUp model over and over as you improve it; doing so develops it.

3D printers are built to print; they don't like to stand idle. Print more often! You'll become an old hand at using your machine, and get to see your design as it evolves in real time.

TIP

Test prints are great for catching errors and mistakes. Test prints are also a great way to document the evolution of a design. It's a good idea to save a version of your SketchUp model that corresponds to each file you 3D print. If the print has an unexpected error, you can look back at that file and understand what went wrong, without having to dig too deeply into the version you have continued to work on. Keep some general points in mind:

» Test prints that use your 3D printer's Low Quality setting will print faster, but with a rougher surface.

» Save test prints as the project goes on. They're a great way to show progress, and clients love to see a physical expression of the work being done.

» Many 3D printing plastics are recyclable or biodegradable. When you're done with your models made of this stuff, toss them in the recycling bin or on the compost heap.

Inside your model

3D printed parts are unique in the world of fabrication. After you've created the outside of your part, you also get to decide what happens on its inside. Usually you let the 3D printer automatically handle the inside of the part, filling it with automatically generated structure. It's also possible to model a part's interior structure to change how it behaves. For example, you might want to hollow out the center of a part to make it lighter or add space for internal components. Some possible variations include

» **Internal voids:** On SLS and stereolithography machines, a common cost-saving strategy is to build parts as a thin shell with an empty interior. The resulting parts have compromised structural strength, but are printed using as little material as possible. Be sure to include drain holes so the un-hardened material you saved can escape from the part.

» **Part density:** FDM printers automatically generate a structure to fill the interior of their prints. The density of the structure is controlled by a setting called fill, which is stated as a percentage. Parts with 100% fill will be solid plastic all the way through, and are as strong as injection-molded parts. Typically, FDM printers default to building parts at 10% fill, meaning that 10 percent of the interior is filled with plastic. Higher fill percentage means more plastic used — and longer print times. Generally speaking, anything over 40 percent is a waste of time and plastic.

» **Outer wall thickness:** Another FDM printer setting, this deals with the amount of material put into the walls of the object before starting the Infill. Look for a setting called Shells, which is the number of layers of plastic the printer will use to make the outside of the model. If you're having trouble with parts crushing, increase the number of Shells; otherwise leave this setting alone.

» **Flexibility:** Flexible materials are available on most 3D printers, usually by using a special flexible plastic filament. You can also make structures flexible by making them very thin with 0 percent infill.

Going beyond Basic 3D Printing

The more you use your 3D printer, the more you may find it affecting your SketchUp designs. Don't be surprised if your designs become a bit more ambitious and mechanically complex. This section of the chapter outlines some possible directions and factors to watch out for.

Designing parts that connect

So you cut your model into parts. Now you need a way to get it to all stay together after it's printed. In this section, you discover different strategies and features, mechanical and otherwise, that you can build into your model for attaching its parts together.

Tolerance and clearance

Before we get into a discussion about mechanical connections, you need to understand two more of those pesky realities that crop up when you move out of SketchUp's idealized environment: tolerance and clearance.

>> *Tolerance* is the difference between the measurement of your part in SketchUp and the measurement of the part produced by your 3D printer. If you draw a 10mm cube in SketchUp and 3D print it, none of the measurements of the printed cube will be exactly 10mm. The differences are small — just a few tenths of a millimeter more or less — but they can cause problems if your 3D printed parts have to connect to parts that already exist in the real world. The 3D printer's manufacturer provides a number for the machine's tolerance as a plus or minus value, usually something like pm0.05mm. This is the *maximum* variation for that machine, and you should be aware of it as you work.

>> *Clearance* is the extra space you need for parts to slide past one another. If you try to install a 10mm peg in a 10mm hole, you're in for a bit of a surprise when the two won't go together. The peg and hole can fit perfectly in SketchUp, but that's not what's going to happen in the real world where you have to contend with friction. The surface of the peg is so much like the surface of the hole that the friction between them will keep the peg from ever going in if the fit is too exact. You need to add a small amount of space called *clearance* so the two parts can slide past each other. How much clearance you use depends on how the part needs to move. A spinning shaft, for example, needs more clearance than a simple snap fitting.

You'll come to an inherent understanding of clearance and tolerance as you do more designing in SketchUp for 3D printing. As you use your 3D printer, you'll be able to find values that work well with your equipment.

As a starting point, add 0.2mm of clearance to all holes and 0.5mm of clearance to any points of rotation.

Glue

Glue, shown in Figure 9-19, is the universal way to stick something to something else. Unfortunately, it's also the weakest and most unreliable method. Glue joints in plastics have very little strength and will tend to break under stress, in response to temperature change, or if you look at them funny. If your part is meant to be anything more than a visual model, use one of the other attachment systems.

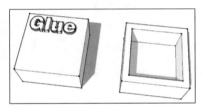

>> The plastics used in 3D printers — ABS, PLA, PVA, nylon, and PETT — all require special glues to bond. These glues are available, but must be ordered from an online retailer.

>> Biodegradable starch plastics such as PLA have a crystalline structure that doesn't work well with liquid superglue. The glue tends to stay liquid and migrate unexpectedly across the surface of the part.

>> When in doubt, use epoxy. Its messy stuff, but will stick to pretty much anything.

>> There are no glues that will stick to the flexible materials that are available for 3D printers. To attach parts made of that stuff, you'll need to look into a process called thermal welding, which is way outside the scope of this book.

Snap fittings

Snap fittings are an awesome way to take advantage of your 3D printer. Properly designed, they'll let you pop your model together as soon as the parts come off the printer. Snap fittings can also be removable, so you can change out various parts of your model as the design evolves.

In SketchUp, you create snap fittings like those shown in Figure 9-20 by following two general steps:

1. Create the tongue with the Line and Push/Pull tools.

2. Create a matching capture point on the opposing part.

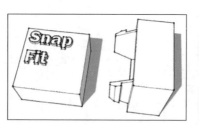

FIGURE 9-20:
A snap fit joint is great for reusable connections.

REMEMBER

As you create your snap fittings, keep these points in mind:

>> Be sure to leave enough space for the tongue to bend backward as it slides into place.

>> Include a clearance of between 0.2mm and 0.5mm, depending on how tight you need the joint to be.

>> Always position snap fittings so they print horizontal to the 3D printer's build platform. Snap fittings printed in the Z direction, perpendicular to the platform, tend to break off.

>> If you want your snap fitting to be re-openable, make sure that you provide a way for the tongue to disengage from the capture. This can either be a ramp in the geometry that forces the tongue backward as you pull on the joint, or an access point that lets you release the tongue manually.

>> Don't make the tongue too thick. It has to bend for the joint to go together.

Press fit

A *press fit* is when two parts are designed with very little clearance between them. When the parts are forcibly pressed together, friction keeps the joint together with no additional hardware or glue.

To make a press fit like the one shown in Figure 9-21, use the Offset tool to create an outer lip on one side of the connection and an inner lip on the other side. Include a clearance of 0.2mm or less between parts, so you can still assemble them. Keep a few points in mind about press fits:

>> For a press fit to work well, it needs to be a tight connection. You might need a small hammer, large clamp, or your whole body weight to press the parts together.

>> A press fit is usually a one-way connection. After you put it together, don't expect to ever get it back apart.

>> Press fits don't scale up well. Always design them at the size at which they'll be printed.

>> The tight clearance of a press fit can make it difficult to get started. Running a hobby knife or deburring tool around the edge of the hole will widen that area a bit and help you get the parts together.

FIGURE 9-21: A press fit is an easy connection to draw in SketchUp.

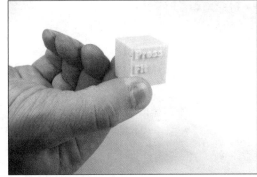

Bolts, screws, and hardware

The strongest connection you can make between 3D printed parts is one held together with metal hardware. These connections are great for things that are more than just prototypes — for example, parts for robots or mechanisms.

When integrating hardware into your design, include the hardware in your SketchUp model. Take measurements of the parts you're planning to use and model them in SketchUp. After you make these components, save them to the component library so that you can use them again with one click. Keep these points in mind:

>> Remember to include enough clearance in your holes for the hardware to be installed.

>> If you're using bolts or screws and don't want to include a matching nut, a trick is to slightly undersize the holes. The threads of the bolt will cut into the excess plastic and hold it firmly in place, as shown in Figure 9-22.

>> Online hardware suppliers like McMaster Carr and Amazon Supply stock every fastener known to the human race. If your local hardware store doesn't have what you're looking for, these online stores will have it.

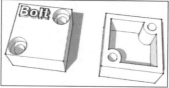

FIGURE 9-22:
Nothing says strength like an exposed bolt.

Testing your model's moving parts

Whatever connection system you are using, always test it first. Before you start printing a giant project, build a small version of the attachment. It only takes a few minutes to design and 3D print, and will give you a chance to make sure the joint works properly. Nothing is worse than modeling a system of joints and then discovering they don't fit together properly.

Designing Things That Move

3D printing something you've designed in SketchUp is cool. 3D printing something that moves is even cooler. This section focuses on a few features you can include to make your creations more than just interestingly shaped hunks of immobile plastic.

Captive joints

A *captive joint* is a moveable connection that comes out of your 3D printer already assembled and working. Captive joints tend to be mechanically simple hinges, ball joints, and chain links. Their simplicity is their power. A 3D printer can quickly build objects with hundreds of captive joints that would take days to construct by hand. Poseable action figures, clothing, and the chainmail in Figure 9-23 are examples of simple captive joints assembled into complex structures.

FIGURE 9-23: Captive joints bring the power of multiplication to life.

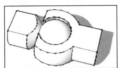 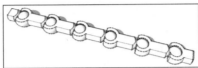 

Creating a captive joint requires trial and error. You'll have to experiment to get the right combination of clearances and shapes. Keep these principles in mind while you work on captive joints:

>> Use components when building structures with captive joints; they let you automatically modify all the joints at once as you work.

>> How you design captive joints depends on the specific 3D printing technology you're using. SLS-based 3D printers can build captive joints that are a few millimeters across. FDM printers can make fantastically strong joints, but the printed objects need to be much bigger.

>> A structure is only as strong as its weakest part. Don't make a joint so fine that it falls apart in your hands.

>> Test print parts of your structure as you work. Remember, 3D printing is cheap, and with captive joints, you're pushing the limits of the technology. Test objects will help you check your work and keep your sanity.

Pins

Pins are small, round snap fittings that are pressed into place to make a connection. They can be a versatile replacement for hardware. In Figure 9-24, a single pin acts as a point of rotation, and two or more will hold parts firmly together.

FIGURE 9-24:
A system of
pin joints used
to make a
simple toy.

Pins are like bolts, except you get to make them in exactly the size and shape you need. You can also print more when you run out.

>> When designing your pins, give them one flat side. The flat side gives you a way to build the pins without using support material — while keeping the tongues horizontal to the build platform. This process also keeps finished pins from rolling off your desk.

>> Make your pins into components so you can easily modify all of them at once if you need to.

>> When designing a project with pin joints, make an effort to standardize around a small number of pin sizes. Standardization helps keep things tidy and simplifies assembly.

Gears

Gears are great for creating complex motions or transferring movement through a mechanism. That is probably the most understated description of the deepest rabbit hole of the industrial age. Gears are in every mechanical device you can imagine. They have existed in some form or other since before recorded history, and are the basis for an incalculable number of clever devices that make everyday life possible.

Making gears is fun and inspires lots of folks to start experimenting with 3D printing. Figure 9-25 shows a simple gear system that can become so much more. To help you get started, here a few basic principles for making gears:

>> Gears need to have clearance between their surfaces to work properly. Gears that are too perfect a fit will bind up. Include a clearance at both the point of rotation and between the teeth of the gear and the teeth of its mate.

FIGURE 9-25:
Welcome
to the New
Industrial
Revolution.
Time to
gear up.

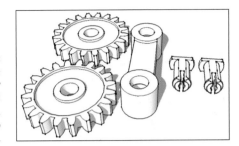 

>> A SketchUp extension called Involute Gears automates the process of making gears. The extension's creator hasn't made it available in the SketchUp Extension Warehouse, so you'll need to locate it by searching *sketchup gear plugin* through Google.

>> Creating optimized gears from scratch is a technical art form that has fallen out of practice. If you want to learn more about designing gears, I recommend getting a copy of *Machinery's Handbook* (Industrial Press). After almost a century in print, this book is the gold standard for anything gear-related.

3

Viewing Your Model in Different Ways

IN THIS PART . . .

Save different looks for a model by applying and customizing styles.

Create realistic shadow studies that reflect the location, day, and time.

Simulate walking through a model.

Save a view of your model as a scene.

Create cutting plans and sections to peek inside a model.

IN THIS CHAPTER

» Giving your model some styles

» Editing, saving, and sharing styles

» Finding out about the Shadows panel

» Using shadows to make models look better

» Displaying and studying accurate shadows

Chapter **10**

Working with Styles and Shadows

S ketchUp is a very capable tool for presenting the stuff you build. Deciding how your models should look — loose and sketchy, quasi-photorealistic, or anything in between — can be lots of fun, and making the right decisions can help your models communicate what they're supposed to.

The first half of this chapter is about styles. If you're the sort of person who likes to draw, you're in for a treat. If you can't draw a straight line with a ruler, you're in for an even bigger treat. SketchUp styles are all about deciding how your geometry — all your faces and edges — will actually *look.*

SketchUp's Shadows feature is another awesome tool for presenting models. Displaying shadows is also an easy operation; it's a matter of clicking a button. When you add shadows to your model views, they look more realistic, more accurate, and more readable. And, well, more *delicious.* You'll see what we mean.

Styling Your Model's Appearance

In SketchUp, a *style* is a collection of settings that control how your model's edges, faces, and background appear. To change a model's whole look, all you need to do is apply a different style. For example, Figure 10-1 shows four different styles applied to the same model of a house. Even cooler, changing a model's style is a one-click operation. Styles also enable you to watermark a model and control how on-screen modeling cues appear.

FIGURE 10-1:
Use styles to make your model look any way you want.

You can also customize styles, which is a little more work than simply applying a style to a model, but arguably more gratifying. This section offers guidelines for using styles and explains how to apply, edit, create, and share styles.

Choosing how and where to apply styles

Styles are endless. With a million permutations of dozens of settings, you can spend all day fiddling with the way your model looks. But you don't have all day, so keep one question in mind: Does this setting help your model say what you want it to say? Focus on what's important. Styles are cool, no doubt, but making them *useful* is the key to keeping them under control.

REMEMBER

To help you make smart decisions about using SketchUp styles, consider at least two factors when you're styling your model:

>> **The subject of your model's level of completeness:** Reserve sketchy styles for models that are still evolving. The message that a sketchy style sends is "this isn't permanent/I'm open to suggestions/all this can change if it has to." As a design gets closer to its final form, styles can make your model appear less rough and more polished. In this way, styles can communicate how much input an audience can have and what decisions still need to be made.

>> **How much your audience knows about design:** An architecture-school jury and a nondesigner client who's building a house for the first time perceive styles differently. Design professionals are more experienced at understanding 3D objects from 2D representations, so they don't need as many visual clues to help them along. Styles' essential purpose is to provide these clues, so here's a guideline: The more your audience knows about design, the simpler you should keep your styles.

Before you dive into styles, remember also that a little style goes a long way. No matter how tempting it is to go hog-wild with the styles settings, please resist the urge. Remember that the purpose of styles is to help your model communicate, *not* to make it look "pretty" or "cool." If the *style* of your work overpowers its content, tone down the styles.

Applying styles to your models

The easiest way to start applying styles is by using the premade styles that come with SketchUp. You find scads of them, which is great because seeing what's been done is the best way to see what's possible. As you go through this section, you'll no doubt get ideas for your own styles, and that's where the fun begins.

Applying a SketchUp style to your model is a three-step process that goes like this:

1. **Open the styles panel by clicking its right-pointing arrow in the Default Tray (Windows) or choosing Window⇨Styles (Mac).**

2. **On the Select tab (which is open by default), choose a styles collection from the Styles Collections drop-down list.**

   We introduce you to the collections that come preinstalled with SketchUp in a moment.

3. **Click a style in the Styles window to apply it to your model.**

TIP

This may come as a surprise, but it's not possible to view your model without any style at all because styles are really just combinations of display settings. Some styles are fancier than others, but no matter what you do, you always have to have a style applied. If you want a relatively neutral view of your model, choose a style in the Default Styles collection.

Wonderfully, SketchUp doesn't leave you out in the cold when it comes to content. SketchUp comes with plenty of examples to get you started. Figure 10-2 shows the Styles Collections drop-down list.

Here's a quick introduction to the most interesting options in the Styles Collections drop-down list:

» **In Model:** The In Model collection shows you all the styles you've applied to your model. The collection keeps track of every style you've *ever* applied to your model, whether or not that style is still applied. To see a current list of styles in your SketchUp file:

1. *Choose the In Model styles collection to show a list of styles you've applied to your model.*

2. *Click the Details flyout menu and choose Purge Unused to get rid of any styles you aren't currently using.*

» **Default Styles:** Think basic. These styles are as minimal as it gets: white background, black edges, white-and-gray front-and-back faces, and no fancy edge effects. Use these styles to get a clean starting point so that you can start simple and build from there.

» **Photo Modeling:** These styles make it easier to work when you're building models that are *photo-textured* — completely covered in photographs. Chapter 8 covers modeling with photos in detail.

» **Sketchy Edges:** These styles use real hand-drawn lines (also called nonphoto-realistic, or NPR, styles) instead of digital ones to render edges, making your models look more like manual sketches than ever before. You can safely use the Sketchy Edges styles to convey any of the following:

- That your design is in process

- That your model is a proposal and not a finished product

- That you welcome feedback in any and all forms

RUNNING FROM REALISM: NPR STYLES

In the world of 3D modeling software, the trend has been toward *photorealism.* Rays of digital light are bounced around a billion times inside your computer until you can see every glint of sunlight in every dewdrop on every blade of grass on the lawn. The standard of perfection is how close the model comes to looking like a photograph, and in a lot of cases, that standard has been met — we've seen computer renderings that look more lifelike than life itself.

But what about models of buildings or other things that aren't completely finished? Perhaps you're an architect who's designing a house for a client. If you aren't sure what kind of tile you'll use on your roof, how are you supposed to make a photorealistic rendering of it? You *could* just go ahead and throw any old tile up there as a placeholder, but that could backfire. Your client could hate the tile and decide not to hire you without ever telling you why, and all because of something you didn't even choose.

What you need is a way to show only the decisions you've made so far, and *that* is exactly why architects and other designers make sketches instead of photorealistic renderings. When you're designing, decisions don't all happen at once. You need to be able to add detail as your design evolves. Sketching allows you to do that because it offers a *continuum* from "cartoony" to photographic, with everything in between. The following figure is an illustration of this.

Programs like SketchUp offer *NPR,* or *nonphotorealistic rendering,* as a way to solve this problem for people who design in 3D. Instead of spending processor power on making representations that look like photographs, the people who make SketchUp went in the opposite direction; they've made a tool that lets you make drawings that are useful throughout the design process. And because SketchUp's NPR engine works in real time, you can make changes on the fly, in front of your audience.

Editing your styles

If you're handy in the kitchen, you've probably heard that cooking is an art and baking is a science. Cooking allows you to experiment — while you're making a sauce, adding a little of this and a dash of that won't wreck anything. Taking liberties with a cake recipe, however, can easily turn the cake into a doorstop. Aidan found this out when he made a lovely chocolate doorstop for his wife's birthday not so long ago. . . .

Luckily, making your own styles has a lot more in common with cooking than it does with baking. Go ahead and fiddle around; you can't do any irreversible harm. Playing with styles doesn't affect a model's geometry. Because styles are just combinations of settings, you can always go back to the way things were before you started.

Of the three tabs in the Styles panel, Edit is definitely the blue whale of the group. Because you find so many controls and settings here, SketchUp's designers broke the Edit tab into the following five sections: Edge, Face, Background, Watermark, and Modeling (for on-screen modeling cues).

REMEMBER

To access each section, first open the Styles panel by clicking the right-pointing arrow in the Default Tray (Windows) or choosing Window ⇨ Styles (Mac). Then click the Edit tab, and select the icon that corresponds to the section whose settings you want to edit.

The following sections explain each part of the Edit tab in detail; we also provide suggestions for using some of the settings.

INTRODUCING STYLE BUILDER

If you're using the Pro version of SketchUp, you have access to Style Builder. It's a completely separate application (just like LayOut) that's put on your computer when you install SketchUp.

Style Builder lets you create NPR styles based on edges *you* draw. Yep, that's right — you can make your SketchUp models look like you drew them by hand with *your* medium of choice (finger paint, Sharpie, bloody knife . . .). All you need is a scanner and a piece of software like Photoshop, and you're good to go. The best thing about the styles you create with Style Builder is that they're completely unique. Unless you share them with someone else, no one can ever make SketchUp models that look like yours.

Because Style Builder is a whole other program and because it's only included in the Pro version of SketchUp, we don't cover Style Builder in depth in this book.

Tweaking edge settings

The Edge section is tricky because it changes a little bit depending on what kind of style you currently have applied to your model. NPR styles have different settings than regular, non-NPR styles. Figure 10-3 shows both versions of the Edge section.

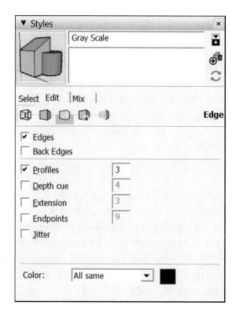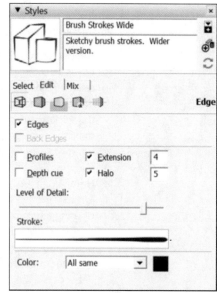

FIGURE 10-3:
The Edge
section comes
in two flavors:
regular (left)
and NPR
(right).

REMEMBER

SketchUp comes with two kinds of styles: regular and NPR. In NPR, SketchUp uses digitized, hand-drawn lines to render the edges in your model. All the styles in the Sketchy Edges collection, as well as all the ones in the Assorted Styles collection, are NPR styles. Because you can create your own styles based on existing ones, all the styles you create using edge settings from one of these NPR styles is an NPR style, too.

Here's the lowdown on some of the less-obvious settings in the Edge section; check out Figure 10-4 for a visual reference:

» **Back Edges:** Switching on this setting tells SketchUp to draw all your model's *obscured* (hidden behind a face) edges as dashed lines. When you display back edges, you can more easily infer edges and points than you can when back edges aren't displayed. Also, there's nothing like a bunch of dashed lines to make a technical drawing look impressive and complex.

» **Profiles:** Selecting the Profiles check box tells SketchUp to use a thicker line for edges that outline shapes in your model. Using profile lines is a pretty standard drawing convention that's been around for a long time. Although models often look better with Profiles on, displaying Profiles comes at a price: drawing Profiles takes more computer horsepower, which can diminish your model's performance. If you're working with a large file, think twice before you turn on Profiles.

>> **Depth Cue:** Using different line thicknesses to convey depth is another popular drawing convention. Objects closest to the viewer are drawn with the thickest lines, whereas the most distant things in the scene are drawn with the thinnest lines.

Depth Cue automatically applies this effect to your models. When its check box is selected, Depth Cue dynamically assigns line thicknesses (draftspeople call them *line weights*) according to how far away from you things are in your model. The number you type is both your desired number of line weights *and* the thickness in pixels of the fattest line SketchUp will use. We recommend a maximum line weight of 5 or 6 pixels.

One more thing: Using Depth Cue and Profiles is overkill. Choose only one.

>> **Halo:** Aidan *really* wishes Halo was available for non-NPR styles because it's just that great. Halo simply ends certain lines before they run into other ones, creating a halo of empty space around objects in the foreground. This keeps your model looking neat and easy to read. In fact, this is a drawing trick that pencil-and-paper users have been using forever to convey depth. Read your favorite comic strips, and you'll likely find this effect. (If you don't have one, Rebecca is a fan of http://xkcd.com.)

The number you type into the Halo box represents the amount of breathing room SketchUp gives your edges. The unit of measure is pixels, but there's no real science to it; just play with the number until things look right to you. For what it's worth, Aidan likes to crank it up.

>> **Level of Detail:** When you slide the Level of Detail controller (which appears only when you've applied an NPR style) back and forth, you're effectively telling SketchUp how *busy* you want your model to look. The farther to the right you slide it, the more of your edges SketchUp displays. Experiment with this setting to see what looks best for your model. The last two images in Figure 10-4 show the Level of Detail slider positioned to the left and right.

>> **Color:** Use the Color drop-down list to tell SketchUp what color to use for all the edges in your model. Here's what each option does:

- *All Same:* This option tells SketchUp to use the same color for all the edges in your model. Select a color by clicking the color well on the right and choosing a color.

- *By Material:* This option turns your model's edges the color of whatever material they're painted with. Because most people don't know that you can paint edges different colors, this setting doesn't get used very often.

- *By Axis:* Now *here's* a useful, but hidden, gem. This option tells SketchUp to make everything that's parallel to one of the colored axes the color of that axis. Edges that aren't parallel to any axis stay black. Why is this so important? When something is screwy with your model — faces won't extrude or lines won't sink in — switching your edge colors to By Axis is the first thing you should do. You'll be surprised how many of your edges aren't what they seem. Have a look at Chapter 15 for more about this problem.

IN A FOG?

If you're looking for something to provide a sense of depth in your model views, look no further than the Fog feature. Fog does exactly what it says — it makes your model look like it's enshrouded in fog (see the accompanying figure). You'd think that a feature this neat would be a little complicated, but it's the opposite. Follow these three steps to let the fog roll into your model:

1. **Open the Fog panel by choosing Window ⇨ Default Tray ⇨ Fog (Windows) or Window ⇨ Fog (Mac).**

2. **Select the Display Fog check box to turn on the fog effect.**

3. **Fool around with the controls until you like what you see.**

We wish the process of controlling how fog looks was more scientific, but it's not. You just play around with the sliders until you have the amount of fog you want. In case you absolutely need to know, here's what the sliders do:

- **Left-hand slider (100%):** This controls the point in space at which the fog is completely opaque. As you move the slider from left to right, you're moving the "completely invisible" point farther away.

- **Right-hand slider (0%):** This controls the point in space at which fog begins to appear in your model. When it's all the way to the right (toward infinity), you can't see any fog.

All edge settings cleared

Edges and Profiles selected

Edges and Depth Cue selected

Edges, Extension, and Halo (2) selected

Edges and Halo (6) selected

Edges, Halo (6), and low Level of Detail selected

FIGURE 10-4:
Choose among the edge settings to give your model the desired look, from realistic to sketchy.

Changing the way faces look

The Face section of the Styles panel, shown in Figure 10-5, is very simple — at least compared with the Edge section (what isn't, really?). This area of the SketchUp user interface controls the appearance of faces, or surfaces, in your model. From here, you can change their color, visibility, and translucency. The following sections describe each element in detail.

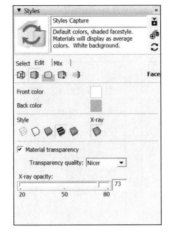

FRONT COLOR/BACK COLOR

In SketchUp, every face you create has a back and a front. To choose the default colors for all new faces you create, click the Front and Back color wells, and then pick a color. We recommend sticking with neutral tones for your defaults; you can always paint individual faces later.

TIP

Sometimes when you model in SketchUp, a face is turned inside out. Follow these steps to flip a face so that the right side shows:

1. **Select the face you want to flip.**

2. **Context-click and choose Reverse Faces.**

**TECHNICAL
STUFF**

Knowing which face is the front and which is the back is especially important if you plan to export your model to another program or create a 3D printable model. Some programs, such as Autodesk 3ds Max, use the distinction between front and back to determine what to display. In these cases, showing the wrong side of a face can produce unexpected results. See Chapter 9 for details about 3D printing models.

STYLE

Face styles provide different modes for viewing the faces in your model. You can switch among them as much as you like without affecting your geometry. Each Face style has its purpose, and all are shown in Figure 10-6:

Wireframe

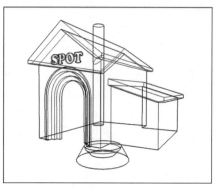

Hidden Line

Shaded

Shaded Using Textures

Shaded Using All Same

Shaded Using All Same in X-Ray mode

FIGURE 10-6:
Use Face styles to change the way your faces appear.

>> **Wireframe:** In Wireframe mode, your faces are invisible. Because you can't see them, you can't affect them. Only your edges are visible, which makes this mode handy for doing two things:

TIP

- When you select edges, switch to Wireframe mode to make sure that you've selected what you meant to select. Because no faces block your view, Wireframe mode helps you select only what you want. The Back Edges setting is handy for this, too.

- After you use Intersect Faces, you usually have stray edges lying around. Wireframe is the quickest way to erase them because you can see what you're doing. See Chapter 4 for details on Intersect Faces.

>> **Hidden Line:** Hidden Line mode displays all your faces using whatever color you're using for the background; it's really as simple as that. If you're trying to make a clean, black-and-white line drawing that looks like a technical illustration, make your background white. (We talk about how later in this chapter.)

>> **Shaded:** This Face mode displays colors on your faces. Faces painted with a solid color appear that color. Faces to which you've added textures are shown with a color that best approximates their *overall color.* If your texture has a lot of brown in it, SketchUp picks a brown and uses that.

TIP

For models with a lot of these textures, choosing the Shaded mode can really speed up orbiting, zooming, and otherwise navigating around. Unless you absolutely need to see textures applied to your model's faces, try staying in Shaded mode as you work on a model.

>> **Shaded Using Textures:** Shaded Using Textures makes textures visible. Because this mode puts a lot of strain on your computer, it can also be the slowest mode to work in. Turn it on only when you work on a small model, or when you need to see the textures. Obviously, if you're going for a photorealistic effect, this is the mode to choose.

>> **Display Shaded Using All Same:** This mode is a quick way to give your model a simplified color scheme. This mode uses your default front and back face colors to paint your model. You can also use this setting to check the orientation of your faces if you're exporting your model to another 3D-modeling program.

>> **X-Ray:** Unlike using translucent materials on only *some* of your faces (such as glass and water), flipping on X-Ray mode enables you to see through *all* your faces. Use X-Ray to see through a wall or a floor and show what's behind it. If you're in a plan (overhead) view, X-Ray mode is a great way to demonstrate how a floor level relates to the one below it.

TRANSPARENCY

Displaying *transparency* (as in translucent materials) is an especially taxing operation for SketchUp and your computer to handle, so you can decide how to display translucent materials:

>> **Enable transparency:** Clear this check box to display translucent materials as opaque. Turn off transparency to speed up SketchUp's performance if you find that it has slowed.

>> **Transparency quality:** If you decide to display transparency, you can further fine-tune your system's performance by telling SketchUp how to render that transparency. In earlier versions of SketchUp, you have the choice of better performance, nicer graphics, or an average of the two. SketchUp 2017 streamlines these options to simply Faster or Nicer; when Nicer is selected, you can adjust the model's opacity with the X-Ray Opacity slider. The lower the opacity, the more see-through your model is.

Setting up the background

In the Background section of the Styles panel, you choose colors and decide whether you want to see a sky and a ground plane. Check out Figure 10-7 to get a view of the Background section, along with an idea of how it works. You have the following options in the Background section:

>> **Background:** For most models, Aidan sets the background to a traditional white.

>> **Sky:** Displaying a sky in your modeling window makes things slightly more realistic, but the real purpose of this feature is to provide a point of reference for your model. In 3D views of big things like architecture, it's nice to be able to see the horizon. Another reason for turning on the sky is to set the mood — keep in mind that the sky isn't always blue. Some beautiful SketchUp renderings are sunset (or maybe nuclear winter) orange.

>> **Ground:** We're not big fans of turning on the Ground feature, and here's why: It's *very* hard to find a ground color that looks halfway good, no matter what you're building. Also, you can't dig into the earth to make sunken spaces (such as courtyards) with Ground turned on. Instead of turning on this feature, try making your own ground planes with faces and edges. This method is more flexible, and we think it looks better.

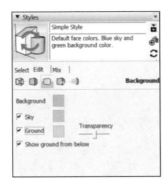

FIGURE 10-7:
Use the
Background
section to turn
on the sky and
the ground
and to choose
colors.

Working with watermarks

Watermarks are much easier to understand if you don't think about them as actual watermarks that are used to brand a model. Instead, think of watermarks as graphics that you can apply either *behind* or *in front of* your model to produce certain effects. Here are a few of the things you can do with SketchUp watermarks:

» Simulate a paper texture, just like some of the styles in the Assorted Styles collection.

» Apply a logo or other graphic to your model view.

» Layer a translucent or cutout image in the foreground to simulate looking through a frosted window or binoculars.

» Add a photographic background like Outer Space or Inside My Ileum to create a unique model setting.

EYEING THE WATERMARK CONTROLS

Figure 10-8 shows the Watermark section of the Styles panel. Here's a brief introduction to what some of the less-obvious controls do:

» **Add, Remove, and Edit Watermark buttons:** The +, –, and gears icons allow you to add, remove, and edit (respectively) watermarks in the style you're editing.

» **Watermark list:** This list shows all your watermarks in relation to *model space,* which is the space your model occupies. All watermarks are either in front of or behind your model, making them overlays or underlays, respectively.

» **Move Up or Move Down arrows:** Use these buttons to change the stacking order of the watermarks in your model view. Select the watermark you want to move in the list and then click one of these buttons to move it up or down in the order.

FIGURE 10-8:
The Watermark
section.

ADDING A WATERMARK

Watermarks are by no means simple, but working with them, miraculously enough, is. Follow these steps to add a watermark to your model view:

1. **Click the Add Watermark button.**

The Choose Watermark dialog box appears.

2. **Find the image you want to use as a watermark and then click the Open button to open the first Create Watermark dialog box shown in Figure 10-9.**

You can use any of these graphics file formats: TIFF, JPEG, PNG, and GIF.

TECHNICAL STUFF

This point is *way* beyond the scope of this book but worth mentioning because you're bound to need this sooner or later: If you want to make a watermark out of an image that isn't a solid rectangle (such as a logo), you need to use a graphics file format that supports alpha channels (such as PNG). An *alpha channel* is an extra layer of information in a graphics file that describes which areas of your image are supposed to be transparent. It sounds complicated, but it's really a straightforward concept. To make an image with an alpha channel, you need software like Photoshop or GIMP (GNU Image Manipulation Program). Try searching for *alpha channels* on Google for more information.

3. **Type a name for your watermark in the Name box.**

4. **Choose whether you want your new watermark to be in the background or in the foreground as an overlay and click the Next button.**

5. **Decide whether to use your watermark as a mask.**

Selecting this check box tells SketchUp to make your watermark transparent, which kind of simulates a real watermark. *How* transparent each part becomes is based on how bright it is. White is the brightest color, so anything white in your watermark becomes completely transparent. Things that are black turn your background color, and everything in between turns a shade of your background color. The possibilities for this feature are interesting, but we haven't found any good uses for it yet.

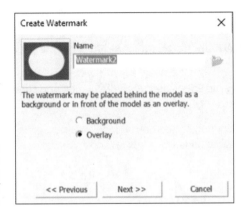

FIGURE 10-9:
The Create Watermark series of dialog boxes.

6. **Adjust the amount that your watermark blends with what's behind it and then click the Next button.**

   In this case, Blend is really just a synonym for Transparency. By sliding the Blend slider back and forth, you can adjust the transparency of your watermark.

TIP

   Blend comes in handy for making paper textures because that process involves using the same watermark twice: once as an overlay and once as an underlay. The overlay version gets blended in so that your model appears to be drawn on top of it. To see how this works, apply one of the Paper Texture styles to your model and then edit each of the watermarks to check out its settings.

7. **Decide how you want your watermark to be displayed and then click the Finish button.**

   You have three choices for how SketchUp can display your watermark: stretched to fit the entire window, tiled across the window, and positioned in the window. If you select Stretched to Fit the Screen, be sure to select the Lock Aspect Ratio check box if your watermark is a logo that you don't want to appear distorted.

EDITING A WATERMARK

You can edit any watermark in your SketchUp file at any time. Follow these simple steps to edit a watermark:

1. **Select the watermark you want to edit in the Watermark list.**

You can find the Watermark list in the Watermark section of the Edit tab of the Styles panel.

2. **Click the Edit Watermark button (it looks like a couple of tiny gears) to open the Edit Watermark dialog box.**

3. **Use the controls in the Edit Watermark dialog box and then click OK when you're done.**

For a complete description of the controls in this dialog box, see the description of the Create Watermark dialog box in "Adding a watermark," earlier in this chapter.

Tweaking modeling settings

In the Modeling section, shown in Figure 10-10, the controls adjust the color and visibility of all your model elements that aren't geometry. The controls are described as follows:

>> **Controls with color wells:** Click the wells to change the color of that type of element.

>> **Section Cut Width:** This refers to the thickness of the lines, in pixels, that make up the section cut when you use a section plane. For more about section cuts, see Chapter 11.

>> **Controls with check boxes:** Use these to control the visibility of that type of element in your model. Three of them are a little confusing:

  • *Color by Layer:* Tells SketchUp to color your geometry according to the colors you've set up in the Layers panel. Check out Chapter 7 for more about layers and this setting.

  • *Section Planes:* This refers to the section plane objects that you use to cut sections. They're gray with four arrows on their corners. Chapter 11 explains how section planes and cuts work.

  • *Section Cuts:* Unlike section planes, this setting controls the visibility of the section cut effect itself. With this deselected, your section planes don't appear to cut anything.

>> **Match Photo settings:** When you photo-match (which you can read all about in Chapter 8), adjusting the visibility of your photograph is sometimes helpful. Use these controls to hide, show, and adjust the photo's opacity in both the background and the foreground.

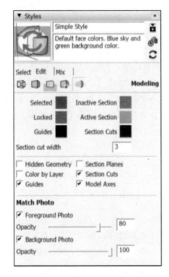

FIGURE 10-10:
The controls in the Modeling section are every bit as simple as they look.

IMPROVING ACCESSIBILITY WITH STYLES

If you have some degree of color blindness, you may have trouble seeing the on-screen modeling cues. However, SketchUp styles enable you to change these colors and improve SketchUp's accessibility.

To start, check whether your version of SketchUp includes the Color Blind style, which you find in the Color Sets collection. The Color Blind style is new in SketchUp 2017.

If you don't have the Color Blind style, you can create your own by selecting a black background and changing the colors in the Modeling section to contrasting colors that are easy for you to see.

In SketchUp 2017, you can also change the axes colors and additional on-screen color cues in the Preferences dialog box. Choose Tools ➪ Preferences (Windows) or SketchUp ➪ Preferences (Mac), and select the Accessibility pane to find and adjust these options.

Mixing styles to create new ones

You can use the Mix tab to combine features of multiple styles to make new ones. Instead of working through the sections of the Edit tab, flipping controls on and off, sliding sliders, and picking colors, the Mix tab lets you build new styles by dropping existing ones onto special "category" wells. In addition to being a nifty way to work, mixing is the only way you can switch a style's edge settings between NPR and non-NPR lines.

REMEMBER

NPR refers to the styles in the Assorted Styles, Sketchy Edges, and Competition Winners collections. These nonphotorealistic rendering styles use scanned, hand-drawn lines to draw the edges in your model. If you have SketchUp Pro, you can use Style Builder to make your own NPR styles from lines you draw and scan in. Take a look at the sidebar "Introducing Style Builder," earlier in this chapter, for more information.

Follow these steps to change a style using the Mix tab, as shown in Figure 10-11:

1. **On the Styles panel, select the Mix tab.**

   When you select the Mix tab, the secondary section opens at the bottom of the panel so that you can view your styles without switching back and forth from the Mix to Select tab.

2. **Find the style you want to sample *from* in the Select section.**

   You can call this your *source* style. Say that you're working on a new style and you want your edges to look just like those in the Marker Loose style that came with SketchUp. In this example, choose the Sketchy Edges collection from the Styles Collections drop-down list, where you'll find the Marker Loose style.

3a. **(Windows) Click the source style from the Styles list in the Select section to sample it and then click the category well that corresponds to the style setting you want to apply.**

3b. **(Mac) Drag your source style from the Styles list in the Select section to the category well that corresponds to the style setting you want to apply.**

   In this case, sample the Marker Loose style from the Select section and drop it on the Edge Settings Category well because you want the edge settings from that style to be applied to the style you're working on.

4. **To save your style after you're done adding all the bits and pieces, see the following section.**

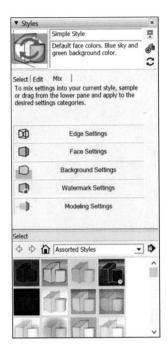

FIGURE 10-11:
Sample from different styles to update the style you're working on.

Creating a new style

Creating a new style adds it to your In Model collection of styles, so you can come back and apply it to your model anytime you like. Follow these steps to create a new style:

1. **Click the Create New Style button in the Styles panel.**

   This duplicates the style that was applied to your model before you clicked the Create New Style button. Your new style appears in your In Model collection as *[name of the original style]*1.

2. **Use the controls in the Edit tab to set up your style the way you want.**

   Frequently, you want to make a new style *after* you already make changes to an existing one. If you want to create a new style that reflects modifications you've made already, just switch Steps 1 and 2.

TIP

3. **In the Name box (at the top of the Styles panel), give your new style a name and press Enter.**

   If you want, you can also give your new style a description in the Description box, though you may want to wait until later.

4. **Click the Update button.**

   This updates your new style with all the changes you made in Steps 2 and 3.

5. **Check the In Model collection in the Select tab to make sure that your new style is there.**

6. **Click the In Model button (which looks like a little house) to see your In Model Styles collection.**

   Your new style appears alphabetically in the list.

TIP

If a bunch of styles exist in your In Model collection that you don't use anymore and that you want to clean up, click the Details flyout menu and choose Purge Unused. This gets rid of any styles that aren't currently applied to any scenes in your model. Chapter 11 has more about scenes.

REMEMBER

Creating a new style *doesn't* automatically make it available for use in other SketchUp files. To find out how to save and share styles, see the next section.

Saving and sharing styles you make

As you work in SketchUp, you'll want to create your own styles and save them so that you can use them in other models. If you're part of a team, everyone will likely want to access the same styles so that all your models look consistent.

Saving the styles you make

When creating your own styles, you can approach things in two ways:

>> **Create New Style:** Clicking this button creates a new style with the currently active settings. When you create a new style, it appears in your In Model collection of styles and is saved with your model. The Create New Style button can be found in the upper-right corner of the Styles panel.

>> **Update Style with Changes:** This button updates the current style with any changes you've made in the Edit or Mix tabs. If you want to modify an existing style without creating a new one, this is the way to go. You can find the Update button right below the Create button in the upper-right corner of the Styles panel.

Updating an existing style

To make adjustments to a style in your model, you need to update it. Follow these steps to update a style:

1. **Apply the style you want to update to your model.**

   If you need help with this, follow the steps in the section, "Applying styles to your models," earlier in this chapter.

2. **Use the controls in the Edit tab to make changes to the style.**

3. **Click the Update Style with Changes button in the Styles panel to update the style with your changes.**

TIP

Use the Update Style with Changes button to rename existing styles, too. Just type the new name into the Name box (at the top of the Styles panel), press Enter, and then click the Update Style with Changes button.

REMEMBER

When you update a style, only the copy of the style that's saved with your model is updated. You aren't altering the copy of the style that appears in every new SketchUp file you create.

Using your styles in other models

TIP

After you update or create a style, you probably want to make that style available in other SketchUp models. To make this happen, you need to create your own styles collections. *Collections* are folders on your computer that contain the styles that appear in the Styles panel. You can create your own collections to keep the styles you invent neat and tidy.

Follow these steps to create a collection to contain your styles:

1. **Open the Styles panel by clicking the right-pointing arrow in the Default Tray (Windows) or by choosing Window⇨Styles (Mac).**

2. **On the Select tab, click the Details menu, and choose Open or Create a Collection. (On a Mac, choose Create a Collection.)**

   A dialog box opens, where you select a location on your hard drive for the collection.

3. **Navigate to the folder on your computer or network where you want to create your collection.**

4. **Click the New Folder button.**

   The new folder you create becomes your new collection.

5. **Type a name for your new collection.**

   For example, you can call your new collection Josephine's Collection. You can call it something else if your name isn't Josephine.

6. **(Mac) Make sure that the Add to Favorites check box is selected.**

7. **Click the Select Folder button (Windows) or the Save button (Mac).**

   The dialog box closes, and your collection is added to the Favorites section of the Collections drop-down list. It will be there in every SketchUp model you open on this computer.

After you create a new collection, you can add styles to it to make them available from any model you work on.

Follow these steps to make a style available for use in other SketchUp files:

1. **Choose Window ➪ Styles.**

The Styles panel appears.

2. **Click the Select tab and then click the In Model button to display your In Model collection.**

The In Model button looks like a little house. The In Model collection contains all the styles you've used in your model, including the ones you've created.

3. **Click the Show Secondary Selection Pane button.**

You find this button in the upper-right corner of the Styles panel. When you click it, a second copy of the Select section pops out of the bottom of the Styles panel, as shown in Figure 10-12. Use this section to drag and drop styles between folders on your computer, which makes it easier to keep them organized.

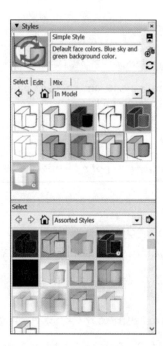

FIGURE 10-12: Use the Select section to manage your styles without leaving SketchUp.

4. **In the Select section, choose the collection to which you want to add your style.**

   If you've created a collection specifically for the styles you make, choose that one; or you can pick any collection in the Collections drop-down list.

5. **Drag your style *from* the In Model styles list *to* the Styles list in the Select section.**

   By dragging and dropping your style from the upper list to the lower one, you make the style available to anyone who has access to that collection. This means that you can use the style in other SketchUp models you build on your computer. To share it with other members of your team, copy your style to a collection where other people can get to it, such as on a network.

Working with Shadows

Typically, you add shadows to a SketchUp drawing for two key reasons:

» **To display or print a model in a more realistic way:** Turning on shadows adds depth and realism, and gives your model an added level of complexity that makes it look like you worked harder than you really did.

» **To study the effect of the sun on what you've built (or plan to build) in a specific geographic location:** Shadow studies are an integral part of the design of any built object. If you're making a sunroom, you need to know that the sun is actually going to hit it, no? You can use SketchUp to show exactly how the sun will affect your creation, at every time of day, on every day of the year.

In this section, we start with a brief, nuts-and-bolts description of how all the controls work, without diving too much into why you'd want to pick one setting instead of another. The second part of this section is devoted to running through each of the preceding scenarios and using the controls to make SketchUp do exactly what you want it to.

Discovering the shadow settings

The basic thing to understand about shadows in SketchUp is that, just like in real life, they're controlled by changing the position of the sun. Because the sun moves exactly the same way every year, you just pick a date and time, and SketchUp automatically displays the correct shadows by figuring out where the sun should be. Hooray for math!

You do all these simple maneuvers in the Shadows panel, as shown in Figure 10-13. The sections that follow introduce how the controls work so you can apply them to your model.

FIGURE 10-13:
Dial up the sun
in the Shadows
panel.

Turning on the sun

Shadows aren't turned on by default, so the first thing you need to know about applying shadows is how to turn them on. Follow these simple steps:

1. **Open the Shadows panel by choosing Window ⇨ Default Tray ⇨ Shadows (Windows) or Window ⇨ Shadows (Mac).**

2. **In the upper-left corner of the panel, click the Show/Hide Shadows button.**

   Clicking it turns on the sun in SketchUp, casting shadows throughout your model and, generally speaking, making everything much more exciting.

Setting a shadow's time and date

The Shadows panel has time and date controls, which you use to change the position of the SketchUp sun. The time and date you choose, in turn, controls the appearance of shadows in your model:

>> **Setting the time:** You don't have to be Copernicus to figure out how to set the time of day; move the Time slider back and forth, or type a time into the little box on the right. Notice the times at each end of the slider? These represent sunrise and sunset for the day of the year you've set in the Date control, described in the next bullet point.

>> **Setting the date:** Just like the time of day, you set the day of the year by moving the Date slider back and forth, or by typing in a date in the little box on the right. If you slide the Date control back and forth, notice that the sunrise and sunset times change in the Time control, in the preceding point.

TIP

To toggle open or closed the extra shadow controls, click the triangular Expand button in the upper-right corner of the Shadows panel.

Choosing where shadows appear

The Display check boxes in the Shadows panel enable you to control *where* shadows are cast. Depending on your model, you may want to toggle these on or off.

>> **On Faces:** Deselecting the On Faces check box means that shadows aren't cast on faces in your model. This is on by default, and should probably be left on, unless you want to cast shadows only on the ground. For what it's worth, we always have it selected.

>> **On Ground:** Deselecting the On Ground check box causes shadows not to be cast on the ground plane. Again, this is on by default, but sometimes you want to turn it off. A prime example is when something you build extends underground.

>> **From Edges:** Selecting the From Edges check box tells SketchUp to allow edges to cast shadows. This applies to single edges that aren't associated with faces — things like ropes, poles, and sticks are often modeled with edges like these.

Adding depth and realism

The neat thing about shadows in SketchUp is how easily you can apply them — and how easy they are to adjust. In the previous sections, you find a dry rundown of the basic controls in the Shadows panel. In the following sections, you learn how to use those controls to add depth, realism, and delicious nuance to your models. If only Caravaggio had had it so good . . .

You often need shadows to make your drawings read better, especially in the following instances:

>> **Indoor scenes:** The sun is the only source of lighting that SketchUp has, so any shadows you use in interior views have to come from it.

>> **Objects that aren't in any particular location:** For things like cars and furniture, it doesn't matter that the shadows are *geographically accurate;* all that matters is that they help make your model look good.

>> **2D views:** Without shadows, reading depth in 2D views of 3D space is next to impossible.

Lighting indoor spaces

Adding shadows to interior views presents an interesting problem: Because SketchUp has no lights besides the sun, how are you supposed to make anything that looks halfway realistic? With a ceiling in your room, everything's dark. If you leave off the ceiling, your model looks ridiculous. Don't despair — here are some tricks:

>> **Decrease the darkness of the shadows.** Sliding the Dark slider to the right brightens your view considerably. You can still see the shadows cast by the sun coming through windows and other openings, but the whole room won't look like something bad is about to happen. Check out Figure 10-14.

>> **Make an impossible ceiling.** As long as you haven't modeled anything on top of the interior you're planning to show, you can tell the ceiling not to cast a shadow. That way, sunlight shines directly onto your furniture, casting gloriously complex shadows all over everything.

Figure 10-15 shows this ceiling method in action. To create this effect yourself, follow these steps:

1. **Adjust the settings in the Shadows panel until the sun shines through one or more windows in your view.**

This ensures that shadows cast by objects in your room look like they're caused by light from the windows.

TIP

To make it seem like overhead lighting is in your space, set the time of day to about noon and the date to about the end of June. The shadows cast by furniture and similar objects will be directly below the objects themselves. One more thing: If you have lighting fixtures on the ceiling, remember to set them not to cast shadows in the Entity Info panel (read on).

2. **Open the Entity Info panel by clicking its right-pointing arrow in the Default Tray (Windows) or choosing Window ⇨ Entity Info (Mac).**

3. **Select any faces that make up the ceiling.**

Hold down the Shift key to select more than one thing at a time.

4. **In the Entity Info panel, deselect the Cast Shadows check box.**

The ceiling now no longer casts a shadow, brightening your space considerably. If you don't see the Cast Shadows checkbox, click the Show Details icon in the upper right.

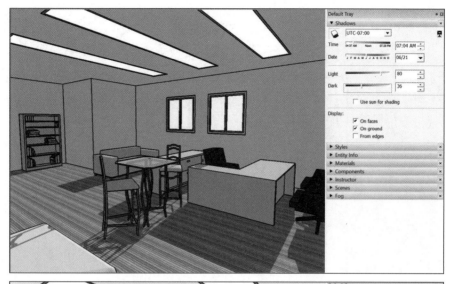

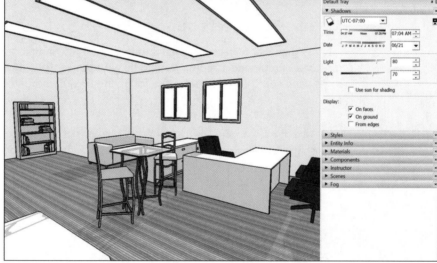

FIGURE 10-14:
Brighten
the room by
decreasing the
Dark slider.

5. **Repeat Steps 3 and 4 for the following faces and objects:**

- The wall with the windows in it

- The windows themselves

- Any walls in your view that cast shadows on the floor of your space

6. **Move the Dark slider to about 50.**

This brightens things even more and makes your shadows more believable.

FIGURE 10-15:
Tell the ceiling not to cast a shadow.

Making 3D objects pop

Adding shadows to freestanding things like tables, lamps, and pineapples is a mostly aesthetic undertaking; just fiddle with the controls until things look good to you and you'll be okay. Keep the following tips, illustrated in Figure 10-16, in mind:

>> **Take it easy on the contrast** — especially when it comes to very complex shapes or faces with photos mapped to them. When your model is too contrasty and dramatic, it can be hard to figure out what's going on. To decrease the contrast

1. *Move the Dark slider over to about 40 or 50.*

2. *Move the Light slider down to 60 or 70.*

>> **Shorten your shadows.** It's strange to see objects lit as though the light source is very far away; overhead lighting looks more natural. To make your shadows look better, follow these steps:

1. *Set the Date slider to a day in the early autumn.*

2. *Set the Time slider to a time between 10:00 a.m. and 2:00 p.m.*

REMEMBER

>> **Don't be afraid to rotate your model.** Remember that you can't get every possible shadow position by using only the controls in the Shadows panel. To get the effect you want, you may have to rotate your model by selecting it and using the Rotate tool.

» **Select the From Edges check box.** Lots of times, modelers use free edges to add fine detail to models (think of a harp or a loom). Selecting the From Edges check box tells SketchUp to allow those edges to cast shadows, which makes complex objects look about 900-percent cooler.

» **Pay attention to the transparency of faces.** When you have a face painted with a transparent material, you can decide whether that face should cast a shadow — chances are that it shouldn't. In SketchUp, the rule is that materials more than 50-percent transparent cast shadows. So, if you don't want one of your transparent-looking faces to cast a shadow, do one of the following:

- *Select the face and then deselect the Cast Shadows check box in the Entity Info panel.*

- *Adjust the opacity of the face's material to be less than 50 percent in the Materials panel.* For more information on how to do this, have a look at Chapter 3.

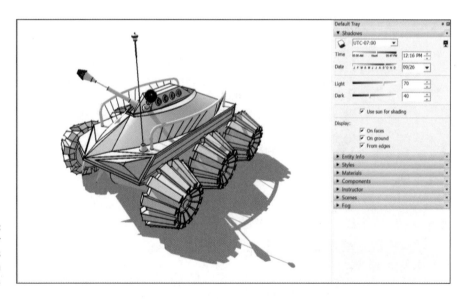

FIGURE 10-16:
Some tips for making objects stand out with shadows.

Creating accurate shadow studies

SketchUp can display accurate shadows, one of its most useful features. To do this, three pieces of information are necessary:

» The time of day

» The day of the year

» The latitude of the building site

The sun's position (and thus the position of shadows) depends on geographic location — that is to say, *latitude.* The shadow cast by a building at 3:00 on March 5 in Minsk is very different from that cast by a similar building, at the same time of day, on the same date in Nairobi.

If you display shadows on a model of a toaster oven, geographic location probably doesn't matter to you; the shadows are just there for effect. But if you try to see how much time your pool deck will spend in the sun during the summer months, you need to tell SketchUp where you are.

Telling SketchUp where you are

Do you know the precise latitude of where you live? We sure don't. It's a good thing SketchUp helps you figure out where in the world your model is supposed to be. You can *geo-reference* your model (give it a geographic location) in two ways; which one you choose probably depends on whether you have an Internet connection:

>> **Using a geo-location snapshot:** This is by far the simplest approach, but it requires that you have a precise idea of where your model is supposed to be on the globe. It also requires that you be connected to the Internet for the operation. If you know exactly where your model is supposed to go, and you're online, use this method. Take a look at Chapter 8 for a complete set of instructions.

>> **Using the Model Info dialog box:** This method is a little more complicated, but it's your only option if you're not online. Read on for all the gory details.

To give your model a geographic location when you're offline, follow these steps illustrated in Figure 10-17:

1. **Choose Window⇨Model Info.**

2. **In the Model Info dialog box that appears, select Geo-Location in the sidebar on the left.**

If you see anything other than This model is not geo-located, stop here. Your model has already been geographically located, and you don't need to go through any of the following steps. Close the Model Info dialog box, make yourself some coffee, and waste the time you just saved avoiding the next steps.

3. **Click the Set Manual Location button to open another dialog box.**

4. **Enter the required information and click OK.**

   What you type in the Country and Location fields is entirely up to you; it doesn't affect your model's geo-location one bit. The Latitude and Longitude fields are the important parts of this dialog box.

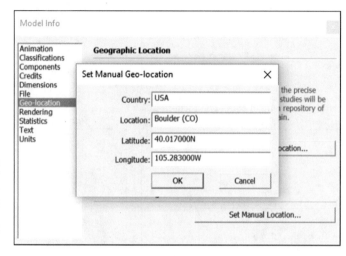

FIGURE 10-17:
Giving your
model a
geographic
location when
you're not
online.

Whether you imported a geo-location snapshot or entered a set of coordinates manually, the next step is to make sure your model is rotated correctly relative to north. If your model faces the wrong way, your shadow studies are completely inaccurate.

REMEMBER

All you really need to know is this: By default, the green axis runs north–south, with the solid part pointing north. If north-for-your-building doesn't line up with the green axis, just select everything and use the Rotate tool to spin the building into place. See Chapter 3 for details about rotating a model.

The following method, illustrated in Figure 10-18, works well:

1. **On the ground somewhere, draw an edge that points to where north** *should* **be.**

2. **Starting at the southern endpoint of the edge you just drew, draw another edge that's parallel to the green axis.**

   You have a V shape.

3. **Select everything in your model** *except* **the edge you drew in Step 2.**

   Your geo-location snapshot (if you have one) should have a red border around it; that's because it's locked. If for some reason it isn't, context-click it and choose Lock — you don't want to rotate it accidentally.

Draw two lines

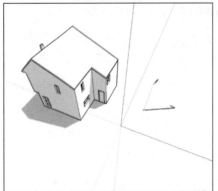

Select all except line parallel to green axis

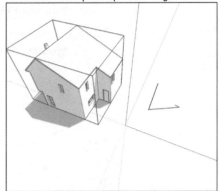

Rotate everything about point where lines meet

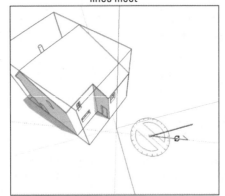

Rotate until lines are parallel

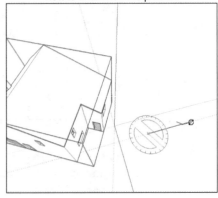

FIGURE 10-18:
Make sure
your model
is correctly
oriented
relative to
north.

4. **Activate the Rotate tool.**

5. **Click the *vertex* (pointy end) of the V to establish your center of rotation.**

6. **Click the north end of the edge you drew in Step 1.**

7. **Click the north end of the edge you drew in Step 2.**

   Now everything's lined up properly.

Displaying accurate shadows for a given time and place

Now that you've told SketchUp where your model is, it's a pretty simple process to study how the sun will affect your project, as shown in Figure 10-19. This is the fun part; all you have to do is move some sliders. If you have an audience, get ready for completely undeserved praise.

To study how the sun affects your project, follow these steps:

1. **Orbit, zoom, and pan around until you have a good view of the part of your project you want to study.**

2. **Open the Shadows panel by clicking its right-pointing arrow in the Default Tray (Windows) or by choosing Window ⇨ Shadows (Mac).**

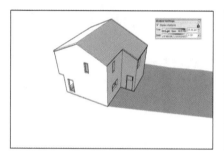 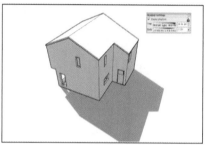

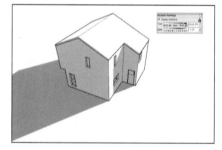

FIGURE 10-19:
Studying the effect of the sun on your model.

3. **Select the Show/Hide Shadows button to turn on SketchUp's sun.**

4. **Make sure the time zone setting is correct for your location.**

   SketchUp doesn't always get the time zone right for every location in the world; time zones don't always map directly to coordinates. If the time zone you see in the Time Zone drop-down list (at the top of the Shadows panel) isn't correct, choose another one.

   Wondering what your time zone is in UTC? Try searching Google for *UTC time zones* to find a list that you can reference.

   TIP

5. **Type a month and day into the box to the right of the Date slider and then press Enter.**

6. Move the Time slider back and forth to see how the shadows will move over the course of that day.

7. Pick a time of day using the Time controls.

8. Move the Date slider back and forth to see how the sun will affect your project at that time of day over the course of the year.

Chapter **11**

Presenting Your Model inside SketchUp

After you make a model, you probably want to show it to someone. How you present your work depends on the idea you want to convey. The tricky part about using SketchUp to present a model isn't actually using the tools; it's choosing the *right* tools to get your idea across without a bunch of extra information distracting your audience. Most 3D models have so much to look at that the real challenge is finding a presentation method that helps you focus on the stuff you want to talk about.

In this chapter, you learn about three ways to show off your models without ever leaving SketchUp. If you've made a building, you can walk around inside it. You can even walk up and down stairs and ramps — just like in a video game. You can create animated slide shows by setting up scenes with different camera views, times of day, and even visual styles. If you want to talk about what's *inside* your model, you can cut sections through it without taking it apart.

As you read this chapter, think about what you want your model to communicate. Think about how you might use each method to make a different kind of point and think about the order in which you want those points to be made. As with everything else in SketchUp (and in life, we suppose), a little bit of planning goes a long way. That said, presenting a model live in SketchUp is undeniably sexy; you can't really go wrong, so have fun.

Exploring Your Creation on Foot

Few experiences in life are as satisfying as running around inside your model. After you make a space, you can walk around it, go up and down stairs, bump into walls, and even fall off ledges. You can check to make sure that the television is visible from the kitchen, say, or experience what it'd be like to wander down the hall. In a potentially confusing building, such as an airport or a train station, you can figure out where to put the signs by allowing someone who's never seen your model to explore the space "on foot." The following sections, uh, walk you through how to use these features.

These tools were made for walking

A couple tools in SketchUp are dedicated to moving around your model as if you were actually inside it. The first step (no pun intended) is to position yourself so that you seem to stand inside your model. This can be tricky with just the Orbit, Pan, and Zoom tools, so SketchUp provides a tool just for this: Position Camera. After you're standing in the right spot (and at the right height), you use the Walk tool to move around. It's as simple as that.

The Position Camera and Walk tools enable you to walk around inside your model.

Standing in the right spot: The Position Camera tool

The Position Camera tool precisely places your viewpoint in SketchUp in a particular spot. That's really all it does, but it works in two ways.

>> **You want to stand right here.** Choose Camera ⟹ Position Camera from the menu bar or click the Position Camera tool. (You find it on the Large Tool Set in both Windows and Mac OS X.) Then click anywhere in the modeling window to automatically position your viewpoint 5 feet, 6 inches above wherever you clicked. Because this is the average *eye height* of an adult, the result is that you are, for all intents and purposes, standing on the spot where you clicked; see Figure 11-1. After you use Position Camera, SketchUp automatically switches to the Look Around tool, assuming that you may want to look around. We talk about Look Around in the "Stopping to look around" section of this chapter.

You're not stuck being five-and-a-half-feet tall forever. After you use Position Camera, type the height you'd rather be and press Enter. Type **18"** to see a golden retriever's view of the world, or type **7'** to pretend you play for the L.A. Lakers. Keep in mind that the Measurements box (the spot in the lower-right corner where numbers appear) displays your eye height as a distance from the ground, and not from whatever surface you're "standing on." To set your eye height to be 5 feet above a platform that's 10 feet high, you'd type **15'**.

FIGURE 11-1:
Drop yourself
into your
model with
the Position
Camera tool.

>> **You want your eyes to be right here, and you want to look in this direction.** Select Position Camera, click the mouse button while in the spot where you want your eyes to be, drag over to the thing you want to look at (you see a dashed line connecting the two points), and release the mouse button; see Figure 11-2. Try this technique a couple times; it takes a bit of practice to master. Use Position Camera in this way if you want to stand in a particular spot *and* look in a particular direction. This technique works great with scenes, covered later in this chapter.

FIGURE 11-2:
Aim your view
by using Posi-
tion Camera in
another way.

Stepping out with the Walk tool

After you use Position Camera to place yourself in your model, use the Walk tool to move through it. You find the Walk tool on the Camera menu or the Large Tool Set.

To walk around, click and drag the mouse in the direction you want to move:

>> Straight up is forward.

>> Straight down is backward.

>> Anything to the left or right causes you to turn while you walk.

The farther you move your cursor, the faster you walk. Release the mouse button to stop. If you've ever played video games, you'll get used to it quickly. If Scrabble is more your speed, it'll take a few minutes to get the hang of things.

TIP

You can even use the Walk tool to walk up and down stairs and ramps. Keep in mind that the highest step you can climb is 22 inches — anything higher and you get the "bump" cursor, just like you walked into a wall. Also, if you walk off a high surface, you fall to the surface below. It's times like these that we wish SketchUp had cartoon sound effects. . . .

Using modifier keys in combination with the Walk tool makes SketchUp even more like a video game:

>> **To run instead of walk,** hold down the Ctrl key (Option on a Mac) while you're using the Walk tool with your mouse. This may be useful if you're trying to simulate what it'd be like if a werewolf were chasing you through your model.

>> **To make the Walk tool change your eye height or move sideways,** use the Shift key. To move straight up like you're growing, hold down the Shift key while you move your mouse up. To get shorter, hold down Shift and move your mouse down. To move sideways like a crab, hold down Shift and move your mouse left or right.

>> **To disable collision detection so that you can walk through walls,** hold down the Alt key (Command on a Mac). Burglars find this handy for entering models without breaking any windows.

Stopping to look around

Look Around is the third tool in SketchUp that's dedicated to exploring your model from the inside. If using Position Camera is like swooping in to stand in a particular spot and Walk is like moving around while maintaining a constant eye height, Look Around is like turning your head while standing in one spot. It's pretty well named, we think; it does exactly what it says.

Using Look Around is so simple it hardly merits these steps:

1. **Choose Camera ⇨ Look Around.**

2. **Click and drag around in the modeling window to turn your virtual head.**

   Don't move too fast, or you'll strain your virtual neck.

TIP

When you're using any of the navigation tools, context-click to access any other navigation tool; this makes switching between them a little easier.

When you use Look Around with the field of view tool discussed in the next section, you get a pretty darned realistic simulation of what it'd be like to stand in your model.

Setting your field of view

Field of view is how much of your model you can see in your modeling window at one time. Imagine your eyesight kind of like a cone, with the pointy end pointing at your eyes and the cone getting bigger as it gets farther away from you. Everything that falls inside the cone is visible to you, and everything outside the cone isn't.

If you increase the angle of the cone at the pointy end, the cone gets wider, and you see more of what's in front of you. If you decrease the angle, the cone gets narrower, and you see less; see Figure 11-3.

Measured in degrees, a *wide field of view* means that you can see more of your model without having to move around. The bigger the angle, the more you can see. A wide field of view comes in handy when you're inside a SketchUp model because working on a model you can't see is hard.

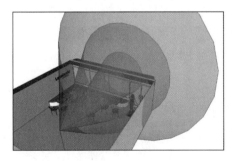

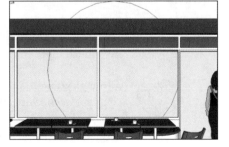

FIGURE 11-3: The wider your field of view, the more you can see.

It's a good idea to fiddle with your field of view while walking around inside your model. Follow these steps to do so:

1. **Choose Camera ⇨ Field of View.**

   Notice that the Measurements box in the lower-right corner of your modeling window says Field of View and that the default value is 35 degrees. This means that you currently have a 35-degree cone of vision, which is kind of narrow.

2. **Type** 60 **and press Enter.**

   Your field of view increases, and you now have a wider view of your model. The trade-off is that you see more distortion at the edges of your modeling window as more information is displayed in the same amount of space.

TIP

A good guideline for setting your field of view is to strike a balance between quantity and quality; a wider view always means more distortion. For views of the *outside* of something, try a field of view of 35 to 45 degrees. For interior views, you can increase the field of view to 60 or 70 degrees.

TECHNICAL
STUFF

If you know something about photography, you can express field of view in millimeters, just like you're using a camera lens. Typing **28mm** gives you a wide-angle view, as if you're looking through a 28mm lens. For people who think about field of view in these terms, this option can be a lot more intuitive than trying to imagine cones of vision.

Taking the Scenic Route

Wouldn't it be great if you could save a particular view of your model? And wouldn't it be even greater if that view could also save things like styles and shadow settings? What if you could come back to any of these saved views by clicking a button on your screen? What if this whole paragraph were just a series of questions?

SketchUp *scenes* are (you guessed it) saved views of your model. It's probably easiest to think of scenes as pre-saved views of your model, except that scenes can save much more than just camera positions.

REMEMBER

Although scenes don't get a lot of space in this book (they don't even get their own chapter), scenes are an important feature in SketchUp for three reasons:

>> **Scenes can save you hours of time.** Returning to exactly the right view with Orbit, Zoom, and Pan isn't always easy. Sometimes a view involves shadows,

styles, sections (you read about those later), and even hidden geometry. Setting up everything the way you need it, every time you need it, can be a pain. It's not that SketchUp's *hard* — it's just that you have a lot of different ways to view your model. Making a scene enables you to apply dozens of settings with a click of your mouse.

>> **Scenes are *by far* the most effective way to present your model.** Saving a scene for each point that you want to make in a presentation allows you to focus on what you're trying to say. Instead of fumbling around with the navigation tools, turning on shadows, and making the roof visible, you can click a button to transition to the next scene (which you've already set up exactly the way you want). Figure 11-4 shows a set of scenes Aidan created to present a house he designed for his dog, Savannah.

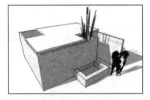
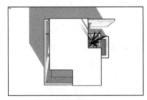
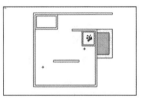

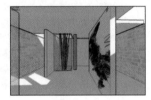

FIGURE 11-4: To show very specific views, create scenes.

>> **Scenes are the key to making animations.** You make animations by creating a series of scenes and telling SketchUp to figure out the transitions between them. The process, explained in later sections, is as simple as clicking a button.

After you get used to scenes, you'll find yourself using them all the time. Here are some of the most common uses for scenes:

>> Showing shade conditions for the same area at different times of the day. (See Chapter 10 for details about shadow studies.)

>> Saving scenes for each floor plan, building section, and other important views of your model

>> Building a walkthrough or flyover animation of your design

>> Creating scenes that show several views of the same thing with different options (the pointy roof or the flat one, madam?)

>> Demonstrating change over time by showing or hiding a succession of components. (Chapter 5 is all about components.)

Creating scenes

Before you start making scenes, know this: Making a scene in SketchUp is *not* like taking a snapshot of your model. If you create a scene to save a view, continue working on your model, and then return to that scene, your model doesn't go back to the way it was when you created the scene. The camera position will be the same, and the settings will be the same, but your geometry won't be. This is a pretty important concept, and one that makes using scenes so powerful.

A *scene* is just a set of view settings, which means that they're automatically updated every time you edit your model. You can make some scenes and use them all the way through your process, from when you start modeling to when you present your design to the president. Or to your mother.

Creating scenes is a simple process. The basic idea is that you add a scene to your SketchUp file whenever you have a view you want to return to later. You can always delete scenes, so there's no downside to using lots of them. Follow these steps to make a new scene:

1. **Choose Window ⇨ Scenes to open the Scenes panel.**

   When the Scenes panel first opens, it doesn't look like there's much to it. Expanding it by clicking the Show Details button in the upper-right corner reveals more options, but don't worry about that right now.

2. **Set up your view however you want.**

   Navigate around until you're happy with your point of view. If you want, use the Shadows and Styles panels to change the way your model looks.

3. **Click the Add Scene button to make a new scene with your current view settings.**

   A new scene is added to your SketchUp file. If this is the first scene you've created, it's called Scene 1, but you can give it a more meaningful name, as explained later in this chapter. As shown in Figure 11-5, the scene appears in two places:

   • As a tab at the top of your modeling window

   • As a list item in the Scenes panel, right underneath the Add Scene button

The scene appears as a tab...   ...and a list item in the Scenes panel.

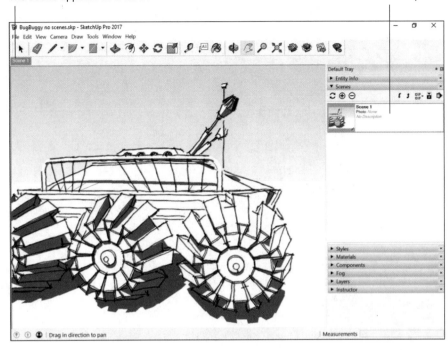

FIGURE 11-5:
A scene appears in two places.

TIP

When you're creating a scene that shows an eye-level view of a building — whether it's an interior or an exterior view — there's a quick, easy step you can take to make the scene look 500 percent better: Choose Camera ➪ Two-Point Perspective to make all the vertical edges in your model appear vertical in the view. Doing so removes the unprofessional, distorted effect that's the hallmark of improperly wielded 3D modeling software.

REMEMBER

Nothing is generated outside of SketchUp when you add a scene; it's not like exporting a JPEG or a TIFF. Scenes are just little bits of programming code that "remember" the view settings in effect when you create the scene. Scenes also don't add much to your file size, so you don't have to worry about using too many of them.

Moving from scene to scene

Activate a scene you've added earlier by doing one of three things:

>> Double-click the name (or thumbnail image) of the scene in the Scenes panel.

>> Click the tab for that scene at the top of the modeling window.

TIP

WHEN SCENES AND STYLES COLLIDE

Sooner or later, you'll be presented with the Warning — Scenes and Styles dialog box shown here. It pops up whenever you try to create a scene without first saving the changes you've made to the style applied to your model. In other words, SketchUp tries to help by reminding you to keep styles in mind while you work with scenes. (The first part of Chapter 10 is all about styles, if you need a refresher.)

This warning dialog box gives you three options; here's some guidance on which one to choose:

- **Save as a New Style:** This option adds a new style to your In Model styles library. When you come back to this scene, it looks exactly the way it did when you created it. Choosing this option is the safest way to proceed because it can't affect any other scene.

- **Update the Selected Style:** Choose this option only if you know what effect updating the style will have on the other scenes in your model. If the style you're updating is applied to any of them, you'll affect the way they look. In models with lots of scenes and styles, updating a style can have big implications.

- **Do Nothing to Save Changes:** This option creates a scene with your current style applied, completely ignoring any changes you may have made to that style. When you come back to this scene, it looks different than it did when you created it. Only choose this option if you really know what you're doing, or if you enjoy doing the same thing more than once.

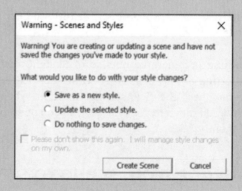

>> Context-click any scene tab and choose Play Animation to make SketchUp automatically flip through your scenes. Choose Play Animation again to make the animation stop.

TIP

Notice how the transition from one scene to the next is animated? You don't have to do anything special to make this happen; it's something SketchUp automatically does to make things look better (and ultimately, to make *you* look better).

You can adjust the way SketchUp transitions between scenes, which is handy for customizing your presentations. Follow these steps to access these settings:

1. **Choose Window ⇨ Model Info.**

2. **On the left side of the Model Info dialog box, choose Animation.**

   The Animation settings panel in the Model Info dialog box isn't very complicated, but it can make a huge difference in the appearance of your scene-related presentations.

3. **In the Scene Transitions area, set how SketchUp transitions from one scene to another.**

   These settings apply to both manual (clicking a page tab) and automatic (playing an animation) scene transitions:

   - *Enable Scene Transitions:* Clear this check box to make SketchUp change scenes without animating the transitions between them. You probably want to do this if your model is so complex (or your computer is so slow) that animated transitions don't look good.

   - *Seconds:* If you've selected the Enable Scene Transitions check box, the number of seconds you enter here indicates the time SketchUp takes to transition from one scene to the next. If you're "moving the camera" very far between scenes, bump up the transition time so that your audience doesn't get sick. Three seconds is a good compromise between nausea and boredom.

TIP

If you're presenting an incomplete model (perhaps you've thought about the garage and the living room, but nothing in between), it can be helpful to turn off scene transitions. That way, your audience won't see the things you haven't worked on when you click a tab to change scenes. It's sneaky, but effective.

4. **In the Scene Delay area, set the length of time SketchUp pauses on each slide before it moves to the next one.**

   If you want the presentation to seem like you're walking or flying, set this to 0. If you want time to talk about each scene in your presentation, bump this up a few seconds.

MAKING WALKTHROUGHS

A really great way to use scenes is to pretend you're walking or flying through your model. By setting up your scenes sequentially, you can give a seamless tour without messing around with the navigation tools. This setup is especially handy when you need to walk and talk at the same time.

Here are some tips that can help you to simulate a person walking or flying through your model with scenes:

- **Adjust your field of view.** For interior animations, make your camera "see" a wider area by setting your field of view to 60 degrees. For exterior views, try a field of view that's between 30 and 45 degrees. See the section "Setting your field of view," earlier in this chapter.

- **Make sure that your scenes aren't too far apart.** Instead of racing through a room like it's on fire, don't be afraid to add more scenes. Your audience will thank you by not throwing up on your conference table.

- **Add scenes at equal distance intervals.** Because SketchUp only lets you control the scene transition timing for all your scenes at once, it's best to make sure that your scenes are set up about the same distance apart. If you don't, your walk-through animations will be jerky and strange, like Aidan's dancing.

- **Don't forget the animation settings in the Model Info dialog box.** Set the scene delay to 0 seconds so that your animation doesn't pause at every scene. For a normal walking speed, set your scene transitions so that you move about 5 feet per second. If your scenes are about 20 feet apart, set your scene transition time to 4 seconds. This gives your audience time to look around and notice things. For flying animations, pick a scene transition time that looks good.

- **Slide around corners.** When you set up a walking animation, you have an easy, reliable way to turn corners without seeming too robotic. The method is illustrated in the following figure. Basically, the trick is to add a scene just short of where you want to turn — in this case, a few feet ahead of the doorway. The key is to angle your view *into* the turn slightly. Set up your next scene just past the turn, close to the inside and facing the new view. This technique makes it seem like you're turning corners naturally.

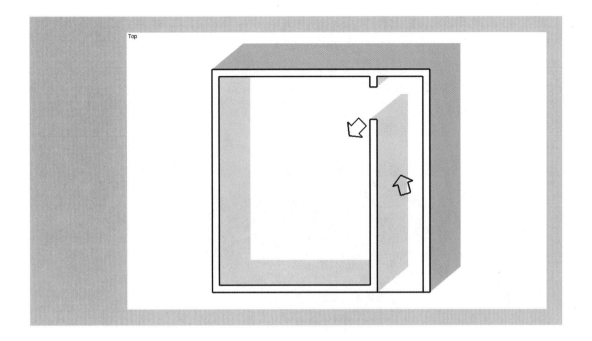

Modifying scenes after you make 'em

After you create a whole bunch of scenes, you inevitably need to fiddle with them in some way. After all, modifying something is almost always easier than making it all over again, and the same thing holds true for scenes. Because your SketchUp model will change a million times, understanding how to make changes to your existing scenes can save you a lot of time in the long run.

WARNING

Certain aspects of the scene-modification process can get a little tricky. This is kind of surprising, given how simple the rest of working with scenes can be. You deal with a lot of complexity when working in SketchUp, and this is just one of the places where that complexity rears its ugly head. The upshot: Pay special attention to the section on updating scenes and don't worry if you take a little while to figure things out. It happens to the best of us.

Reordering, renaming, and removing scenes

Making simple modifications to scenes, such as reordering, renaming, and removing them, is easy. You can accomplish each of these in two ways: You either context-click a scene tab at the top of your modeling window or use the Scenes panel menu (click the menu arrow in the upper right). See Figure 11-6.

Context-click a tab.   Open the Scenes panel menu.

FIGURE 11-6:
You can modify scenes by context-clicking scene tabs or by using the Scenes panel.

Here's how to reorder, rename, or remove scenes:

>> **Reordering scenes:** You can change the order in which scenes play in a slide show. If you're using scenes, you need to do this often — trust us. Use one of the following methods:

- Context-click the tab of the scene you want to move (in the modeling window) and choose Move Right or Move Left.

- In the expanded Scenes panel, click the name (or thumbnail image) of the scene you want to move to select it. Then click the Move Scene Up or Move Scene Down arrow at the top of the panel to change the scene's position in the scene order.

REMEMBER

>> **Renaming scenes:** Give your scenes meaningful names: Living Room, Top View, and Shadows at 5:00 P.M. are descriptive enough to be useful. Scene 14 lacks a certain *je ne sais quoi*. Use one of the following methods:

- Context-click the scene tab and choose Rename (this works only on the Mac, for some reason).

- In the Scenes panel, select the scene you want to rename and type something into the Name field below the list. If you don't see the Name field, click the Show Details button in the upper right. If you're feeling really organized, go ahead and give the scene a description, too — more information never hurts.

>> **Removing scenes:** If you don't need a scene anymore, feel free to delete it. However, if you have a scene that you don't want to appear in slide shows, you don't have to get rid of it. Use one of the following methods to remove a scene:

- Context-click the scene tab and choose Delete to get rid of it permanently.

- In the Scenes panel, select the scene you want to ax and click the Delete button.

To exclude a scene from slide shows without getting rid of it, select its name (or thumbnail) and clear the Include in Animation check box.

Working with scene properties

Okay. Turn off the television. Send the kids outside to play. Do whatever you need to do to concentrate because wrapping your head around the concept of scene properties isn't altogether straightforward. We do our best to explain it.

Basically, a scene is just a collection of saved viewing *properties.* Each of these properties has something to do with how your model looks:

>> **Camera Location:** Camera Location properties include the camera position, or *viewpoint,* and the field of view (discussed earlier in this chapter).

>> **Hidden Geometry:** Hidden Geometry properties are really just one thing: what elements are hidden and what elements aren't. These properties keep track of the visibility of the lines, faces, groups, and components in your model.

>> **Visible Layers:** Visible Layer properties keep track of the visibility of layers in your model.

>> **Active Section Planes:** Active Section Plane properties include the visibility of section planes and whether they're active. We talk about sections in the last part of this chapter.

>> **Style and Fog:** Style and Fog properties are all the settings in the Styles and Fog panels, and there are a lot of them. (See Chapter 10.)

>> **Shadow Settings:** Shadow Settings properties include whether shadows are turned on and the time and date for which the shadows are set. They also include all the other settings in the Shadows panel.

>> **Axes Location:** Axes Location properties are very specific. They keep track of the visibility, location, and orientation of the main red, green, and blue axes in your modeling window. It's sometimes useful to move the axes around when

you're working, such as when you're working with a rotated street grid in an urban-scale model.

REMEMBER

Here's the tricky part: Scenes can *save* (remember) any combination of the preceding properties — it's not an all-or-nothing proposition. After the full impact of this information soaks in, you'll realize that this means that scenes are *much* more powerful than they first appear.

TIP

By creating scenes that save only one or two properties (instead of all seven), you can use scenes to do some pretty nifty things. Here are three of our favorites:

» Create scenes that affect only your camera location, allowing you to return to any point of view without affecting anything else about the way your model looks (such as styles and hidden geometry).

» Create scenes that affect only styles and shadows, letting you quickly change between simple and complex (hard on your computer) display settings without affecting your camera location.

» Create scenes that have different combinations of Hidden Geometry to look at design alternatives without changing your model's style and camera location.

The key to working with scene properties is the expanded Scenes panel, visible in Figure 11-7. Although this panel is pretty simple, folks who understand it are few and far between. Prepare to join the informed minority.

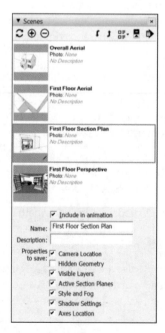

FIGURE 11-7: Choose which scene properties to save in the expanded Scenes panel.

Follow these steps to set which properties a scene saves:

1. **In the Scenes panel, select the scene whose properties you want to fiddle with.**

   You don't have to view this scene when you edit it; you can edit properties for any scene at any time.

2. **If not already expanded, click the Show Details button in the upper-right corner of the Scenes panel.**

3. **Select the check boxes next to the properties you want to save.**

   That's it. You don't have to click Save anywhere to make your changes stick. A little anticlimactic, no?

One terrific use of scene properties is to create scenes that help you show off different *iterations* (versions) of your design. You do this by making a different layer visible with each scene in your model. See Chapter 7 for details about controlling layer visibility.

TIP

Updating scenes

If you want to *update* (make changes to) an existing scene, you have a couple options:

» Update all the scene's properties at once, which is a piece of cake.

» Update the scene's properties selectively, which isn't quite as simple. Read on for both sets of instructions.

After you update a scene, you can't use Undo to return the scene back to the way it was. Instead, save your SketchUp file right before you update a scene and choose File ⇨ Revert if you don't like the results.

WARNING

UPDATING ALL THE SCENE PROPERTIES AT ONCE

The simplest way to modify a scene is to not worry about individual properties. If all you want to do is update a scene after you make an adjustment to the appearance of your model, you're in luck. Follow these steps:

1. **Click the tab of the scene you want to update.**

   The tabs are at the top of the modeling window.

2. **Make whatever styles, shadows, camera, or other display changes you want to your model.**

3. **Context-click the current scene tab and choose Update.**

WARNING

Be careful not to accidentally double-click the tab, or you'll reactivate the scene and lose all the changes you made. However, after you update the scene, the new scene properties replace the old ones, and you're home free.

UPDATING SCENE PROPERTIES SELECTIVELY

Here's where things get complicated. At times in your SketchUp life, you'll want to update a scene without updating all its properties.

WARNING

When you update scenes selectively, you make changes that you can't see immediately, which means disaster might strike. Copy your SketchUp file before you update more than one scene at a time, just in case something awful happens.

Maybe you've used scenes to create a tour of the sunroom you're designing for a client, and you want to change the shadow settings to make your model look brighter. You have 30 scenes in your presentation, and your meeting's in 5 minutes. You don't have time to change and update all 30 scenes one at a time. What to do? Follow these steps:

1. **Adjust the Shadow properties to where you want them to be for all the scenes you want to update.**

   Although this example deals with shadows, this same method applies to any scene properties changes you want to make.

2. **In the Scenes panel, select all the scenes you want to update.**

   Hold down the Shift key to select a group of consecutive scenes. Hold down Ctrl (Command on the Mac) to select noncontiguous scenes.

3. **Click the Update Scenes button in the Scenes panel.**

   The Scene Update dialog box appears, as shown in Figure 11-8.

4. **Select the Shadow Settings check box and click the Update button.**

   If all you want to update are the Shadow Settings, make sure that only that check box is selected. More generally, you'd select the check box next to each of the properties you want to update. All the selected scenes are updated with those new properties, and all the properties whose check boxes are clear remain unchanged.

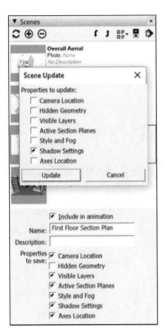

FIGURE 11-8:
Updating only
certain scene
properties is
a little more
involved.

Mastering the Sectional Approach

Software like SketchUp has a funny way of providing moments of perfect simplicity, moments when you sit back, scratch your head, and think to yourself, "That's it? That's all there is to it?"

Sections in SketchUp offer one of those moments. To put it simply, *sections* are objects that cut away parts of your model so you can look inside. However, the sections don't actually split or otherwise alter a model's geometry. A section is temporary and easily hidden or removed, so that you can see your whole model again just as easily as you created the cutaway.

You place sections wherever you need them, use them to create views you couldn't otherwise get, and then delete them when you're done. When you move a section plane, you get instant feedback; the cut view of your model moves, too. If you want to get fancy, you can embed sections in scenes and even use sections in animations. Sections are the icing on the SketchUp cake: easy to use, incredibly important, and impressive as all get-out.

People use sections for all kinds of things:

>> Creating standard orthographic views (such as plans and sections) of buildings and other objects

>> Making cutaway views of complex models to make them easier to understand

>> Working on the interiors of buildings without moving or hiding geometry

>> Generating sectional animations with scenes

Cutting plans and sections

The most common use for sections is to create straight-on, cut-through views of your model. These views often include dimensions and are typical of the drawings that architects make to design and explain space.

Straight-on, cut-through views are useful because

>> They're easy to read.

>> You can take measurements from them (if they're printed to scale).

>> They provide information that no other drawing type can.

REMEMBER

The following terms (illustrated in Figure 11-9) can help you create different views of your model more easily:

>> **Plan:** A *planimetric* view, or plan, is a top-down, two-dimensional, nonperspectival view of an object or space. Put simply, a planimetric view is every drawing of a house floor plan you've ever seen. You generate a plan by cutting an imaginary *horizontal* slice through your model. Everything below the slice is visible, and everything above it isn't.

>> **Section:** Not to be confused with sections (the SketchUp feature), a *sectional* view, or *section*, is a from-the-side, two-dimensional, nonperspectival view of an object or space. You make a sectional view by cutting an imaginary *vertical* slice through your model. Just like in a plan view, everything on one side of the slice is visible, and everything on the other side is hidden.

FIGURE 11-9:
A plan is a horizontal cut, whereas a section is a vertical one.

CUTTING LIKE AN ARCHITECT

In architecture, the convention is to *cut* plans at a height of 48 inches, meaning that the imaginary horizontal slice is made 4 feet above the floor surface. This ensures that doors and most windows are shown cut through by the slice, whereas counters, tables, and other furniture are below it, and thus are fully visible. You can see what we mean in Figure 11-9. These details are important when you try to explain a space to someone. After all, architectural drawings are two-dimensional abstractions of three-dimensional space, and every little bit of clarity helps.

When it comes to architectural sections (as opposed to sections, the SketchUp feature), there's no convention for where to cut them, but you should follow a couple rules:

- **Never cut through columns.** If you show a column in a section, it looks like a wall. This is bad because sections are supposed to show the degree to which a space is open or closed. You can walk around a column, but you can't walk through a wall (at least we can't).

- **Try your best to cut through stairs, elevators, and other vertical circulation.** Showing how people move up and down through your building makes your drawings a lot more readable, not to mention interesting. See Figure 11-9 for an example.

You cut plans and sections by adding section planes to your model. These are a little abstract because nothing like them exists in real life. In SketchUp, *section planes* are objects that affect the visibility of certain parts of your model. When a section plane is active, everything in front of it is visible and everything behind is hidden. Everywhere a section plane cuts your model, a slightly thicker section cut line appears.

TIP

If you're using Windows, open the Section toolbar by choosing View ⇨ Toolbars ⇨ Section. If you're on a Mac, the Section Plane tool is in the Large Tool Set, which you can activate by choosing View ⇨ Tool Palettes ⇨ Large Tool Set. On both platforms, Section Plane looks like a white circle with letters and numbers in it. To add a section plane, follow these steps:

1. **Choose Tools ⇨ Section Plane to activate the Section Plane tool.**

You can also activate Section Plane by choosing its icon from the Large Tool Set (or if you prefer, the Section toolbar on SketchUp for Windows).

2. **Move the Section Plane tool around your model.**

   Notice how the orientation of the Section Plane cursor (which is quite large) changes to be coplanar to whatever surface you hover over.

3. **After you figure out where you want to cut, click once to add a section plane.**

   To create a plan view, add a horizontal section plane by clicking a horizontal plane like a floor. For a sectional view, add a vertical section plane by clicking a wall or other vertical surface. You can, of course, add section planes wherever you want; they don't have to be aligned to horizontal or vertical planes. Figure 11-10 shows a section plane being added to a model of a house.

4. **Choose the Move tool.**

5. **Move the section plane you just added by clicking it once to pick it up and again to drop it.**

   You can slide your section plane back and forth in only two directions so that the section plane remains perpendicular to its cutting plane. When you're deciding where to locate your cut, the nearby sidebar, "Cutting like an architect," offers helpful pointers.

   After you add a section plane and move it to the desired location, you can rotate and even copy it, just like any other object in your model. The section plane never affects your geometry — just the way you view it.

6. **If you need to rotate your section plane, select it and use the Rotate tool.**

   Why rotate a section plane? In certain circumstances, rotating a section plane (instead of creating a brand-new one) can help explain a complex interior space. Showing a plan view *becoming* a sectional one is a powerful way to explain architectural drawings to an audience that doesn't understand them.

   Read more about the Rotate tool in Chapter 3.

7. **To make a new section plane by copying an existing one, use the Move or Rotate tool to do it the same way you'd make a copy of any other SketchUp object.**

   Chapter 3 explains these basic actions in detail.

   Copying section planes is a great way to space them a known distance apart. Spacing sections planes consistently can be trickier if you use the Section Plane tool to keep adding new ones, instead.

   Figure 11-11 shows moving, rotating, and copying a section plane.

When the section plane you've added is in position, you're ready to control how it affects visibility in a number of other ways. See the following sections for details.

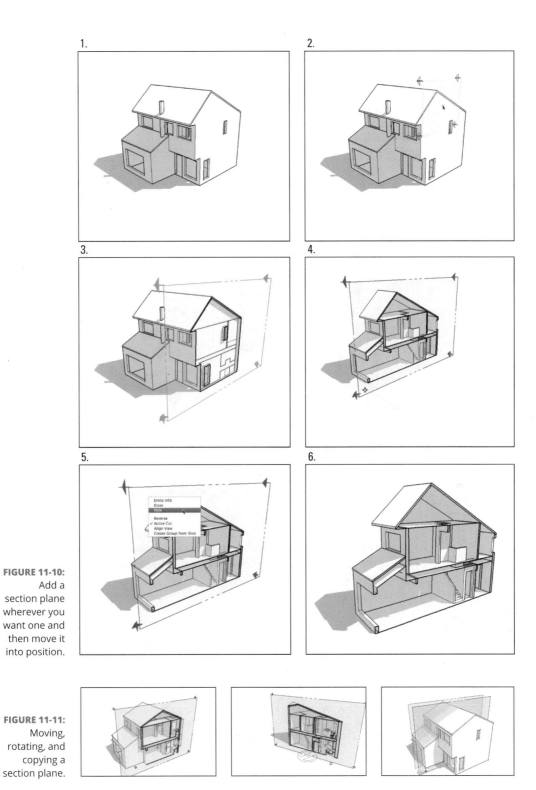

1.

2.

3.

4.

5.

FIGURE 11-10:
Add a
section plane
wherever you
want one and
then move it
into position.

6.

FIGURE 11-11:
Moving,
rotating, and
copying a
section plane.

Controlling individual section planes

You can control the way section planes behave by context-clicking them to bring up a context menu, as shown in Figure 11-12. You see examples of what the following options do in the same illustration:

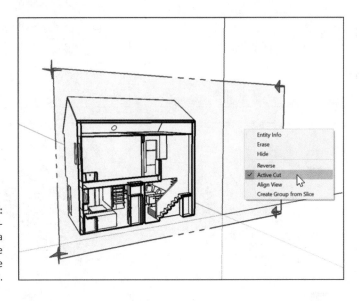

REMEMBER

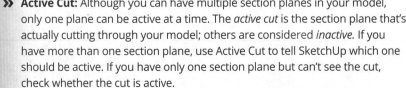

>> **Reverse:** This option flips the direction of the section plane, hiding everything that was previously visible, and revealing everything that used to be behind the cut. Use this when you need to see inside the rest of your model.

>> **Active Cut:** Although you can have multiple section planes in your model, only one plane can be active at a time. The *active cut* is the section plane that's actually cutting through your model; others are considered *inactive*. If you have more than one section plane, use Active Cut to tell SketchUp which one should be active. If you have only one section plane but can't see the cut, check whether the cut is active.

You *can* have more than one active section plane in your model at a time, but doing so requires that you nest, or embed, each section plane in a separate group or component. You can achieve spiffy effects with this technique, but explaining how they work in detail is beyond the scope of this book. You can read all about groups and components in Chapter 5.

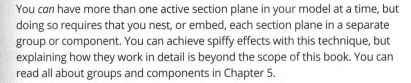

TECHNICAL
STUFF

>> **Align View:** When you choose Align View, your view changes so that you look straight on at the section plane. You can use this option to produce views like the ones described in "Getting different sectional views" later in this chapter.

>> **Create Group from Slice:** This option doesn't have much to do with the other choices in this context menu; it's really a modeling tool. You can use the Create Group from Slice command to do exactly what it says: Create a group from the active slice, or section plane. The command is handy for creating filled-in section cuts for final presentations.

Setting section-plane visibility

REMEMBER

If you want to control the visibility of all your section planes at once, a couple menu options can help. Use both of these toggles in combination to control how section cuts appear in your model. These two options, shown on the View menu, are illustrated in Figure 11-13:

>> **Section Planes:** This choice toggles the visibility of section-plane objects without affecting the section cuts they produce. More simply, deselecting Section Planes hides all the section planes in your model, but doesn't turn off the section cut effect, as shown in the middle image in Figure 11-13. This view is how you probably want to show most of your sectional views, so this toggle is pretty important.

>> **Section Cuts:** This option toggles the section cut effect on and off without affecting the visibility of the section-plane objects in your model. This choice is sort of the opposite of Section Planes, in the previous point, but it's every bit as important.

Getting different sectional views

Using section planes, you can create a couple useful and impressive views of your model without much trouble. The second builds on the first, and both are shown in Figure 11-14. A section perspective (left) is a special view of a three-dimensional space. The second type, an orthographic view (right), is straight on and doesn't use perspective.

MAKING A SECTION PERSPECTIVE

If you imagine cutting a building in half and then looking at the cut surface straight on while looking inside, you have a section perspective. The *section* part of the term means that the building has been cut away. The *perspective* part indicates that objects inside the space seem smaller as they get farther away.

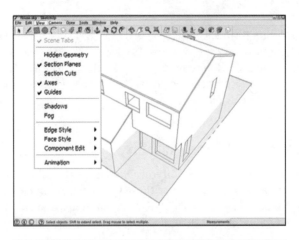

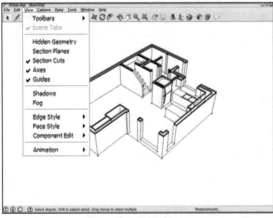

FIGURE 11-13:
Control section
plane visibility
with Section
Planes and
Section Cut.

FIGURE 11-14:
Turn on
Perspective
for a section
perspective;
choose Parallel
Projection to
produce an
orthographic
view.

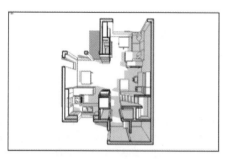

Section perspectives show interior space in a way most people can understand — and section perspectives look incredibly cool, too. To create a section perspective using the Section Plane tool in SketchUp, follow these steps:

1. **Select the section plane you want to use to make a section perspective by clicking it with the Select tool.**

    When the section plane is selected, it turns blue, (assuming that you haven't changed the default colors in the Styles panel).

2. **If the selected section plane isn't active, context-click it and choose Active Cut.**

    Active section planes cut through their surrounding geometry. If your section plane is visible but isn't cutting through anything, it's not active.

3. **Context-click the selected section plane and choose Align View.**

    This aligns your view so that it's straight on (perpendicular) to your section plane.

4. **If you can't see your model properly, choose Camera ⇨ Zoom Extents.**

    This zooms your view so that you can see your whole model in the modeling window.

GENERATING AN ORTHOGRAPHIC SECTION

Ever seen a technical drawing that included top, front, rear, and side views of the same object? Chances are that was an *orthographic projection*, which is a common way for 3D objects to be drawn so that they can be built.

Producing an orthographic section of your model is pretty easy; it's only one extra step beyond making a section perspective. Here's how to do it:

1. **Follow Steps 1 through 3 in the preceding section, as if you're making a section perspective.**

2. **Choose Camera ⇨ Parallel Projection.**

This switches off Perspective, turning your view into a true orthographic representation of your model. If you printed an orthographic view at a specific scale, you could take measurements from the printout.

TIP

To print a plan or section view of your model at a particular scale, have a look at Chapter 12, which explains the whole process. If you have SketchUp Pro, see Chapter 14; printing to scale is among the things LayOut was created to do.

Animating sections with scenes

Combining section views with scenes to create an animation is both a useful and impressive way to show off your model. The basic idea is that you can use scenes to create animations where your section planes move inside your model. Here are a few reasons you may want to use this technique:

» If you have a building with several levels, you can create an animated presentation that shows a cutaway plan view of each level.

» Using an animated section plane to "get inside" your model is a much classier transition than simply hiding certain parts of it.

» When you need to show the relationship between the plan and section views for a project, using an animated section plane helps to explain the concept of different architectural views to 3D beginners.

Follow these steps to create a basic section animation; a simple example is illustrated in Figure 11-15:

1. **Add a section plane to your model.**

For help with this step, see "Cutting plans and sections," earlier in this chapter.

2. **Add a scene to your model.**

The earlier section "Creating scenes," explains how to add scenes.

3. **Add another section plane to your model.**

You can add another section plane in one of two ways:

● *Use the Section Plane tool to create a brand-new one.* This is probably the easiest option, which makes it ideal for beginners.

● *Use the Move tool to copy an existing section plane.* The earlier section "Cutting plans and sections" introduces this technique.

Make sure that your new section plane is active; if it is, it cuts through your model. If it's not active, context-click the section plane and choose Active Cut from the context menu.

4. **Add another scene to your model.**

   This new scene remembers which is the active section plane.

5. **Click through the scenes you added to view your animation.**

   You see an animated section cut as SketchUp transitions from one scene to the next. If you don't, make sure that you have scene transitions enabled: Choose Window➪Model Info and then choose the Animation panel in the Model Info dialog box. Make sure the Scene Transitions check box is selected.

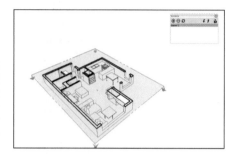 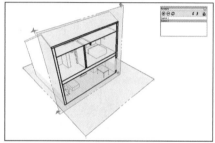

FIGURE 11-15: Making a section animation is a fairly straightforward process.

TIP

If you don't like seeing the section-plane objects (the boxy things with arrows on their corners) in your animation, switch them off by deselecting Section Planes on the View menu. Then you see the section cuts without any ugly rectangles flying around.

REMEMBER

The hardest thing to remember about using scenes and section planes to make section animations is this: *You need a separate section plane for each scene that you create.* That is to say, SketchUp animates the transition from one active section plane to another active section plane. If all you do is move the same section plane to another spot and add a scene, this animation technique won't work.

4

Sharing What You've Made

Print from a Windows or Mac computer, and discover how to print a model at a specific scale.

Share a model with other SketchUp users via the 3D Warehouse.

Export images of your model as raster image files, or create a simple animation of your model.

Design a presentation of your model or create a construction document in LayOut, which comes with SketchUp Pro.

Chapter **12**

Paper or Cloud? Printing and Uploading Your Work

You live at a time in history when it is often necessary to inscribe an image of your design onto dried and bleached wood pulp, and then, in a few seconds, send that same design, in the form of ones and zeros, thousands of miles to a series of data centers, where it's available in its entirety to anyone with an Internet connection.

Printing on paper and uploading to the cloud may seem like diametric opposites, but they're really just points on the same continuum of sharing.

In the first part of this chapter, you learn how to print views of your SketchUp model. Because the Windows and Mac versions of this procedure are so different, each operating system has its own section.

The second part of this chapter is dedicated to the SketchUp 3D Warehouse. It's a giant online repository of models made (mostly) by everyday SketchUp modelers. Uploading your own creations to the 3D Warehouse is useful for sharing and archiving your work.

Printing Your Work

As much as everyone likes to pretend that we live in an all-digital world, the truth is that we don't. Some clients simply prefer looking at printouts. Aidan loves having a printout to stick to the wall. Rebecca likes to brainstorm and sketch out potential changes on a printout, as a way of developing a roadmap for the changes she really wants to make before further changing a digital file.

TIP

If you're using the Pro version of SketchUp, you can always use LayOut to print views of your models. Making both scaled and nonscaled prints is easier in LayOut than in SketchUp; take a look at Chapter 14 for all the juicy details.

Printing from a Windows computer

Printing from SketchUp is easy, as long as you're not trying to do anything too complicated. By complicated, we mean printing to a particular scale, which can be a harrowing experience the first couple times you attempt it. Fortunately, printing to scale is something most people almost never have to do, so we save the instructions for how to do it for the end of this section.

Making a basic print (Windows)

Most of the time, all you need to do is print exactly what you see on your screen. Follow these steps to do that:

1. **Make sure that the view you want to print appears in your modeling window.**

Unless you're printing to scale, SketchUp prints exactly what you see in your modeling window.

2. **Choose File ⇨ Print Setup.**

The Print Setup dialog box opens, which is where you choose what printer and paper you want to use.

3. **In the Print Setup dialog box shown in Figure 12-1, do the following:**

  a. *Choose the printer you want to use.*

  b. *Choose a paper size for your print.*

  c. *Choose an orientation for your print; most of the time, you want to use Landscape because your screen is usually wider than it is tall.*

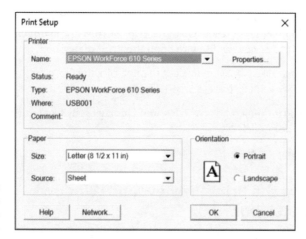

FIGURE 12-1:
The Print Setup
dialog box in
Windows.

4. **Click OK to close the Print Setup dialog box.**

5. **Choose File ⇨ Print Preview.**

TIP

   The Print Preview dialog box opens. Print Preview lets you see an image of what your print will look like before you send it to a printer. Lots of trees thank you for saving paper by using Print Preview every time you print.

6. **In the Print Preview dialog box, do the following:**

   a. *In the Tabbed Scene Print Range area, choose which scenes you want to print, if you have more than one.*

   If you need to, you can read all about scenes in Chapter 11.

   b. *Tell SketchUp how many copies of each scene you need.*

   c. *Make sure that the Fit to Page check box is selected.*

   d. *Make sure that the Use Model Extents check box isn't selected.*

   e. *Choose a print quality for your printout.*

   We recommend High Definition for most jobs.

TIP

   For a complete description of all the knobs and doohickeys in the Print Preview and Print dialog boxes, have a look at the next section in this chapter.

7. **Click OK.**

   The Print Preview dialog box closes, and you get an on-screen preview of what your print will look like.

8. **If you like what you see, click the Print button in the upper-left corner of the Print Preview window to open the Print dialog box.**

   If you *don't* like what you're about to print, click the Close button (at the top of the screen) and go back to Step 1.

9. **In the Print dialog box (which should look exactly like the Print Preview dialog box), click OK.**

   Your print job goes to the printer.

Decoding the Print Preview and Windows Print dialog box

Three cheers for simplicity! The Print Preview and Print dialog boxes in SketchUp are exactly the same. Figure 12-2 shows the former because that's the one we advocate using first every time, but the descriptions in this section apply to both.

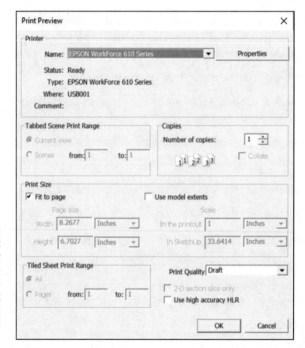

FIGURE 12-2:
The Print Preview dialog box in Windows. The Print dialog box looks exactly the same.

PRINTER

If you used the Print Setup dialog box first, you shouldn't need to change the settings in this section. If you want, from the drop-down list, you can choose which printer to use. If you know something about printers, you can even click the Properties button to make adjustments to your printer settings. (Because settings are different for every printer on Earth, that's between you and your printer's user manual.)

TABBED SCENE PRINT RANGE

Use this area to tell SketchUp which of your scenes you want to print, if you have more than one. This option is really handy for quickly printing all your scenes. Select the Current View option to print only whatever's currently in your modeling window.

COPIES

This one's pretty basic: Choose how many copies of each view you want to print. If you're printing multiple copies of multiple scenes, select the Collate check box to print *packets*, which can save you from assembling them yourself. Here's what happens when you print three copies of four scenes:

>> Selecting the Collate check box prints the pages in the following order: 123412341234.

>> Deselecting the Collate check box prints the pages like this: 111222333444.

PRINT SIZE

This is, by far, the most complicated part of this dialog box; Print Size controls how your model will look on the printed page. Figure 12-3 shows the effect of some of these settings on a final print.

My SketchUp screen   Fit to Page   Fit to Page and Use Model Extents

FIGURE 12-3:
Different Print Size settings applied to the same view in SketchUp.

The Print Size controls are as follows:

>> **Fit to Page:** Selecting this check box tells SketchUp to make your printed page look like your modeling window. As long as the Use Model Extents check box isn't selected, you can see exactly what you see on your screen — no more, no less.

>> **Use Model Extents:** This option tells SketchUp to zoom in to make your model (excluding your sky, ground, watermark, and whatever else may be visible on your screen) fit the printed page. If we want this effect, we prefer to choose Camera ⇨ Zoom Extents from the menu bar before printing a model. Doing so ensures we know exactly what we're getting.

>> **Page Size:** As long as you don't have the Fit to Page check box selected, you can manually enter a page size using these controls. If you type a width or height, SketchUp figures out the other dimension and pretends it's printing on a different-sized piece of paper.

The Page Size option is especially useful if you want to make a big print by tiling together lots of smaller pages. See the next section in this chapter, "Tiled Sheet Print Range," for more details.

TIP

REMEMBER

>> **Scale:** Here's where printing gets a little complicated. To print to scale, you must do two things before you go anywhere near the Print or Print Preview dialog boxes:

- Switch to Parallel Projection mode.

- Make sure that you're using one of the Standard views.

Take a look at the section "Printing to scale (Windows and Mac)," later in this chapter, for a complete rundown on printing to scale in SketchUp.

TILED SHEET PRINT RANGE

Perhaps you're printing at a scale that won't fit on a single page, or you've entered a print size that's bigger than the paper size you chose in the Print Setup dialog box. The Tiled Sheet Print Range area lets you print your image on multiple sheets and then attach them together later. You can get posters from your small-format printer!

PRINT QUALITY

To be honest, selecting a print quality for your image involves a little trial and error. What you get with each setting depends a lot on your model, so try a couple different settings if you have time.

>> Draft and Standard are really only useful for checking how your model appears on the printed page.

>> For a finished-looking print, try High Definition first and then bump up to Ultra High Definition if your computer/printer setup can handle it.

OTHER SETTINGS

You can control the following odds-and-ends settings in the Print Preview dialog box, too:

» **2-D Section Slice Only:** If you have a visible section cut in your model view, selecting this check box tells SketchUp to print only the section cut edges. Figure 12-4 shows what the same model view would look like without (on the left) and with (right) this option selected. You can use this option to produce simple plan and section views.

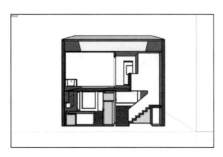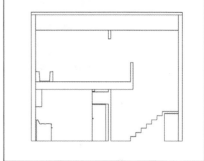

FIGURE 12-4:
Printing only the 2D section slice yields a simple drawing that's easy to sketch over.

» **Use High Accuracy HLR:** The bad news is that we have no idea what HLR stands for. The good news is that it doesn't really matter. Selecting this check box tells SketchUp to send *vector* information to the printer instead of the usual *raster* data. (Check out Chapter 14 for a description of what these terms mean.) Why should you care? Vector lines look much smoother and cleaner when printed, so your whole model will look better — with one condition: *Gradients* (those nice, smooth shadows on rounded surfaces) don't print well as vectors. If you have a lot of rounded or curvy surfaces in your model view, you probably don't want to choose this option. Try to print both ways and choose the one that looks better. Thank goodness for Print Preview, huh?

TIP

If your model view includes a Sketchy Edges style, don't use high accuracy HLR; you won't see any of the nice, sketchy effects in your final print.

Printing from a Mac

If you're using a Mac, the printing story is a little simpler than it is for folks who use Windows computers — but only by a little. The first part of the following sections lays out a procedure for generating a simple, straightforward print of what you see in your modeling window.

The second part can be called "Gross anatomy of the Mac dialog boxes." In these sections, we explain what each and every setting does.

Making a basic print (Mac)

Follow these steps to print exactly what you see in your modeling window on a Mac:

1. **Make sure that your modeling window contains whatever you want to print.**

SketchUp prints exactly what you see in your modeling window, unless of course you're printing to scale. Because printing to scale is complicated, the topic has its own section later in this chapter.

2. **Choose File ⇨ Page Setup.**

The Page Setup dialog box opens, where you decide what printer and paper size to use.

3. **In the Page Setup dialog box shown in Figure 12-5, do the following:**

a. Choose the printer you want to use from the Format For drop-down list.

b. Choose a paper size for your print.

c. Choose an orientation for your print.

Landscape is the most common choice, because SketchUp's modeling window is usually wider than it is tall.

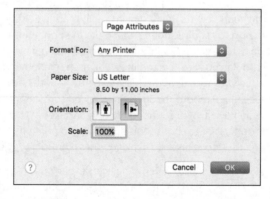

FIGURE 12-5:
The Page Setup dialog box on a Mac lets you select a printer, a paper size, and a page orientation.

4. **Click OK to close the Page Setup dialog box.**

5. **Choose File ⇨ Document Setup.**

The Document Setup dialog box opens.

6. **In the Document Setup dialog box, make sure that the Fit View to Page check box is selected.**

   Check out the next section in this chapter for a full description of what everything does.

7. **Click OK to close the Document Setup dialog box.**

8. **Choose File ⇨ Print to open the Print dialog box.**

   In the Print dialog box, you see an on-screen preview of what your print will look like on paper.

9. **If the preview suits you, click the Print button to send your print job to the printer.**

   If you're not happy with the preview, click the Cancel button and start again at Step 1. Isn't printing fun?

The Document Setup dialog box

You use the settings in the Document Setup dialog box shown in Figure 12-6 to control how big your model prints. Here's what everything does:

TIP

» **Print Size:** This one's pretty self-explanatory, but here are some details just in case:

  - *Fit View to Page:* Select this check box to tell SketchUp to make your printed page look just like your modeling window on-screen. It's really that simple.

  - *Width and Height:* If the Fit View to Page check box is deselected, you can type either a width or a height for your final print. This is the way to go if you want to print a tiled poster out of several sheets of paper; just enter a final size, and you'll have a poster in no time flat.

FIGURE 12-6:
The Mac
Document
Setup
dialog box.

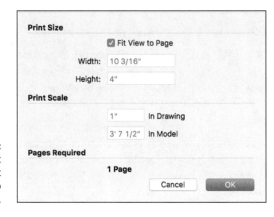

>> **Print Scale:** Use these settings to control the scale of your printed drawing, if that's the kind of print you're trying to make. Because printing to scale is a bit of an ordeal, we devote the last section of this chapter to the topic. See that section for a description of what these settings do.

>> **Pages Required:** This is really just a readout of how many pages you need to print. If you have selected the Fit View to Page check box, this is 1. If your print doesn't fit on one sheet, it's tiled onto the number of sheets displayed in this section of the dialog box.

The Print dialog box

The Print dialog box on the Mac is something of a many-headed beast; several panels are hidden underneath the SketchUp drop-down list. Luckily, you don't need to adjust those options unless you're managing color or other printing technicalities that are beyond the scope of this book. The options on the SketchUp panel, shown in Figure 12-7, are described in the following list:

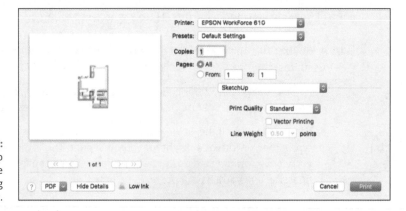

FIGURE 12-7:
The SketchUp panel of the Print dialog box.

>> **Copies:** Tell SketchUp how many copies you'd like to print.

>> **Pages:** If the Pages Required readout at the bottom of the Document Setup dialog box (refer to Figure 12-6) said that you need more than one sheet to print your image, you can choose to print all or some of those pages right here.

>> **Print Quality:** This setting may require some trial and error, because each printer handles the quality setting in its own way. To start, try the High setting and adjust from there. In general, Draft or Standard is only good for checking how the page will look. If you have time, try both High and Extra High and see which one looks the best.

>> **Vector Printing:** When you select this check box, SketchUp sends *vector* (instead of *raster*) information to the printer. Have a look at Chapter 14 for a description of these terms.

REMEMBER

The upshot here is that vector printing makes edges look much smoother and cleaner but does a lousy job on *gradients* (the shadows on your curved surfaces). Use vector printing if your model view is made up of mostly flat faces, but try printing both ways (with vector printing on and off) to see which looks better.

TIP

If your model view includes a Sketchy Edges style, don't select Vector Printing; you won't see any of the nice, sketchy effects in your final print.

>> **Line Weight:** This option works only if you've selected the Vector Printing check box. The number in this box represents the thickness of edges in your print; any edges that are 1-pixel thick in your model view will be drawn with a line as thick as what you choose for this option. The default is 0.50 points, but feel free to experiment to see what looks best for your model.

Printing to a particular scale

Here's where printing gets interesting. Sometimes, instead of printing exactly what you see on your screen so that it fits on a sheet of paper, you may need to print a drawing *to scale*. See the nearby sidebar "Wrapping your head around scale" for more information about drawing to scale.

TIP

Keep in mind that if you have SketchUp Pro, you can use LayOut to generate scaled views of your model very easily. Take a look at Chapter 14 for more information.

Preparing to print to scale

Before you can print a view of your model to a particular scale, you have to set up things properly. Keep the following points in mind:

>> **Perspective views can't be printed to scale.** If you think about it, this makes sense. In perspectival views, all lines appear to "go back" into the distance, which means that they look shorter than they really are. Because the whole point of a scaled drawing is to be able to take accurate measurements directly off your printout, views with perspective don't work.

>> **Switch to Parallel Projection if you want to print to scale.** We know, we know — this is the same as the last point. But it's important enough to mention twice. To change your viewing mode from Perspective to Parallel Projection, choose Camera ⇨ Parallel Projection.

>> **You have to use the Standard views.** SketchUp lets you quickly look at your model from the top, bottom, and sides by switching to one of the Standard views. Choose Camera ⇨ Standard and pick any of the views except Iso.

WRAPPING YOUR HEAD AROUND SCALE

When you print to scale, anyone with a special ruler (called a *scale,* confusingly enough) can take measurements from your drawing, as long as he knows the scale at which it was printed. You can use three kinds of drawing scales:

Architectural: In the United States, most people use feet and inches to measure objects. Most architectural scales substitute fractions of an inch for a foot. Three common examples of architectural scales follow:

- ½ inch = 1 foot (1 inch = 2 feet)
- ¼ inch = 1 foot (1 inch = 4 feet)
- ⅛ inch = 1 foot (1 inch = 8 feet)

Engineering: When measuring big things like parcels of land and college campuses, U.S. architects, engineers, and surveyors still use feet, but they use engineering scales instead of architectural ones. Three common engineering scales follow:

- 1 inch = 20 feet
- 1 inch = 50 feet
- 1 inch = 100 feet

Metric: Outside the U.S., virtually everyone uses the metric system. Because all measurement is based on the number 10, metric scales can be applied to everything from very small things (blood cells) to very big things (countries). Metric scales use ratios instead of units of measure. Here are three examples:

- 1:10 (The objects in the drawing are 10 times bigger in real life.)
- 1:100 (The objects in the drawing are 100 times bigger in real life.)
- 10:1 (The objects in the drawing are 10 times smaller in real life.)

Printing to scale (Windows and Mac)

The steps in this section allow you to produce a scaled print from SketchUp. The Windows instructions appear first and then Mac details. When the user-interface elements are different for the two platforms, the ones for Mac are shown in parentheses. Figure 12-8 shows the relevant dialog boxes for printing to scale in Windows and on a Mac.

When printing to scale, don't worry about these numbers

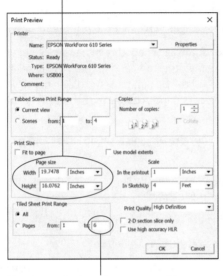

To print at 1 inch = 4 feet, you need 6 pages

REMEMBER

Before you begin, make sure that you've switched to Parallel Projection and that your view is lined up the right way. See the preceding section of this chapter for help with your model view for scaled printing. Follow these steps to produce a scaled print:

1. **Choose File ⇨ Print Setup (Page Setup).**

2. **Select a printer, paper size, and paper orientation, and then click OK.**

3. **Choose File ⇨ Print Preview (Document Setup).**

4. **Clear the Fit to Page (Fit View to Page) check box.**

5. **Windows: Make sure that the Use Model Extents check box is clear.**

   Mac users don't have this option.

6. **Enter the scale at which you want to print your model view.**

If you want to print a drawing at ¼ -inch scale, enter the following:

- **1 Inches** into the In the Printout (In Drawing) box
- **4 Feet** into the In SketchUp (In Model) box

If you want to produce a print at 1:100 scale, enter the following:

- **1 m** into the In the Printout (In Drawing) box
- **100 m** into the In SketchUp (In Model) box

7. **Take note of how may pages you'll need to print your drawing.**

If you're using Windows, you can check this in the Tiled Sheet Print Range area of the dialog box. On a Mac, the number of pages you'll need appears in the Pages Required section of the Document Setup dialog box. If you want to print on a different-sized piece of paper, change the setting in the Print Setup (Page Setup) dialog box.

8. **If you want to print your drawing on a single sheet and it won't fit, use a smaller scale.**

Using the ¼ inch = 1 foot example, try shrinking the drawing to $^3\!/_{16}$ inch = 1 foot scale. To do this, enter the following:

- **3 Inches** into the In the Printout (In Drawing) box
- **16 Feet** into the In SketchUp (In Model) box

9. **When you're happy with how your drawing will print, click OK.**

10. **Perform the step based on your operating system:**

- *Windows:* If you like what you see in the Print Preview dialog box, click the Print button (in the upper-left corner) to open the Print dialog box.
- *Mac:* Choose File ⇨ Print.

11. **In the Print dialog box, click OK to send your print job to the printer.**

See this chapter's earlier "Making a basic print" section (for your operating system) for the whole story on basic printing from SketchUp.

Working with the 3D Warehouse

The *3D Warehouse* is a huge online collection of 3D models that is searchable and, most importantly, free for everyone to use. To access the 3D Warehouse, all you need is an Internet connection. If you have a SketchUp model that you want to share with the world, share with just a few people, or store on SketchUp's servers for safekeeping, the 3D Warehouse is where you put it.

Why Warehouse?

TIP

Before we go on, let us dispel a popular misconception right away: When you upload a model to SketchUp's 3D Warehouse, you aren't automatically donating your hard work to the world — you can make uploaded models and collections private.

With that understanding, here are some awesome reasons to use the 3D Warehouse:

>> **Sharing is good for your self-esteem.** To be clear, we don't subscribe to the *nouveau tech* mindset that all information wants to be free of charge. If you spent a lot of time on something and you don't want to give it away, you shouldn't have to. But if you're proud of what you made, and sharing it with others would make you feel good, the 3D Warehouse offers a great way to contribute to the 3D modeling community.

>> **Create your own personal component library.** Because SketchUp can download models directly from the 3D Warehouse into the model you're working on, making your own online collections is incredibly handy. Everything you upload is accessible anywhere you happen to be working.

For example, you can maintain a collection of the furniture in your house. Whenever you need a model of your sofa, you can just download it — no matter what computer you're using.

>> **Explore uploaded models in 3D without having to download them.** You can orbit, pan, and zoom around any model you can see on the 3D Warehouse — *without* having to download it into SketchUp first. If you want to show someone your model in 3D, you can just send her its 3D Warehouse link. Better yet, you can embed a 3D viewer window on your web page; anyone who visits your page can poke around.

>> **It's never a bad idea to have a backup.** If all you're looking to do is save a copy of your work in the cloud (where you can't spill your coffee all over it), services like Dropbox, Google Drive, and Microsoft OneDrive are great choices. None of these, however, give you direct access to your models inside of SketchUp. When you upload something to the 3D Warehouse, it's both safe *and* readily available.

Getting to the 3D Warehouse

You can get to the 3D Warehouse in two ways:

>> **From SketchUp:** Choose File ➪ 3D Warehouse ➪ Get Models; when you do, a mini web browser opens right in front of your modeling window.

>> **From the web:** Browse to https://3dwarehouse.sketchup.com.

Accessing the 3D Warehouse from the web is a great way to hunt for 3D models without opening SketchUp first.

TIP

Go ahead and poke around the 3D Warehouse. It's amazing what you find; thousands of people add new content every day. Much of it isn't very useful, but you still find plenty of interesting things to download and look at.

Taking apart strangers' models is a great way to figure out how they're built.

TIP

Refer to Chapter 5 for plenty of information about grabbing what you need from the 3D Warehouse.

Uploading a model

Follow these steps to upload your model to the 3D Warehouse:

1. Open the model you want to upload in SketchUp and fiddle around with your view until you like what you see.

When you upload a model to the 3D Warehouse, SketchUp automatically creates a preview image that's a snapshot of your modeling window.

2. Choose File ➪ 3D Warehouse ➪ Share Model.

A mini-browser window opens, and it shows the logon screen for the 3D Warehouse. If you want to upload models, you need a Trimble ID or a Google account. Both types of accounts are free; you just need a valid e-mail address to get one. If you don't already have one, follow the on-screen instructions to sign up.

3. Enter your account information, click the Sign In button, and fill out the Upload to 3D Warehouse form as completely as you can:

- *Privacy:* You can choose to make your model Public or Private. Checking the Public option gives anyone the right to find, download, and use your model however he likes. If you select Private, your model stays hidden (from everyone but you). Flip ahead to "Managing models online," in this chapter, for more about this topic.

- *Title:* Enter a title for your model. If it's a public building, you may enter its name. Something like Royal West Academy would do nicely.

- *Description:* Models with complete descriptions are very popular among people who hunt around the Warehouse. Try to use complete sentences here; the more you write, the better.

- *URL:* If you have a website address that you want people who view your model to visit, enter it here. For example, if your model is a historic building, you may include the website that provides more information about that building.

- *Tags:* Type a string of words that describe the thing you modeled. The 3D Warehouse search engine uses whatever you enter here to help people find your model. To increase the number of people who see what you made, add lots of tags. For example, if you were uploading a modern coffee table, you might enter the following tags: coffee table, table, coffee, modern, living room, furniture, glass, chrome, metal, and steel. You get the idea — be exhaustive.

4. **Click the Upload button to add your model to the 3D Warehouse.**

   If everything works properly, you see a page with your model on it, along with all the information you just entered. Congratulations — you're now a full-fledged member of the SketchUp universe.

TIP

It takes a while for the 3D Warehouse's robots (its *backend*, in geek parlance) to process your model after you upload it. You won't be able to search for it, see it in your collections, or even preview it in 3D for a few minutes. But that's okay — just sit back and reflect on what your great-grandfather would say if he heard you complaining. He *did* have to walk 50 miles to school, after all.

CONNECTING WITH A TRIMBLE ID

If you share SketchUp models as part of your office workflow or with your clients, using a Trimble ID offers some advantages over a Google account. Both types of accounts enable you to log in to SketchUp's online services, such as 3D Warehouse and Extension Warehouse. However, a Trimble ID gives you access to Trimble Connect, which has a few extras that might be helpful to you:

- Other people, whether they're project team members or clients, can review and comment on models in a web browser. This capability enables people to review models without having to download SketchUp. (Another option with this capability is SketchUp Viewer, introduced in Chapter 16.)

- Trimble Connect offers a bunch of project-management and workflow tools, such as an activity tracker and to-do items.

Managing models online

The 3D Warehouse isn't a free-for-all of individual models floating around in cyberspace. It's actually a pretty organized place. Take a look at any model's individual details page to see what's possible. Figure 12-9 is a screenshot of Aidan's couch in the 3D Warehouse, taken in March 2014 (it may look slightly different by the time you read this).

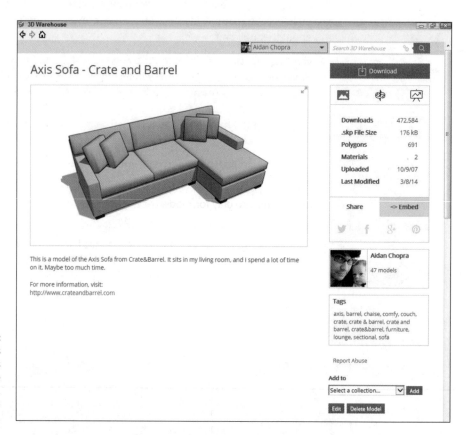

FIGURE 12-9:
Aidan's couch's details page on the 3D Warehouse, circa March 2014.

Here's a list of the less-obvious doodads and gadgets on the 3D Warehouse that you'll want to know about:

>> **Account drop-down menu:** With options for going to a page full of your own models, creating a new collection (more on that later), and signing out of your account, this is a critical part of the Warehouse interface.

>> **Search bar:** Type in keywords to find models; there's nothing magical here — *except* if you click the little icon in the bar that looks like a couple of machine gears. This icon reveals options for searching for collections (instead

of models), and a link to an advanced search page. This is your ticket to precision searching nirvana.

>> **Viewer settings:** These three icons let you choose between static images, a 3D view, and a chart that shows the model's popularity (views and downloads) over time.

Of the three views, 3D view (the middle icon) is the most revolutionary. Being able to orbit around a model without having to download it first will save you tons of time and energy.

>> **Statistics panel:** The numbers that appear on this section of the page are all interesting and useful, but the ones you should pay closest attention to are Polygons and Materials. These tell you the model's size in the two metrics that count most:

- *Polygons* is 3D modeling shorthand for faces; the more you have, the harder SketchUp has to work to display your model. If you're thinking about downloading a tree with 350,000 polygons, consider taking a vacation to Tahiti while SketchUp opens it.

- *Materials* are similarly taxing on your computer's performance, but they only come into play for models that have been heavily photo-textured.

>> **Share:** Shout out to Twitter, Facebook, Google Plus, and Pinterest here. Upload your model, and then tell your social networks about it.

>> **Embed:** Click here and the 3D Warehouse serves up some HTML code that you can use to embed the model on a web page.

The Embed feature is especially important for product manufacturers, designers, and anyone else who wants to let the public explore a model in 3D without leaving his or her website.

>> **Add to Collection:** One of the most productive things you can do on the 3D Warehouse is collect models — your own *and* other people's. Make yourself empty collections for things like chairs, scale figures, trees, and star destroy-ers. Then fill them with the amazing models you find as you're exploring. Back in SketchUp, in the Components panel, choose My Collections from the Collections drop-down menu, and there they are, ready to use in your own work.

>> **Edit:** Clicking the Edit button turns most of the text areas on the page into editable text fields; to change your model's title, just type a new one right where the old one was. Simple.

While we're on the subject of collections, here's how to create your own:

1. **Make sure you're logged in to the 3D Warehouse.**

   If you're logged in, you'll see your username on the account drop-down menu at the top of every page in the Warehouse. If you're not logged in, click Sign In (also at the top of every page) and put in your account credentials.

2. **Choose Create Collection from the Account drop-down menu at the top of any page.**

   You can create a collection in a couple of other ways, but this is the most universal one; it works no matter where you are in the 3D Warehouse.

3. **Choose a Privacy setting for your new collection.**

   Public means everyone on the Warehouse can see it. Private means only you can see it, and only when you're logged in.

4. **Give your new collection a title.**

5. **Write a brief but meaningful description of what your collection will contain.**

   Keep in mind that collections can contain both models and other collections.

6. **Add a URL (web address), if it's relevant.**

7. **Type in tags that might help others find your collection.**

   Tagging is especially relevant for collections marked Public.

8. **Click Create Collection at the bottom of the page.**

TIP

Chapter **13**

Exporting Images, Animations, and CAD Files

Awesome 3D models need to be shared. The folks who create SketchUp understand this, and the software includes a multitude of ways to share your models with other people and programs. Want to send a JPEG of your newly modeled custom home to your parents? How about a movie that shows what it's like to walk through that home? Need to turn your house model into a CAD-friendly DWG file for the builder? SketchUp can do all this and more.

SketchUp Make (the free version) can export raster images and movies. SketchUp Pro can export raster images and movies, along with vector images, CAD files, and a bunch of other 3D formats. This chapter covers the basics that most SketchUp Make or Pro beginners will need: common raster image formats, basic video formats, and CAD files.

Exporting 2D Images of Your Model

Both SketchUp Make and Pro can export 2D views of your model as *raster* images, which are images made of lots of tiny pixels. When you're exporting an image, it's helpful to know a little bit about graphics file formats in general. If you're already an aficionado about these sorts of things, or if you're in a big hurry, you can skip ahead to the section "Exporting a raster image from SketchUp."

TIP

If you have SketchUp Pro, you also have LayOut, which offers a much better way to export images. In fact, LayOut may be able to replace whatever application is the reason you're trying to export an image in the first place. Take a look at Chapter 14 for an introduction to LayOut.

Introducing raster versus vector files

Pictures on your computer are divided into two basic flavors: *raster* and *vector*. The difference between these two categories of file types has to do with how they store image information. Here's the one-minute version:

- >> **Raster:** Raster images are made up of dots. (Technically, these dots are *pixels,* just like the pixels that make up images you take with a digital camera.) Raster file formats consist of information about the location and color of each dot. When you export a raster, you decide how many dots (pixels) it should include, which directly affects how big the image can be displayed. SketchUp exports TIFF, JPEG, and PNG raster images; the Windows version also exports BMPs, although that's nothing to get excited about. You can read more about raster images in the sidebar "Understanding rasters: Lots and lots of dots," later in this chapter.

- >> **Vector:** Vector images consist of instructions written as algorithms. These algorithms describe *how* to draw the image to whatever software tries to open it. The major advantage of using vector imagery (as opposed to raster) lies in its *scalability* — vectors can be resized larger or smaller without affecting their image quality, whereas rasters lose quality if you enlarge them too much.

TECHNICAL STUFF

SketchUp Make can export only raster images, but SketchUp Pro can export vectors in both PDF and EPS file formats.

Exporting a raster image from SketchUp

The process of exporting an image of your SketchUp model is fairly straightforward. Depending on which format you choose, the export options are slightly different, but we address them all in this section.

Follow these steps to export a raster image from SketchUp:

1. Adjust your model view until you see exactly what you want to export as an image file.

SketchUp's raster image export is *WYSIWYG* — What You See Is What You Get. Basically, your entire modeling window view is exported as an image, so use the navigation tools or click a scene to set up your view. Use styles, shadows, and fog to make your model look exactly the way you want it to. To change the proportions of your image, resize your SketchUp window. Follow these steps to do so:

a. *Windows only: If your SketchUp window is full screen, click the Minimize button in its upper-right corner.*

b. *Drag the Resize tab in the lower-right corner of your SketchUp window until the modeling window is the right proportion.*

In Figure 13-1, we want to export a wide view of a house, so we adjust the proportions of the modeling window until things look right.

TIP

You may be wondering whether *everything* in your modeling window shows up in an exported raster image. The red, green, and blue axes don't, which is good, but guides do, which is usually bad. If you don't want your guides to be visible in your exported image, deselect Guides on the View menu.

SketchUp modeling window

Exported image

FIGURE 13-1: Adjust your view and your modeling window until things look the way you want them to in your exported image.

2. **Choose File ➪ Export ➪ 2D Graphic.**

The File Export dialog box opens.

3. **Select the file format you want to use from the Format drop-down list.**

TIP

Before you choose JPEG by default, know that this file type isn't always the best choice. For a complete description of each format (as well as recommendations for when to choose each), see the section "Looking at SketchUp's raster formats," later in this chapter.

4. **Choose a name and a location on your computer for your exported image.**

5. **Click the Options button.**

The Export Options dialog box opens, where you can control how your image is exported. Figure 13-2 shows what this dialog box looks like for each of SketchUp's raster file formats.

Export options for TIFF, PNG, and BMP files

Export options for JPG files

FIGURE 13-2:
The Export
Options dialog
boxes for
TIFFs, PNGs,
and BMPs (left)
and JPEGs.

6. **Adjust the settings in the Export Options dialog box.**

Here's a description of what the settings do:

- *Use View Size:* Selecting this check box tells SketchUp to export an image file that contains the same number of pixels as are currently being used to display your model on-screen. If you plan to use your exported image in an e-mail or on-screen presentation (such as PowerPoint), you can select Use View Size. However, manually setting the width and height is better.

- *Width and Height:* When you don't select the Use View Size check box, you can manually enter the size of your exported image. Because this process requires a fair amount of figuring, we devote a whole section to it; take a look at "Making sure you export enough pixels," later in this chapter, to find out what to type into the Width and Height boxes.

- *Anti-Alias:* Because raster images use grids of colored squares to draw pictures, diagonal lines and edges can sometimes look jagged and, well . . . lousy. *Anti-aliasing* fills in the gaps around pixels with similar-colored pixels so that things look smooth. Figure 13-3 illustrates the concept. In general, you want to leave anti-aliasing on.

- *Resolution (Mac only):* This is where you tell SketchUp how big each pixel should be, and therefore how big (in inches or centimeters) your exported image should be. Pixel size is expressed in terms of pixels per inch/centimeter. This option is available only when the Use View Size check box isn't selected. See "Making sure you export enough pixels," later in this chapter for help choosing a resolution.

No anti-aliasing   With anti-aliasing

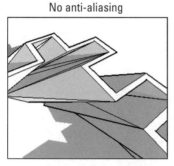

FIGURE 13-3:
A view of
the same
image with
anti-aliasing off
(left) and on.

- *Transparent Background (not for JPEGs):* You can export a TIFF or PNG file with a transparent background, which can make selecting your model in an image editor easier. Exporting your image with a transparent background is also a nice way to use image-editing programs like Photoshop to drop in a sky and ground plane later.

- *JPEG Compression (JPEG only):* This slider lets you decide two things at the same time: the file size of your exported image and how good the image will look. The two are, of course, inversely related; the farther to the left you move the slider, the smaller your file will be, but the worse it will look. Never set JPEG compression to less than 8 — your models take too long to build for you to make them look terrible on export.

7. **Click OK to close the Export Options dialog box.**

8. **Back in the File Export dialog box, click the Export button to export your raster image file.**

You can find your exported file in whatever location on your computer you specified in Step 4. What you do with it is entirely up to you — you can e-mail it, print it, or use it in another software program to create a presentation.

Don't be alarmed if the export process takes longer than you think it should. If you export a pretty big image (one with lots and lots of pixels), the export takes a while. Take the opportunity to call your mother — she'll appreciate it.

UNDERSTANDING RASTERS: LOTS AND LOTS OF DOTS

When you look at a photograph on your computer, you're really looking at a whole bunch of tiny dots of color, or *pixels.* These are arranged in a rectangular grid called a *raster.* Digital images that are composed of pixels arranged in a raster grid are *raster images,* or *rasters* for short. Have a look at the first image in the figure below for a close-up view of a raster image. Here are some things to keep in mind about rasters:

- **Rasters are everywhere.** Almost every digital image you've ever seen is a raster. TIFF, JPEG, and PNG are three of the most common raster file formats, and SketchUp exports them all.

- **Rasters are flexible.** Every two-dimensional image can be displayed as a raster; a grid of colored squares is an incredibly effective way of saving and sharing picture information. As long as you have enough pixels, any image can look good as a raster.

- **Rasters take up a lot of space.** If you think about how raster images work, it takes a lot of information to describe a picture. Digital images are made up of anywhere from thousands to millions of pixels, and each pixel can be any one of millions of colors. To store a whole picture, a raster image file needs to include the location and color of *each* pixel; the bigger the picture is, the more pixels are needed to describe it, and the bigger the file size gets.

- **Rasters are measured in pixels.** Because every raster image is made up of a specific number of pixels, you use a raster's *pixel dimensions* to describe its size. If we told you that we e-mailed you a photograph that was 800 x 600, you could expect to receive a picture that is 800 pixels wide by 600 pixels tall. (See the following figure.) Pixels don't have a physical size on their own — they're just dots of color. You determine a picture's physical size by deciding how big its pixels should be; this is referred to as *resolution* and is generally expressed in terms of *pixels per inch (ppi).* Check out the section "Making sure you export enough pixels," later in this chapter, for the whole scoop.

Why use pixels instead of inches or centimeters to describe the size of a digital image? It all has to do with how computer screens work. Because not all screens display things at the same size, it's impossible to predict how *big* an image will look when it shows up on someone's computer. Depending on the person's display settings, an 800-x-600-pixel image may be a few inches across, or it may take up the whole screen. Giving a digital image's dimensions in pixels is the only accurate way of describing how "big" it is.

Individual pixels

600 pixels

800 pixels

Looking at SketchUp's raster formats

So you know you need to export a raster image from SketchUp, but which one do you choose? You have four choices in Windows; three of them are available on the Mac. The following sections give you the details.

REMEMBER

When you export a raster image, you're saving your current view in SketchUp to a separate file somewhere on your computer. As a raster image, that file consists of tiny, colored dots, or *pixels* — more pixels than you can shake a stick at. When you look at all the pixels together, they form an image.

Tagged Image File (TIFF or TIF)

TIFFs are the stalwarts of the raster image file format world; everyone can read them and just about everyone can create them. *TIFF* stands for Tagged Image File Format, but that's hardly important. Here's everything you need to know about TIFFs:

>> **When image quality is important, choose TIFF.** Unless file size is a concern (because, for example, you need to send an image by e-mail), always export a TIFF if you need a raster image. For everything from working in Photoshop to creating a layout in InDesign or QuarkXPress, a TIFF can provide the image quality you need.

>> **TIFFs don't compress your image data.** That means they don't introduce any garbage like JPEGs do, but it also means that they're really big files.

>> **Pay attention to your pixel count.** If you're exporting a TIFF, you're probably looking for the best image quality you can get. And if that's the case, you need to make sure that your TIFF is "big" enough — that it includes enough pixels — to display at the size you need. Have a look at "Making sure you export enough pixels," later in this chapter, for more information.

Joint Photographic Experts Group (JPEG or JPG)

JPEG stands for Joint Photographic Experts Group, which makes it sound much fancier than it really is. Almost every digital image you've ever seen was a JPEG (pronounced *JAY-peg*); it's the standard file format for images on the web. Check out these JPEG details:

>> **When file size is a concern, choose JPEG.** The whole point of the JPEG file format is to compress raster images to manageable file sizes so that they can be e-mailed and put on websites. A JPEG is a fraction of the size of a TIFF file with the same number of pixels, so JPEG is a great choice if file size is more important to you than image quality.

>> **JPEGs compress file size by degrading image quality.** This is known as *lossy* compression; JPEG technology basically works by tossing out a lot of the pixels in your image. JPEGs also introduce a fair amount of pixel garbage; these smudges are *artifacts,* and they're awful.

WARNING

>> **JPEG + SketchUp = Danger.** Because of the way the JPEG file format works, JPEG exports from SketchUp are particularly susceptible to looking terrible. Images from SketchUp usually include straight lines and broad areas of color, both of which JPEG has a hard time handling. If you're going to export a JPEG from SketchUp, make sure that the JPEG Compression slider is *never* set less than 8. For more details, see the section "Exporting a raster image from SketchUp," earlier in this chapter.

Portable Network Graphics (PNG)

REMEMBER

Hooray for PNG! Pronounced *ping,* this graphics file format is our hero. Unfortunately, it isn't as widely used as it should be. If we had our druthers, every raster export from SketchUp would be a PNG. Why? Because, at least as far as SketchUp is concerned, PNG combines all the best features of TIFF and JPEG. PNG details are as follows:

>> **PNGs compress image data *without* affecting image quality.** As a *lossless* compression technology, PNGs are smaller files than TIFFs (just like JPEGs), but they don't mess up any pixels (totally unlike JPEGs). Granted, PNGs aren't as small as JPEGs, but the difference in image quality is worth a few extra bits.

>> **If you're exporting an image for someone who knows a thing or two about computers, choose PNG.** The truth is that some software doesn't know what to do with a PNG, so using it involves a risk. If you plan to send your exported image to someone who knows what he's doing, go ahead and send a PNG — he'll be impressed that you're "in the know." If the recipient of your export is less technologically sophisticated, a JPEG or TIFF file may be a safer choice.

TECHNICAL STUFF

The PNG file format wasn't developed to replace JPEG or TIFF; it was supposed to stand in for *GIF* (Graphics Interchange Format), which is a file type that SketchUp doesn't export. Without going into too much detail, folks use JPEG for images like photographs and GIF for things like logos. Because exported SketchUp views usually have more in common with the latter, PNG (the replacement for GIF) is the better choice. So why can't PNG replace JPEG and TIFF? For most photographs (which are the majority of images on the web), JPEG is better than PNG because it produces smaller files, which in turn yields faster load times when you're surfing the Internet. TIFF is more versatile than PNG because it supports different *color spaces*, which are important to people in the printing industry. For reasons that are beyond the scope of this book and that aren't relevant to exports from SketchUp, PNG is still the best — if not the safest — choice.

Windows Bitmap (BMP)

Windows Bitmap, or BMP, files are old school; they can be used only on Windows, and they're big. If a BMP were a car, it would be an old van with a rusted-out floor. As you can probably guess, we don't recommend using BMPs for anything.

Making sure you export enough pixels

With raster images, it's all about pixels. The more pixels your image has, the sharper the image is, and the bigger it can be displayed or printed. Figure 13-4 shows the same image three times. The first image is 150 x 50, meaning that it's 150 pixels wide by 50 pixels high. The second image is 300 x 100, and the third is 900 x 300. Notice how the image with more pixels looks a lot better? That's the whole point of this section.

TIP

Why not always export a truckload of pixels, just in case you need them? There are two reasons:

>> Image exports with lots of pixels take a long time to process.

>> Raster images are very big files. If you want to share an image digitally via e-mail or the web, you want enough pixels to make the image look good on-screen but not so many that your recipient acquires a few gray hairs or gums up their Internet connection trying to download the image.

 150 x 50 pixels

 300 x 100 pixels

FIGURE 13-4:
More pixels
yield a much
more detailed
image.

 900 x 300 pixels

How many pixels you need to export depends on what you're going to use the image *for*. Very broadly, you can do two things with your image:

>> Display or project it on a screen, digitally.

>> Print it.

In the next two sections, we talk about each of these possibilities in detail.

Exporting enough pixels for a digital presentation

If you plan to use your exported image as part of an on-screen presentation, it's helpful to know what computer monitors and digital projectors can display:

>> The smallest, oldest devices currently in use have images that are 1024 pixels wide by 768 pixels high.

>> At the other end of the spectrum, high-end, 30-inch LCD monitors display 2560 x 1600 pixels.

So it stands to reason that if you're exporting an image that will be viewed only on-screen, you need to create an image that's somewhere between 800 and 2500 pixels wide. Table 13-1 provides some guidelines on image sizes for different digital applications.

TABLE 13-1

Suggested Image Sizes for On-screen Use

How the Image Will Be Used	Image Width (Pixels)
E-mail	400 to 800
Website, large image	600
Website, small image	200
PowerPoint presentation (full screen)	800 or 1024 (depends on projector)
PowerPoint presentation (floating image)	400

Understanding resolution: Exporting images for print

REMEMBER

Images that you want to print need to have lots more pixels than ones that are going to display only on-screen. That's because printers — photo, inkjet, laser, and offset — all operate very differently than computer monitors and digital projectors. When you print something, the pixels in your image turn into microscopic specks of ink or toner. To make a decent-sized print of your exported image, it needs to contain enough *pixels per inch* of image. An image's pixel density, expressed in pixels per inch (ppi), is its *resolution*. What kind of resolution you need depends on three things:

>> **The kind of device you print to:** For home inkjet printers, you can get away with a resolution of as little as 150 ppi. If your image will be appearing in a commercially produced book, you need a resolution of at least 300 ppi.

>> **How far away the image will be from the audience:** There's a big difference between a magazine page and a trade-show banner. For close-up applications, a resolution of 200 to 300 ppi is appropriate. Large graphics that will be viewed from several feet away can be as low as 60 ppi.

>> **The subject matter of the image:** Photographic images tend to consist of areas of color that blur together a bit; these kinds of images can tolerate being printed at lower resolutions than drawings with lots of intricate detail. For images with lots of lines like SketchUp models, it's best to work with very high resolutions — 300 to 600 ppi — especially if the image will be viewed close-up.

Table 13-2 provides some guidelines for exporting images that will be printed.

TIP

Keep in mind that the biggest raster image that SketchUp can export is 10,000 pixels wide or tall (whichever is greater). This means that the largest banner image, printed at 100 ppi, that SketchUp can create is about 100 inches wide. To make larger images, you need to export a *vector* file, which requires SketchUp Pro and is beyond the scope of this book.

TABLE 13-2   **Recommended Resolutions for Prints**

How the Image Will Be Used	Image Resolution (Pixels/Inch)	Image Resolution (Pixels/Centimeter)
8.5-x-11 or 11-x-17 inkjet or laser print	200 to 300	80 to 120
Color brochure or pamphlet	300	120
Magazine or book (color and shadows)	300	120
Magazine or book (linework only)	450 to 600	180 to 240
Presentation board	150 to 200	60 to 80
Banner	60 to 100	24 to 40

Follow these steps to make sure that you export enough pixels to print your image properly:

1. **In the Export Options dialog box, make sure that the Use View Size check box is deselected.**

   To get to the Export Options dialog box, follow Steps 1–6 in the section "Exporting a raster image from SketchUp," earlier in this chapter.

2. **Decide on the resolution that you need for your exported image. (Refer to Table 13-2.)**

   Keep the resolution in your head or scribble it on a piece of paper.

3. **Decide how big your exported image will be printed, in inches or centimeters.**

   Note your desired physical image size, just like you did with the resolution in the preceding step.

TIP

4. **Multiply your resolution from Step 2 by your image size from Step 3 to get the number of pixels you need to export:**

   Resolution (pixels/in or cm) × Size (in or cm) = Number of pixels

   In other words, if you know what resolution you need to export, and you know how big your image will be printed, you can multiply the two numbers to get the number of pixels you need. Here's an example: 300 pixels/inch × 8 inches wide = 2400 pixels wide.

   To export an image that can be printed 8 inches wide at 300 ppi, you need to export an image that's 2400 pixels wide. Figure 13-5 gives an illustration of this example.

TIP

SketchUp's default setting is to make your exported image match the proportions of your modeling window; that is, you can type only a width *or* a height, but not both. If you're on a Mac, you can manually enter both dimensions by clicking Unlink (which looks like a chain). You can always click it again to relink the width and height dimensions later.

8 inches wide x 300 ppi = 2400 pixels

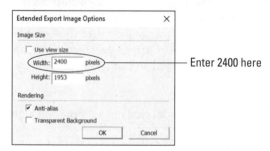

Enter 2400 here

FIGURE 13-5: To figure out how many pixels you need to export, multiply the resolution by the physical size.

5. Type the width *or* height of the image you want to export, in pixels.

It's usually pretty hard to know *exactly* how big your image will be when it's printed, and even if you do, you probably want to leave some room for cropping. For these reasons, you might add 15–25 percent to the number of pixels you'll need. For example, if an image calls for 2400 pixels, you might export 3000 pixels, just to be safe.

TIP

If you're on a Mac, things are a little easier because SketchUp's designers built a pixel calculator into the Export Options dialog box. Just enter your desired resolution in the appropriate spot, change the Width and Height units from pixels to inches or centimeters, and type your desired image size. SketchUp does the arithmetic for you.

6. **Click OK to close the Export Options dialog box.**

Making Movies with Animation Export

When it comes to having nerdy fun, exporting movie animations of your SketchUp models is right up there with Pokémon GO and store-bought fireworks. Like both these things, what's so great about animation export is how *easy* it is to do.

That's not to say that animation and digital video are simple topics — they're not. It'd take a freight elevator to move the books that have been written about working with video on the computer, but in this section, we keep it simple. What you find here is only what you need to know in order to export an animation of a 3D SketchUp model.

Getting ready for prime time

The key to exporting animations of your SketchUp models is using scenes; if you haven't read it already, now's the time to check out Chapter 11. *Scenes* are saved views of your model that you can arrange in any order you want. When you export an animation, SketchUp strings together the scenes in your model to create a movie file that can be played on just about any computer made in the last several years.

Follow these steps to get your model ready to export as an animation:

1. **Create scenes (as described in Chapter 11) to build the "skeleton" of your animation.**

2. **To adjust the animation settings in the Model Info dialog box, choose Window ⇨ Model Info and then select the Animation panel.**

   Chapter 11 explains all the controls; see the section about moving from scene to scene.

3. **Select the Enable Scene Transitions check box to tell SketchUp to move smoothly from one scene to the next.**

4. **Enter a transition time to tell SketchUp how long to spend moving between scenes.**

   If your Scene Delay is 0 (below), you can multiply your transition time by your number of scenes to figure out how long your exported animation will be.

5. **Enter a scene delay time to pause at each scene before moving on to the next one.**

   If you plan to talk about each scene, use the scene delay time to pause before each one. If your animation is supposed to be a smooth walkthrough or flyover, set this to 0.

TIP

6. **Adjust the proportions of your modeling window to approximate the proportions of your movie.**

   Unlike SketchUp's 2D export formats, the proportions of your exported movie don't depend on those of your modeling window; that is to say, making your modeling window long and skinny won't result in a long and skinny movie. You choose how many pixels wide and tall you want your movie to be, so to get an idea of how much you'll be able to see, make your modeling window match the proportions of your exported file. (The 16:9 aspect ratio is common for video formats.) Have a look at Step 1 in the section "Exporting a raster image from SketchUp," earlier in this chapter, for guidance on adjusting your modeling window.

7. **When your project is ready to go, move on to the next section to export your animation.**

Exporting a movie

SketchUp offers a veritable alphabet soup of video export formats: You can choose from seven on Windows and six on Mac. The list can seem daunting, so here's a cheat sheet that should save you some mental anguish:

» **H.264 (`.mp4`):** This video format is as close to an industry standard as it gets. Everyone with a Mac and anyone with QuickTime on her Windows computer can readily view H.264 movies without any hassle. It's also the upload format of choice for popular video-sharing websites like YouTube and Vimeo. SketchUp's exported H.264 files are nicely compressed, which keeps them smallish and good-looking.

» **AVI (`.avi`):** All Windows machines and Macs with a special plugin can play AVI movies. Popular video-sharing websites like YouTube and Vimeo let you upload AVI files, but they tend to prefer H.264. SketchUp's exported AVI animations are *uncompressed,* meaning that they look nice and clean but the files can get huge quickly. If you're planning to send someone your movie file, AVI might not be your best choice.

» **VP8** (`.webm`) : Not too many years ago, the tech world started getting nervous about H.264's dominance as a file format used to display video on websites. H.264 is *proprietary,* meaning that big companies have to pay licensing fees to its owner (Apple) if they want to use it. WebM is a free alternative, backed by Google, and made for use on websites that use HTML5. Translation: You don't need to worry about WebM unless you're planning to embed your movie on a modern website *without* first uploading it to YouTube or Vimeo.

» **Theora** (`.ogv`) : Theora is another free, open source format meant for videos that will be embedded on websites. Unlike WebM, Theora is managed by an independent foundation that tries to keep important multimedia file formats out of the hands of big, private corporations like Apple (H.264) and Google (WebM).

» **JPEG, PNG and TIFF:** Choosing to export in any of these formats won't give you a movie file that you can watch — they aren't video file formats. Instead, you'll get a pile of image files that each represent one frame in your anima-tion; for a 3-second video at 30 frames per second, SketchUp would export 90 individual images. These options are useful for serious video editors who need lots of control, but most folks shouldn't need to use them.

Although exporting animations in SketchUp is a pretty simple operation, figuring out how to set all the animation export controls can seem like landing the space shuttle.

Follow these steps to export a movie file from SketchUp:

1. **Prepare your model for export as an animation.**

   See the section "Getting ready for prime time," earlier in this chapter, for a list of things you need to do before you export an animation.

2. **Choose File ➪ Export ➪ Animation ➪ Video.**

   Choosing Video provides you with file formats that yield video files. If you pick Image Set instead, you'll see options for creating sets of still images. We explain the difference between these a little later on in this section. If you're on a Mac, there's no bifurcation of the Animation submenu; just choose File ➪ Export ➪ Animation, and you see all your format choices.

3. **Give your movie file a name and then choose where to save it on your computer system.**

4. **Make sure that the correct file format is selected.**

   From the Format drop-down list, select the file format you want SketchUp to export. In most cases, this is either H.264 or AVI, but take a look at the descrip-tions earlier in this section for more detailed info.

5. **Click the Options button to open the Animation Export Options dialog box.**

6. **Adjust the settings for the type of animation you want to export. (See Figure 13-6.)**

   How you set up everything in this dialog box depends on how you plan to use the animation you create. Check out the next section in this chapter for a list of settings and their implications.

7. **Click OK in the Export Options dialog box.**

   You return to the Animation Export dialog box.

8. **Check to make sure that everything looks right and then click the Export button.**

   Because exporting an animation takes a while, it pays to double-check your settings before you click the Export button. When the export is complete, you can find your animation file in the location you specified in Step 3. Double-clicking the file causes it to open in whatever movie-playing software you have that can read it.

Figuring out the Animation Export Options settings

As we say earlier, digital video can be complicated. Lucky for you, you don't really have to know exactly what everything means to export the right kind of movie; you just have to know how to set up everything. The Animation Export Options dialog box (shown in Figure 13-6) is the same for each of the video file formats that SketchUp offers; here's a brief guide to the settings:

>> **Resolution:** This use of the word *resolution* refers to the pixel dimensions — the physical size — of your video. SketchUp Make (the free version) lets you choose from three standard sizes, whereas SketchUp Pro provides a Custom option for more flexibility. Here's what the terms mean:

- *1080p Full HD* yields a video that is 1920 pixels wide and 1080 pixels high. This is the highest resolution that most newer televisions can display, and it's even higher than a lot of laptops can handle natively. Choose this option only if you know you'll need it; exporting this many pixels takes a long time.

- *720p HD,* which is 1280 pixels wide by 720 pixels high, is the most common resolution for high-quality exported video. This size looks good on computer screens and televisions, and it's the recommended upload resolution for YouTube and Vimeo. Chances are good that this is the resolution for you.

- *480p SD,* at only 854 pixels wide by 480 pixels high, will probably look small on most computer screens. This is the resolution used for DVDs, which every 16-year-old knows are weird artifacts from the distant past. (Aidan has a huge collection, unfortunately.) Use 480p if file size is a concern.

- *Custom* is available only if you're using the Pro version of SketchUp. Choosing this option "unlocks" settings for Aspect Ratio and Frame Size, which we describe later in this list.

>> **Aspect Ratio:** This refers to the proportions of your video frame; the first name refers to the width and the second to the height. Common aspect ratios for film and video are 16:9 (which is wide) and 4:3 (which is more square). If you're using SketchUp Pro, you can choose Custom and put whatever you want into the Frame Size fields below this setting.

>> **Frame Size:** Pro users can pick their own video frame dimensions. Go nuts, big spender.

>> **Preview Frame Size:** This is actually an incredibly handy button. Click it to see a green box preview of how big your video will look on your screen. Click the preview to make it go away when you're done.

>> **Frame Rate:** Different video technologies use different frame rates. Using more frames/second (fps) results in smoother motion but bigger files and longer processing times. Generally speaking, 30 fps is a good sweet spot. If you're worried about big files, try 15 fps and see how that looks.

- >> **Restore Defaults:** Replaces your hard drive's contents with a looping, 8-second video montage of Keanu Reaves's greatest cinematic moments. Just making sure you're still paying attention — this button puts everything in Export Options back the way it was before you started messing around.

- >> **Loop to Starting Scene:** Automatically ends your video on the scene you started with, rather than the last scene in the sequence. This option is handy if you want your movie to end exactly how it started.

- >> **Anti-alias Rendering:** Choosing this doubles the amount of time it takes for your animation to export, but it makes your edges look much smoother in the final movie. You'll almost certainly want to select this option.

- >> **Transparent Background (Mac only):** If you're planning to use your exported movie with advanced video editing software, this is something that might interest you. Otherwise, you should probably leave this option deselected.

- >> **Always Prompt for Animation Options (Windows only):** Select this to force SketchUp to show you the Animation Export Options dialog box every time you export a movie.

Exporting a CAD File

AutoCAD and other CAD-based software are popular among architects, engineers, and anyone who needs to build or make super-precise stuff. Although some professionals have totally replaced AutoCAD-based workflows with SketchUp and LayOut, others still use AutoCAD.

If you ever need to export a SketchUp model to a DWG file that works with CAD-based software, SketchUp Pro has the inner workings to translate your SKP file into a DWG file. (You cannot export a CAD file from SketchUp Make; you have to plunk down the money for Pro.) Because the SKP-to-DWG process is fairly advanced, this section mostly gives you a high-level overview of the export process so that you have a basic understanding of how it works.

Preparing your file

First, a few tasks can produce a cleaner exported file. Here's how to prepare your file before you export it as a DWG file:

- >> **Check your units.** If the unit format (inches or decimals, for example) of your SketchUp file matches the desired units for the DWG file, the export process goes much more smoothly. To check your model's units, choose Window⇨Model Info and select the Units pane on the left.

>> **Turn off problematic styles.** Line styles that use endpoints or extensions don't always translate well in the export process. If you have problems with endpoints or extensions in you exported file, try turning them off. You turn off the line styles on the Edit tab of the Styles panel. See Chapter 10 for details.

>> **Set your view.** If you're exporting a 2D DWG file, you're likely exporting a floor plan that may need to reflect a specific scale. If that's the case, make sure the model is in Parallel Projection view (choose Camera⇨Parallel Projection) and uses one of the standard views, such as Top or Front. (Any standard view but Iso is okay.)

Keep in mind that SketchUp layers may not translate directly to CAD layers.

Exporting a 2D DWG file

To export a SketchUp model as a 2D CAD file, follow these steps:

1. **Prepare your file, as explained in the preceding section.**

   We don't want you to miss those tips.

2. **Choose File⇨Export⇨2D Graphic.**

3. **In the export dialog box that appears, choose to export your file as a DWG file. Then click the Options button.**

4. **Choose your desired options.**

   The Drawing Scale and Size section enables you to choose scale options. If your model uses profile lines (See Chapter 10), then you can select options here that export the profile lines as CAD polylines and customize the line width if you like. The Separate on a Layer check box, when selected, places profile lines or section cut lines on a separate layer.

5. **Click OK in the Export Options dialog box. Then click the Export button.**

   Depending on how big your SketchUp file is, this process can take a while.

Exporting a 3D DWG file

When you export a SketchUp file to 3D DWG file, you can select what entities you want to export. For example, you may want to export only edges and leave out faces, dimensions, and text. Follow these steps to export your SketchUp model to a 3D DWG file:

1. **Remember to prepare your file, as explained at the beginning of this section.**

2. **Choose File ⇨ Export ⇨ 3D Model.**

3. **In the Export Model dialog box that appears, select the DWG file type.**

4. **Click the Options button to select what entities you want to export. When you're done, click OK.**

5. **Click the Export button.**

   SketchUp's gears start converting your file into a CAD-friendly format.

IN THIS CHAPTER

» Managing pages and layers

» Inserting and updating SketchUp models

» Adding graphics

» Creating labels and dimensions

» Customizing LayOut with your own templates and scrapbooks

» Printing, exporting, or presenting your work

Chapter **14**

Creating Presentations and Documents with LayOut

I f you're lucky enough to have SketchUp Pro, you also have LayOut, a separate application for presenting 3D SketchUp models. LayOut was designed to be easy to use, quick to learn, and tightly integrated with SketchUp.

The people who built LayOut want you to use it to create all your design presentations. Here are examples of what you can make:

» Design packs, presentation boards, and posters

» Construction drawings with scaled views and dimensions

» Storyboards for planning camera shots

LayOut gives you the tools to add company branding, accurate dimensions, shading and hatching patterns, and more — whatever needs to accompany views of your model. You can create presentations that are just about any physical size and export them as PDFs or images to send to other people.

REMEMBER

Best of all, when your design changes in SketchUp, you can easily update your model views in LayOut to reflect the changes. If you make your living designing and presenting ideas in 3D, LayOut can save you boatloads of time.

Although this book can't dig into all that LayOut can do, this chapter helps you start using LayOut's key features for presenting your models.

Building a LayOut Document

To help you get your bearings in LayOut, this section helps you put together a LayOut document. Take a deep breath, put a fresh battery in your mouse, and prepare for your presentation-making life to get much easier than it's ever been. . . .

When you launch LayOut (or each time you start a new LayOut document), the Getting Started dialog box appears and asks you to select a template. You can change this default behavior if you like, but the templates are usually the easiest way to begin.

In Figure 14-1, all the template options are expanded so you can have a look at all the categories of options. The template selected in Figure 14-1 is a Titleblock template that uses simple serif fonts and a standard U.S. letter document size (8 ½ x 11 inches). Whether you start with a prebuilt template or create your own, the following sections walk you through the basics of creating a presentation in LayOut.

Customizing a document's pages and layers

Many LayOut templates have multiple pages and layers, as shown in Figure 14-2. When you use pages and layers together, they give you a lot of control over what appears where in your document:

>> **Pages:** Your document can have as many pages as you like. In the Pages panel on the right, you can customize the number and sequence of pages. To add a page, click the plus sign icon. To duplicate a page, click the Duplicate Selected Page icon. To delete a page, click the minus sign icon. To change the order of the pages, click and drag a page up or down in the sequence.

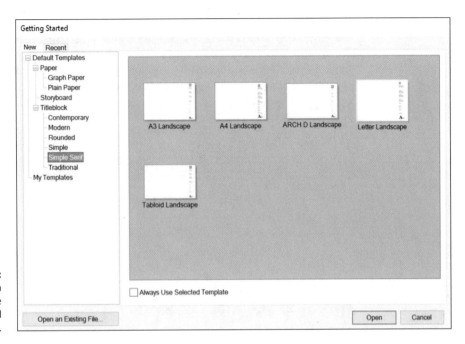

FIGURE 14-1:
Select a
template in the
Getting Started
dialog box.

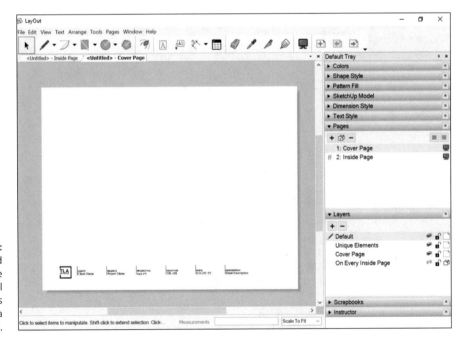

FIGURE 14-2:
Pages and
layers enable
you to control
what appears
where in a
document.

>> **Layers:** In LayOut, the layers work like sheets of acetate stacked one on top of another. (This functionality is *very* different from SketchUp layers, covered in Chapter 7.) In the Layers panel, you can add layers that control what does or doesn't appear on each page. Two features enable you to manage layers: layer visibility (the eye icon) and layer sharing (the single or double page icon).

In a template, layers may be locked by default so that you can't accidentally move things. To customize the template with your own information, unlock each layer by clicking its little lock icon. Figure 14-3 helps you find these important controls in the Layers panel.

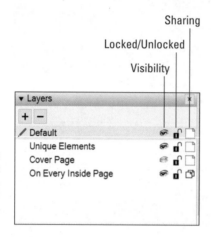

FIGURE 14-3:
In LayOut's Layers panel, icons control sharing and visibility.

To add an element on almost every page, follow these steps:

REMEMBER

1. **In the Layers panel, create a layer or select an existing layer.**

   The layer with the little red pencil next to it is your active layer.

2. **Click the layer's sharing icon so that it looks like two pages (not one).**

   This step shares whatever you add to this layer on every page in your document.

3. **Create an element, such as typing text, drawing a shape, or inserting a SketchUp model or image.**

   You discover how to add items to a page in the upcoming sections.

4. **In the Pages panel, select any page on which you don't want the item to appear.**

5. **Back in the Layers panel, click the eye icon so that the eye closes and the layer is toggled to its hidden state.**

   The element becomes hidden on the selected page. In Figure 14-2, notice that Cover Page is selected in the Pages panel. To create a custom cover page, the On Every Inside Page layer is hidden.

REMEMBER

In the Layers panel, when a layer is shared among all your pages, you can control the layer's visibility on the selected page by toggling the eye icon.

Conversely, if you want an element to appear on only one page, follow these steps:

1. **In the Pages panel, select the page on which you want the element to appear.**

2. **In the Layers panel, click the plus icon to create a new layer or select a layer that displays elements only on the selected page.**

3. **Click the layer's sharing icon so that it looks like a single page.**

4. **With the page and layer selected, create the element on the new layer.**

TIP

As you create a document, keeping your elements organized with pages and layers can save your sanity. Here are a few tips to help you on your way:

» **To keep track of what each page and layer does,** give each one a descriptive name, similar to the names you see in the template shown in Figure 14-2. To name a page or layer, double-click its name, and the name becomes editable.

» **To see what layer an element is on currently,** select the element and look for the tiny blue dot in the Layers panel. If you select two elements on two different layers, you see two blue dots.

» **To change which layer something is on,** select the destination layer in the Layers panel. Then context-click the element you want to move and choose Move to Current Layer. Selecting multiple elements, context-clicking one of them, and choosing Move to Current Layer moves them all.

» **Move several elements from multiple layers to a single layer with Copy and Paste.** Copying elements from multiple layers and pasting them pastes them all on the same layer — the active one.

Adding and editing text

 LayOut enables you to add plain old text with the Text tool, and it's easy to do. Labels and dimensions, covered later in this chapter, have a few whiz–bang features that regular text does not.

Text boxes in LayOut are classified into two broad types, depending on how you create them:

>> **Bounded:** If you click and drag with the Text tool, the text box you create is *bounded.* Any text you enter into it that doesn't fit isn't visible, and you get a little red arrow at the bottom. That arrow tells you that there's more in your text box; you need to use the Select tool to make the box bigger to show everything that's inside. Use a bounded text box whenever your text needs to fit into a precise space in your design.

>> **Unbounded:** If, instead of creating a text box with the Text tool, you simply click to place your cursor somewhere on your page, the text you create is *unbounded.* It stays inside a text box, but that text box automatically resizes to accommodate whatever text you put inside it. To turn an unbounded text box into a bounded one, just resize it with the Select tool or choose Text ⇨ Make Unbounded.

Naturally, you control things like text size, color, alignment, and font using the Text Style panel (Fonts dialog box on a Mac). Select the text you'd like to format and choose your desired settings in the panel.

TIP

As you add and edit text in LayOut, here are a few tips to help you along the way:

>> To edit text, double-click a text element with the Select tool. When you're done, click elsewhere on the page.

>> Zoom into your document if you need to add or edit text precisely. See the nearby sidebar, "Get zooming," for details.

>> Choose Text ⇨ Insert Auto-Text to insert a tag that displays automatically generated text. For example, you can insert page numbers or a company name. To customize the text that appears for a specific Auto-Text tag, choose Text ⇨ Customize Auto-Text, and in the dialog box that appears, select the tag at the top and type your desired text in the specified area at the bottom.

>> On a Mac, choosing Text ⇨ Show Rulers does more than just display ruled increments at the top of your drawing window. It also enables extra controls for paragraph spacing and lists — bulleted and numbered. Just select text in your document to see them appear above the ruler.

Inserting SketchUp model views

With every other page-layout program in the universe, the only way to include a view of a SketchUp model is to export that view from SketchUp as an image file and then place it in the layout program. Changing the SketchUp file means going through the whole export-and-place process again. If your presentation includes lots of SketchUp model views, this process can take hours.

REMEMBER

This brings us to LayOut's *raison d'être*: Instead of exporting views from SketchUp to get them into LayOut, all you do is insert a SketchUp file. From within LayOut, you can pick the view you like best. You can also use as many views of the same model as you want. When your SketchUp file is modified, LayOut knows about it and (using the References panel in the Document Setup dialog box) lets you update all your views at once by clicking a single button. If you need to pause for a minute to let the timesaving aspects of this feature sink in, we understand.

Follow these steps to insert a SketchUp *viewport* (model view) into your document:

1. **In SketchUp, create a scene for each view of your model that you want to show in your LayOut document. When you're done, save your document.**

   Take a look at Chapter 11 for a refresher on using scenes. Be sure to give them meaningful names.

2. **In LayOut, on the Pages panel, select the page where you want to insert a viewport.**

3. **Choose File ⇨ Insert.**

4. **In the Insert dialog box that appears, find the SketchUp file on your computer that you want to insert and click the Open button.**

   The Insert dialog box closes, and your SketchUp model is placed on your current LayOut document page.

5. **With the Select tool, context-click your viewport, choose Scenes, and then choose the name of the scene you want to appear in this viewport, as shown in Figure 14-4.**

   TIP

   If you don't see a list of scenes, you probably forgot to save your SketchUp file in Step 1. Save your SketchUp file; then context-click your viewport (in LayOut) and choose Update Reference.

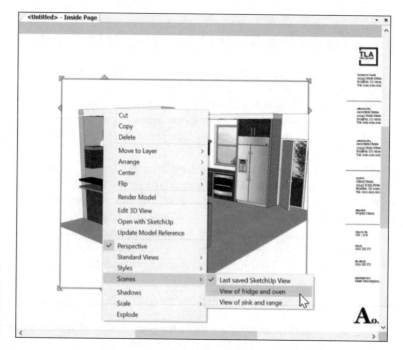

FIGURE 14-4: Associate a scene from your model with a viewport in LayOut.

6. **(Optional) Assign a drawing scale to your model view if that's appropriate.**

   If the scene you picked in Step 5 is an *orthographic* view (top, front, side) where perspective is turned off, you likely want to show your model at a particular drawing scale. See "Creating scaled orthographic views" later in this chapter for details.

7. **Use the Select tool to position or resize your model view.**

Click and drag to move any element in your document on the page. Click and drag the Rotation Grip (the little blue stick in the center of your image when it's selected) to rotate. You can resize anything by clicking and dragging any corner.

TIP

If a bright yellow exclamation mark icon appears in the lower-right corner of a viewport, you need to tell LayOut to render that viewport so that it reflects whatever changes you've made. Context-click the viewport, choose Render Model from the context menu, and you're good to go.

Repositioning a model view in LayOut

In LayOut, when you're working inside a model viewport, you're working in 3D. You can do a couple of things to change your viewport's point of view: Use the Camera tools or edit scenes with the Model panel.

Double-clicking a viewport with the Select tool is a little bit like activating SketchUp from inside LayOut. When you're in this SketchUp-like mode, the thick blue border around the model viewport becomes a thin blue border. When you're in this model, you can change your point of view as follows:

» Orbit, zoom, and pan around using your mouse, exactly the way you do in SketchUp.

» Context-click the viewport and choose a specific Camera tool from the context menu (Orbit, Pan, Zoom, Zoom Window, Look Around, or Walk).

» On the SketchUp Model panel's View tab, shown in Figure 14-5, choose an option from the Scenes or Standard Views drop-down lists.

FIGURE 14-5:
The SketchUp Model panel in LayOut.

When you're done repositioning your model, click somewhere else to stop editing the viewport. LayOut re-renders the view, and your model goes back to looking nice and crisp.

Making your models look their best

The SketchUp Model panel's second tab — Styles — contains one of the most important settings in all of LayOut: the Line Weight field. The number you put into the Line Weight field tells LayOut how thick to draw the thinnest lines in your viewport. Entering **2** yields edges that are 2 points wide. Typing **0.25** makes your edges a quarter point wide — much thinner and (in many cases) much nicer. Figure 14-6 illustrates how adjusting this setting changes how a model looks.

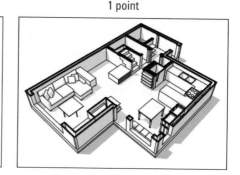

FIGURE 14-6: Use the Line Weight field to make your models look their very best.

REMEMBER

Changing the Line Weight number is the single best thing you can do for your models in LayOut. The line weights you use depend entirely on the size of your viewports and the complexity of your drawings. Try to avoid making anything look too wispy or too chunky — the key here is readability.

TECHNICAL STUFF

If the style that's applied to your viewport has Profiles enabled, some edges look thicker. To change the thickness of Profiles in a viewport, edit the style that defines the Profiles in the SketchUp model. Profile thickness is always a multiple: A setting of **4** produces Profiles that are four times as thick as regular edges. Check out Chapter 10 for more about styles and how to edit them.

How LayOut renders a model can also have a big impact on your model's appearance. You control the rendering on the SketchUp Model panel's Styles tab: In the lower right, a drop-down list enables you to select Vector, Raster, or Hybrid. Here's how selecting each option impacts how your model is rendered (and check out Figure 14-7 to see examples of each rendering style):

>> **Raster:** Renders your viewport as an image comprising many, many little dots. If your model is rendered as a raster, it can display sketchy styles, shadows, and other effects that make it look like it does in SketchUp. On the other hand, printing or exporting a raster image at large sizes involves truckloads of pixels, and that can make LayOut choke. See the nearby sidebar "Balancing performance and quality" to find out more.

>> **Vector:** Renders your selected model viewport as a vector image. Lines appear smooth and crisp, but things like shadows, textures, and sketchy styles don't appear. Also, choosing vector rendering for really complex models can take a long time to process.

>> **Hybrid:** Combines clean vector lines with rich raster faces, shadows, and other goodies. Behind the scenes, LayOut renders the model twice — once as a vector and once as a raster. Hybrid rendering takes even longer than vector rendering but produces very nice results. If you have time, try hybrid rendering to see how it looks.

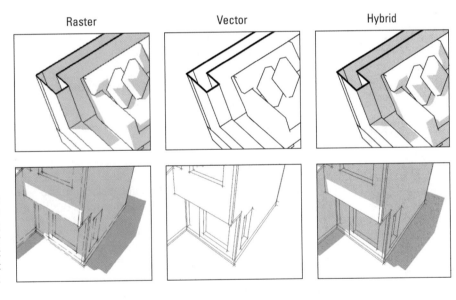

FIGURE 14-7: Choose a rendering method for each viewport in your LayOut document.

TIP

Try raster rendering for models with Sketchy Edges styles and for any model with a lot of geometry. Select hybrid or vector rendering for any plans, sections, or other views that feature a lot of line work.

BALANCING PERFORMANCE AND QUALITY

The more complex your SketchUp model is, the longer it takes to render in LayOut. If LayOut is sluggish, adjusting a couple of rendering settings might put a little spring in its step. Try the following:

- Select File ⇨ Document Setup ⇨ Paper. From the Display Resolution drop-down list, select Low, which corresponds to a resolution of 72 ppi (pixels per inch).

- On the SketchUp Model panel, clear the Auto check box in the lower left. Doing so tells LayOut not to render a model viewport each time you edit it. Instead, LayOut waits until you click the Render button (next to the check box) before it does any rendering.

Creating scaled orthographic views

The first step in creating a dimensioned drawing is to turn your viewport into a 2D orthographic view of your model. (See Chapter 11 for an introduction to orthographic views.) Although you can use the controls in the SketchUp Model panel to accomplish this, a better way is to go back to the model and create a scene.

Follow these steps to save an orthographic scene in your SketchUp model and assign it to a viewport in LayOut:

1. **In LayOut, context-click (with the Select tool) the viewport that contains your model and choose Open with SketchUp.**

2. **If you plan to have an active section cut in your view, add it to your model (if you haven't already).**

   Chapter 11 explains how to make section cuts.

3. **In SketchUp, choose Camera ⇨ Parallel Projection; then choose Camera ⇨ Standard Views ⇨ Top (or any other option from this list except Iso).**

4. **Zoom and pan (but don't orbit) until you have the view you want and then choose View ⇨ Animation ⇨ Add Scene.**

5. **Save your model and close it.**

6. **In LayOut, context-click the viewport and choose Update Reference.**

7. **In the View tab of the SketchUp Model panel, choose your new scene to associate it with the viewport.**

Now that you have an orthographic view of your model, you can assign a scale to it. Here's everything you need to know about that:

>> **Assign a scale using the Scale drop-down list in the SketchUp Model panel.** Don't forget to select the viewport you're working on first. Alternately, with the Select tool, context-click your viewport, choose Scale, and then choose one from the list that appears, as shown in Figure 14-8.

FIGURE 14-8: Assign a precise drawing scale to any orthographic viewport.

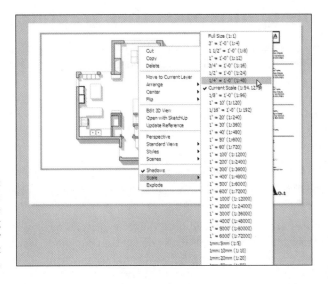

>> **Create your own scales if you want.** Need a scale that doesn't appear in the default list? Choose Edit ⇨ Preferences (LayOut ⇨ Preferences on a Mac) to open the Preferences dialog box; then click Scales on the left. Click the plus sign to add a new scale to the list. Scales you add are available for any LayOut file you're working on.

TIP

>> **Make sure Preserve Scale on Resize is selected.** After you assign a scale to a viewport, you probably want to manually resize its boundaries with the Select tool. Before you do, make sure the Preserve Scale on Resize check box (in the SketchUp Model panel) is selected. If it's not, you change the scale of your model view when you try to resize its viewport.

LayOut lets you assign a scale to any old view, but that doesn't matter. Drawing scales apply only to nonperspectival, straight-on views of your model.

REMEMBER

Updating model references

If you ever aren't sure whether your SketchUp viewports reflect the latest changes to your SketchUp model file (the .skp file), LayOut enables you to check. Select File ⇨ Document Setup ⇨ References. You see a list of files that the LayOut document references and whether those references are current. To update any SketchUp model file manually, select it in the list and click Update. The SketchUp file must be saved to your hard drive for the update process to work.

Adding photos and other graphics

Inserting images into your LayOut document is a straightforward affair. Just choose File ⇨ Insert and take it from there. A few more things to know about images you insert:

>> **LayOut can insert raster images.** Raster images are made of pixels, or tiny dots. TIFF, JPEG, GIF, BMP, and PNG are all graphics file formats that save pictures as lots of tiny dots.

>> **The Mac version of LayOut can also insert PDFs.** This is indisputably the best way to bring in vector art, such as logos. You can use a program like Adobe Illustrator to save any AI (Illustrator) or EPS file as a PDF.

>> **Images are a lot like viewports.** The techniques for moving, resizing, and rotating images work just like they do for SketchUp model views; use the Select tool to do everything. Remember to hold down the Shift key when you resize to maintain your image's aspect ratio.

Unfortunately, LayOut offers no easy way to import editable vector (such as AI, EPS, and SVG) graphics. If you want to use vector graphics in your LayOut document, you have two choices:

>> **Make your own.** LayOut is a fantastic vector illustration tool. The upcoming section, "Drawing with LayOut's vector tools," helps you get started.

>> **Borrow shamelessly from the Scrapbooks panel.** One of the best things about LayOut is the hundreds — maybe thousands — of predrawn graphical elements you can find in the Scrapbooks panel (shown in Figure 14-9). You find things like

- *Symbols:* Arrows, section markers, north indicators, graphic scales, and column grids

- *Entourage elements:* Trees, cars, and people at various scales and levels of detail

- *Color palettes:* To help with producing attractive documents quickly

To use something you see in the Scrapbooks, just click it with the Select tool to sample it and then click again to stamp it onto your page. You can keep clicking to stamp more copies. Press the Esc key when you're ready to exit stamping mode.

FIGURE 14-9: Scrapbooks contain all sorts of images you can insert into a LayOut document.

Drawing with LayOut's vector tools

LayOut includes a full slate of drawing tools that you can use to create logos, title bars, north arrows, graphic scales — anything you want. The drawings you create are vectors, meaning that you can do the following:

>> Scale the drawings without losing quality.

>> Change the fill and stroke (outline) colors.

>> Split lines and then rejoin them to make new shapes.

Because we don't know what you want to draw, a step list would be pretty pointless here. Instead, here are a few pointers to get you started:

>> **Create shapes the same way you create them in SketchUp.** Lines, arcs, rectangles, circles, polygons — you see the same or similar tools, and you can (for the most part) click-move-click to create the shapes just as you do in SketchUp.

>> **Type measurements and angles.** LayOut has a Measurements box (in the lower-right corner of your screen), just like the one in SketchUp. Take a look at Chapter 3 for tips on working accurately with this box.

>> **Build complex shapes out of simpler ones.** For example, with the Split tool and the Join tool, you can combine a triangle and a rectangle to create a thick, blocky arrow.

>> **Use the right kind of snaps.** You can snap to objects or to a grid via the Arrange menu.

>> **Open the Shape Style panel.** Use the Shape Style panel to change the fill and stroke characteristics of the selected shape(s). In plain English, double-click the Fill, Pattern, or Stroke swatches to open a panel where you can pick colors and patterns for the things you draw. The controls are straightforward, so you don't need much from us; just experiment and see what happens. You can also select dashed lines or add arrows to the beginning or end of a line.

If you're a pro, such as an architect or engineer, who needs to represent different materials using standardized patterns called *hatches*, LayOut has you covered — and more importantly, helps you cover your drawing. LayOut includes some of the most common hatches (which it calls Material Symbols), as well as hatches for Geometric Tiles, Site Patterns, and Tonal Patterns (which include dots and lines of various sizes). To apply these hatches (or any pattern) to a shape in your LayOut document, select the shape, double-click the Pattern swatch in the Shape Style panel. In the Pattern Fill panel that opens, select a category from the drop-down list at the top, and then select your desired hatch or pattern among the swatches that appear. Figure 14-10 shows this process in action.

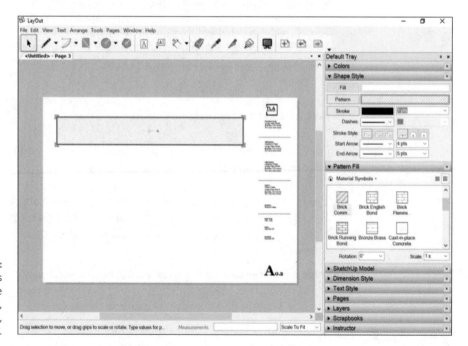

FIGURE 14-10:
Draw shapes and customize their outlines, fills, pattern, and color.

Annotating with labels

 In LayOut, labels are the easiest way to add *callouts* (notes with leader lines) to models and drawings. With the Label tool, you can add labels wherever you need them. Here are six important points about one of the most useful tools in LayOut:

» **Activate, click, click, type, and click.** Activate the Label tool, click once to pin the end of the leader line to an element in your drawing, click again to place your text cursor, type something, and click somewhere else to finish your label, as shown in Figure 14-11.

If you want, you can create *curved* leader lines. They often do a better job of standing out when most of the shapes in your drawings have straight edges. In LayOut, you curve a leader line by *click-drag-releasing* your mouse when you're placing its endpoints. (You can also do this with lines created with the Line tool.)

» **Save time with auto-filled text.** When you label certain kinds of entities in a model viewport, LayOut automatically fills in the text part for you. Labeling a component gives you its name. Labeling a face gives you its area. If you don't want LayOut's suggestion, just type something else.

» **Leader lines stick to drawing elements.** When you move the thing your leader line is pinned to, the line moves with it.

» **Use the Shape Style panel to edit the look of your leader lines.** You can change the color, thickness, and endpoints (arrowheads, slashes, and dots) of any leader line very easily after you create it.

» **Save time by sampling.** After you edit a label, making every subsequent label match is easy:

a. *Activate the Label tool and then press the S key.*

b. Your cursor changes into an eyedropper.

c. *Click the text part of the label you sample and then click S again.*

d. *Click the leader line of the label you sample.*

Now every label you create looks just like the one you sampled.

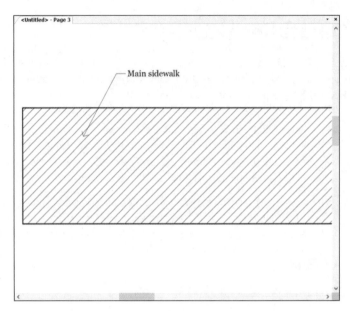

FIGURE 14-11:
Add text
callouts with
the Label tool.

Displaying dimensions

Dimensions can display exact measurements based on your model or drawing.

REMEMBER

The dimensions tools work hand-in-hand with inserted models to save you hours of work. For example, if you add a dimension to an inserted SketchUp model and later change the dimension of your model, LayOut can know about those changes and update the inserted model and the dimension accordingly.

TIP

Before you use either dimension tool, make sure Object Snap is turned on. (It's on by default.) With Object Snap on, your dimension leader lines can "see" the points to which they're supposed to attach. On the Arrange menu, you can check the status of Object Snap.

To create a linear dimension, follow these steps:

1. **Select the Linear Dimension tool.**

2. **Click a start point, and then click an endpoint.**

3. **Click to define an offset, and you're done.**

TIP

After you create your first dimension and while the tool is still active, double-click the next point you want to dimension. This technique duplicates the offset that you set for the first dimension.

Angular dimensions are a little trickier than linear dimensions. Follow these steps to make it work (see Figure 14-12):

1. Activate the Angular Dimension tool.

2. Click somewhere along the first line for the angle you want to mark, and click again along that line.

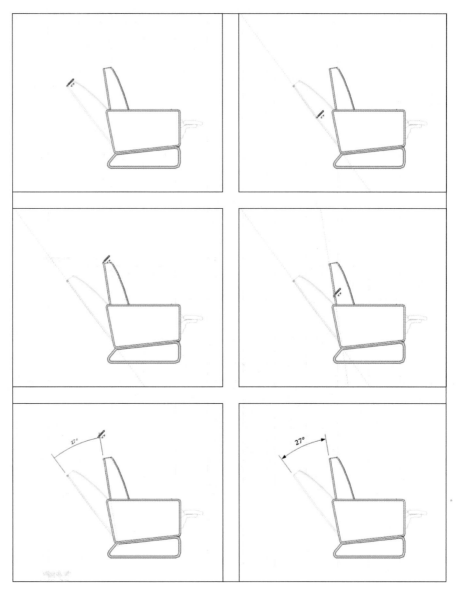

FIGURE 14-12:
Creating
an angular
dimension
takes some
getting
used to.

You create two "pin points" that establish the first line of the angle you want to mark.

3. **Click somewhere along the second line that creates the angle, and click again.**

   You create second set of pin points that tells LayOut where the other line of the angle is.

4. **Click one last time to position the text of your angular dimension.**

Creating separate layers for text, labels, and dimensions saves time in the long run. See "Customizing a document's pages and layers" earlier in this chapter for details.

Editing dimensions

After you actually draw a dimension — linear or angular — on your page, you can do an awful lot to change what the dimension looks like. To begin with, take a look at the anatomy of a dimension. Figure 14-13 shows an example of each kind.

Now that you're clear on nomenclature, here's some advice on editing a dimension's appearance (basically, everything except its text box):

>> **Use the Shape Style panel** to change colors, line styles, line weights, and arrow styles (the things at the ends of dimension lines).

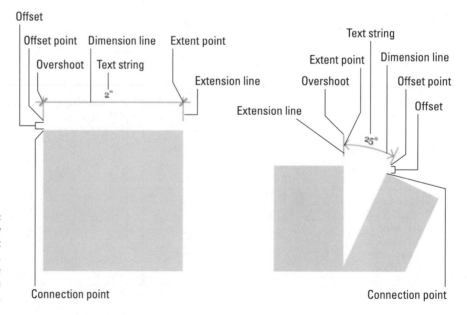

FIGURE 14-13: The anatomy of a LayOut dimension. Linear on the left, angular on the right.

>> **Use the Text Style panel** to change the font, text size, and so on.

>> **Use the Style tool to copy formatting and other settings from one dimension to another.** Activate the Style tool, click your "source" dimension, and then click each dimension you want to change.

>> **Double-click a dimension to access all its internals.** After they become editable, you can click and drag the dimension's connections points, offset points, extent points, or text all you like.

>> **Select individual lines to edit them.** After you double-click a dimension, you can select its constituent lines to edit them. Aidan likes to draw dimension lines slightly thicker than extension lines, so he selects the dimension line and increases its width in the Shape Style panel.

>> **Overshoots can be tricky.** The *overshoot* (as shown in Figure 14-13) is the part of an extension line that extends beyond the dimension line. You can adjust your overshoot's length if you like. Here's how:

   a. *Double-click a dimension to edit it.*

   b. *Click to select the extension line whose overshoot you want to adjust.*

   c. *Change the number beside the End Arrow setting in the Shape Style panel.*

   Unfortunately, there's no way to alter both extension lines' overshoots simultaneously. After you change one line, choose Edit ⇨ Copy Style; then select the other and choose Edit ⇨ Paste Style.

REMEMBER

After a dimension looks just the way you like, copying a dimension's style and applying it to your other dimensions is pretty easy. Just use the Style tool to transfer formatting from one dimension to the other.

To sample a dimension's style so that every new dimension you draw matches it, select the Style tool (or press the S key) and click your source dimension before you draw the next one.

Take a gander at the Dimension Style panel, as shown in Figure 14-14. Most of the controls here are obvious, but some definitely aren't. Diving right in:

>> **Text position:** Choose to display a text string above, below, or right smack dab in the middle of its corresponding dimension line.

>> **Text alignment:** Force a text string to always be horizontal or vertical on the page, or aligned (parallel) or perpendicular to its dimension line.

>> **Display units:** People who use the Imperial system of measurement tend to show the units on their dimensions. Metric folks tend not to. You have the choice.

- **Auto Scale button:** Here's where dimensions start to get a bit complicated. For a full discussion of what the heck this button does, see the next section.

- **Scale drop-down list:** This is available only when Auto Scale is deselected. Skip ahead to read all about model space and paper space. Getting your head around this topic takes time.

- **Length:** Different professions have different conventions for the dimensions they put on their drawings. Choose the one that suits you best.

- **Precision:** If you dimension the overall length of an airport runway, you probably don't need to be accurate to the 1000th of an inch. However, if you design an artificial heart valve . . .

- **Angle:** Degrees or radians — you decide. Sometimes, software reminds you that math nerds create it.

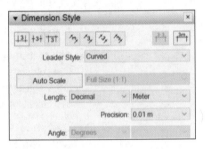

FIGURE 14-14:
The Dimension Style panel.

Keeping track of model space and paper space

When you place a SketchUp model viewport on your page, you end up with two types of space in your LayOut document:

- **Paper space:** Distances that pertain to the physical sheet of paper you're working on are said to be in *paper space.* A 4-x-4-inch blue square in paper space is 4 inches long.

- **Model space:** Distances within a model viewport have nothing to do with the size of the sheet of paper the viewport is on. An 80-x-80-foot building shown at 1 inch = 8 feet scale is 80 feet long in model space. In paper space, it's 10 inches long.

REMEMBER

A dimension you draw in LayOut is either in paper space or in model space. Which one the dimension is in by default depends on what the dimension is connected to:

- **Viewports:** When you draw a dimension between two points in a model viewport, LayOut is smart enough to presume that you want to display the length between the points *in the model* (in model space).

- **Everything else:** When you create a dimension between two points that have nothing to do with a viewport, LayOut assumes that you want to see the *actual length on the page* (in paper space).

Figure 14-15 illustrates the difference between model space and paper space. Both dimensions are exactly the same physical length on the page: 3 inches. However, the dimension on the left is attached to two points on a SketchUp model that's shown at 1 inch = 8 feet scale. This dimension displays the *model space* length of 24 feet (3 x 8), whereas the dimension on the right shows its *paper space* length of 3 inches.

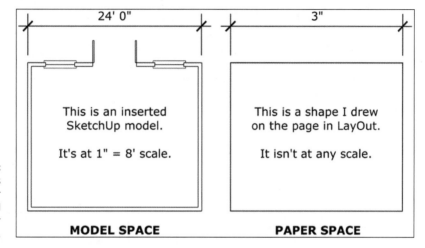

FIGURE 14-15: Dimensions can either show model space or paper space.

TIP

The Auto Scale button in the Dimension Style panel is automatically selected whenever you create a new dimension. If your dimension touches a point in a model viewport, the text string displays the length in model space. If it doesn't touch any model viewport at all, you get a length in paper space.

Turning off Auto Scale lets you assign a scale to the dimension you select. Choosing 1 inch = 60 feet for a dimension that's physically 4 inches long makes its text string read **240 feet** — no matter what the dimension is attached to.

Creating tables

If you create construction documents, the Table tool is for you. New in LayOut 2017, the table feature enables you to easily add construction schedules, area and quantity takeoffs, legends, or whatever you need in order to help others understand your LayOut document.

To start creating tables, here are the basics:

>> To create a table, select the Table tool, click to set the upper-left corner, move the cursor until your desired number of rows and columns appears, click to set the table's lower-right corner, and click one more time to adjust the table dimensions.

>> To add text to a table, double-click the table to access the table cells. Click in a cell and type the text you want to appear.

>> To edit a table's line width and background, select the table and use the Shape Style panel.

>> To edit the rows, columns, and cells, double-click the table and then context-click to see a menu of options.

LayOut tables include a few cool features for creating and managing table data:

>> If your table data is already saved as an Excel (.xlsx) or CSV (.csv) file, then you can import that data into LayOut and save yourself a bunch of time. To import the file, choose File ➪ Insert, select the file, make sure the correct sheet is selected, and click OK. You can also choose to import the table formatting from Excel.

>> After you import a table, managing changes between your table's source file and LayOut is super easy. If you need to update the source file, then you can update your table in LayOut by context-clicking the table and choosing Update Table Reference from the menu that appears.

Creating Your Own Templates

Most of the design presentations that you (or your firm) put together probably look alike — after all, they're part of your brand identity. If the presentation documents you make are all variations on a couple themes, why not build your own templates and use them every time you start a new project? You can set up LayOut so that your templates appear in the Getting Started dialog box, making it easier to build consistent presentations, quicker.

Follow these steps to turn any LayOut file into a template:

1. **Build a LayOut file that includes all the elements you want.**

    These elements may include a title block, a logo, page numbering, and a cover page. You probably also want to set up things you can't see, such as Auto-Text tags, a layering system, and even premade, empty pages for content. To make sure your template captures everything, you can strip all the content out of a LayOut document that you've already made and then save the resulting shell as a template.

TIP

Before you move to Step 2, make sure you're viewing the page that you want to use as the thumbnail preview in the template list.

2. **Choose File ⇨ Save as Template.**

The Save As Template dialog box opens.

3. **Type a name for your template and then choose a location for your new template.**

In the list at the bottom of the dialog box, click the folder (they're all folders) in which you want to include the template you're adding.

4. **Click OK (Save on a Mac).**

The next time the Getting Started dialog box appears, your new template will be in it.

Putting Together Your Own Scrapbooks

Most hardcore LayOut users make their own scrapbooks of scale figures, cars, trees, drafting symbols, typography — anything they need to use again and again.

Like templates, *scrapbooks* are just LayOut files that have been saved in a special folder on your system. When you open the program, it checks that folder and displays the files it finds in the Scrapbooks panel.

Follow these steps to build your own LayOut scrapbook:

1. **Build a LayOut file with the elements you want to include in your scrapbook.**

2. **Choose File ⇨ Save As Scrapbook.**

3. **Type a name for your scrapbook.**

In the Save As Scrapbook dialog box, the Scrapbook Folder list shows the location of the folder where your new scrapbook will be saved. If you prefer to use another folder, you can add one using the Folder panel of the Preferences dialog box.

4. **Click OK (Save on a Mac).**

   The next time you restart LayOut, your scrapbook appears at the top of the Scrapbooks panel.

A few notes about making your own scrapbooks:

>> **A good size is 6 x 6 inches.** You can choose any paper size for the file you plan to save as a scrapbook, but smaller sheets work better. The scrapbooks that come with LayOut are 6 inches square.

>> **Scrapbooks can have multiple pages.** In fact, just about all the default scrapbooks in LayOut do. The first page in your document becomes the cover page for the scrapbook; all subsequent pages appear below it in the list. Pay attention to your page names, which appear in the Scrapbooks panel, too.

>> **Use locked layers.** Anything you put on a locked layer can't be dragged out of the scrapbook. Take a look at the People scrapbook that comes with LayOut — the word *People* and the information next to it are on a locked layer. Notice how you can't drag them into your drawing?

>> **You can put model viewports into scrapbooks.** Open the Arrows ⇨ 3D ⇨ Curved scrapbook. Drag one of the arrows onto your page. Now double-click it — it's a model! Aidan created that scrapbook specifically to provide story boarders with orbitable arrows that they could pose however they liked. The moral of this story is that you can put *anything* into a scrapbook: graphics, images, viewports, and text.

Getting Your Document Out the Door

After you create a LayOut document, you can do the following four things to show it to someone else:

>> Print it.

>> Export it as a PDF or image files.

>> Export it as a DWG or DXF (CAD) file.

>> View it as a full-screen presentation.

Simple, huh? The next four sections provide more detail on each of these options.

Printing your work

Chapter 12 is about printing from SketchUp; notice that it's more than ten pages long. The instructions for printing from LayOut, on the other hand, would easily fit on a business card:

1. **Choose File ➪ Print.**

   In the Print dialog box, choose which pages to print and how many copies you want.

2. **Click OK to send your document to the printer.**

And that, dear reader, is why you should always insert your SketchUp models into a LayOut document if you need to print them.

TIP

That said, Aidan almost never prints directly from LayOut. Ninety percent of the time, he exports a PDF and uses Adobe Acrobat (or Reader) to send the actual job to the printer. The settings in Adobe's Print dialog box give you more control over the finished product.

Exporting a PDF or image files

Anyone with Adobe Reader software (which is free and is already loaded on millions of computers) can look at a PDF document you create; all you have to do is email it to your recipient.

Or you can export the pages of your file as individual raster images in either JPEG or PNG format. Take a look at Chapter 13 for more information on the differences between JPEG and PNG if you need to.

Follow these steps to export your LayOut document as a PDF file or images:

1. **Choose File ➪ Export ➪ PDF or File ➪ Export ➪ Images.**

   On a Mac, choose File ➪ Export and then make sure PDF, PNG, or JPEG is selected in the Export dialog box. An export dialog box opens.

2. **Name your file and tell LayOut where to save it on your computer. If you're saving an image, select the file format for the image.**

3. **Click the Save button (Windows) or the Options button (Mac).**

4. **In the dialog box that appears, set the options for your PDF or images.**

Here's what each option does:

- *Pages:* Choose which pages you want to export. If you're exporting images, each page in your LayOut document exports as a separate image file.

- *Image resolution:* If you're exporting a PDF, you can select High, Medium, or Low. Here's a good guideline: For documents that are small enough to be handheld, we recommend a setting of High. For anything bigger, go with Medium. If you're exporting an image, you can specify a width or height in pixels or type a resolution in pixels per inch (ppi). 96 ppi works well on screens, and 300 ppi works well for prints.

- *Image compression:* You see this option only if you're exporting a PDF. Select this setting to apply JPEG-style compression to images.

- *Layers:* You see this option only if you're exporting a PDF, because PDFs can have layers, just like LayOut documents do. If it makes sense to do so, you can export a layered PDF so that people who view it can turn the layers on and off.

- *Finish:* Select this check box to view your PDF or images after they're exported.

5. **Mac only: Click OK to close the Options dialog box.**

6. **Click the Export button (Save button on a Mac) to export your document as a PDF or images.**

Exporting a DWG or DXF file

You'd be hard-pressed to find a piece of professional computer-aided drawing (CAD) software that can't read the DWG and DXF formats, which are the industry standard for exchanging CAD files with people who use apps like AutoCAD. Here's how to turn your LayOut document into a CAD file:

1. **Set all your SketchUp viewports to vector rendering mode.**

   Viewports that are rendered as rasters export to DWG/DXF as raster images. That's usually not what you want to happen — especially if you're exporting a CAD file. See "Making your models look their best" earlier in this chapter for details about setting a viewport's rendering mode.

   TIP

   If a viewport contains a view whose edges you don't want to manipulate in CAD (such as a glitzy rendering), leave it as a raster.

2. **Choose File ⇨ Export ⇨ DWG/DXF.**

   On a Mac, choose File ⇨ Export and make sure DWG/DXF is selected in the Export dialog box.

3. **Name your file, tell LayOut where to save it on your computer, and click the Save button (Options on a Mac).**

   The DWG/DXF Export dialog box opens.

4. **Set the DWG/DXF Export options.**

   Here's what all the knobs and switches do:

   - *Format:* Unless you know you need a DXF, export a DWG file. As for which version, stick with the most recent one in the list.

   - *Pages:* Choose which pages you want to export. Keep in mind that each page in your LayOut document exports as a separate file.

   - *Layers:* If you want LayOut to export your layers as DWG/DXF layers select that option. If you want to export hidden layers, select Export Invisible Layers. See "Customizing a document's pages and layers" for details about layer visibility.

   - *Other:* Select the check box for any option you like. Color by Layer exports each layer as a different color. You can export the LayOut entities as native DWG/DXF entities. If you tell LayOut to ignore fills, shapes that are drawn in LayOut and filled with a color or pattern don't appear in the exported file.

5. **Mac only: Click OK to close the DWG/DXF Export dialog box.**

6. **Click the Export button (Save button on a Mac) to export your document as one or more DWG/DXF files.**

   If your LayOut file included any inserted raster images (such as JPEGs or PNGs) you also end up with a folder that contains copies of those. They're necessary for the DWG/DXF files you produce.

Going full screen

REMEMBER

Many times, design presentations for clients go beyond printed boards and booklets. These presentations include a digital slide show that usually involves a few hours of work in a program like PowerPoint or Keynote. LayOut helps you skip the PowerPoint step by letting you display your presentation in a full-screen view. You can move back and forth between pages with the arrow keys on your computer, and you can even double-click SketchUp model views to orbit them. Follow these tips:

>> **Switching to Presentation mode takes less than a second.** Choose View ⇨ Start Presentation to view your presentation full screen. Press the Esc key to exit Presentation mode.

>> **Specify where you want your presentation to appear.** Use the Presentation panel in the Preferences dialog box to tell SketchUp which monitor (or projector) you want to use to show your presentation.

>> **Move from page to page.** Use the left- and right-arrow keys.

>> **Choose which pages to show full screen.** You can decide not to show certain pages in full-screen mode by toggling the Show Page in Presentations icon to the right of those page names in the Pages panel. (You have to be in List view to be able to do this.)

>> **Double-click to change your view of a SketchUp model.** When you're in full-screen mode, you can double-click any SketchUp model viewport to orbit and zoom around inside it. Click anywhere outside the view to exit.

>> **Draw while you're in full-screen mode.** Try clicking and dragging while you're in full-screen mode; doing so lets you make red annotations right on your presentation. If a client doesn't like the porch you designed, scrawl a big, red *X* over it to let her know you understand. When you press Esc to exit Presentation mode, you can choose to save your annotations as a separate layer.

>> **Play scene animations in full-screen mode.** You can double-click and then context-click a model view with scenes that you've set up in SketchUp; then choose Play Animation. LayOut transitions from scene to scene. You can read more about scenes in Chapter 11.

5

The Part of Tens

Find tips for handling common problems that new users have as they create 3D models.

Discover resources for improving your SketchUp modeling skills.

Check out other SketchUp modeling tools, including Extension Warehouse and a browser-based version of SketchUp called my.SketchUp.

Chapter **15**

Ten SketchUp Traps and Their Workarounds

The bad news is that every new SketchUp user encounters certain problems, usually in the first couple hours using the software. You can call these problems growing pains. The good news is that, because these problems are common, we can write a chapter that anticipates a lot of the bad stuff you'll go through. This chapter offers tips that help you make sense of what's going on so you can get on with your life as quickly as possible.

SketchUp Won't Create a Face Where You Want It To

You've dutifully traced all around where you want SketchUp to create a face, but nothing's happening. Try checking whether your edges aren't all on the same plane.

REMEMBER

Ninety percent of the time, when SketchUp doesn't create a face where you think it should, an edge isn't on the plane you think it's on. To check whether your edges are coplanar, draw an edge that cuts diagonally across the area where you want a face to appear. If a face appears now, your edges aren't all on the same plane. To fix the problem, you have to figure out which edge is the culprit, and the Color By Axis option may help you see this information at-a-glance. Here's how Color By Axis works:

1. **In the Styles panel, change your edge color from All Same to By Axis.**

   See Chapter 10 for details. SketchUp draws the edges in your model the color of the axis to which they're parallel; edges parallel to the red axis are red, and so on.

2. **Look carefully at the edges that you wanted to define your desired face.**

   Are all the edges the color they're supposed to be? If they're not all supposed to be parallel to the drawing axes, this technique doesn't do much good. But if they are, and one (or more) of them is black (instead of red or green or blue), that edge (or edges) is your problem child. Fix it and switch back to All Same when you're done.

If the plane isn't the problem with your edges, then check whether one edge is part of a separate group or component. To check whether you have a component problem, try hiding groups or components and checking the edges to make sure that they're all in the group or component you think they're in. See Chapter 5 for details.

Your Faces Are Two Different Colors

REMEMBER

In SketchUp, faces have two sides: a front and a back. By default, these two sides are different colors.

When you do certain things like use Push/Pull or Follow Me on a face, sometimes the faces on the resulting geometry are "inside out." For some people, the issue is just bothersome. If you want to 3D-print your model, the issue needs to be fixed so that your model will print correctly.

To fix this issue, context-click the faces you want to flip and choose Reverse Faces from the context menu. If you have lots of faces to flip, you can select them all and then choose Reverse Faces to flip them all at once.

In 3D printing, this process is called checking your model's normals. See Chapter 9 for details about preparing a model for 3D printing.

Edges on a Face Won't Sink In

This tends to happen when you're trying to draw a rectangle (or another geometric figure) on a face with one of SketchUp's shape-drawing tools. Ordinarily, the Rectangle tool creates a new face on top of any face you use it on; after that, you can use Push/Pull to create a hole, if you want.

When the edges you just drew don't seem to cut through the face you drew them on, try these approaches:

» **Retrace one of the edges.** Sometimes that works — you'd be surprised how often.

» **Select Hidden Geometry from the View menu.** You're checking to make sure that the face you just drew isn't crossing any hidden or smoothed edges; if it is, the face you thought was flat may not be.

» **Make sure that the face you drew on isn't part of a group or component.** If it is, undo a few steps and then redraw your shape while you edit the group or component.

SketchUp Crashed, and You Lost Your Model

Unfortunately, SketchUp crashes happen sometimes.

The good news is that SketchUp automatically saves a copy of your file every five minutes. The file that SketchUp autosaves is actually a *separate* file, AutoSave_*your filename*.skp. If your file ever gets corrupted in a crash, an intact file is ready for you.

The problem is that most people don't even know that the autosaved file is there. Where do you find it?

» **If you've ever saved your file,** it's in the same folder as the original.

» **If you never saved your file,** it's in your Documents folder — unless you're on a Mac, in which case it's here:

```
User folder/Library/Application Support/SketchUp 201X/
    SketchUp/Autosave
```

TECHNICAL STUFF

Simple, right? Not so fast. On a Mac, you may need to change your Library folder from hidden to visible. In the Finder app, hold down the Option key while you choose Go ➪ Library. If you don't hold down the Option key, Library may not appear on the menu.

When you close your model, SketchUp typically assumes nothing untoward has happened and cleans up after itself by deleting the autosaved file.

TIP

To minimize the amount of work you lose when software (or hardware) goes south, always do two things:

>> **Save often — compulsively, even.**

>> **Use the Save a Copy As command on the File menu.**

When you're working on a big project, the following steps can help ensure you don't lose any work:

1. **Save the original version of your file as** *yourfilename*_Master.skp.

    That's the file you'll always be working on.

2. **Create a folder that lives in the same place as your Master file; call the folder something like** *Your file's name* Archive.

3. **Every half-hour or so, choose File ➪ Save a Copy As and save a numbered version of your file to the Archive folder.**

    When Aidan is building a big model, he often has 40 or 50 saved versions of it in his Archive folder, dating back to when he first started working on it.

SketchUp Is Soooooo Slooooooooooow

The bigger your model, the worse your computer's performance. What makes a model big? In a nutshell, faces.

TIP

Do everything in your power to keep your model as small as you can. Here are some tips for doing that:

>> **Reduce the number of sides on your extruded circles and arcs.** See Chapter 6 for instructions.

>> **Use 2D people and trees instead of 3D ones.** Three-dimensional plants and people have *hundreds* of faces each. Consider using 2D ones instead, especially if your model won't be seen much from overhead.

Some models are just big, and you can't do much about it. Here are some tricks for working with very large SketchUp models:

>> **Make liberal use of the Outliner and layers.** As we explain in Chapter 7, these SketchUp features were specifically designed to let you organize your model into manageable chunks. Hide everything you're not working on at the moment — doing so gives your computer a fighting chance.

>> **Substitute simple forms for large numbers of complex components.** For example, insert sticks as placeholders for big sets of 3D trees, cars, and other big components. The tips for replacing components in Chapter 5 explain how to swap the placeholders with more complex components.

>> **Turn off shadows and switch to a simple style, such as Shaded in the Default Styles collection.** It takes a lot of computer horsepower to display shadows, edge effects, and textures in real time on your monitor. When you're working, turn off all that stuff. Chapter 10 is all about styles.

>> **Use scenes to navigate between views.** Scenes aren't just for presenting your model — they're also great for working with it. If you create scenes for the different views you commonly use and with different combinations of hidden geometry, then you don't have to orbit, pan, and zoom around your gigantic model. To speed up things even more, deselect Enable Scene Transitions (in the Animation panel of the Model Info dialog box). Chapter 11 is full of tips on working efficiently with scenes.

You Can't Get a Good View of the Inside of Your Model

It's not always easy to work on the inside of something in SketchUp. You can do these things to make it easier, though:

>> **Cut into your model with sections.** SketchUp's Sections feature lets you cut away parts of your model — temporarily, of course — so that you can get a better view of what's inside. Take a look at Chapter 11 for the whole story on sections.

>> **Widen your field of view.** *Field of view* is the part of your model you can see on-screen at one time. A wider FOV is like having better peripheral vision. You can read all about it in Chapter 11.

A Face Flashes When You Orbit

If you have two faces in the same spot — maybe one is in a separate group or component — you see a *Z-fighting* effect. SketchUp is deciding which face to display by switching back and forth between them; it's not a good solution, but certainly a logical one — at least for a piece of software. The only way to get rid of Z-fighting is to delete or hide one of the faces.

You Can't Move Your Component the Way You Want

When you insert some components into your model, the components by default *glue* to faces. A glued component instance isn't actually glued *in one place*. Instead, it's glued to the plane of the face you originally placed (or created) it on. For example, if you place a sofa component on the floor of your living room, you can move it around only on that plane — not up and down.

This gluing behavior comes in handy when you deal with things like furniture; it allows you to rearrange things with the Move tool without accidentally picking them up.

If you can't move your component the way you want to, context-click it and see whether Unglue is an option — if it is, choose it. Now you can move your component around however you want.

Bad Stuff Happens Every Time You Use the Eraser

When you use the Eraser tool, it's pretty easy to delete stuff accidentally. Worse yet, you usually don't notice what's missing until it's too late. Here are some tips for erasing more accurately:

>> **Orbit around.** Try to make sure that nothing is behind whatever you're erasing; use SketchUp's navigation tools to get a view of your model that puts you out of danger.

>> **Switch on Back Edges.** When you're doing a lot of erasing, choose View ⇨ Edge Style ⇨ Back Edges. That way, you can see every edge in your model, and you're less likely to erase the wrong ones.

>> **Double-check.** After you do a lot of erasing, give your model a quick once-over with the Orbit tool, just to make sure that you didn't get rid of anything important. Put a sticky note on your computer monitor that says something like *Check after Erase!* just to remind you.

All Your Edges and Faces Are on Different Layers

WARNING

Using Layers in SketchUp is a dangerous business. Chapter 7 has tips you should follow when using layers, so we don't repeat them here, but here's the short version: Always build everything on Layer0, and put whole groups or components on other layers only if you really need to.

If you used layers and now things are messed up, here's what you can do to recover:

1. **Make sure that everything is visible.**

   Select Hidden Geometry on the View menu; then (in the Layers panel) make all your layers visible. Just make sure that you can see everything in your model.

2. **Choose Edit ⇨ Select All.**

3. **In the Entity Info panel, move everything to Layer0.**

4. **In the Layers panel, delete your other layers. When prompted, tell SketchUp to move anything remaining on them to Layer0.**

5. **Create new layers and follow the rules in Chapter 7.**

Chapter **16**

More Than Ten Ways to Learn About SketchUp

SketchUp is like a little digital universe where anything is possible. With all the creative possibilities, you can almost always learn more about new modeling methods, tips, tricks, and tools.

In this chapter, we share a few resources, tools, and topics that help you take the modeling skills you learn in this book even further. Some of the stuff we cover is free, and we think the stuff that costs money is totally worth it.

Free Online Resources

At fancy receptions, Rebecca samples every item on the dessert buffet, and Aidan is the one stuffing his suit pockets with *hors d'oeuvres* wrapped in napkins. We love free stuff *that much*. So without further ado, what follows are five complimentary sources of SketchUp help.

> » **SketchUp training resources:** SketchUp publishes first-rate materials right on its website (www.sketchup.com/learn):
>
> • *Video tutorials:* When SketchUp first launched in 2000, it became known for its excellent video tutorials. Figure 16-1 shows the series for beginners. We

can't recommend them highly enough; there's nothing like seeing SketchUp in action.

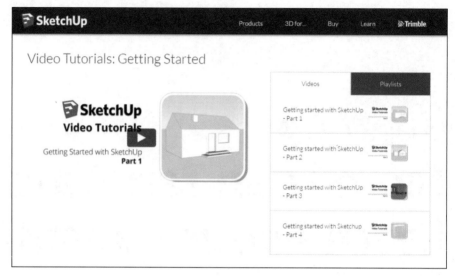

FIGURE 16-1:
SketchUp training videos help beginners see how 3D modeling works.

`http://www.sketchup.com/learn/videos/58?playlist=58`

- *Self-paced tutorials:* These are SketchUp files that use scenes to teach different aspects of the program in a "follow along with me" style. If this is how you like to figure things out, have a look.

- *Online Help Center:* The SketchUp Help Center includes hundreds of articles created specifically to help new users along. (Rebecca helped to write many of them.) The easiest way to get to the SketchUp Help Center is to choose Help➪ Knowledge Center from the SketchUp menu bar.

- *SketchUp Community Forum:* SketchUp's online forum is a thriving online community and a great place to learn from other SketchUp users. When a 3D modeling issue has you stumped, the folks here can lend you a hand.

» **SketchUcation:** You find discussions, tutorials, plugins, news, and piles of other good stuff at SketchUcation. You'll also find a large and active forum of users from around the world. (`www.sketchucation.com`)

» **SketchUp School videos:** This is a terrific YouTube channel. The free videos are first rate, and you can buy a subscription to watch over a hundred more on SketchUp School's website. (`www.youtube.com/4sketchupgo2school`)

The School designers have also produced some of the world's finest SketchUp educational/training videos; you can pay for a subscription to watch them on the School website (www.sketchupschool.com). The production quality on these things is outstanding, and Mike Tadros and Alex Oliver (two of the School guys) do an amazing job of teaching SketchUp for both the Windows and Mac operating systems.

>> **MasterSketchUp.com:** Matt Donley has put together a nice site dedicated to helpful tips and tricks, videos, and other tutorials. He also self-published a book about LayOut; you can read about it in the next section. (www.mastersketchup.com)

>> **The SketchUpdate blog:** Visit the SketchUp blog regularly for news, case studies, tips and tricks, modeler profiles, plugins, and other updates. (http://blog.sketchup.com/)

The Ultimate SketchUp Reading List

These books and resources cost a bit of money, but they're worth every penny:

>> **Bonnie Roskes's books:** Bonnie's *The SketchUp Book* (published by 3DVinci) was the first book available, and now she has several titles, including SketchUp books for kids. If you think you want to get another, bigger book about SketchUp (written with architects and other design pros in mind), check out Bonnie's books at www.3dvinci.net.

>> **Daniel Tal's books:** Daniel Tal focuses on specific techniques that can help build advanced 3D-modeling skills. *SketchUp for Site Design: A Guide to Modeling Site Plans, Terrain and Architecture,* 2nd Edition (Wiley) is, simply put, a great book. Dan's latest book (also published by Wiley) is *Rendering in SketchUp: From Modeling to Presentation for Architecture, Landscape Architecture and Interior Design.* It demystifies the dark art of photorealistic rendering in a way that might finally get you to try it. When you're ready to take the next step in your SketchUp relationship, get Dan's books.

>> **Michael Brightman's book:** A recent addition to the SketchUp bookshelf, Michael's *The SketchUp Workflow for Architecture: Modeling Buildings, Visualizing Design, and Creating Construction Documents with SketchUp Pro and LayOut* (Wiley) is a watershed in the history of SketchUp publishing. He came up with a viable workflow for using SketchUp Pro (including LayOut) to produce complete construction document sets that look just like the ones you'd

normally use AutoCAD or Revit to make. The stuff in this book is insanely clever — you have to read it to believe it.

>> **Alex Schreyer's book:** The title of *Architectural Design with SketchUp: Component-Based Modeling, Plugins, Rendering, and Scripting* (Wiley) certainly implies that it's a book for architects. That's not strictly true; it's actually a great resource for anyone looking to find out more about all the topics in the subtitle. Alex deserves special credit for his skillful introduction to Ruby scripting for nonprogrammers.

>> **Matt Donley's book:** The man behind MasterSketchUp.com has written an e-book called *SketchUp to LayOut: The Essential Guide to Creating Construction Documents with SketchUp Pro and LayOut*. Unlike Mike Brightman's book (which we mention earlier), Matt's book approaches the subject from more of a beginner's perspective. It also shows woodworking and kitchen and bath examples, which should appeal to people who aren't architects.

>> **Dennis Fukai's books:** Three words: jaw-dropping detail. Dennis's books are hard to describe. He's written seven of them, each is fully illustrated in SketchUp, and each teaches a different subject. If you want to discover more about using SketchUp in building construction or more about construction itself, or you just want to be completely inspired by what you can do with SketchUp, have a look at these books. Search for his name on Amazon (www. amazon.com) or go to his company's website, www.insitebuilders.com.

Other Tools from the Makers of SketchUp

The folks who make SketchUp offer a mindboggling suite of products and tools for 3D modeling and sharing what you model. We introduce the main extras, the 3D Warehouse and LayOut, in Chapters 5, 12, and 14. The following list is a whirlwind tour of your other options:

>> **my.SketchUp:** This free version of SketchUp runs in a web browser. my.SketchUp debuted in 2016 with a limited toolset, but the main cast of drawing tools is all there, as shown in Figure 16-2. You can expect to see more features as the product evolves. All the tools that are available work almost exactly as they do in SketchUp, although you will find some minor differences to accommodate working in a browser instead of in an application installed on your computer. To get started, visit http://www.sketchup.com/products/my-sketchup.

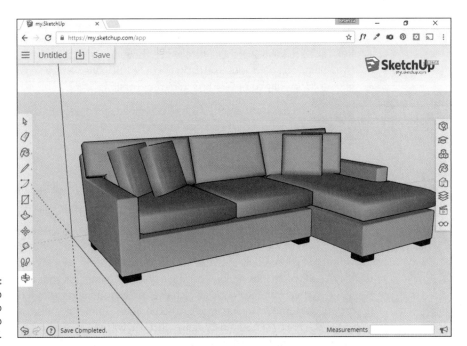

FIGURE 16-2:
my.SketchUp
enables you to
model in a web
browser.

>> **Extension Warehouse:** Extensions typically add little bits of functionality for specialized tasks, such as 3D printing. Indeed, it's no coincidence that most of the discussion about extensions occurs in Chapter 9, which is all about 3D printing. Whether you use SketchUp for architecture, woodworking, interior design, movie sets, or something else, you can find whole categories of extensions designed to make specific tasks a little bit easier. Start exploring at `http://extensions.sketchup.com/` or within SketchUp, choose Window ⇨ Extension Warehouse. To actually install an extension in SketchUp, you need to login with a Trimble ID or Google account. When you log in through SketchUp (that is, by choosing Window ⇨ Extension Warehouse), installing an extension is usually pretty easy: Just click the red Install button in the upper left of the extension's details page.

TIP

After you install a few extensions, SketchUp 2017 enables you to choose Window ⇨ Extension Manager for help managing your extensions and keeping them up to date. In earlier versions of SketchUp, you can manage extensions through the online Extension Warehouse online interface.

>> **SketchUp Viewer:** If you need to show models to your clients (who are not likely to have SketchUp installed on their computers), SketchUp Viewer may help you share your SketchUp files. SketchUp Viewer is a separate application that actually comes in three different versions:

- The desktop version is a free download (get it here: http://www.sketchup.com/products/sketchup-viewer).

- The mobile version is an inexpensive app (about $10) that you download for iOS or Android.

- The virtual reality version transports you to Star Trek Holodeck so that you can protect the galaxy within the 3D model of your choice.

  Okay not really. The third version does enable you to immerse yourself in a 3D model using virtual reality. As this book goes to press, the virtual reality version is only available via the Microsoft Store on a Microsoft HoloLens. If you're looking for a cutting-edge way to impress your clients, definitely check out the ways in which you can view holograms of models on a table or jump from one floor to another in the immersive view. If you can't afford a pricey virtual reality viewer just yet, you can at least get a preview of the possibilities in the SketchUp Viewer for HoloLens YouTube video (https://youtu.be/c2HIrT3Nshs).

Index

bounded text boxes, 408

bridging, 262

Brightman, Michael (author)

The SketchUp Workflow for Architecture: Modeling Buildings, Visualizing Design, and Creating Construction Documents with SketchUp Pro and LayOut, 445

building

bottles, 155–157

collections, 380

complex objects, 198

components, 131–133

document pages/layers in LayOut, 404–407

documents in LayOut, 404–426

a doghouse, 19–25

doors, 135–136

eaves for pitched roofs, 109–110

exterior walls, 92–96

extruded shapes, 157–162

flat roofs with parapets, 107–109

freeform hills/valleys, 185–187

gabled roofs, 110–112

groups, 121

guides with Tape Measure tool, 63–64

gutters, 157–162

handrails, 157–162

hip roofs, 112–113

interior walls, 83–84

lathed forms, 156–157

linear dimensions, 420

models in layers, 260–262

new terrain models, 177–184

paths, 190–193

a quick model, 19–25

roads, 190–193

scaled orthographic views, 414–415

scenes, 336–337

scrapbooks in LayOut, 427–428

shadow studies, 323–328

spheres, 155–157

styles, 313–314

tables in LayOut, 425–426

templates in LayOut, 426–427

terrain models, 177–184

textures projected, 239–241

windows, 135–136

buildings

about, 71

floors, 72–101

roof, 106–117

stairs, 101–106

walls, 72–101

C

CAD files

cleaning up imported data, 247–250

exporting, 399–401

importing into SketchUp Pro, 245–247

modeling on top of imported CAD data, 251–257

working with imported, 245–257

callouts, 419

Camera Location property, 343

captive joints, 287

changing

color of modeling cues, 55

field of view, 340

modeling settings, 310–311

scene transitions, 339

scenes, 341–347

views, 85–86

Cheat Sheet (website), 3

checking

model normals, 269–270

model size, 270–271

choosing

guides, 65

items, 52–53

Match Photo images, 231–232

with Move tool, 58–59

shadows, 319

Circle tool, 75

Classifications feature, 204

Classifier, 134

cleaning up imported data, 247–250

CleanUp[3], 266–267

clearance, in 3D printing, 282–283

M

Macs
  accessing tools, 15
  Magic Mouse, 14
  printing from, 367–371
  printing to scale, 373–374
Magic Mouse, 14
Make Unique option, 134
MakerBot Replicator (website), 278
managing
  layers with scenes, 213
  models online, 378–380
  section planes, 352–353
  visibility, 207
mapping faces with photographs, 216–230
MasterSketchUp.com, 445
Match Photo feature, 231–238
materials, 216
Materials panel, 65–66
Measurements box, 13, 14, 49–51
Measurements box (LayOut), 417
Menu bar, 12–13, 14
metal, 3D printing and, 280
metric scale, 372
Mix tab (Styles panel), 312–313
mixing styles, 312–313
Model Info, 97
Model Info dialog box, 15–16, 324, 340
model space, 424–425
model views
  inserting in LayOut, 409–416
  repositioning in LayOut, 411
modeling
  curved and irregular forms, 255–257
  directly from photographs, 230–238
  with repeated elements, 149–151
  right-angled walls, 253–254
  symmetrically, 143–149
  on top of imported CAD data, 251–257
  on top of textures, 239–241
  walls that meet at non-right angles, 254–255
modeling axes, 19
modeling cues, changing color of, 55

modeling section (Styles panel), 310–311
modeling window, 12, 14
models
  accuracy of, 48–51
  checking normals, 269–270
  checking size, 270–271
  geo-locating, 241–244
  managing online, 378–380
  preparing for 3D printing, 263–276
  presenting. *See* presenting models
  scaling, 224–225
  splitting, 272–276
  subtracting from, 163–166
  updating references, 416
  uploading, 376–377
  viewing in Google Earth, 244
modifier keys, 13
mouse, 14
Move tool
  copying with, 59–60
  preselecting with, 58–59
  selecting with, 58–59
  shaping forms with, 56–57
Move Up/Down arrows, 307
Move/Scale/Rotate/Shear/Distort Texture mode, 220
movies, exporting, 395–397
moving
  entities to different layers, 209–210
  guides, 65
  items, 55–56
  between scenes, 337–340
  selections, 58
  textures, 221–222
.mp4 (H.264), 395
multi-direction curves, 226–227
my.SketchUp, 446–447

N

naming groups, 121
navigation tools, 27
nesting order, 207
nonphotorealistic rendering (NPR), 11

About the Authors

Aidan Chopra has always had a thing for computers — his parents thoughtfully sent him to Apple camp instead of hockey lessons like every other 8-year-old in Montreal — but he learned to draft and build physical models the old-fashioned way, working for his architect father. In the twelve years since he graduated with a Master of Architecture degree from Rice University, he's done a lot of writing and lecturing about the way software is used in design. These days, Aidan is the co-founder and Chief Creative Officer at Bitsbox, where he's been since he left the SketchUp team in 2014. At Google, and then at Trimble, and now at Bitsbox, he works on ways to mediate between complexity and usability; he believes the best technology in the world isn't worth a darn if nobody can figure out how it works. Aidan lives in Boulder, Colorado, with his wife Sandra and their sons Chatham and Cedar.

Rebecca Huehls loves graphics and drawing technology. She has fond memories of illustrating physics concepts in the old Macintosh HyperCard program for her eighth-grade science class and still remembers her excitement when she was paired with Aidan to edit the original edition of this book, *Google SketchUp For Dummies*. Today, as the owner of Comet Dog Studio, Rebecca writes and edits technical content for several global brands, publishers, and organizations, including the SketchUp Help Center, which is the online help and support documentation for SketchUp, LayOut, 3D Warehouse, Extension Warehouse, and more. She has more than 17 years of experience in technical writing and editing and is thrilled to join Aidan as coauthor for this edition of the book. She lives in Indianapolis, Indiana, with her family.

Dedication

Aidan: For my parents, Jenny and Shab, and my brother, Quincy, because I love them very much

Rebecca: For Mason, Bear, and Halle

Authors' Acknowledgments

Aidan: For helping in all the ways that it is possible to help with a book — offering technical advice, lending a critical ear, providing moral support and encouragement — I'd like to thank my wife, Sandra Winstead. It's rare to find everything you need in a single person, and I can't imagine having written this book without her.

Rebecca: A huge thank you to Aidan for the opportunity to help write this book

Both of us: Thanks to Michael Curry for writing Chapter 9 of this book. As a 3D Printing Evangelist who also happens to know SketchUp inside and out, there simply isn't anyone on the planet who's better qualified.

We'd like to thank J.V. Lee for agreeing to be the Technical Editor for this volume. As a SketchUp Sage and experienced architect, we knew he'd do a bang-up job of keeping us honest, and he did.

We thank Steve Hayes and Colleen Diamond, our editors at Wiley. It was a delight to work with a team of such intelligent, thoughtful, and well-meaning professionals.

Finally, we need to thank the very long list of individuals who provided critical help: Tommy Acierno, Brad Askins, John Bacus, Brian Brown, Todd Burch, Mark Carvalho, Chris Cronin, Tasha Danko, Steve Dapkus, Jonathan Dormody, Marc Durant, Joe Esch, Rich Feit, Jody Gates, Toshen Golias, Scott Green, Mark Harrison, Adam Hecht, Preston Jackson, Barry Janzen, Alex Juhola, Tyson Kartchner, Chris Keating, Patrick Lacz, Scott Lininger, Catherine Moats, Allyson McDuffie, Millard McQuaid, Tyler Miller, Parker Mitchell, Simone Nicolo, Steve Oles, Drew Parker, Bruce Polderman, Alok Priyadarshi, Peter Saal, Brad Schell, Gopal Shah, Matt Simpson, Mike Springer, Tricia Stahr, Bryce Stout, Vicky Tait, Daniel Tal, James Therrien, Mason Thrall, Nancy Trigg, Tushar Udeshi, John Ulmer, David Vicknair, Jeremy Walker, Greg Wirt, and Tom Wyman.

Publisher's Acknowledgments

Executive Editor: Steve Hayes

Project Manager: Colleen Diamond

Development Editor: Colleen Diamond

Copy Editor: Colleen Diamond

Technical Editor: J. V. Lee

Editorial Assistant: Serena Novosel

Sr. Editorial Assistant: Cherie Case

Production Editor: Tamilmani Varadharaj

Cover Photo: Courtesy of Nicholas Sonder